The Art of Reading The Novel

PHILIP FREUND

THE ART

THE

OF READING
NOVEL

(Original title: How to Become a Literary Critic)

New, revised edition

COLLIER BOOKS, New York, N. Y.

Library of Congress Catalog Card Number: 64-21331

First Collier Books Edition 1965

This edition revised for Collier Books is published by arrangement with the author.

The Art of Reading the Novel was originally published under the title *How to Become a Literary Critic*

Acknowledgment is made to Alfred A. Knopf, Inc. for permission to quote from the following:
Albert Camus, *The Fall,* © Alfred A. Knopf, Inc., 1956 translated from the French by Justin O'Brien
Albert Camus, *The Plague,* copyright Alfred A. Knopf, Inc., 1948 translated from the French by Stuart Gilbert

The Macmillan Company, New York
Collier-Macmillan Canada Ltd., Toronto, Ontario
Printed in the United States of America

For

FRIEDA TALMEY GALLUN

The great question as to a poet or novelist is, How does he feel about life? What, in the last analysis, is his philosophy? . . . This is the most interesting thing their works offer us. Details are interesting in proportion as they contribute to make it clear.

HENRY JAMES

Table of Contents

A ROOM IN ROME

Chapter 1

A Room in Rome

THIS BOOK was begun in a room in Rome, when I was twenty-one years old. A small inheritance had made it possible for me to travel abroad. It was July, and Rome was very hot; but my room was cool because the house was stone, the windows were shuttered. Noise from the street intruded, but the sun and dust did not.

If you want to feel always young, I think you might live in Rome, where so much is very old. Many tourists to the "Eternal City" experience this. Walking through streets that men have trod for thousands of years, you cannot be convinced that your own twenty, or forty, or sixty years amount to very much. At twenty-one, of course, this is especially true.

The sights of Rome were very impressive, and very much in my mind. Sometimes when we confront the great memorials of the past we become restive and uncertain about the present and future. Our simple, natural faith in what is contemporary falls away from us; we begin to question.

That was my mood on that July morning as I stood in my room; the past was in my thoughts when I recalled scenes of the day before, and the present was in my ears while the traffic's discord floated through the window. My room was a modest one, with new plumbing along the wall; it was "modern" in an ancient city, just as I was modern too, yet lived in a world of old ideas.

Rome has a long history—perhaps the longest of any important city in the Western world—and when I remembered that, the din outside my window sounded rather meaningless: taxi horns and children shouting, the whistles of policemen; and once there was even a martial tread as a company of *fascisti* went by in black shirts and olive tunics. But the marchers did not seem very important, for all their valiant show. The armies of the popes, and before them the armies of the Caesars, had also marched here; and in the perspective of history they did not seem very important either. I had not come to Rome because of anything they had done.

13

If the past lives at all, it is because of the artists and thinkers who worked then. Of all that men accomplished in the vanished centuries only a small part is left, and surprisingly it is mostly the good and beautiful.

Only works that embody certain proved values endure, remain wonderful to our eyes: what is heroic and handsome in stone, glowing and inspired in paint, lyric in word; virtuous and honest in conception, whatever the medium. The past gives us legend and experience, and these are the materials of art and philosophy, and thus the artist and philosopher are mankind's historians.

That is why, as I stood in that room in Rome on a hot July morning, feeling younger than ever with the visible past surrounding me, art and philosophy suddenly became urgent matters. I lived in a world of which I knew too little. Perhaps, if I could learn more about art and philosophy, I might find in them an inkling of man's purpose and historic direction. Then my own young energy in the contemporary world might be put to better use.

Books and travel are the means by which one learns about the past. I thought about all the books that I had read, many of which had brought the wonders of forgotten times to me. I was grateful to them for having done that. And I was filled with remorse for the many books that I had not read.

Thinking of those unread books gave me the same feeling I had when I passed a Tuscan hilltown without stopping to wander a little through its cobbled streets. Or I would find in my Baedeker a reference to some dingy chapel which contained an isolated masterpiece of a long-dead artist; but I would continue on without seeing it, bringing to my mind a vision of a dusty, local church, bolted at the hot noon hour, where I would have to ring a bell, summon the sacristan, press a coin in his palm, and then follow him for a moment's glimpse of a painting too dimly lit above an altar. But, of course, I could not visit every hilltown in Italy, or see every faded painting, or read every book ever written.

Once, when I was sixteen and a first-year student, I had actually tried to read every book ever written. Does that sound preposterous? At a certain hour each afternoon I hastened to the university library to pore over yellowed books; my idea was that in four years' reading I could at least skim through all the important works put on paper. I began with

Beowulf, that first English classic (for some reason I slighted, even in translation, all the Greeks, Romans, Italians, and French Medieval Romancers), and persisted steadily for twelve months, when I found myself somewhere near the middle of *Piers Plowman,* a century or two further on. Then I quit, owning to myself that I was thoroughly bored. Of all that I read during those twelve months, I cannot now recall a single word.

Even in Rome, at twenty-one, I looked back with a smile at that absurd, youthful dream. Yet several of my friends tell me of having had the same ambitious reading plan. None ever carried it through. How could he? Even if a man had time and patience enough, what good would that do? The human mind cannot hold so much.

What had inspired me to try reading all the books in the world was a deep curiosity about the men who had written them, and about the past and present. I had not waited until now to experience that. But this particular morning, the street cries of the sunlit twentieth century through my shuttered window prompted a decision. Those bright noises from the ancient street were deeply stirring . . . they taunted me because they were alien noises.

Just why was I in Rome contemplating all these unseen pictures and unread books with regret? Actually, I knew, I was thinking about myself, contemplating with regret all the experiences I was destined to miss, and all the different sorts of people I might have been but was not. People like those outside the window. And whenever I began to analyze those other sorts of life, I realized that I knew them chiefly from having read about them. Sometimes a great sculpture or painting suggested much, but a book told far more.

It could not be otherwise. One youth is not long enough to experience all youth, to study all, to travel everywhere; and my predestined three-score-years and ten could never teach me all wisdom. A life spent mostly in reading books would not be satisfactory, but surely a life without books would be so dull, limited, uninformed, as to seem almost impossible. Yes, even though it be indirectly, most of us owe the better part of our *self* to the accumulated knowledge of life contained in books.

Then to read without plan was to live chaotically, or at least carelessly, and for a long time I had been sensing that. It is astonishing how much time the average man spends reading. If, during my student years when I had much leisure, I had read only two books a week, that would have meant that in the years from ten to twenty I had read more than a thousand books of all kinds, good and bad; but actually I had read far more books in that period, as had most other students, without being aware of it. The number was doubtless several thousands, and yet, when I questioned myself, I found that my knowledge was still very small, nor had I oriented myself to any permanent truth. The heritage of several thousand books was merely confusion.

In vague ways I had attempted to plan during those years. I had "discovered" authors, pursuing them through many books. For a period my thoughts would be completely under their sway. A good book, and especially a good novel, is very compelling. That excellent dramatist and critic, Harley Granville-Barker, has described this when he speaks of "the moral hypnosis latent in the solitary and silent enjoyment of the narrative form. . . . It is said that the Russian peasant believes whatever he sees in print must, in virtue of the printing, be true." At moments, in the grip of enthusiasm over some new author, I had not been much better than the Russian peasant.

We have all of us, indeed, seen many people whose whole lives have been affected by books they admire; esthetes, who in college have come under the sway of Oscar Wilde; tersely cynical followers of Aldous Huxley and Ernest Hemingway, who fancy that their sophistication is properly accepted as a symbol for a secret nostalgia; enthusiasts for the doctrine of D. H. Lawrence, of André Gide.

"Certain novels are like great but temporary bereavements; they abolish our habits, bring us in contact once more with the reality of life, but for a few hours only, like a nightmare; since the force of habit, the oblivion that it creates, the gaiety that it restores to us because our brain is powerless to fight against it and to recapture the truth, prevails to an infinite extent over the almost hypnotic suggestion of a good book, which, like all suggestions, has but a transient effect." So remarks Marcel Proust in *The Sweet Cheat Gone*.

It had been bewildering and often difficult to combat this transient "moral hypnosis" as one novelist succeeded another. I could not very well combine the ways of life suggested to me in Wilde and Hemingway, but owned to myself merits in both, the one a pagan idealization of beauty, profound and original; the other an idealization of emotional honesty that is also profound and original, yet in outward expression very different. I did not desire to borrow a way of life from anyone, but with each such writer I discovered potentialities in myself I had not known of before, and this indeed is the value of reading. You can hardly call such immersion in literature "escape." It is perpetual discontent.

That, the stirring of discontent, had been the rôle of books in my life. Reading brings delights, but not all reading is delightful. It is also disturbing, mentally provocative. Books are a call to mental action. They hint at the marvels of the world. Sometimes, naturally, I sought "escape," but for that strangely I did not turn to fiction—where I saw portrayed only a world of problems reiterative of my own—but to science, clean, shining with hope, always bringing encouragement.

So, with vague purpose and growing discontent, I had read and read, and all the time I had felt the need of a plan. And finally, that need had drawn me to the works of the professional literary critics.

But I was disappointed. The critics are truly professional and they are concerned with technical matters of limited interest to an unprofessional reader; they analyze structure, literary innovations and borrowings; they fix an author's place in the literary scene. I could see that amateur criticism would be quite a different thing: it would be *autobiography*. I was interested in a critic who might show me what use I could make of the authors I read.

George Bernard Shaw has said that he is the greatest playwright who ever lived, because he stands on the shoulders of all the playwrights who have gone before him. That, with allowance for my native limitations, was how I was feeling about the development of my personality. That was what I was searching for in books, in addition to vicarious experience: the enhancement of my own personality. Nor in so doing was I asking too much of the books I read. I could not become Tolstoi simply by going through his novels. On the other hand, I could absorb a good deal of Tolstoi's wisdom by *understanding* him. But even for that task I deemed myself inadequate, and that was why I had turned to the professional critics for help.

You might say that my bent had become philosophical, and I was really looking in the novel for philosophy. I cared very little, therefore, for three-hundred-page books of literary criticism that distinguished between chronicle novels and dramatic

novels, that explained—as they all explained at great length—
how Henry James had introduced the practice of telling a
story from only one point of view; when I read Henry James
myself it was for a quite different purpose. Henry James had
some ideas about life that were valid, highly civilized; he was
a very honest writer; he had an emancipated mind that still
loved refinement and delicacy. He was a romantic cosmopolitan with the same fine manners in life that he had in
literature. To overlook those qualities would be like reading
Shakespeare's sonnets only to comment on their difference
in form from those of Petrarch, a matter of not the slightest
concern to me. Yet essays on Henry James dealt chiefly with
his interesting technical innovations.

And so—though I was less than twenty-one, or perhaps for
that very reason—I found myself much more serious about
literature than the professional critics.

But perhaps the novel is not the right place to look for
philosophy. That had also occurred to me, and I turned to
proper philosophy itself. But I turned right back again to the
novel.

For what I found in proper philosophy was an abstract
intellectualism that led me nowhere and contributed nothing
to my understanding of human nature or the world about me.
It is a realm of metaphysical systems that seems at distant
removes from actuality.

But at least proper philosophy does formulate; it does
produce plans. I thought to myself, "If only some critic would
attempt a like formulation in the realm of art. Not esthetics
That would involve the same polysyllabic intellectualism. No,
a reading plan that would be cognizant of some sort of
philosophical purpose."

II

Was I right to search for philosophy in the novel?

I was in Rome. I was listening to foreign street voices I
could not understand. I was trying to resolve the confusion of
an inquiring but immature mind and spirit, challenged by the
vastness of this noisy, sun-drenched spectacle, and I was hopefully deciding that I might find my answer in the birth of a
new kind of "literary criticism."

I was sure it could be done. My respect for imaginative literature was deep enough. Its proper study, embraced in a more

penetrating literary criticism, would be philosophy. It would be even more than that. It would be an exciting adventure.

I was certainly not the first to think so. Anatole France, who was intellectually and sensually one of the richest of men, had defined criticism as "the soul's adventure among masterpieces."

That is not only an illuminating definition but also a tempting one. Anatole France is ever the great tempter.

I had seen attractive pictures of him, a bowed hulk of a man with a luxuriant beard and the light of a *bon vivant* in his eyes. It would have been a rare privilege to discuss books with him. For there are certain men who see truth keenly. We do not even begin to live until we have spent time in their company.

Such men, as France has indicated, are the world's great novelists. I thought of them, and of Anatole France, as I stood in my room in Rome, and I was certain of the wisdom of my course.

III

When Anatole France was a small and serious-eyed youngster, as we know from his uncanny and sensitive memoirs, his parents began to describe him as "bookish." That is not exceptional. The world is full of small, serious-eyed youngsters who are "bookish."

In childhood we live in a fabulous world. Some never outgrow it. Our Andersens, Wildes, and Cabells write fairy tales long into their maturity. They compose them not only for children but for grown men and women in whom there still remains an element of the fantasy that enkindled their earlier days. It is to the imagination that all literature, even the most realistic, makes its appeal. When, however, the imagination directs itself to the creation of a fable that shall have a closer resemblance to our actual lives and announces that it possesses a definite moral purpose, literature takes on a new dignity, perhaps the highest dignity accruing to any of the works of man.

Very little of this moral purpose is perceived by the average reader. He buys books to enjoy them, but his appreciation is limited to that of a concert-goer who is held by a lyric melody alone. To that concert-goer there is small difference between a melody by Beethoven and one by Offenbach. Both are lovely.

He likes both. And that is all. He misses the deeper beauty and communicable meaning of the greater work.

The serious-eyed grow up to be a different sort of concert-goer. They are introspective. Since they are always seeking for an inner meaning in their own lives, they seek for it also in the works of important artists.

That is what I meant to do, starting all over again in my reading. But just how?

You cannot spend all your time reading books. If you did, you would gain little. You become tone-deaf after you have listened to music too long; besides, there is always the necessity of earning a living. Apart from that, there is the second necessity of knowing what you are reading about. I should consider my life well-spent if my experiences helped me to understand, to the very last word, one of the great books we shall discuss in this essay. But I knew, in that Roman room, that I could never arrive at that by rereading the book twenty times. There are many professors who lecture on Shakespeare, conning every obscure phrase, who have not the least notion of what Shakespeare was trying to say. They are pedants. Only by living fully can we fully understand a good book, and only by reading fully, and understanding most of what we read, can we realize all the possibilities that living presents.

For a time, that notion of making a thorough study of one great book did attract me. My heart sank when I thought of going back over all those thousands of volumes which lay behind me. But I saw the other dangers of reading one book alone. The experience of doing that would be too narrow, considering how wide the world is. Some religious people have said that a man could profitably spend all his years reading that most impressive of anthologies, the Bible, but I was inclined to think them wrong. There is much wisdom and beauty in the Bible, and also much inspiriting melodrama. It must be observed, however, that many who conduct themselves most rigorously by its precepts are still ungracious bigots.

Then I played that mental game, popular and amusing, of telling myself that I was on a desert isle and asking myself what six or twelve books I would choose to have with me. Most often, when this inconsequential question is asked of people of consequence, the Bible is always the first mentioned, with invariable public piety; and *Robinson Crusoe* next, or some other practical guide to living most comfortably on a desert isle. Then the works of Shakespeare are usually included.

Since I did not have to appear pious, not even to myself, and since I did not have to anticipate the actual physical difficulties that beset a castaway, I had more liberty in my choice.

My original discontent, I had perceived, had been born of the realization that I had only one life to live: that I was one sort of person and not another. "Now," I said to myself, "I am not an earthy sort of person like Fielding's Tom Jones." Yet it seemed to me that about all that could be said for an earthy sort of person has been said for Tom Jones. And that is why he is an important person to meet in literature. On any desert island containing typical representatives of the varied human race, Tom Jones would have to be at hand.

I began to think of others like him in literature, whom I had found important to meet, and they came quickly to mind: Melville's Billy Budd, whom I was nothing like; and Hardy's Jude, in whom I could recognize something of myself. The books in which these typical young men appear as characters were ones that I would most certainly restudy.

And then, proceeding much as Noah had done when selecting passengers for his Ark, I worked out my reading plan.

But the plan had possibilities that I did not realize in that first moment. They appeared to me later, when I set to it in earnest. For although I was not a professional critic in any sense of the word, I had now a persuasive notion of what amateur criticism entails. Anatole France had suggested it to me. "The soul's adventures among masterpieces." One's autobiographical development. It might lead me somewhere. And thereafter my reading, because I had a sense of direction, was always more enjoyable.

At odd moments, in the years since I was in Rome, I have been compiling this book.

Chapter 2

A Quarrel with the Critics

BEFORE WE can have new ideas we must often rid ourselves of old ones.

Remembering my disappointment when I had approached the works of critics, before I went to Rome, but willing to accept the blame for it, I now investigated their essays again.

But most books of criticism are intended for writers and other critics. Few have any meaning to the average reader, although there is one short book by Arnold Bennett which teaches the almost illiterate how to develop a liking for Charles Lamb by a series of easy reading exercises.

A book with a plan such as I had in mind existed nowhere. Perhaps professional critics had never considered a book of this sort within their province. Their neglect to produce such a work made it seem so, but in that event I was ready to quarrel with them.

Mary Colum, in a recent book, has spoken of our age as one without criticism in the greater sense.

At all times in literary history, good professional critics have been rarer than good writers. This suggests an amusing paradox, that there is more good writing than there are critics to appreciate it; hence the possibility of many undiscovered masterpieces.

Observation does not let us cherish that hope. It must seem, to any follower of literary news, that contemporary masterpieces are quite the opposite of undiscovered; indeed no week passes without the trumpeted arrival of a new work of genius, which for some reason is forgotten by the year's end.

If the professional critics err on the side of generosity, that is the better fault. We are not treated any longer to such hounding as pursued the luckless Keats, nor such indifference as met Melville. At least, one presumes not; for it is not every day that a Keats or Melville appears.

But these—who praise so indiscriminately—are not the best professional critics; they are reviewers who write hurriedly at the time of the book's publication. We may suppose there is a difference between a professional critic and a reviewer;

practically, the former sees his pronouncements finally issued in book form, while the reviewer's opinion, most times fortunately for him, is published only on perishable newsprint. The literary critic is more often concerned with writers recently dead—and hence no longer able to confound forecasts—or contemporaries of substantial reputation, whose importance he is anxious to measure, fixing them in the historic scene.

These professional critics are most perceptive. But usually they pride themselves on their intellectual detachment, which really means that they are concerned with demonstrating to their readers how clever they are (and they are clever), how sound are their own ideas, and how vividly accomplished is their prose. They are fond of catching authors in witty, mellifluous phrases. Thus the much quoted Mr. Chesterton has described Thomas Hardy as "the village atheist brooding and blaspheming over the village idiot." That is a happy example, to which we might return later.

We cannot despise the professional critics for writing vividly. But we can despise them for not thinking as vividly; they seldom declare themselves for an author, as do the reviewers, but are content to study literary influences and contributions. After warming their subject in the pan, they delicately hand him over to their public.

What qualifies them as critics, aside from their intelligence and wit? They know the rules of writing, which is to some extent an apprehensible craft. But they do not presume on this to announce any fixed standard as the one by which they guide themselves, unless they have a radical political or religious allegiance; and on the whole they are to be commended on their tolerance. Many of them conceive their function to be that of interpretation rather than judgment; and indeed criticism has a special warrant for interpretation in these days of obscurant James Joyce and T. S. Eliot, both of whom are worthy of explanation, and about whom so much has already been written that each might better be described as not an artist in his own right, but a collaborator.

Some authors would regret the need for critical collaboration and even resent it as intrusive. But Joyce and Eliot, I believe, would be quite lost without it. Their debt to professional criticism is considerable, though Eliot himself has lessened that debt by becoming perhaps one of our most notable professional critics.

Delving in the complex depths of Verlaine, Mallarmé, Joyce, or Eliot is no easy task. But just as I had convinced myself that the primary function of criticism is not a study of literary technique, so I am convinced that fundamentally criticism is even less interpretation. The author interprets. Should I have to interpret the author? Then most likely he is a poor artist. It is different with Joyce and Eliot, for there interpretation concerns itself with the author's manner, rather than his content. A new manner, like anything else new, may need explanation.

And I was sure, from having met scholarly critics in the universities, that mere scholarship is not a sufficient qualification for the critic, although it does provide a necessary background. The lecturers on Shakespeare tell us the meaning of archaic words and allusions, they annotate texts, but they speak with dry voices.

Criticism, appearing in any of these forms, did not affect me vitally. How could it? Wit, interpretation, scholarship . . . what more? Something was lacking. As an amateur critic, I was sure of my ground. There should be a book written for me, because my desire was a genuine one. And unless it satisfied my desire, a book of criticism was not complete.

Earlier I said that I was more serious about literature than are the critics. That is true. They talk about the literary value of books and the literary importance of authors; that is why their audience is small. They are not concerned, as most readers are, with relating art to everyday life.

II

What Is Art? is the title of a brilliant, wrong-headed, and even self-annihilating essay by Tolstoi. It contains a great deal of glorious nonsense, but also one of the most profound observations on art ever written. *"Art,"* says Tolstoi, *"is the transmission of emotion."*

You have only to ask yourself what happens when you look at a work of art to learn how true that is.

Something "happens"—that is your first discovery. You are not tranquil before a work of art. It communicates something to you, excitement and usually a persuasive excitement.

And criticism involves excitement. That was what I had been feeling every day during my stay in Rome, as I walked through the noble corridors of the Vatican, staring at the ceiling of the Sistine Chapel, gazing upon the earth-yellowed marbles of Greek antiquity. That is where, as an amateur critic, I differed from the professional critics. They were afraid to get excited. Enthusiasm is indiscreet.

The qualified amateur critic, as well as the good professional critic of literature, has to be many things. He must be an experienced reader, with some sophistication in the world of books. If he wishes the fullest esthetic pleasure, he must have a sufficient knowledge of literary craft. He must be, to a lesser extent, an interpreter and scholar. But he is only a complete critic when, in addition to his proven qualifications in these other roles, he is still capable of experiencing—and, if professional, communicating—an informed, excitant enthusiasm. The moment that in emulation of the professional critics he proudly intrudes his "intellectual detachment," he has lost what makes a work of art. He no longer has the work of art before him. The emotion, the communicable excitement, has disappeared.

It is the emotional quality in a novel that induces a "moral hypnosis." That emotional quality is the result of the author's profound conviction.

If you are a good amateur critic you differ from the professional—in degree, not in kind—in your capacity for fervor. Since you are not doing so in public, you may indulge your enthusiasm to the fullest. You are like the man casting his ballot in a political conflict; you either vote for the author or you do not. You plunge.

But you do so in private.

The professional critic has to be more careful. He is the bondsman of discretion. But then, the professional critics know the tricks whereby they can say everything and say nothing, seldom committing themselves. Their wit protects them.

"Hardy . . . the village atheist brooding and blaspheming over the village idiot."

Thus Mr. Chesterton turns a phrase seemingly so apt and memorable that you cannot despise him; you envy him for writing so brightly. You forget to ask whether the village atheist *should* not weep over the village idiot. Most decidedly, in my opinion, he should.

On the other hand, Mr. Chesterton was not an atheist; he was exceedingly devout. He was the Catholic apologist brooding over the literary atheist, no less subject to ridicule by someone of an opposite mood.

Professional criticism as practiced, you perceive, is a game of words and ideas, sometimes very illuminating, but usually at the expense of someone's reputation.

Amateur criticism goes straight to the heart of literature. Is it important to you, the village atheist weeping over the idiot? It is. You can become quite excited about it. Because the idiot concerns Hardy—he sees the poor creature as the victim and symbol of a senseless, malign Nature proceeding blindly on her way—and he is a great artist and communicates his conviction to you.

The next time you read a book of professional criticism ask yourself how much enthusiasm its author has, and how indiscreet he dares to be.

III

The whole conception of the critic's rôle has been vitiated by the attractive legend of Dr. Johnson.

Dr. Johnson presided pontifically over the letters of his day, an epigrammatic dictator of rules and morals. But the truth is, Dr. Johnson is not a great critic. He is not even a very good one. He is rather a great talker, an impressive lexicographer, a monumental personality. He knew very little about literature; he made unpardonable mistakes. He read *Tom Jones*, the greatest book of his age, and declared it bad. Nothing "happened" to Dr. Johnson when he encountered a masterpiece. He had no humility.

You have only to compare him to men who are truly great critics—Matthew Arnold, Coleridge, Pater—to see all that Dr. Johnson is not; for these men are seers; they combine knowledge of craft with scholarship and emotional insight, such as comes only to those who have a creative compulsion of their own. Coleridge communicates his enthusiasm —and this is the point—not to the reader alone, but to his fellow authors as well! The greatest critic is a Janus in his enthusiasm: he faces both ways.

Great criticism is always acknowledged to be creative. It inspires reader and writer alike.

And finally you see that it is Boswell who is the great critic, but of Dr. Johnson. He plunges. He communicates *his* enthusiasm; and creatively he does so in both directions. Dr. Johnson was inspired by that enthusiasm; he must have sat beaming, talking and talking, while the enchanted Boswell listened. A divine garrulity.

Actually, Dr. Johnson talks too much. Like most incompetent critics at all times, Dr. Johnson is always ready with an "opinion." An "opinion" about a work of art is often superfluous—since a work of art "happens." Emily Dickinson explains that in her famous account of how she knew that she had read a good poem. She felt as though her head had blown off. We need not go quite that far; Emily's was an extremely passionate nature.

Nor can we say that one should never question what has happened, or why. But most of us rush in, and especially the critics into print, without waiting for anything to "happen." If time were allowed to pass, there might be no need for an opinion. If last week's book is already forgotten, that is criticism enough. But time also gives space for the explosion. Sometimes a work of art does not "happen" at once. Frequently we dislike a good book when we are actually reading it. Only in involuntary retrospect do we come to like it exceedingly.

On the whole, we could do famously with having opinions on less than one of ten books or plays or paintings we see. We are wiser simply to experience and enjoy, not bothering to cast a vote unless the work has so affected us that a decision is urgent. (It does not happen often.) Then we should be prepared to go the full way, or not at all. That is the way of esthetic enjoyment. It also leaves the esthetic sensibilities fresh. It makes the critical process a rite. For having opinions about everything is tiresome and probably unwarranted. An opinion, to have value, should be reached slowly, with full information.

We should work, nine times out of ten, for understanding rather than judgment. The two are not synonymous. The rest of my quarrel with the professional critics is that they have deadened their emotional response to a genuine work of art when it comes by having already had too many opinions on trivial works. They hurry too much. They cannot afford the enthusiasm that comes from deliberation and deep conviction. They are host to no explosions.

IV

This does not advocate enthusiasm as an omnibus for criticism. There can be enthusiastic bad critics as well as enthusiastic good critics. It is possible for the critics to have enthusiasm for bad literature because their knowledge of the craft is fallible, or their knowledge of life, and consequently their values. That accounts for the numerous masterpieces discovered weekly by incompetent reviewers.

It is not always possible either—especially for amateur critics—for enthusiasm to be Janus-like, so that it encourages the practicing writer. For the author is likely to be out of the amateur's reach, and of the professional too, since the latter is so often concerned with writers long dead. I have only suggested that a *great* critic of his contemporaries would be such a man as Ruskin was with his painters. He helped them; he lent them his zeal, his knowledge, and fought for them.

Yet to a lesser extent such criticism obtains among practicing writers themselves. It was so in the salons of Paris, where George Moore and Turgenev and Zola met and discussed their art. It explains the fondness writers have for the company of other writers, their tendency to form cliques and colonies, where there is creative sympathy.

It obtains, also, this Janus-like exchange, when the amateur critic talks to himself about art, and that meeting—of the amateur critic with himself—is, to my mind, far more important and exciting. It is an individual experience, but a creative, enthusiastic one.

Perhaps no work of art is fully realized until such amateur criticism occurs. It marks the completion of the novelist's task. He challenges criticism. He demands that the intelligent reader shall enthusiastically come to a decision. If he can win an opinion, he has succeeded. The reader must confess to himself that *if* he has been driven to pass judgment on a work, even though his decision may be unfavorable in the light of some moral or philosophical prejudice, he has admitted the author's artistic success. He disapproves of what the artist has to say, but the necessity of his reaching an opinion gives testimony to how efficaciously the artist has delivered himself.

Thus we observe again that two things every work of art requires are excitement, compulsion.

This does not imply violence. Perfection, in whatever shape, holds us. Some authors—like Elinor Wylie—have a feeling for what is small and attractive, not important, but pleasant. If my mind contemplating the author's artificial, miniature world—the world of *Mr. Hodge and Mr. Hazard* and *The Venetian Glass Nephew*—shares some of its creator's enthusiasm, I experience one of the small excitements of art.

I may look breathlessly from the height of Mann's *Magic Mountain*.

But there must be excitement in art, an excitement that the critical process must help to engender, not dispel.

What—for the intelligent reader of the novel—is the critical process?

Chapter 3

The Search for Amateur Criticism

BUT FIRST, what is the novel?

There can be as much unwisdom in too many definitions as in too few. I shall not attempt one. But I do not suppose anyone will fail to understand what I am talking about.

Matthew Arnold says that the highest literature contains "criticism of life."

It follows that in order to criticize such literature competently, our criticism itself must involve a "criticism of life." Both writing and reading a book entail that task.

That is the difficulty of criticism. But perhaps it is easier to arrive at a sound conclusion about life when judging a great book, than at any other time.

One reason is that the novel may show us worlds we do not know, but should know. Or a novel may correct our perspective toward the world with which we are too well acquainted. The function of art has often been spoken of as a helpful attempt to make the new seem familiar; and the old, new. Both ways, when we read a great book our minds are stimulated.

Such books—that stimulate our minds—are philosophical; they interest us because they illuminate character and consciously or unconsciously interpret reality; and when they do this, they achieve a condensation of truth.

But when they stimulate our minds, they also stir our emotions; otherwise we are no longer in the realm of art, but of history, biography, or proper philosophy.

Please observe that I have inserted the word *unconsciously,* for after all that is how the novelist usually works; he sits at his desk to tell a story, not to write a moral tract or an out-and-out philosophical discussion. I hold no brief for such moral tracts and simple philosophical discussions. Quite the contrary. But when we limit the novel to the bounds of an art-form, we invest it with all the authority of imaginative literature, which by its nature must draw on life and mirror it concretely, in order to be successfully vivid, to convince.

We should look next at this authority—the authority of imaginative literature, of art. From it the novel derives its philosophical warrant.

Most popularly it is held that when a novel is philosophical, it is not a good novel, but a dull, didactic one.

Well, *Tom Jones* is a philosophical novel!

II

The first question I asked myself, in formulating my reading plan, was not "Why do I read?"—I could always answer that —but "Why do authors write?" Their motive was important to me.

The answer is a simple one. "Because they cannot help themselves. . . . They *have* to write."

Why?

Well, what is art? It did not seem that I could reach a simple answer to that. I did not attempt a simple answer. Too many books have been written, establishing one definition or another; so many arguments have been held, but seemingly in vain, that I was not reckless enough to emulate their proponents. I had read too many pages of esthetics, many of them emblazoned with intuitive flashes into some small part of art, but most of them sterile, to care much for esthetic talk or to approach the subject reverently.

On a certain wet evening in New York, very late, I was returning home when I passed a young man on a bench laden with books and manuscripts. The sight of that tousled young man in the dark drizzle surrounded by such unusual luggage interested me, and I sat down next to him.

He answered my first question by saying ingenuously, "I am a playwright." Before I could ask further, he assured me that he was a genius. He then handed me a manuscript copy of a play to prove his claim, and by the flickering light of a match held in the faint rain, I was able to read a few lines of the composition he described as his favorite.

"It sounds a bit like Synge," I remarked, not knowing whether this was an intentional echo of the Irish dramatist.

He made no comment. Instead, he told me his story. He had come to New York from California, walking part of the way. He was penniless. His plays, stories, and novels were great works of art, but he could not sell them. The landlord had locked him from his room; he was coatless and hatless in the rain, but—as I could see—he had contrived to salvage some of his books and manuscripts, which was better than nothing. He laughed at his plight and said it amused him. He was young, strong, and lank. Seen in the wet night, his cheerful self-confidence impressed me. He reminded me a little of Thomas Wolfe; not the actual, mature Thomas Wolfe, whom I did not know, but the youthful swaggering Gant of Wolfe's confessedly autobiographical novel, *Look Homeward, Angel!* And a few moments later, in answer to a query about the kind of novels he wrote, my new friend said instantly, "Like Thomas Wolfe's." Literature obviously has its effect. Since my encounter with this damp but romantic young genius was so brief, I cannot pretend to know whether the general acceptance of Thomas Wolfe's gospel, that of a vigorous vagabondage in life, was wholly responsible for this young man's behavior— as, at the end of an earlier century, Goethe's *Sorrows of Young Werther* had set all the wan youth of Europe to doleful sighing after death—or whether a natural affinity had merely been further strengthened by his meeting with a popular author through the medium of print. He shared Wolfe's verbosity, though. This discouraged me. My duty was clear; my sympathy was active. "You can't stay in the rain. Come home with me," I said. "I'll give you something to eat and find some place or other for you to sleep."

My premises were cold and still, and I was tired. But hot coffee and food revived my companion. His brown eyes lit with exuberant appreciation of his youth, momentary shelter, warmth, and companionship. "It's late. Are you sleepy? Let's talk! In the morning, I'll be gone."

"What shall we talk about?" I asked.

"Life and Art."

He was persuasive and eager. His was the ruthlessness that belongs to youth and genius alike. Nothing availed with him, my reference to the hour, my plans for the next day, the coldness of the room, my weariness. He talked, argued, expounded. He cajoled: "It is not often that two persons like us meet, under such unusual circumstances. We must make the most of this opportunity to exchange ideas." This was flattering, even though he did all the talking, while I listened. But his self-belief, the exploits he recounted, the naïve revelation of his self as an artist and person, were as compelling as sleep. I dared not close my heavy eyes and surrender: I was subject to two antagonistic magics. He sat in a blue chair across the room from me, his energetic voice loud, his garrulity ceaseless. In the dream-like, half-consciousness in which my attendant senses drifted, I envied him and wondered whether he might not be the genius he represented himself. Yeats, I remembered, had once had the peace and privacy of his rooms invaded by a scolding, pedagogic youth who had finally announced that his name was James Joyce, and who then fled into the night. Galsworthy, the lone passenger on a tramp steamer in Eastern waters, had made the acquaintance of the ship's mate, a young Pole who called himself Joseph Conrad. Such meetings were rare, but exciting to think about. My respect for Yeats and Galsworthy was so great that I would be grateful to experience adventures like theirs. So I strove for wakefulness. For my reward, I have since seen one of the young man's plays in print—he is still very young—in the company of works by several acknowledged masters. Who knows what the future holds for him?

But at last the protesting nerves and flesh could stand no more.

"May I say something?" I begged.

He paused, his gesticulating, outlined figure vague against the drawn shade and the early morning light shining coldly through the glassy margin of the window.

"I am very tired. You are an incredible bore. And please, when you speak of Life and Art, say instead, 'My life' and 'My literary work.'"

This was rude but excellent advice, but the young man did not take it, for I now observed that the moment he had stopped the effort of talking, he had instantly fallen asleep, his handsome brown head fallen forward on his chest.

III

This is a true story and may explain why, at the very mention of the words Life and Art, by an associative process I stifle a yawn, as it may be you, the reader, do too.

But when, of necessity, I came to that question in Rome, asking again, but modestly, "What is art?" it seemed to me that in their long vexatious attempt at a handy explanation of art and philosophy, the relation between the two, and their separate relations to life, supposedly wise men have erred in seeking epigrammatic phrases.

Thus Tolstoi says, "Art is the transmission of emotion." Or Roger Fry declares, "Art is significant form."

Philosophy has fared as badly.

I had read enough to perceive that any attempt to circumscribe the whole meaning of art in a pert sentence is presumptuous and futile, because art represents a hemisphere of human activity of which no easy census can be taken. There are a thousand communities in which men bring to art and ask of art a thousand things.

The same is true of philosophy.

The whole realm of esthetics resembles a Pirandello play, the characters without an established identity; it is like a fantastic village of two hundred souls, and for those two hundred souls, one family name; and the lay reader's the difficulty of anyone who attempts to go about in that village and ask for people by their last names only.

Anyone who wants to recapitulate the more important of the many esthetic theories should read Tolstoi's comprehensive essay, wherein he wanders backstage at the Imperial Opera House, observes the ballet making ready for a performance amid an expensive clatter and bustle of activity, and wonders what sane purpose all this feverish talent serves. None, Tolstoi thinks. He traces the history of art, summarizes the opinion of philosophers and estheticians since the beginning, refutes them all, and proceeds to a mélange of humanitarianism, mysticism, and pietism of his own as irrelevant to a true depiction and understanding of art as anything ever set down. Pathetically, Tolstoi not only dismisses Shakespeare but is even forced to renounce the works that made him, too, revered and famous: all this in a book that, despite its great faults, is still our best modern treatise on its subject.

Then, whether one reads Tolstoi or goes independently to other estheticians, one learns that many of them think that art derives from life, but distorts life in some measure, according to the genius of the artist, who illuminates a portion of reality to us in the light of his own flame. As we may see reality through the eyes of enchanted Keats . . . the hoarfrost world of St. Agnes' Eve.

Others like Nietzsche believe that life molds itself to art, that men alter the incomplete pattern of their ways to fit an ever-growing law laid down by those more perceptive than themselves. As once women, having read Rousseau, tore their babies from their nurses' arms and put them to the breast, to vindicate their challenged motherhood. . . . Two theories that are contradictory, yet not incompatible. Art in both of these is a dynamic exchange, borrowing from reality and contributing to it.

But there are also Realists who would not permit art to be anything more than simple imitation; and at the other extreme "Presentationalists," like Mr. Gordon Craig, who deem art to be "illusion," and who, proceeding by far-fetched logic, would even substitute marionettes for living actors on an abstract stage. I rather fancy that Mr. Craig is lucky to come after Tolstoi and thus escape inclusion in his essay and the patriarchal wrath; yet "Presentationalism" is an idea whose very lifelessness has a strange vitality; for Gordon Craig has given us "pure theater," which has led to Expressionism and Constructivism, contributions to the virility and color of contemporary plays.

In the world of philosophy, one finds William James berating all his predecessors as barren intellectualists, much as did Tolstoi in esthetics.

The professional critics, whom we have already described as tolerant, survey this battling scene and observe there nothing but confusion, but they know that this confusion results from little more than a poverty of words to cover a wealth of interesting ideas. They do not find it hard to reconcile all these theories. There is no question, for example, that what Gordon Craig describes as art is something at pleasant but ineffectual removes from what he means by life; but also no question that his art is not the only art, nor his vision of life the only possible vision. This having been admitted, the critics find themselves still free to agree with Plato, Kant, Schopenhauer, Pater, Ruskin and others who preceded Mr. Craig; and so an esthetic pragmatism is established, one suggestion considered about as valuable as the next, depending on which is momentarily the most useful.

You cannot blame the modern critics for recommending that we have only to learn the first names of those for whom we search, that we must speak of Tolstoi's "Art," Nietzsche's "Art," or Schopenhauer's "Art," and ungrudgingly admit a place to all of them.

Still, I think the problem is not quite as difficult as it has been made to seem. There is a constant—the word "art," and here we are speaking only of imaginative literature, holds a fixed shape. It is valuable to expose it.

Who is anxious to open shop alongside Plato? Not mine, such effrontery. But perhaps as amateurs we should take a chance, however brash, than with the professional critics go out of business altogether.

IV

Most definitions of art are not definitions at all—they are, as with Tolstoi, propaganda. They usually include a *pronunciamento* of the purpose to which art should be wielded. They help us to distinguish moral art, immoral art, amoral art, judged by its effect. But though art, if it has an effect, must work for good or bad (and there can be no doubt that the highest art is moral, and the most popular art immoral), we beg the esthetic question, or rather never ask it at all, when we succumb to such moral propaganda. We decide that a man is a poor artist because, like Zola, he writes of street women; or because, like Baudelaire, he loves the morbid; or because, like Galsworthy, he pities men at the "top of his voice," when these are for the moment irrelevant considerations. We are judging the artist as a man, not as an artist.

The artist is a man. He is subject to moral judgments. Art is also liable to moral and social judgments. But because an artist or a work of art has a high or low morality does not mean that the result is artistically more or less successful. Zola, once condemned for his immorality, is today praised for his social conscience. But Zola's merit as an artist has been fixed; it is neither as high nor as low as successive generations, with altering mores, have acclaimed it. They are hailing the moralist, the sociologist, not the artist. Who now remembers which Greek dramatists were honored, which exiled from Athens for their religious attitudes? When we read Wilde and Baudelaire, we forgive them for their personal transgressions. We are even grateful to them. They have, in a sense, produced art of the greatest morality, because as artists they are disciplined, sincere, effective. They also celebrate avenues of experience hitherto closed to us: above all, they help us to understand.

I would like to make myself clear about this. It was Oscar Wilde who said that a man might be a poisoner without affecting his prose style. Even a good Catholic philosopher like Jacques Maritain agrees with Wilde on this. Maritain is also ready to forgive the personal faults of the errant artist. ("We do not have to judge him. God will work it out with him, somehow or other.") Furthermore, a great many other critics and estheticians argue—and this is going on to another point—that an "evil book" should be judged only for the skill with which it is written. Such books as Nabokov's *Lolita* and Genet's *Thief's Journal* are defended in this spirit. Elizabeth Drew has stated this position very well:

> The artist takes as much pains and is as much absorbed in his creation of evil as of good, of ugliness as of beauty. He lavishes as much work and care, and exactly the same *sort* of work and care, on Iago as on Othello, on Medea as on Alcestis, on a gargoyle as on the Venus of Milo. He looks upon experience as an end in itself, while the moralist regards it as a symptom which must be treated in relation to some general manifestation of truth, and requires that a book shall conform to some special ethical formula.

Most commentators on art, fearful of interference by the too easily shocked and censorious, hold fast to this position. Santayana does; he does not want busybody puritans taking over the realm of art, which he deems to be chiefly concerned with the bright and holiday side of life.

Much as I dislike hypocrisy and overzealous puritanism, I still find myself lined up with the moralists. For it was also Wilde who declared most perceptively that life—and even nature—imitates art, as much as the opposite. So that, it seems to me, art cannot ever disclaim its moral responsibility. If evil is made too attractive in art, because the artist himself is consciously or unconsciously corrupt, who can deny that the work will seduce and lead astray? Shall he be granted that license? The important question, Wilde aside, is not whether the poisoner's prose style is good, but what ideas he uses his prose to convey—and if his ideas purport to be ethical ones, the fact of his being a poisoner—or a thief, or lecher—is likely to be much to the point. Personally, I do not see how the rôles of the artist and the moralist can be completely separated; though again—as I have said just above—the circumstance that a writer is moral does not alone make a true artist of him. He may be well-intentioned and virtuous, a saint, yet wholly ineffectual at his craft. I am convinced, moreover, that any moralizing in art should be done subtly and implicitly, never explicitly; for the latter method is bad art. To sum up: the artistic success of a book is one thing, its moral worth is another, yet they are inextricably connected. It is preposterous to claim otherwise.

This necessary and yet temporarily irrelevant concern with morality arises chiefly in a discussion of the art of imaginative literature. That art is different from the art of music, the art of painting or sculpture. All the fine arts have certain impulses and ends in common, but each works through a different medium and is at last inseparable from that medium. What we decree for the art of imaginative literature cannot be taken as the rule for any other. But this is not a return to pragmatism. There is an absolute truth about the art of imaginative literature.

What is art? Here is the answer. Art is the *control* of experience: a control of the artist first over himself, then over the medium he has selected, and finally over the reader or observer of his artistic work. Art is something compulsive. It is something hypnotic.

This is not an epigram. As it stands, it can be instantly reduced to absurdity (as Tolstoi's "transmission of emotion" is ridiculed). Control of experience? If I should take a club and hit someone on the head, would that be the art of imaginative literature? It would affect the recipient's experience in just the way I intended! He would be compelled. He would be hypnotized. The answer could be, when Dickens created Dotheboys Hall, to expose the intolerable evils at English public schools, he did just that, took a club and hit the English public on the head. So too Ibsen, in *An Enemy of the People*. Art had excitement.

But no, *control of experience* remains a meaningless phrase until it shall be qualified for pages beyond number. By then it would assume a more wieldy shape. But since I have no ambitions to become an esthetician, nor—I anticipate—has the reader, we shall proceed more quickly and assume that we know exactly what is meant by the artist's control, or discipline, or projected self-hypnotism. Many so-called definitions of art, stated epigrammatically, describe means by which this control or compulsion may be established; and here, as I have said before, we find that Tolstoi's "transmission of emotion" is perhaps the most effective of them all.

Control: the word is dynamic. It suggests, as our picture of the artist, the master of self-discipline, jealous of his skill—which includes his ability to think clearly and express himself, with a courageous devotion to what is honest. Since art never deals with the ordinary—save in an extraordinary manner—his control over his medium transcends the usual and is

partly measured by the alertness and compassionate understanding with which he gathers, from observation of life, and
from his own living, the truths that are to be his artistic
resources, the plots, the metaphors, that go into his story.

Perfection, we have suggested, compels. Only by his
approach to perfection shall the artist earn control over his
reader, in whom he shall summon up a suspension of disbelief.
By then the reader is quite his to do with as he will, by
the exertion of that "moral hypnotism" of which Granville-
Barker spoke. Thomas Mann, when he writes of the evil
Magician who casts his spell over the hapless Mario, dramatizes this. Does not Mario at last rebel and murder the
necromancer, who admits to no ethical obligation?

This postulates art as hypnotic? Yes. And is not perfection
hypnotic? We act at the artist's bidding. Our heart beats
faster as the musician dictates. Dreams come at his command.
The architect determines what lines our eyes shall follow.
The painter presents colors in a composition which we enter,
losing ourselves, subject to the artist's dominant vision. The
great dramatist works through his players to order the emotions of his audience: we weep when the tragic poet wills, or
laugh with the satirist; the members of the audience are really
the characters of the play. Thus we have some modern dramatists, as O'Neill in *Emperor Jones,* who even use physical
means to achieve control: aside from Brutus Jones's revealed
emotions being so primitive that we share them naturally, we
know he is afraid, because we see and hear what he is afraid
of, even what is imagined or supernatural. We hear the tom-
toms, the rattle of the ghostly dice-bones, the clinking of the
road-gang chains, and we too wait lost in darkness. Shakespeare has no need for such devices, but by knowing men
so well that the revelation of his characters is for each of us
self-revelation, he gathers us to him as a beacon gathers
moths, a light to which we cannot close our eyes. So with the
poet, he must select just those words, Stendhal says, that will
cause in us the emotion which he wishes.

This way art provides us with vicarious experience, and that
alone may be the end of art. Vicarious experience instinct with
"sweetness and light." . . . So a great many of the Victorians
envision art. Vicarious experience tantalizingly evil. . . . So the
French decadents and the Wildes and Beardsleys dwell on its
ripe promise. "It is the revelation—impossible by direct and
conscious means—of the qualitative differences in the way the

world appears to us, differences which, but for art, would remain the eternal secret of each of us," speaks Marcel Proust wisely. "Thanks to art, instead of seeing only one world, our own, we see it under multiple forms."

But art is something more than vicarious experience.

It may also serve with ideas as a medium of exchange, man to man, nation to nation—as with national art.

Yet art is something more than an exchange of ideas, a cultural expression of national and racial temperaments.

It may order reality for man's understanding, as Nietzsche argues. Or to put it better, I should say it may interpret reality to men, and men to themselves.

V

Considering art as a hypnotic control, may we not say things about it which are true, without prefixes? Yes, I think we may.

Our next question should be something of a complaint: "What a meddlesome fellow, this artist! Who is this self-chosen arbiter of other people's lives, this man who sits up to all hours, burns midnight-oil, to discover how he can persuade us, first this way, then that? For very likely, half the time the self-appointed artist—seldom the great man he believes himself—gets us into trouble."

True enough. I am not always sure that I like a man better after he has come from wandering in Joyce's grubby night-town—though Joyce is a genius, his courage and sincerity to be envied, and his *Portrait* a fine book. Yet here, and in the dead odor of Baudelaire's decadent flowers, the steam of Swinburne's fleshpots, the paranoid landscapes of Dali, are ways of life some would deem better never opened. Tolstoi thought that if the world could be cleansed of three-quarters of the dishonest or unwholesome art which clutters our halls and minds, existence would be sounder, the tangle of mental experience simplified. Though Tolstoi is partly wrong, because vicious art is not the sole cause of vicious living, and just as much the result of it. . . . You cannot deny the dishonest or the unwholesome either. They too belong with us, picturing our world as it is.

But these artists, why do they do it? Self-importance? Perhaps vanity accounts for eight-tenths of this production, good and bad—a vanity too often put to practical purpose. For the artist combines leisure—or a freedom from routine that an eight-hour-a-day world calls leisure—with occasionally sufficient reward to bring him a living.

Yet we do not so readily throw over even the minor artist as a presumptuous or self-seeking interloper in the daily scheme of things. Deeper than vanity or self-interest, there is an urge, bound up with inner articulateness and a power of expression, one springing from the other, which exercises a compulsion over him. This compulsion of inner articulateness is one which the artist cannot deny. He is like the student who, almost before he knows what he is doing, raises his hand in class to a question for which he has the answer. He must speak out the things he knows and feels. Before he compels others, he is himself compelled.

He must speak out, for still another reason, which is that at some time all thinking men must speak out in answer to one question forever asked of them. That question is: What is for him, for other people, the most fruitful way of living? The artist, as I look upon him, is one who publishes his personal experience in attempting a solution of that question, and he publishes his experience not only because of vanity, but also because his is that born articulateness not to be gainsaid.

It is the question I asked myself in Rome. It is a question usually called philosophical. Only, instead of turning to philosophy for an answer, I was proposing to search for it in novels. Therein, I was soon told, lay my heresy.

VI

What is philosophy?

Once I wrote a short play called *Simon Simon* which was filled with absurd and fantastic logic and intended to poke fun at certain modern philosophical fads. On the night the play was produced, I observed to my horror that not only were the actors taking my play seriously, but so also were the audience and newspaper critics, whose columns the next day earnestly pointed out that much of my thought was sophistical and my argument unconvincing.

Thus I was taught that one has only to pronounce the word "philosophy" and immediately everyone looks respectful and worried.

Such solemnity is often incongruous. It once prompted me to set up an "improper philosophy" of my own, reasonably called a "Philosophy of the As If and the What of It," that was still accepted with quite enough gravity. (Perhaps I should explain that what I was rather youthfully proposing—though the title of my essay may have seemed somewhat too flippant—was to formulate an approach to problems by combining ideas included in Vaihinger's stimulating *Philosophy of the As If* and William James's *Pragmatism*. I was in earnest, and my title was appropriate, but there was no need to be too sober about it.)

Many of the great philosophers were not serious or even respectable: the henpecked Socrates, the cowardly Montaigne, the scoundrelly Bacon, the mad Nietzsche. It remained for the ponderous German Idealists to establish a tradition of "proper" philosophy, the tradition at which William James laughed.

"Philosophy," the proper philosopher would say, "is the creation of a metaphysical system."

Yet has it not always been suspect that in systems our best minds have wasted their energies by raising answers to unanswerables? Was that not why William James, because he sought less pretentiously, was perhaps the noblest among his kind?

"An attempt to settle the most fruitful way of living"—James, I am sure, would have considered that a sufficient task for a philosopher. He might even have described it as the most important work that philosophy could undertake; and I wonder if he would not think that a good novel is one which joins in this work, and as such is the most vital and effective of all imaginative and intellectual endeavors: more effective by far than so-called systematic philosophy, with her webs of dialectic which, like the beauteous virgin in Veronese's allegory, she spins on her long fingers and holds aloft to her enraptured gaze.

To realize this, it is worthwhile to reach our own simple definition of art, as amateur critics, thereby finding that its ultimate function is quite the same as the ultimate function of philosophy.

The gracious Sir Philip Sidney, in the days before there were any novels to speak of, and imaginative literature was called "poesy," deplored proper philosophy in this manner:

For the philosopher, setting down with thorny arguments the bare rule, is so hard of utterance and so misty to be conceived, that one that hath no other guide but him (*to virtue*) shall wade in him till he be old, before he shall find sufficient cause to be honest. For his knowledge standeth so upon the abstract and general that happy is the man who may understand him, and more happy that can apply what he doth understand. . . .

Could that be said of proper philosophy today? Sir Philip continues:

Now doth the peerless poet perform both; for whatsoever the philosopher saith should be done, he giveth a perfect picture of it in someone by whom he presupposeth it was done, so as he coupleth the general notion with the particular example. [And,] For conclusion, I say the philosopher teacheth, but he teacheth obscurely, so as the learned only can understand him; that is to say, he teacheth them that are already taught. But the poet is food for the tenderest stomachs; the poet is indeed the right popular philosopher. Whereof Aesop's tales give good proof; whose pretty allegories, stealing under the formal tales of beasts, begin to hear the sound of virtue from those dumb speakers.

Yes, it had been with the tenderest of stomachs, the gullibility of the Russian peasant, the strongest of philosophical yearnings, that I had read thousands of novels after proper philosophy had repelled me.

Yet Sir Philip Sidney, in his charming *Defense of Poesy,* has not said all that I wanted to say. He differentiates the philosopher's method from that of the artist where the ethical end toward which they work is to all purposes the same; one is a passionless research through logic, rather than through experience and intuition, and hence remote from the real. One function of the artist, as Sidney sees him, is to act as mediator between philosopher and layman, transmuting for the people the words of wisdom poured and cooled in the logical crucible. So Chapman, after Sidney, propounds that "Poetry can discover philosophy retired to darkest caves."

That was not acceptable to me.

Shelley says it better: "Poetry is philosophy teaching by example."

Poetry *is* philosophy—honest imaginative literature is philosophy—and the artist of necessity, a philosopher. And as for the artist running back and forth, in the rôle of mediator, let us commend that to the weaker spirits; to those who write or paint not in response to some compulsion too strong for them, but merely as squires to the ideas of other men.

VII

The true artist is philosopher in his own right. He should never admit the proper or closet-philosopher superior to him. For the material of thought must be gathered from experience, and that is the field in which the artist, by virtue of his calling, is preëminent. Furthermore, the artist must carry his ideas through to experience again, in that world which he creates and which only carries conviction by its resemblance to nature; but the closet-philosopher has a freedom which frequently disperses itself in license. Nietzsche, locking himself in his room, could become the loudest anarchist in the world, propounding theories which incite other men, similarly locking themselves in their rooms, to a dangerous moral nihilism. But the artist Dostoevski, in *Crime and Punishment,* shows us what is likely to happen to a man who really achieves an end by living without conventional scruple, without "slave morality," the Nietzschean doctrine put to practice.

Philosophy can do harm, as in our days the purely meant but misapprehended Nietzschean concept has done, but in art is a safer testing ground for philosophical ideas, where they are brought face to face with appropriate circumstance. Tolstoi threshes out his problems on that stage, as do Dante, Shakespeare, Milton, Leonardo, Michelangelo, and Rembrandt. And probably nothing so inspired them to seek this stage as a desire to test their doubts and their conclusions in real terms, but more vividly than they could in their own lives. William Saroyan, that most spontaneous writer, calls his art a "correction of error—of personal error—the world's error." Robinson Jeffers, in his *Apology for Bad Dreams,* speaks of himself as poet and tells us what his poems are to him. Of the poet, Jeffers says:

He brays humanity in a mortar to bring the savor
From the bruised root: a man having bad dreams, who
    invents victims . . .

But of the man who has no dreams:

He being sufficient might be still.

This is probably why we so often have testimony from artists that they do not choose their subject, but that instead their subject has apparently chosen them. Some, like Marcel Proust, have a quite mystical conviction of this. Their subject seems to come to them from some empyrean, but more likely it has come from their subconscious. This is also why, in the opinion of some psychologists, an artist may encounter a "block," an inability to proceed with his work. He harbors something in himself too painful to disclose. He may be prevented from confronting it for a long time, even from admitting its existence in himself, until with his further maturity his feeling about his secret has lessened, disturbs him not as much; or, possibly, until he has found some artful symbolic disguise for it. If his problem is actually a neurotic one, we may observe him developing ritualistic habits—as Schiller needed to smell rotten apples before working, and a writer of my acquaintance requires his pencils to be arranged on his desk in just one way, and his paper piled just so—to help him exorcise an irrational fear or doubt in himself; such rituals are atavistic, akin to fetishes.

But I do not think that artists are more neurotic than the rest of mankind. And I do not believe that all their subjects come to them from their subconscious. In most major works, the themes set before us are to a great extent consciously chosen ones, treated by men of large intellect. What haunts men with bad dreams is not alone their irrational content, though that counts, too; but what can be clearly read in them, that which has a very discernible troublesome meaning. So the work of art is for them a "controlled dream," which corrects the irrational excesses of the night-time one, and seeks to bring illumination and sense to what might otherwise be personal distress and anarchy.

Any serious work of art, then—and, particularly, a novel—is a crucible, a meeting place of experience and philosophical ideas, where men who have dreams and cannot be still, imagine a situation which essentially resembles their own, though some outward details of this story may be superficially different. In that "plot," the characters come into conflict with one another, or with their pictured environment, to resolve the problem which has long troubled the author, perhaps obsessively. The conflict is one which the reader watches, held wordless by the artist's strong sense of conviction. The artist's honesty should be far greater than ours, and the deepest emotions of his characters presented with a candor we could never attain. Thus a superb work of art, a matchless expression of the human spirit, may put us to shame at our own unworthiness, when we compare ourselves, with all our human shortcomings, to the figures stripped of subterfuge that he courageously sets before us. But afterward we may rediscover ourselves with exaltation. Whatever has been accomplished here, in this brave and beautiful work of art, bestows its human glory on us; for we, too, share the artist's humanity—what has been achieved by him is potential in all men, in us, in others. This is one of our principal joys in art, this rediscovery of ourselves, of the promise inherent in mankind, before an embodiment of the artist's great sincerity. He has discovered some truth about human nature —he brilliantly demonstrates it, and helps us to know ourselves better. His conviction about it has first exerted itself on him, before he sends it through his medium to exert hypnotic control of us. Then we can stand before Rembrandt's *Inspiration,* and identifying ourselves with his St. Matthew, can hear the angel whispering at our ear.

The artist's conviction may be a single one, as with genius, whom we set apart from other men as warped, completely given to one cause, one compulsive idea. The establishment of the artist's dominion may indeed be in many ways unconscious. Shaw, explaining the *Ring* and contradicting Wagner's own account of what the *Ring* was meant to be, exclaims that Wagner probably knew no more about what he intended than Henry VIII, in the days before Harvey, knew about the circulation of his blood; although that king had a surprisingly brilliant surmise as to how his arteries served him.

(Very nice. I wonder could the same be said about Shaw's own work!)

VIII

The novel is the broadest stage in all the realm of art for the testing of philosophical or ethical ideas. The art of the novel is control, perhaps first of a writer over himself, and then of the observer who steps within the circle of the writer's strong conviction; and what concerns the novelist in this circle is a grappling with one aspect or another of our fundamental question, the most fruitful use of the years allotted to us.

His problem, squarely faced in a personally projected situation, emotionally embodied, cannot fail to hold us. Here is the crowded, struggling world we call the novel, for what purpose brought together, in what direction goes it—the eternal question asked this time of a creator not beyond our reach. But his answers are not compelling unless we see the method by which he has obtained them; that method not merely logical or abstract, but also impulsive, dramatically experiential.

So the novel is a vessel of life, transparent, like a chemist's test tube. The quintessence of the novel would be the *purpose* of the experiment, the writer's mortal hope. That hope is as inspired as the hope of any scientist. It is the pure essence of life, this controlled experience which the novelist heats before us in his marvelously transparent vessel. Yet he is not so much the chemist as the ancient magician: he is Faust peering at forbidden secrets, or Paracelsus almost consumed in the alchemic flame of his imagination.

It is for such a quintessential purpose in each book that the amateur critic must learn to search: its discovery and recognition *is* amateur criticism, autobiography. From then on, he can make use of the author's resolution of the fundamental problem; and when the reader is able to find it for himself in every novelist, he shall almost literally, like Martin Luther, hurl an inkpot at the Devil.

In *Lady Chatterley's Lover,* one of the great novels which we shall discuss later, D. H. Lawrence begins by saying: "Ours is essentially a tragic age, so we refuse to take it tragically. The cataclysm has happened, we are among the ruins, we start to build up new little habitations, to have new little hopes. It is rather hard work: there is now no smooth road into the future: but we go round, or scramble over the obstacles. We've got to live, no matter how many skies have fallen."

To hurl an inkpot at the Devil, be he death, futility, or disillusion. To seek "new little habitations": that is probably the quintessential purpose of Lawrence's novel, as of so many others. My plan then is to study Lawrence for a little of what he has to tell us; but first—and more important—I want to study the novels of four other men who precede him both in time and in some sort of chronological development. These men are Henry Fielding, Herman Melville, Thomas Hardy, Joseph Conrad, and I have chosen them along with Lawrence because in each of them we discover singularly advocated one of the four fundamental directions that claim the inkpot in its flight: or in less fanciful terms, one of the four fundamental approaches to our whole problem; a coördinated attitude, emotional and intellectual, to our question what is the fruitful life. The Realist, the Idealist, the Skeptic, the Romantic.

Others—Dante, Shakespeare, Milton, Dostoevski, and Tolstoi—offer riper wisdom, but perhaps we could not anywhere find four men who so clearly let us know just where they stand. And finally, here are four who as individuals are no closet-weaklings, no Prousts given over to introspection only, but men of eventful histories; men whose ideas take on an appearance of additional validity because they are derived from conflict with the actual world.

My plan was also to indicate an approach to the whole field of literature. To create a mythical young reader, seeking such an approach, who might say to himself what I finally and enthusiastically said to myself in Rome: "I have asked what I should read first, and why I want to read, and for a long time I have come to no conclusion. Now if I agree that the question these men are asking is of real interest to me; and if I read them in this order, and am not afraid to give way to the 'moral hypnotism' of each book as I read it; and if literature is all it claims to be, is there not a chance that I will emerge at the end with some formula for personal integration, having shared in part with five great men the spiritual development of the human race?"

FIVE NOVELS: A READING PLAN

Chapter 4

How to Read a Novel

THE NOVELIST often asks himself, "Let us suppose a young man starting out into the world." He then prepares the world for that young man and follows him on his journey.

Two hundred years ago, Henry Fielding set himself this formula and wrote *Tom Jones.* He took an "open and unsuspicious lad, of good disposition and a full allowance of natural appetites," deprived him of father and mother, and finally of protector, and sent him on the great high road to eighteenth-century London. Tom Jones's travels, his adventures in London, his recapture of his country sweetheart and of the good graces of his patron: these form the content of a thousand marvelous pages. They are marvelous because Tom Jones is real, the world he meets is real, and his adventures are amusing and exciting. But more than real, amusing, and exciting, they illuminate for us the eternal strengths and weaknesses of youth.

Herman Melville set himself the same formula when he wrote *Billy Budd;* Thomas Hardy, when he wrote *Jude the Obscure;* and Joseph Conrad, in *Lord Jim.* The young man who follows these four young men, giving himself over in turn to each of them, sharing imaginatively their adventures, has a good deal of life thrown open to him. His task, as reader, is to realize first how his four authors differ among themselves, how they view their heroes and the world through the lens of different temperaments; his further task as reader is to identify himself with the temperament most clearly his own. He must not accomplish this identification, however, with too much positiveness; the world is too varied a place to be seen through a single lens; perhaps that is wherein Tom Jones and Billy Budd and Jude and Lord Jim fail. He must avoid the fatal error of the sheepdog in Hardy's *Far from the Madding Crowd,* who in blind exuberance drives his whole flock off a cliff's head; whereupon,

> having done his work so thoroughly, he was considered too good a workman to live, and was, in fact, taken and

tragically shot at twelve o'clock that same day—another instance of the untoward fate which so often attends dogs and other philosophers who follow out a train of reasoning to its logical conclusion, and attempt perfectly consistent conduct in a world made up so largely of compromise.

The identification of the reader's predominant temperament is chiefly important to him as the pole star to a mariner, who needs a light by which to steer, even when his ship is heading anywhere but North. His task, then, is to learn which direction is for him most truly magnetic, but to discover this with caution, keeping in mind that there is likely to be more truth wherever his five authors come to agreement, than where they come to five separate conclusions.

This is only a beginning. Our young man must read these five novels in no ordinary way if he is to emerge at the end with something more than what the stories at first glance offer. He must read critically, and criticism sets up knowledge as its requisite; no work of art exists in isolation, but must be seen against the background of the artist's personal history and his earlier and later works. Much of the opportunistic humor of *Tom Jones* is missed, unless one knows something of Fielding's rivalry with Richardson; nor is any understanding of *Billy Budd* complete, unless the reader has first gone with Melville through *Typee* and *Moby Dick*. The prologue to *Jude* is found in an entry in Hardy's Journal, which reads, "Woke before it was light. Felt that I had not enough staying power to hold my own in the world." Just as surely we must remember enough of Conrad's life to see that in some aspects *Lord Jim* is not an Englishman at all, "but a passionate and melancholy Pole."

The need of such knowledge is greatest in appraisal of imaginative literature, among all the arts, because its explicit medium forbids an author to repeat himself; he can only go forward on the assumption that he shares with the reader all that he has already written; to readers who do not come so prepared he is often partly unintelligible. Then to read these five novels critically, one shall have to read other novels, to be listed at the end of this chapter. He will have to read biographical sketches too; or better, autobiographical sketches, wherever possible.

This small research, kept to the minimum, will be incommensurately rewarded; our young man will have disclosed to him the histories of five great men, and soon after he can see for himself by collation what meaning those five great men read into their histories: that meaning added on to life will represent the interpretative addition of art to reality. Or rather —since the word "addition" connotes something less than my intention—the *realization* of reality by art.

One of the advantages of imaginative literature over closet-philosophy, we have claimed, is that literature is so often autobiographical, with its materials spread where we can see them. The novel is not autobiographical, but it derives from autobiography, and its borrowings are frequently enough apparent. Philosophy hides its head. We are not supposed to know anyone is there, beneath the logical system. The philosopher's impersonal expression attempts to deny his temperamental prejudices. The novelist cannot do that.

Perhaps the thousand pages of *Tom Jones* tell us all we need to know about Henry Fielding, the author's character is so explicit in his work. That is all our amateur critic need read of Fielding. Yet there is an imposing and informative *History of Henry Fielding*, by Wilbur Cross, very long, but very delightful, that is worth his attention. Fielding's life was an unusual one, quite as astonishing and violent as that of his hero: he was a prolific playwright, a scurrilous pamphleteer, a politician, an earnest magistrate. Governor Cross's book re-creates Fielding's England with a sympathetic zest of its own. The reader who has time will also enjoy the two novels that preceded *Tom Jones: Joseph Andrews* and *Jonathan Wild*. They are good fun. *Amelia* is quite dull and sentimental, and Fielding's plays have only an academic interest today, though they were bawdy and lively enough in their time. The author's last book, *A Voyage to Lisbon*, is short and little famed: it is an unfinished travel diary, kept by Fielding when he knew himself dying. The reader will find it affecting, with many vignettes of eighteenth-century life, and always deserving of an hour's perusal.

Herman Melville's career was one of the most amazing ever recorded. He has written much of it in *Typee*, which tells of his experiences in the South Seas, where he took part in a ship mutiny and lived as a captive among cannibals. His family was an aristocratic one, descended from Dutch forbears, and noted in early American society. Melville taught school, sailed on a whaling ship, served in the United States Navy, clerked, and for a short time played the rôle of a popular author. But his popularity declined as his works grew better. He finally entered into long obscurity and died almost unknown, the greatest and least appreciated of American novelists. The best short biography of him is an English one by John Freeman; it should be read. *Typee* and *Moby Dick* should also be read, and *Billy Budd*, of course. The latter will be found in the *Shorter Novels of Herman Melville*, which also contains *Benito Cereno*, a story increasingly praised, and *Bartleby the Scrivener*, a story that might be praised even more. I particularly commend it to those who find Melville congenial.

The reader should be cautioned against Raymond Weaver's Introduction to the *Shorter Novels*. Professor Weaver's discovery and transcription of *Billy Budd* (which was not published in its author's lifetime) was a work of notable scholarship, but his attempt to interpret Melville's character is a misbegotten one. One might even call it an unscrupulous one, because to make his point he reprints lines from an almost inaccessible poem by Melville, wholly disregarding the actual use Melville made of the quoted words. The poetic passage, torn from its context, is misleading, and Professor Weaver's deduction from it quite unwarranted. In the poem, the words are the lament of a peasant girl repining with love for a young nobleman and regretting her desire for him; Professor Weaver, without explaining where they occur or by whom they are spoken, cites them to prove Melville had a hatred of his own sexuality. The reader of *Typee* will find that hard to believe.

Besides *Jude*, the amateur critic will want to read two other great novels by Hardy, *Tess of the D'Urbervilles* and *Far from the Madding Crowd*. They lack some of the bleakness of *Jude*, which is a work of unrelieved tragedy. The *Life* by the second Mrs. Hardy is too long but contains engrossing and invaluable extracts from his personal journal. Then there is Hardy's verse! He is a masculine poet: his work is stern, lyric, ironic, profoundly intellectual by turns. An acquaintance with it is essential to anyone who wants to know what anti-romantic modern poets are writing, because Hardy is the founder of their school. My favorite among the Hardy books is *Under the Greenwood Tree*. It is the pastoral Hardy, not the philosopher. But for the purposes of our reading plan, the three novels will suffice.

Joseph Conrad was a hot-tempered, eccentric Pole who

deliberately made a mystery of his career. The son of a famous Polish revolutionary, and later the ward of a rich uncle, he studied in France and passed his youth as an African trader, a Carlist arms smuggler, a world-wandering seaman, before he suddenly married an English girl and settled down to middle age and a literary career in a wholly strange language in rural England. He was soon the friend and intimate of most of the great writers of America and England, Henry James, John Galsworthy, ill-fated Stephen Crane, and others, so that the story of his later life contains many pictures of these interesting men. His vague but fascinating *Personal Record* should be inspected by our amateur critic, and his important novels *Victory* and *Nostromo,* as well as *Lord Jim.* But all his work is superb. If our reader is young, perhaps *Youth* and *The Shadow Line* will please him most.

The courts of England and America have finally lifted a ban on the sale of D. H. Lawrence's *Lady Chatterley's Lover* in its unexpurgated form. Formerly one could order it by mail from Paris booksellers, though the chances were that the customs men would seize it.

The book is not scandalous, but merely frank. It is not pornography, but a work of genuine poetry; Lawrence simply tired of euphemisms and wrote freely at last.

Those who could not buy or borrow the book had perforce to content themselves with the Lawrence found in *Sun* and *Glad Ghosts,* two stories contained in a volume called *The Woman Who Rode Away.* These did not shock the most conventional and should still be read. His ideas are also well expounded, though less beautifully, more verbosely, in *The Plumed Serpent.* His *Letters,* collected by Aldous Huxley, give the best picture of the man. They are resplendent with his fiery thought and response to life. The most revealing biography of him is *Son of Woman*—an objectionable title—by John Middleton Murry, who knew him well. But Mr. Murry lets his personal dislike of Lawrence—who made no secret of his distrust of Murry—color his explanation. This is unfortunate, because Murry has unusual critical gifts and understood Lawrence clearly. The novel that made Lawrence famous, *Sons and Lovers,* relates an incident important to the history of its troubled author.

We shall also look rather quickly at a book by Hervey Allen.

Here, then, is our reading plan:

The History of Tom Jones, by Henry Fielding
The History of Henry Fielding, by Wilbur Cross
(optional)
Typee, by Herman Melville
Moby Dick, by Herman Melville
Herman Melville, by John Freeman
Billy Budd, by Herman Melville (in *Shorter Novels*)
Far from the Madding Crowd, by Thomas Hardy
Tess of the d'Urbervilles, by Thomas Hardy
Jude the Obscure, by Thomas Hardy
Collected Poems of Thomas Hardy (optional)
Nostromo, by Joseph Conrad
Victory, by Joseph Conrad
Personal Record, by Joseph Conrad
Lord Jim, by Joseph Conrad
Youth, by Joseph Conrad (optional)
The Shadow Line, by Joseph Conrad (optional)
The Arrow of Gold, by Joseph Conrad (optional)
Lady Chatterley's Lover, by D. H. Lawrence
Sun, Glad Ghosts, by D. H. Lawrence (in *The Woman
Who Rode Away*)
The Letters of D. H. Lawrence, by Aldous Huxley
(optional)
The Plumed Serpent, by D. H. Lawrence (optional)
Son of Woman, by J. M. Murry (optional)
Not I But the Wind, by Frieda Lawrence (optional)
Anthony Adverse, by Hervey Allen

There are fifteen prescribed books. They are the ones I read,
or reread, along with many others, in the years after I left
Rome. What follows, in the rest of this part of my essay, are
the notes I made as I went through them.

Chapter 5

Earth: Fielding

DESCENDED from Rabelais of an earlier era in France, there is an eighteenth-century English literary school which includes such varied members as Defoe, the Scottish doctor Smollett, and Parson Laurence Sterne, and which emphasizes the lusty, the physical—the less delicate aspects of life. We call them the "natural." Full of belly laughs and phallic humor, this assorted company has regaled ten generations with *Moll Flanders, Peregrine Pickle, Tristram Shandy*. The more weary and complex becomes our modern existence, the more we are inclined to turn back to these "primitives," grateful that they have provided English letters with a frank and vigorous strain.

The noblest expression of the philosophy of life embodied in their books is found in *Tom Jones*. Fielding tells his young man to live to the hilt, but to remember always that satiety blunts the edge; he chides him to pay heed to the just demands of society. He offers him the golden rule: do no harm to anyone.

This is the inspired and matured realist speaking.

With *Tom Jones* the sun of English story telling came splendidly over the horizon. There had been earlier novels, such as Richardson's *Pamela*, but most of them were picaresque stories in the rollicking tradition founded by Cervantes' *Don Quixote* and Le Sage's *Gil Blas*. *Tom Jones* was the first philosophical novel, as we have now defined it. Until Fielding appeared, philosophy in imaginative literature had been mostly confined to the play and epic. *Tom Jones* incorporated the picaresque story, catching up its gay action and rapid pace, but set it in a firm and masterly plot. This was wholly new. The novel took on form; it was to be no longer a loosely strung series of incidents. Fielding had already declared in a preface to an earlier book that he was contemplating an epic in prose: he had Homer as well as Cervantes in mind.

This was a new democracy in literature. Consider how original Fielding was: his was to be an epic in comedy and prose, not in tragic verse. Ben Jonson had said: "Comedy is an imitation of the common errors of our life . . ." and Fielding was now to practice what Jonson preached. He was to be one of the first English writers, after Chaucer, to return to simple, particularized characters. Shakespeare generalized his melancholy Dane and tragically heightened Lear; Milton pretentiously justified the ways of God to man. Fielding was to justify the ways of men to God; he elevated the simple man; he substituted Parson Adams, whose goodness transcended absurdity, for Spenser's Arthurian knights; healthy Tom Jones, for introspective Hamlet. The host of Restoration writers preceding him, and headed by Dryden, sought to model on nobility—not Fielding; to him, the natural goodness of Parson Adams and Squire Allworthy needed no royal mantles.

He wrote so much from the earth, so little from literary manners, that his every word remains alive today. He is modern. Search through his book, the first great novel in English history: you find no archaisms in it. In his strong hands, our novel is full-born as from the brow of Jove. His advance over Cervantes and Defoe and *Pamela* is so imposing that the novel's progress through the two hundred years since then, even with the efforts of the most daring experimentalists, seems miniscule by comparison. We have not gone as far in two centuries as Fielding in one decade in the middle of the eighteenth century.

II

The quintessence of *Tom Jones* is robustness: robust feeling guided to robust action by a robust morality, which in turn is derived from experience.

There are moral issues successively raised for Tom Jones in his career. The amateur critic will see that these are the essence of the story. As a boy, Tom Jones decides that a lie to shield the gamekeeper Black George from incommensurate punishment is the better part of truth (did ever an author preach a more immoral doctrine!); he chooses between Sophia, whom he loves, and Molly Seagrim, to whom he feels himself duty-bound, because he is supposedly the father of her child. Both times his impetuous generosity, which helps him to his decision, only serves to increase his troubles. He rescues a Mrs. Waters, who is no better than she should be, and humanly succumbs to her charms; later, arrived penniless in London, he permits the amorous Lady Bellaston to purchase some part of his affections. The money thus earned he gives away in lavish charity.

Fielding's point is that Tom Jones is naturally good, but that he does not know wherein he is likely to fail, until after he has experienced the actual world.

When Tom has learned his lesson, he stiffens his morality. He is able to resist Lady Bellaston, the second offers of Mrs. Waters and a Mrs. Fitzpatrick, and even a flattering proposal of marriage from a rich widow, Mrs. Hunt. His chief reason for doing this is because he does not want to risk losing Sophia Western. By this time, his affairs have reached a crisis, in which he finds himself jailed for dueling and suffering under the horrible suspicion that the middle-aged Mrs. Waters is his unknown mother.

So Fielding propels his young man into experience, portraying him to us without cant or sentimentality. He finally proves to him that life cannot be fully lived without restraint. "The wise man gratifies every appetite and every passion, while the fool sacrifices all the rest to pall and satiate that one." This is what life had shown Fielding himself. "Wisdom, in short, whose lessons have been represented as so hard to learn by those who never were at her school, only teaches us to extend a simple maxim universally known and followed in the lowest life, a little further than that life carries. And this is, not to buy at too dear a price."

Perhaps you thought "philosophy" was something more profound than this? Is this not merely common sense? But the wonderful simplicity of Fielding's moral misleads us as to his true originality. It is not enough to admit that probably no one personifies robustness so happily as Fielding; the message to live fully by light of the golden rule comes first from him as well. Observe that he does not preach denial, no divinely sanctioned curb on the senses, but only a healthy caution. The Platonic-Christian teaching is an ascetic one; Fielding translates it into something very different from asceticism.

That, again, is realism.

III

We make a common mistake if we think that Henry Fielding lived in an age more realistic or natural than our own. If only, like the hero of Henry James's *The Sense of the Past* (so vividly dramatized as *Berkeley Square* by John Balderston), we could walk eighteenth-century streets and enter eighteenth-century taverns and drawing rooms, staring at them with twentieth-century eyes, we should learn that while this was a time of physical vigor—the brawling age which Fielding has depicted with such strong and memorable strokes in his living accounts of chase, and road, and post-house—it was also a time effeminate and artificial in its soul; a time of persisting superstitions, of gallantries that cloaked harsh social injustice. Too many of our notions of the eighteenth-century come from Fielding himself. Too little justice is done until we see him against the world as it really was, rather than in that world his own manly genius created. The clean and wholesome air that blows through his novel is a "Somerset air." That of the city is heavy with hypocrisy, with the close scent of boudoirs and gaming-rooms and powder from the bewigged heads of wits and courtiers, and Fielding despised it.

Richardson, the author of *Pamela,* is a better spokesman of the middle eighteenth century: in *Pamela* he teaches the passions of his heroine to move at the behest of a calculating virtue. The century, priding itself as the Age of Reason, the Age of Voltaire, substituting sentiment for passion, clasped Pamela to its heart and wept over her disappointments.

It was too much for Fielding, the young man about London. He protested. His protest took the form of a gaily picaresque, deriding paraphrase of *Pamela* called *Joseph Andrews.* It was Richardson who started him on his career as a novelist. In a forthright preface to *Joseph Andrews,* the scoffing Fielding wrote that "the only source of the true Ridiculous (as it appears to me) is affectation. . . . Now affectation proceeds from one of these causes, vanity or hypocrisy. . . ." And the young author, in his tale of the supremely virtuous Joseph, a male Pamela, exposed Richardson to ridicule so unsparing that the other author became his life-long enemy.

In *Jonathan Wild,* which followed the success of *Joseph Andrews,* Fielding turned from Richardson to other public figures and defined that which the world calls "greatness" as an admired capacity for murder and thievery, such as had elevated Charles of Sweden and particularly England's Prime Minister, Robert Walpole, in public esteem. Fielding elevates Jonathan Wild in public esteem—at the end of a rope.

His thoughts deepened, his outlook on life settled—and next through a thousand hours he wrote *Tom Jones,* broadening his satiric purpose to include all the meritless spiritual and intellectual pretensions of his day. The sharp humor becomes even more alert, incarnating in the pedantic persons of Thwackum and Square, Tom Jones's two tutors, the deism and conventional theology whose noisy warring filled the Voltairean era. Fielding repays every switching of poor Tom, with a redoubled whacking of Thwackum and Square before his book is done.

But *Tom Jones,* the apotheosis of his career, interests us today for its universal rather than its topical characterizations. A masterpiece will do that: it will have meaning for its own time, but no less meaning for the future. It loses color because many contemporary allusions are dropped, but it gains by the mysterious intervention of time. Centuries have passed. Through all those years, readers have chuckled over the same incidents. We are conscious of that, when our turn comes to go through it. All that is old and long past is poignant too, for centuries of life and death overlay every scene.

Even when we read the same book over, we find new pleasures in it. Colors appear in it that hardly seemed there before. Some books are like meerschaum pipes, that grow more beautiful when used.

IV

Perhaps one of the reasons we like *Tom Jones* so much is that Fielding himself enjoyed telling it. He did not write it easily, we have his testimony to that, but his anxious heart was in it. Later he described it boldly as "a living monument to incontinence." Was that a gibe at his critics? But he meant perhaps an incontinence of the spirit rather than of the flesh, for *Tom Jones* is hardly that bawdy. On the contrary, it has the dignity of all great literature, as Fielding himself had the dignity of the great man that he was. Few books let us know their author so well. He speaks to us directly. When the story prevents him from conversing with us, he forgets his story for the moment; whereby he set the rule for the informal English novel, so ably exemplified later in Thackeray and Trollope. Some object to this personal intrusion of the author. But I would sooner agree with George Eliot, who is grateful that Fielding "seems to bring his armchair to the proscenium and chat with us in all the lusty ease of his fine English."

I shall have a chapter on "Technique" later in this book, but this might be a place to digress and ask whether Henry

James, for all that he admirably enhanced the shape of the novel, did narrative a true service in denying an author a minimum of self-consciousness. Perhaps those who deem James's "authorless" novels superior in form to those of Fielding and Thackeray are mistaken when they insist that art which pretends to be life will for that pretension be more convincing. A little observation shows us that art willing to be accepted at its face value as art, equally well performs its function. The picture that pretends to be an actual extension of space, rather than what it is, a picture in a frame, interests us more for its achievement in perspective than for its more important qualities: by pretending to be too real, it has broken down "esthetic distance." We like to lose ourselves in something, but not be actually lost in it. We never care for a painting in which a window opens directly toward us, as though to let us look into a room; or in which an arm or leg extends too violently in our direction; we are too much aware that the artist is trying to trick us. We resent the presence of actors among us in the audience. The play must keep its place behind the proscenium arch; the picture frame of the theater is part of the dramatic esthetic experience. In other terms, a sense of the picture frame can be part of the esthetic experience of reading a novel as well. The qualification is this: the author should not intrude in the action; James is right about that, and Fielding seems to agree with him; he stays strictly within the narrow confines of his preface and introductory essays; but within those confines, his presence has artistic legitimacy. The essays serve another purpose: they deliberately delay the action, which otherwise would gather too much momentum; and finally the essays, even though the reader accepts Fielding's permission to skip them, by their very presence help the author to create the sense of passing time, that most difficult of literary problems.

Perhaps whether we welcome an author or not in a book depends mostly on his personality. Who is not glad to meet Fielding?

v

This is the most utterly honest novel written in any age. How was it received by his contemporaries? Let us look.

Horace Walpole sniffed at Fielding's easy democracy. Dr. Johnson, the "Great Cham of Literature," rebuked poor Hannah Moore for having read anything "so vicious" as *Tom Jones,* and announced his preference for Richardson.

Richardson himself wanted to know, "What reason had he to make his Tom illegitimate, in an Age where Keeping is become a Fashion? Why did he make him a common—What shall I call it? And a Kept Fellow, the Lowest of all Fellows, yet in Love with a Young Creature who was traping after him, a Fugitive from her Father's House?—Why did he draw his Heroine so fond, so foolish, and so insipid?—Indeed he has one Excuse—He knows not how to draw a delicate Woman—He has not been accustomed to such Company,—And is too prescribing, too impetuous, too immoral, I will venture to say, to take any other Byass than that a perverse and crooked Nature has given him; or Evil Habits, at least, have confirmed in him. Do Men expect Grapes of Thorns, or Figs of Thistles?"

The history of *Tom Jones* after its printing is almost as amusing as the novel itself. From belief that the book was "coarsely titled" (people were displeased at the author's having made the hero a foundling) Fielding's offering encountered rising disfavor that found climax in the voice of *Old England,* a political weekly, and his relentless enemy. Two earthquakes had rocked England; "chairs shook, pewter rattled, chimneys tumbled, people ran into the streets." The cause of this supernatural disturbance, a heavenly judgment, was the reading of "lewd novels, especially one called *Tom Jones.*" Paris had purified herself by suppressing the novel, and so avoided the earthquake and meteors.

The "moral persuasion" of the philosophical novel was truly recognized at its very inception. Art had its excitements!

We have attested, once again, the true measure of his originality. How difficult it always is to be natural!

VI

There is a scene in *Tom Jones* in which a fashionable young man is about to abandon a girl whom he has betrayed, to contract a socially better marriage; our hero remonstrates with him.

"Tom, Tom," answered Nightingale, "remember last night—"

"Lookee, Mr. Nightingale," said Jones, "I am no canting hypocrite, nor do I pretend to the gift of chastity. . . . I have been guilty with women, I own it; but am not conscious that I have ever injured any; nor would I, to procure pleasure to myself, be knowingly the cause of misery to any human being."

The point of the passage does not appear to the casual reader. On November 27, 1747, while he was at work upon *Tom Jones,* the widower Fielding shocked his family and the London world by marrying Mary Daniel, his housekeeper, a woman much below him in social position and mental endowments. The reason was soon obvious; their eldest son was born but three months afterward. The mores of his day exempted gentlemen of honor from obligations of this sort.

Richardson, had he heard the story, would not have approved. He could hardly have commended a social move so emotional, so impolitic. He would not have understood; for Richardson, like Walpole and Johnson—and all the rest of us —was but a creature of his age. He was a rationalist after all, with moral ideas for heart.

What we find in Fielding is this wonderful balance of reason and feeling that places him far ahead of his century. His was the time when the schism of the intellect and emotions first began to widen, to give in turn a century in which reason was predominant, and next a century in which feeling more strongly manifests itself; a change evidenced in literature by the surrender of the neo-Classicism of Dryden and Pope to the rising Romantic movement of Wordsworth and Coleridge, and Byron, Shelley, and Keats. Fielding is one of the last to span the two, intellect and emotions, and again by virtue of that, one of the first we might call modern. For that schism continued, and we notice later how the late nineteenth and early twentieth centuries—as typified by Thomas Hardy in verse, and Joseph Conrad and D. H. Lawrence in prose— seek to bring it to an end. That is why in essence Fielding's work is so closely akin to theirs.

There is finally the brief *Voyage to Lisbon.* Proudly, yet without pride, a dying man reveals himself to us, still serenely good-humored, interested, and unafraid.

We might say it in other words. The quintessence of Henry Fielding is manliness.

Chapter 6

Sea and Sky: Melville

THE EXAMPLE of Tom Jones has been put first, because it is a touchstone. That it is no more than a touchstone is apparent; and further, to Fielding's credit, he himself was aware of this. We have submitted to the "hypnotism" of *Tom Jones* and accepted its doctrine of the natural, robust life; but now, coming to Herman Melville, let us lay side by side a merry paragraph in *Joseph Andrews*, which tells of a theological discussion between Parson Adams and the host at one of the inns where Joseph and quixotic Adams have taken shelter, and a short passage from one of Melville's autobiographical novels, *Redburn*. The conversation between Adams and the host goes like this:

"Why," says Adams very gravely, "do you not believe in another world?"

To which the host answered, "Yes, he was no atheist."

"And you believe you have an immortal soul?" cries Adams.

He answered, "God forbid he should not."

"And heaven and hell?" said the Parson.

The host then bid him not to profane, for those were things not to be mentioned nor thought of but in church. Adams asked him, why he went to church if what he learned there had no influence on his conduct in life?

"I go to church," answered the host, "to say my prayers and behave godly."

"And dost not thou," cried Adams, "believe in what thou hearest at church?"

"Most part of it, master," returned the host.

"And dost thou then tremble," cried Adams, "at the thought of eternal punishment?"

"As for that, master," said he, "I never once thought about it. But what signifies talking about matters so far off? The mug is out, shall I draw another?"

That is Tom Jones as well, who does not think of matters so
far off, but rather draws the mug. He is after all an unaspiring
young man; he is, in fact, set rather heavily on earth. Redburn,
another young man, is making his first sea voyage, amid the
most adverse circumstances; still such moments as this come
to him by way of compensation:

> At last we hoisted the Stun'-sails up to the topsail-yards;
> and as soon as the vessel felt them she gave a sort of bound
> like a horse, and the breeze blowing more and more she
> went plunging along, shaking off the foam from her bows,
> like foam from a bridle-bit. Every mast and timber seemed
> to have a pulse in it that was beating with life and joy; and
> I felt a wild exulting in my own heart, and felt as if I would
> be glad to bound along so round the world.
>
> Then I was conscious of a wonderful thing in me, that
> responded to all the wild commotion of the outer world;
> and went reeling on and on with the planets in their orbits,
> and was lost in one delirious throb at the centre of All. A
> wild bubbling and bursting was at my heart, as if a hidden
> spring had just gushed out there; and my blood ran tingling
> along my frame, like mountain brooks in spring freshets.

Our first question, while we are still under the spell of Fielding's compelling matter of factness, would be how seriously
should we take such idealistic outbursts. Melville's own immediate answer follows:

> But how soon these raptures abated, when after a brief
> interval, we were again set to work, and I had a vile
> commission to clean out the chicken-coops, and make up
> the beds of the pigs in the long-boat.
>
> Miserable dog's life is this of the sea! commanded like
> a slave, and set to work like an ass! vulgar and brutal men
> lording it over me, as if I were an African in Alabama.
> Yes, yes, blow on, ye breezes, and make a speedy end to
> this abominable voyage!

II

The novelist's warrant for philosophy, we have maintained,
is his great experience of life. There have been idealists from

Plato to Hegel, to Bosanquet and Bradley, but none who ever put idealism so harshly to the test as Herman Melville—and still continued an idealist. For that renunciation by Redburn, who is Melville, is not a lasting renunciation: the "abominable voyage" is not to be Melville's final voyage: *Moby Dick* is to follow *Redburn;* and forty years after *Moby Dick* comes *Billy Budd.*

The problem, to return to *Tom Jones,* might be put this way: What is the road to the fruitful life? The high road that Fielding points, is after all a dubious one. Tom Jones finds himself, near the end of his journey, in all sorts of apparently irremediable troubles, which miraculously disappear before his essential goodness and simplicity. The story is so persuasive, that we fail to ask whether there is a compulsion in Tom Jones's essential goodness and simplicity which brings the beneficent truth to light at last, or whether it is not the kindly, relenting intervention of the author. Then reëxamine the final book of *Tom Jones* and you will discover what a chain of happy accident, *deus ex machina,* comes to extricate our lucky Tom; the horrible likelihood is that should Tom Jones, or anyone like him, ever attempt the same adventures again, and without the helping hand of an author, no miracle would be forthcoming. There is small real inner defense against the force of hostile circumstance: this is Melville's view; his Billy Budd, who starts life with an equal innocence, is hanged from the main-yard, "facing aft."

I have already said that Fielding later caught sight of this real human defenselessness; Captain Booth, in *Amelia*—written some years after—is Tom Jones married and grown older, and brought to a conviction of his own inadequacy, in order that Dr. Harrison, Parson Adams's and Allworthy's homiletic successor, may lead him to Christianity.

Booth's hesitation on the threshold of orthodoxy has been based on this belief, " 'that, as men appeared to me to act entirely from their passions, their actions could have neither merit nor demerit.' " That is the author of *Tom Jones* speaking.

The author of *Amelia* replies with a clumsy attempt at dialectic:

"A very worthy conclusion truly!" cries the doctor; "but if men act, as I believe they do, from their passions, it would be fair to conclude that religion to be true which applies to the strongest of these passions, hope and fear; choosing rather to rely on its rewards and punishments than on that beauty of virtue which some of the ancient philosophers thought proper to recommend to their disciples."

Surely Fielding's natural robustness here lays rather violent hands on Christian doctrine. But we should remember that in his later years—and during the time *Amelia* was written—he was energetically serving as a London magistrate. Perhaps something of the weary asperity of the magistrate shows itself in this pronouncement of a religion of rewards and punishments. The realist on the bench, facing the dregs of London, could hardly place much faith in "contemplation of the beauty of virtue" as a practical means of keeping men decent.

Melville was never interested in Christianity, which is notably a practical scheme of ethics. He was not a practical man; yet a better formulation of idealism, I believe, is come upon in him, who was no late convert, but a true idealist all his life. And so seeking, we turn from a touchstone to a lodestone, though not toward a brightening vision.

III

Melville is a strange man.

I think excerpts may help to explain him, and that he has given us a veiled picture of himself, with shy immodesty, when in a passage in *Moby Dick* he speaks of Nantucket whaling men, who though of Quaker origin, "from the audacious, daring and boundless adventure of their subsequent lives, strangely blend with these unoutgrown peculiarities, a thousand bold dashes of character, not unworthy a Scandinavian sea-king, or a poetical Pagan Roman. And when these things unite in a man of greatly superior force, with a globular brain and a ponderous heart; who has also by the stillness and seclusion of many long night-watches in the remotest waters, and beneath constellations never seen here at the North, been led to think untraditionally and independently; receiving all nature's sweet or savage impressions fresh from her own virgin voluntary and confiding breast, and thereby chiefly, but with some help from accidental advantages, to learn a bold and nervous lofty language—that man makes one in a whole nation's census—a

mighty pageant creature formed for noble tragedies. Nor will
it at all detract from him, dramatically regarded, if either by
birth or other circumstances, he have what at bottom seems a
half wilful overruling morbidness at the bottom of his nature.
For all men tragically great, are made so through a certain
morbidness."

He is "tormented with an everlasting itch for things
remote."

The sea fascinates him.

"Why is almost every robust healthy boy with a robust
healthy soul in him, at some time or other crazy to go to sea?
Why upon your first voyage as a passenger, did you feel such
a mystical vibration, when first told that you and your ship
were now out of sight of land? Why did the old Persians hold
the sea holy? Why did the Greeks give it a separate deity, and
own brother to Jove? Surely all this is not without meaning.
And still deeper the meaning of that story of Narcissus, who
because he could not grasp the tormenting, mild image he saw
in the fountain, plunged into it and was drowned. But that
same image, we ourselves see in all rivers and oceans. It is the
image of the ungraspable phantom of life; and this is the key
to it all."

He gives himself away even more in a letter to his friend
Hawthorne, in which he tells of his impressions of Emerson,
after having heard him lecture. (How often this happens when
we pass judgment on another!) The letter is dated March 3,
1849, when Melville was thirty years old.

Nay, I do not oscillate in Emerson's rainbow, but prefer
rather to hang myself in mine own halter than swing in any
other man's swing. Yet I think Emerson is more than a
brilliant fellow. Be his stuff begged, borrowed, or stolen,
or of his own domestic manufacture, he is an uncommon
man.

Swear he is a humbug—then he is an uncommon humbug. Set it down that had not Sir Thomas Browne lived,
Emerson would not have mystified—I will answer that had
not Old Zach's father begot him, Old Zach would never
have been the hero of Palo Alto. The truth is that we are
all sons, grandsons, or nephews or great-nephews of those
who go before us. No one is his own sire.

I was very agreeably disappointed in Mr. Emerson. I

had heard of him as full of transcendentalism, myths and oracular gibberish . . . to my surprise, I found him quite intelligible, tho' to say the truth, they told me that night he was unusually plain.

Now, there is something about every man elevated above mediocrity, which is for the most part instantly perceptible. This I see in Mr. Emerson. And, frankly, for the sake of the argument, let us call him a fool—then had I rather be a fool than a wise man.

I love all men who *dive*. Any fish can swim near the surface, but it takes a great whale to go down stairs five miles or more; and if he don't attain the bottom, why, all the lead in Galena can't fashion the plummit that will. I'm not talking of Mr. Emerson now, but of the whole corps of thought-divers that have been diving and coming up again with blood-shot eyes since the world began.

I could readily see in Emerson, notwithstanding his merit, a gaping flaw. It was the insinuation that had he lived in those days when the world was made, he might have offered some valuable suggestions. These men are all cracked right across the brow. And never will the pullers-down be able to cope with the builders-up. . . . But enough of this Plato who talks thro' his nose. . . .

You complain that Emerson tho' a denizen of the land of gingerbread, is above munching a plain cake in company of jolly fellows, and swigging off his ale like you and me. Ah, my dear sir, that's his misfortune, not his fault. His belly, sir, is in his chest, and his brains descend down into his neck, and offer an obstacle to a draughtful of ale or a mouthful of cake. . . . Goodbye.

H.M.

I have quoted these last two paragraphs, because they reveal the saving personal humor always Melville's, and that goes far to discount the momentary petulance of *Pierre*, of which I think too much is made. For the rest, he characterizes himself well, this proud village schoolmaster "who lived with cannibals," who loved to *dive*, and who did in a sense hang himself in his own halter, saying that if this be fame, "let me be infamous," and praying God "if his soul missed its haven that it might, at least, end in utter wreck."

The history of Melville is easily followed in his books,

beginning with *Redburn,* of which Mr. John Freeman has said, in prose that matches Melville's own: "The troubles of *Redburn* are material troubles, for the spiritual has scarce been born; as yet, hunger and cold are much more vital enemies than fatalism, and mysteries are still unconfronted. The peculiar radiance of *Redburn* comes from its innocence: it is a chapter of innocent biography, and the light that shines from within it, as from under water, is very pure and clear. The as yet unvexed puritanism that lay beneath Melville's heritage is seen in that verdant light like a softer rock, shaping the current of his thoughts and making them actual and quick to every man who remembers his own youth—shy and ardent, frank and secret, bold and suppressive. Such is the character that *Redburn* displays." Then through *Typee* and its sequel *Omoo,* which incredible though they sound—and lately subject to more close investigation—are still faithful in my opinion to the known facts of Melville's life; important because they show the opportunities given to this man, four months restless captive on a Polynesian isle, to observe civilization stripped: the unwilling Utopian in a friendly Utopia. Finally through the allegorical *Mardi,* with these rewarding sentences: "We have had vast developments of parts of men, not of any wholes. Before a full-developed man, Mardi would fall down and worship."

Melville's goal was not too far beyond himself; and it was that perhaps that led him on honest and unwinking to the maelstrom that is *Moby Dick.*

IV

John Macy, a few decades ago, dismissed *Moby Dick* as a "madly eloquent romance of the sea"; and Ludwig Lewisohn, only the day before yesterday, described it as the work of an eccentric, a less than minor writer, which was somewhat foolhardy of Mr. Lewisohn. These criticisms are the natural prologue and epilogue, I suppose, to the enthusiasm that seized America when, in our time, thirty years after its author's death, a great book was discovered; now found, the true greatness of *Moby Dick* will not diminish, and needs no defense. But I would join with the hostile critics of *Moby Dick* this far, not to deny its explicit merits, but to express the opinion that in *Billy Budd,* a yet-to-be famous work of Melville's later maturity, he has written an even better story, which though it lacks the sweep of *Moby Dick,* shows greater humanity; more penetrating psychology, couched in exalted prose; and a more steadfast philosophy of life. And with it, as I have complained before, most Americans have yet to discover those two shorter masterpieces, *Bartleby the Scrivener* and *Benito Cereno.* The first is of that rare genre of satire which attains to the tragic; the second is artistically wonderful, with deep color, and a suspended movement worthy of Conrad, and the solemnity of Hardy. The air of *Benito Cereno* has that shining stillness which hangs over a glassy sea.

I do not find fault with *Moby Dick,* having made this comparison, for what has been called its chaos; Melville's theme is a chaotic one and could not have been otherwise presented; the long digressions, the over-heightened style, the mass of realistic detail, are all integral to the effect, which could not have been achieved in any other way; they are imperceptive who blame Melville for having succeeded where and by means with which anyone else would have failed. His originality, his recognition of his problem, pronounce the at-all-times conscious master. But *Moby Dick,* having reached its last great scene, is without an end; the disaster that engulfs monomaniac Captain Ahab and his *Pequod,* that little universe, leaves no one satisfied, least of all Melville himself. *Billy Budd,* written forty years afterward, in the last months of Melville's life, accomplishes such an end; accomplishes in fact a tragic catharsis, which *Moby Dick* does not. The secret of the tragic catharsis lies in an exalted acceptance of defeat; there must always be that upward thrust, the human head held high, the shining eyes that find victory in themselves, in the resignation that consummates a long resistance. Captain Ahab fights cruelty with cruelty; but Billy Budd, hanged from the main-yard, with "God bless Captain Vere" upon his lips, looks like "an angel."

The stories are essentially the same, except that in *Billy Budd* the symbolism has been translated into human terms; the struggle of innocence and evil is retold, with Claggart fulfilling the rôle of Moby Dick; and with this further difference, that what is dark in *Moby Dick* is here shot through "with a soft glory as of the fleece of the Lamb of God seen in mystical vision"; when "simultaneously therewith, watched by the wedged mass of upturned faces, Billy ascended; and ascending, took the full-rose of the dawn."

V

The time is that of the Great Mutiny. Billy Budd, an impressed American, the "handsome-sailor," has been condemned to death for the murder of Claggart, the Master-at-Arms, who has falsely accused the boy of treason, moved against him by "his significant personal beauty." When Claggart's "unobserved glance happened to light on belted Billy rolling along the upper gun-deck in the leisure of the second dog-watch, exchanging passing broadsides of fun with other promenaders in the crowd, that glance would follow the cheerful sea-Hyperion with a settled, meditative, and melancholy expression, his eyes strangely suffused with incipient feverish tears." For "the Master-at-Arms was perhaps the only man in the ship intellectually capable of adequately appreciating the moral phenomenon presented in Billy Budd, and the insight but intensified his passion which, assuming various secret forms within him, at times assumed that of cynic disdain—disdain of innocence. To be nothing more than innocent! Yet in an esthetic way he saw the charm of it, the courageous free-and-easy temper of it, and fain would have shared it, but he despaired of it." The absurdly simple tragic flaw in Billy Budd is that he stutters; called to the Captain's cabin and confronted with the accusation of treason, he is unable to speak, and in a choked, inarticulate moment strikes out, causing his accuser's death. Discipline ordains his punishment, no matter how much his officers, especially the kind, perceptive Captain Vere, would like to save him.

The real world for Melville, as for Fielding, is possessed of calculable—and for Melville, incalculable—evil. He is informed of this by instinct even more than reason. His peculiar genius made him create this world anew—outside himself—in titanic and transcendent images.

Thus in *Moby Dick,* he has glimpses "of that mortally intolerable truth; that all deep, earnest thinking is but the intrepid effort of the soul to keep the open independence of her sea; whilst the wildest winds of heaven and earth conspire to cast her on the treacherous, slavish shore."

But beyond the real world is an ideal one. His instinct—

the godhead in man—also tells him of it. Then "gazing down from the boat's side into that same golden sea," he is moved to murmur,

> "Loveliness unfathomable, as ever lover saw in his bride's eye!—Tell me not of thy teeth-tiered sharks, and thy kidnapping cannibal ways. Let faith oust fact; let fancy oust memory; I look deep down and do believe." [For,] "As in landlessness alone resides highest truth, shoreless, indefinite as God—so better is it to perish in that howling infinite, than be ingloriously dashed upon the lee, even if that were safety!"

Melville's vision of that infinite—with the sureness of the true mystic, who has words for everything he feels—has been set down in his magnificent chapter on the whiteness of the whale, too long to be quoted, and in this separate paragraph from *Moby Dick*, resounding like the finest poetry of Francis Thompson:

> How nobly it raises our conceit of the mighty, misty monster, to behold him solemnly sailing through a calm tropical sea; his vast, mild head overhung by a canopy of water, engendered by his incommunicable contemplations, and that vapor—and you will sometimes see it—glorified by a rainbow, as if heaven itself had put its seal upon his thoughts. For d'ye see, rainbows do not visit the clear air; they only irradiate vapor. And so, through all the thick mists of the dim doubts in my mind, divine intuitions now and then shoot, enkindling my fog with a heavenly ray. And for this I thank God; for all have doubts; many deny; but doubts or denials, few along with them have intuitions. Doubts of all things earthly, and intuitions of some things heavenly; this combination makes neither believer nor infidel, but makes a man who regards them both with equal eye.

That is his vision, divine intuitions—like a rainbow—"through all the thick mists of the dim doubts in my mind," but given to him for what purpose? Captain Ahab, the hunted hunter, cries:

What is it, what nameless, inscrutable, unearthly thing is it; what cozening, hidden lord and master, and cruel, remorseless emperor commands me; that against all natural lovings and longings, I so keep pushing, and crowding, and jamming myself on all the time; recklessly making me ready to do what in my own proper, natural heart, I durst not so much as dare? Is Ahab, Ahab? Is it I, God, who lifts this arm? But if the great sun move not of himself; but is as an errand-boy in heaven; nor one single star can revolve, but by some invisible power; how then can one small heart beat; this one small brain think thoughts; unless God does that beating, does that thinking, does that living, and not I. By heaven, man, we are turned round and round in this world, like yonder windlass, and Fate is the handspike. And all the time, lo! that smiling sky, and this unsounded sea! Look! see yon Albicore! who put it into him to chase and fang that flying-fish? Where do murderers go, man! Who's to doom, when the judge himself is dragged to the bar? But it is a mild, mild wind, and a mild looking sky; and the air smells now, as if it blew from a far-away meadow; they have been making hay somewhere under the slopes of the Andes, Starbuck, and the mowers are sleeping among the new-mown hay. Sleeping? Aye, toil we how we may, we all sleep at last on the field. Sleep? Aye, and rust amid greenness; as last year's scythes flung down, and left in the half-cut swathes—

VI

Now let us turn to the serene surcease of *Billy Budd*.

Melville himself, and his career, had almost gone down in the wake of *Moby Dick;* he was to enter that long obscurity, with all its disappointments, and "the twilight of his eyes," fast failing him; but if he was to reach the feeling expressed in his disillusioned poem, *Clarel,* that:

> The world is portioned out, believe:
> The good have but a patch at best,
> The wise their corner; for the rest—
> Malice divides with ignorance.

He was to emerge from "the last whelming sea," admonishing himself:

> Then keep thy heart, though yet but ill resigned—
> Clarel, thy heart, the issues there but mind;
> That like the crocus budding through the snow—
> That like a burning secret which doth go
> Even from the bosom that would hoard and keep . . .

Unambitious Captain Vere is Melville, looking back at his lost youth; but Billy Budd is something more than youth; he is youth informed by innocence with all the wisdom of life and age.

The chaplain comes for a last conference with his charge, and finds him thus, awaiting his last dawn:

> On the starboard side of the *Indomitable's* upper gun-deck, behold Billy Budd under sentry lying prone in irons in one of the bays formed by the regular guns comprising the batteries on either side. . . . Over him, but scarce illuminating him, two battle-lanterns swing from two massive beams of the deck above. Fed with the oil supplied by war-contractors (whose gains, honest or otherwise, are in every land an anticipated portion of the harvest of death), with flickering flashes of dirty yellow light they pollute the pale moonshine all but ineffectually struggling in obstructed flecks through the open ports from which the tompined cannon protrude. Other lanterns at intervals serve but to bring out somewhat the obscurer bays which, like small confessionals or side-chapels in a cathedral, branch from the long, dim-vasted broad aisle between the two batteries of that covered tier.
> . . . Through the rose-tan of his complexion, no pallor could have shown. It would have taken days of sequestration from the winds and the sun to have brought about the effacement of that young sea-bloom. But the skeleton in the cheek-bone at the point of its angle was just beginning delicately to be defined under the warm-tinted skin. In fervid hearts self-contained some brief experiences devour our human tissue as secret fire in a ship's hold consumes cotton in the bale.
> But now, lying between the two guns, as nipped in the vice of fate, Billy's agony, mainly proceeding from a generous young heart's virgin experience of the diabolical incarnate and effective in some men—the tension of that

agony was over now. It survived not the something heal-
ing in the closeted interview with Captain Vere. Without
movement, he lay as in a trance, that adolescent expression
previously noted as his, taking on something akin to the
look of a slumbering child in the cradle when the warm
hearth-glow of the still chamber night plays on the dimples
that at whiles mysteriously form in the cheek, silently
coming and going there. For now and then in the gyved
one's trance, a serene happy light born of some wandering reminiscence or dream would diffuse itself over his
face, and then wane away only anew to return.

The Chaplain withdraws, "peradventure feeling that even
he, the minister of Christ, though receiving his stipend from
wars, had no consolation to offer which could result in a peace
transcending that which he beheld."

Billy Budd, then, is divine, because wholly instinct. Tom
Jones represents one sort of "natural" man, Billy Budd another. The one is simply unintelligent, the second trustfully
unreasoning.

Yet can we believe that Melville ever found these mystical
flights wholly satisfying—at least until those last months of
his life devoted to the composition of *Billy Budd*? Therein
lay his tragedy. His intelligence was too strong to accept with
full complaisance the endowments of unreason.

Still, those last months brought "revelation" to Melville.
That is why *Billy Budd* is idealism's most complete document.

Here, perhaps, the aged Melville anticipated his own death.
Certainly he must have welcomed his own end in something
of this same exalted spirit. His defeated life now embodied
the upward-thrusting formula of tragic catharsis.

He was a man, this Melville, for whom "courage was not a
sentiment; but a thing simply useful to him, and always at
hand upon all mortally practical occasions"; and for whom—
since in *Moby Dick* he identifies himself with all his characters, little mad black Pip, as well as valiant Starbuck—God's
foot is visible upon "the treadle of the loom." Poor Pip! "The
sea had jeeringly kept his finite body up, but drowned the
infinite of his soul. Not drowned entirely, though. Rather carried down alive to wondrous depths, where strange shapes of
the unwarped primal world glided to and fro before his
passive eyes; and the miser-merman, Wisdom, revealed his

hoarded heaps; and among the joyous, heartless, ever-juvenile eternities, Pip saw the multitudinous, God omnipresent, coral insects, that out of the firmament of waters heaved the colossal orbs." Thereafter, as Melville anticipated, "his shipmates called him mad."

Chapter 7

Mind: Hardy

THE REMAINDER of Billy Budd's brief tragedy can serve for our next transition. Billy stands facing aft. "At the penultimate moment, his words, his only words, words wholly unobstructed in the utterance, were these—'God Bless Captain Vere!' Syllables so unanticipated coming from one with the ignominious hemp about his neck—a conventional felon's benediction directed aft towards the quarters of honor; syllables, too, delivered in the clear melody of a singing-bird on the point of launching from the twig, had a phenomenal effect, not unenhanced by the rare personal beauty of the young sailor, spiritualized now through late experiences so poignantly profound.

Without volition, as it were, as if indeed the ship's populace were the vehicles of some vocal electric current, with one voice, from alow and aloft, came a resonant echo— "God Bless Captain Vere!" And yet, at that instant, Billy alone must have been in their hearts, even as he was in their eyes. . . .

The hull, deliberately recovering from the periodic roll to leeward, was just regaining an even keel—when the last signal, the preconcerted dumb one was given. At the same moment it chanced that the vapoury fleece hanging low in the East, was shot through with a soft glory as of the fleece of the Lamb of God seen in mystical vision. . . .

This should be compared to the death of the young hero of Thomas Hardy's *Jude the Obscure*. He leaves no benediction.

As soon as he could speak he murmured, his eyes still closed: "A little water, please."

Nothing but the deserted room received his appeal, and he coughed to exhaustion again—saying still more feebly: "Water, some water, Sue. Arabella!"

The room remained still as before. Presently he gasped

again: "Throat—water—Sue—darling—drop of water—
please! O please!"

No water came, and the organ notes, faint as a bee's hum,
rolled in as before.

While he remained, his face changing, shouts and hurrahs
came from somewhere in the direction of the river.

"Ah—yes, the Remembrance games," he murmured.
"And I here. And Sue defiled."

The hurrahs were repeated, drowning the faint organ
notes. Jude's face changed more; he whispered slowly, his
lips scarcely moving:

"Let the day perish wherein I was born, and the night in
which it was said, There is a man child conceived."

II

Melville once wrote a letter to a friend praising James
Thomson's poems. "As to pessimism, although neither pessimist nor optimist myself, nevertheless I relish it in the verse,
if for nothing else than as a counterpoise to the exorbitant
hopefulness, juvenile and shallow, that makes such a muster
these days—at least in some quarters."

Thomas Hardy was one who seeing life as clearly as did
Melville, perhaps even more clearly, was unable to accept Melville's compensatory idealism and mysticism as a valid solution. The difference between the two men, contemporaries,
was more than temperamental: it lay in intellectual environment. Melville called himself Ishmael; but Hardy's world, like
that of most men, was not the deck of a whaling-ship; his sea
was rather that which spread at Matthew Arnold's feet, a re-
ceding tide of faith, an English world of tradition and intellectual rumor. Jude, unlike unthinking Tom Jones, and innocent,
inarticulate Billy Budd, is possessed of a clear intelligence: he
faces the world with scientific eyes.

Jude's author was to write in his Journal, underscoring the
words: *"Let every man make a philosophy for himself out of
his own experience."* And then to enter next, "A Pessimist's
apology. Pessimism (or rather what is called such) is, in brief,
playing the sure game. You cannot lose at it; you may gain. It
is the only view of life in which you can never be disappointed. Having reckoned what to do in the worst possible
circumstances, when better arise, as they may, life becomes
mere child's play."

III

The young Hardy was an architect. Marcel Proust finds in his work a "stonemason's geometry" and traces many other parellelisms to that craft. We have glimpses in his own Journal of the apprentice Hardy descending on London to make his fortune, and one memorable picture of him, in the performance of his duties as a church-renovator, standing guard in a cemetery while by lantern-light bursting coffins were disinterred.

There is a fine poem of his, *The Church Builder*, a bitter account of a man who loses faith and hangs himself in a church of his own Gothic design.

The poem is symbolic, of course, but its symbolism is more than personal. It bespeaks a skeptical age. Hardy insisted that his philosophy was intuitive only; nevertheless, like Housman and the others of his mordant generation, he was enabled to find sufficient confirmation outside himself in that doubting nineteenth century: exiles of immortality, one might call them, paraphrasing Rupert Brooke.

Much as he would like to, he cannot deny sensitivity to these influences. His correspondence and Journal betray him. To the Reverend Dr. Grossart, who strangely asked him how to reconcile the horrors of human and animal life "with the absolute goodness and non-limitation of God," the author regretfully replied that he was "unable to suggest any hypothesis which would reconcile the existence of such evils as Dr. Grossart describes with the idea of omnipresent goodness." Whereupon this novelist, who wanted his pessimism to be considered as merely intuitive, goes on to suggest: "Perhaps Dr. Grossart might be helped to a provisional view of the universe by the recently published *Life of Darwin*, and the works of Herbert Spencer and other agnostics." Hardy was in the nineteenth-century materialist tradition. His Journal tells us: "Reading in the British Museum. Have been thinking over the dictum of Hegel—that the real is the rational and the rational the real—that real pain is compatible with a formal pleasure—that the idea is all, etc., but it doesn't help much. These venerable philosophers seem to start wrong; they cannot get away from a prepossession that the world must somehow have been made to be a comfortable place for man. If I remember, it was Comte who said that metaphysics was a mere sorry attempt to reconcile theology and physics."

The essence of the problem for Hardy is discovered in a simple note, in which he has set down a possible subject for a poem: "We (human beings) have reached a degree of intelligence which Nature never contemplated when framing her laws, and for which she consequently has provided no adequate satisfactions." Turning his back on the "sorry attempt" of theologians, he records for himself "infinite" effort "to reconcile a scientific view of life with the emotional and spiritual, so that they may not be interdestructive."

He found his solution in frank acceptance of defeat. "If Law itself had consciousness, how the aspect of its creatures would terrify it, fill it with remorse!" So in *Tess* he comes to the conclusion that "Nature does not often say 'See!' to her poor creatures at a time when seeing can lead to happy doing; or reply 'Here!' to a body's cry of 'Where?' till the hide and seek has become an irksome outworn game."

Therefore one should not play the game; other than skeptical withdrawal, there is no sane reply. Tess has countered bravely, but in vain; Jude, wiser, simply gives in. The President of the Immortals has little sport with him, who scarcely answers back.

IV

Our young man will have discovered in Fielding and Melville their quintessential qualities of reality and ideality: the one an approach to life, the other a compensation for those many things wherein life fails us, who forever seek something out of human sight. He may observe in Hardy how once again in the novel, that broadest testing-ground in all the field of art, the artist comes to terms with himself; this time a turning away from life, dramatically justified. Hardy promised to himself, in an early jotting, that he would write the "story of a young man—'who could not go to Oxford'—His struggles and ultimate failure. Suicide. There is something (in this) the world ought to be shown, and I am the one to show it to them—though I was not altogether hindered going, at least to Cambridge, and could have gone up easily at five-and-twenty."

He deviated very little from this design, and indeed the jotting is precious to us, exposing not only the artist's search for something in experience more objective than his autobiography affords, but also his deep inner conviction: "There is something the world ought to be shown, and I am the one to show it to them."

The boy Jude is passionately in love with learning. He wants, in particular, to master Latin and Greek. He is poor and by an ingenious device begs a Latin grammar from a school-master in a nearby town.

Jude waited days and weeks, calling every morning at the cottage post-office before his great-aunt was stirring. At last a packet did indeed arrive at the village, and he saw from the ends of it that it contained two thin books. He took it away to a lonely place, and sat down on a felled elm to open it.

. . . When, having noted that the packet bore the post-mark of Christminster, he cut the string, opened the volumes, and turned to the Latin grammar, which chanced to come uppermost, he could scarcely believe his eyes.

The book was an old one—thirty years old, soiled, scribbled wantonly over with a strange name in every variety of enmity to the letter-press, and marked at random with dates twenty years earlier than his own day. But this was not the cause of Jude's amazement. He learned for the first time that there was no law of transmutation, as in his innocence he had supposed (there was, in some degree, but the grammarian did not recognize it), but that every word in both Latin and Greek was to be individually committed to memory at the cost of years of plodding.

Jude flung down the books, lay backward along the broad trunk of the elm, and was an utterly miserable boy for the space of a quarter of an hour. As he had often done before, he pulled his hat over his face and watched the sun peering insidiously at him through the interstices of the straw. This was Latin and Greek, then, was it, this grand delusion! The charm he had supposed in store for him was really a labor like that of Israel in Egypt.

What brains they must have in Christminster and the great schools, he presently thought, to learn words one by one up to tens of thousands! There were no brains in his head equal to this business; and as the little sun-rays continued to stream in through his hat at him, he wished he had never seen a book, that he might never see another, that he had never been born.

Somebody might have come along that way who would have asked him his trouble, and might have cheered him by saying that his notions were further advanced than those of his grammarian. But nobody did come, because nobody does; and under the crushing recognition of his gigantic error Jude continued to wish himself out of the world.

The remainder of Jude's story is deep with sorrow and pitiless in the telling. He is an orphan. Early in his life he learns that his mother's death had been at her own willing; she had drowned herself through the ice. Jude walks toward home from his old aunt's, who has told him this. He passes a large, round frozen pond.

The frost continued, though it was not particularly sharp, and the larger stars overhead came out slow and flickering. Jude put one foot on the edge of the ice, and then the other; it cracked under his weight; but this did not deter him. He ploughed his way inward to the centre, the ice making sharp noises as he went. When just about the middle he looked around and gave a jump. The cracking repeated itself; but he did not go down, He jumped again, but the cracking had ceased. Jude went back to the edge and stepped upon the ground.

It was curious, he thought. What was he reserved for? He supposed he was not a sufficiently dignified person for suicide. Peaceful death abhorred him as a subject, and would not take him.

What could he do of a lower kind than self-extermination: what was there less noble, more in keeping with his present degraded position? He could get drunk. Of course that was it. . . .

A good part of Jude's bitter, brooding character is depicted in this scene. In him we see always, as in Hardy himself, what later psychologists call the "death-wish," an ever-intrusive force in our human thought and feeling. In Jude's history we find Hardy. There has occurred for him, in words that Guy de Portalès dedicates to Liszt, "the sudden crystallization that inevitably takes place in the life of an artist, that determines the scale of its values and outlines the spiritual profile of his personality."

Jude seeks to educate himself, but he cannot succeed; the gates of the university are rudely closed to him. Frustrated, laughing at himself, he quits his studies. Indeed, as we follow Jude's career, from his stark childhood to his maturity, we behold few fruitions vouchsafed him. His every desire is denied to him, chiefly by a brief, unhappy marriage, into which he is tricked by the time-old stratagem of a scheming woman. His wife, Arabella, deserts him. He really loves his cousin Sue, and she loves him, but their attempt at a life together is harried by scandal. In fact, Jude is the victim of every kind of snobbery. His brilliant dreams end when he becomes a cathedral mason, then finally a simple cutter of headstones for the very poor. (Hardy was enamored of this symbol.) Jude himself, the obscure, is poorer than ever. His children die. One of them—nicknamed "Little Father Time" because of his precocious melancholy—emulates his grandmother in suicide. He leaves a heart-rending explanation, written in a childish hand. *"Done because we are too menny."* But here the tragedy is heightened almost beyond bearing.

Hardy's climax is remorseless; few who read it will ever forget it.

v

It is a far cry from the hanging of Billy Budd to the suicide of Little Father Time.

Melville's Redburn looked upward from his task of making up the beds of pigs in the long-boat, but we see Jude—if we may look back a moment at his childhood—going out, and, feeling more than ever his existence to be "an undemanded one," lying down "upon his back on a heap of litter near the pig-sty. The fog had by this time become more translucent, and the position of the sun could be seen through it. Growing up brought responsibilities, he found. Events did not rhyme quite as he had thought. Nature's logic was too horrid for him to care for. As you got older, and felt yourself to be at the centre of your time, and not at a point in its circumference, as you had felt when you were little, you were seized with a sort of shuddering, he perceived."

The *All,* of which Melville's Redburn caught sight, is for Hardy, borrowing from the evolutionary theory, only a senseless, unconscious force slowly growing conscious of itself. One can expect nothing of it, this something that does one's thinking for one.

VI

Hardy's poems help to carry the skeptical burden. They are without the supposed faults of the novels—weak causality, and a consequent lack of inevitability—but that could be because they demand much less of their author. The success of a lyric is hardly comparable to the success of a novel. The poems however succeed in a separate way: they mark the meeting in verse of that schism of the intellect and emotions of which we spoke when we looked at Fielding. The lyricism of the early nineteenth century, following Wordsworth, was not so much an expression of life, as an emotional refuge. Hardy and Browning, and after them the twentieth-century poets, have brought Shelley's skylark back to earth. These two are Wordsworth and Coleridge over again, the one revivifying the near, the other recapitulating the far and strange in recognizable terms.

The oft-mentioned faults in Hardy's novels can be defended. His emphasis upon chance in motivating his plots is only consistent with his philosophical attitude: nothing is inevitable in a world without a conscious first cause, unless disillusion. His artistic theories, carefully thought out, account for other apparent shortcomings sometimes impetuously decried. The chief criticism of *Jude* is that its hero is too unfortunate to be credible; Hardy's profound answer is he desires simply that, to spare his readers. "There is mercy in troubles coming in battalions—they neutralize each other. Tell a man in prosperity that he must suffer the amputation of a limb, and it is a horror to him; but tell him this the minute after he has been reduced to beggary and his only son has died: it hurts him but feebly."

Jude, the story of a young man of "tempestuous and self-harrowing nature," spares us that way.

Our amateur critic will appreciate and respect Hardy. In him skepticism and pessimism—born of intense honesty and intellectuality—attain to an exemplary heroism.

VII

But if *Jude* spares us, wherein does it help? Its author wanted to show "the contrast between the ideal life a man wished to lead, and the squalid real life he was fated to lead."

That is what the skeptic does: plays off idealism against realism. "The throwing of the pizzle, at the supreme moment of his young dream, is to sharply initiate this contrast. But I must have lamentably failed, as I feel I have, if this requires explanation and is not self-evident. The idea was meant to run all through the novel. It is, in fact, to be discovered in *everybody's* life, though it lies less on the surface perhaps than it does in my poor puppet's." (The italics are his own.)

Hardy felt that he had lamentably failed. He failed, but not lamentably. I do not think his failure results from any artistic flaw, but rather from something deeper. George Meredith speaks of Hardy's "twilight view of life." Jude's melancholy tale and the thesis affirmed there are obvious enough; the reader, even though he may reject the thesis, understands it. But the young reader does reject it—he feels that something is lacking; he feels that the author's temperament, though courageous, is impoverished. Hardy never fully attained the end which he set up for art, when he determined: "There is enough poetry in what is left in life, after all the false romance has been abstracted, to make a sweet pattern: *e.g.*, the poem by H. Coleridge:

> *'She is not fair to outward view.'*

So, then, if Nature's defects must be looked in the face and transcribed, whence arises the *art* in poetry and novel-writing? which must certainly show art, or it becomes mere mechanical reporting. I think the art lies in making these defects the basis of a hitherto unperceived beauty, by irradiating them with 'the light that never was' on their surface, but is seen to be latent in them by the spiritual eye." How utterly he failed to do that for himself, is betrayed in this confession: "I have attempted many modes of finding it. For my part, if there is any way of getting a melancholy satisfaction out of life it lies in dying, so to speak, before one is out of the flesh; by which I mean putting on the manners of ghosts, wandering in their haunts, and taking their views of surrounding things. To think of life as passing away is a sadness; to think of it as past is at least tolerable. Hence even when I enter a room to pay a simple morning call I have unconsciously the habit of regarding the scene as if I were a spectre not solid enough to influence my environment; only fit to behold and say, as another spectre said: 'Peace be unto you!'"

D. H. Lawrence once proposed writing a study of Hardy. He was interested and even envious of the man, hidden in Wessex, while the village church "chimed away the hours." Hardy, the skeptic, had an odd perception of Time. The later years of his life, engulfed in its impalpable flow, bore out his relentless fidelity to the truth of existence as he saw it. His days passed in endless quiet; he faced them indifferent even to the fame that for once visited a great man in his lifetime.

Chapter 8

Dream: Conrad

FOR LIFE Hardy never cared greatly. He saw that "Romanticism will exist in human nature as long as human nature itself exists. The point is in imaginative literature to adopt that form of romanticism which is the mood of the age." Hardy believed and recognized this, but he himself was not the man to do it; and where he failed, I think, Joseph Conrad has succeeded.

From the beginning of his career it was fashionable to speak of Joseph Conrad as a poet, but it took longer for him to be respectfully spoken of as a philosopher.

Perhaps his first readers were unprepared to look for philosophy in the exotic tales that are the dynamic expression of his ideas. His peculiar genius, like Melville's, drew on the incredible adventures of his own life.

At bottom, Joseph Conrad shared Hardy's skepticism, but his temperament was infinitely richer and would not permit of either withdrawal or defeatism. He came to grips magnificently with these themes in three great novels: *Victory, Lord Jim, Nostromo.*

For he accepted Hardy's challenge by facing Nature's defects and making them "the basis of a hitherto unperceived beauty, irradiating them with 'the light that never was' on their surface, but is seen to be latent in them by the spiritual eye."

But first, let us hear him:

The ethical view of the universe involves us at last in so many cruel and absurd contradictions, where the last vestiges of faith, hope, charity, and even reason itself, seem ready to perish, that I have come to suspect that the aim of creation cannot be ethical at all. I would fondly believe that its object is purely spectacular: a spectacle for awe, love, adoration, or hate, if you like, but in this view alone—never for despair! These visions, delicious or poignant, are a moral end in themselves. The rest is our affair—the laughter, the tears, the tenderness, the indignation, the high tranquillity of a steeled heart, the detached curiosity of a subtle

89

mind—that's our affair! And the unwearied self-forgetful attention to every phase of the living universe reflected in our consciousness may be our appointed task on this earth —a task in which fate has perhaps engaged nothing of us except our conscience, gifted with a voice in order to bear true testimony to the visible wonder, the haunting terror, the infinite passions, and the illimitable serenity; to the supreme law and abiding mystery of the supreme spectacle.

This is Joseph Conrad's vision, as revealed in his *Personal Record*. It is a definition of romanticism in splendid terms.

The thing we must observe is that this is not a facile romanticism, but a difficult and ironic one. To the charge of Gustave Kahn, that he was *"un puissant reveur,"* Conrad unblushingly replied:

So be it! Who would cavil at the words of a friendly reader? Yet perhaps not such an unconditional dreamer as all that. I will make bold to say that neither at sea nor ashore have I ever lost the sense of responsibility. There is more than one sort of intoxication. Even before the most seductive reveries I have remained mindful of that sobriety of interior life, that asceticism of sentiment, in which alone the naked forms of truth, such as one conceives it, such as one feels it, can be rendered without shame. It is but a maudlin and indecent verity that comes out through the strength of wine. I have tried to be a sober worker all my life—all my two lives. I did so from taste, no doubt, having an instinctive horror of losing my sense of full self-possession, but also from artistic conviction.

There you have an artist, I think. And there, for sure, you have a philosopher. Who would challenge his warrant?

II

Three stories of Conrad, two short and one long, contain succinct expression of the irony that chastened his romantic impulse.

A Smile of Fortune unfolds with melancholy humor. A young sea captain, mentally becalmed in the romantic atmosphere of the isles, is pursued by an unwanted profit in potatoes. *Because of the Dollars* is more cruel. A man risks death, a woman sacrifices her life—the rewards of generosity and heroism are an unjustified loneliness and suspicion.

Typhoon is a swirling epic—Melville himself could not have done better. Deified by their conflict with the storm, the end of the journey finds Conrad's men returned to their small, ordinary stature. The irony here is as beautifully subtle as the story's color, and the two are dynamically blended by the superb invention of the scrambling Chinamen in the hold.

Then in *Heart of Darkness*, Conrad looked deeply. It is a study of atavism in Africa, of the darkness that is also within us. (A striking parallel to O'Neill's *Emperor Jones*.)

My destiny! Droll thing life is—that mysterious arrangement of merciless logic for a futile purpose. The most you can hope for it is some knowledge of yourself—that comes too late—a crop of unextinguishable regrets. I have wrestled with death. It is the most unexciting contest you can imagine. It takes place in an impalpable grayness, with nothing underfoot, with nothing around, without spectators, without clamour, without glory, without the great desire for victory, without the great fear of defeat, in a sickly atmosphere of tepid skepticism, without much belief in your own right, and still less in that of your adversary. If such is the form of ultimate wisdom, then life is a greater riddle than some of us think it to be. I was within a hair's breadth of the last opportunity for pronouncement, and I found with humiliation that probably I would have nothing to say. That is the reason why I affirm that Kurtz was a remarkable man. He had something to say. He said it. . . . He had summed up— he had judged. "The horror!"

But these are minor exercises—judged philosophically. The true depth of Conrad's skepticism and the exalted heights of his affirmation are come upon in *Victory*; and here too we learn that this skepticism and compensating romanticism were not apperceptions, but inherited. To understand Conrad fully, one must read the story of Apollo Korzeniowski, his father; and of his mother, Evelina. The same imaginative conscience that motivated their tragic history was their legacy to their early orphaned son. A portrait of Apollo Korzeniowski, the self-betrayed visionary, appears in *Victory* in the absent yet dominant character of the elder Heyst.

He [the son] stirred impatiently in his chair, and raised the book to his eyes with both hands. It was one of his father's. He opened it haphazardly, and his eyes fell on the middle of the page. The elder Heyst had written of everything in many books—of space and of time, of animals and of stars; analyzing ideas and actions, the laughter and the frowns of men, and the grimaces of their agony. The son read, shrinking into himself, composing his face as if under the author's eye, with a vivid consciousness of the portrait on his right hand, a little above his head; a wonderful presence in its heavy frame on the flimsy wall of mats, looking exiled and at home, out of place and masterful, in the painted immobility of profile.

So is the example of Apollo Korzeniowski always present to his son. There is another scene, where Heyst sits alone, remembering the night his father died. (The actual death of his father, with whom the boy Conrad lived alone, left an ineradicable impression on him, to which he frequently refers.)

He [Heyst] suffered. He was hurt by the sight of his own life, which ought to have been a masterpiece of aloofness. He remembered the thin features, the great mass of white hair, and the ivory complexion. A five-branched candlestick stood on a little table by the side of the easy chair. They had been talking a long time. The noises of the street had died out one by one, till at last, in the moonlight, the London houses began to look like the tombs of an unvisited, unhonoured cemetery of hopes.

He had listened. Then, after a silence, he had asked—for he was really young then:

"Is there no guidance?"

His father was in an unexpectedly soft mood on that night, when the moon swam in a cloudless sky over the begrimed shadows of the town.

"You still believe in something, then?" he said in a clear voice, which had been growing feeble of late. "You believe in flesh and blood, perhaps? A full and equable contempt would soon do away with that too. But since you have not attained to it, I advise you to cultivate that form of contempt which is called pity. It is perhaps the least difficult—

always remembering that you too, if you are anything, are as pitiful as the rest, yet never expecting any pity for yourself."

"What is one to do, then?" sighed the young man, regarding his father, rigid, in the high-backed chair.

"Look on—make no sound . . ."

That could be Hardy speaking. "Action—the first thought, or perhaps the first impulse, on earth! The barbed hook, baited with the illusion of progress, to bring out of the lightless void the shoals of unnumbered generations!" thinks Heyst. Yet he is in the end heedless of his father's counsel, just as the young adventurer Conrad, smuggling arms in South American and Mediterranean waters, was heedless of his own father's fate. The swift tragedy follows with its reckoning, and yet the book is titled *Victory*. The victory is in the assertion of life, whatever its human cost.

The spirit of the girl which was passing away from under them clung to her triumph convinced of her victory over death.

. . . Heyst bent low over her, cursing his fastidious soul, which even at that moment kept the true cry of love from his lips in its infernal mistrust of all life. He dared not touch her, and she had no longer the strength to throw her arms about his neck.

"Who else could have done this for you?" she whispered gloriously.

"No one in the world . . ." And at last, convinced like her that defiance of death is the victory of life, he plunges into the burning bungalow. Davidson explains: "I suppose he couldn't stand his thoughts before her dead body—and fire purifies everything."

III

The same warning against aloofness, the same self-conscious embrace of action, is explicit in the character of Martin Decoud, in *Nostromo*. Decoud is left by his fellow-conspirator on an unvisited isle to wait for rescue. The cloudless sky, the waveless sea, the bright sun—and always the silence—mirror him to himself.

The brilliant "Son Decoud," the spoiled darling of the family, the lover of Antonia and journalist of Sulaco, was not fit to grapple with himself singlehanded. Solitude from mere outward condition of existence becomes very swiftly a state of soul in which the affectations of irony and skepticism have no place. It takes possession of the mind, and drives forth the thought into the exile of utter unbelief. . . . In our activity alone do we find the sustaining illusion of an independent existence as against the whole scheme of things of which we form a helpless part. . . . The vague consciousness of a misdirected life given up to impulse whose memory left a bitter taste in his mouth was the first moral sentiment of his manhood. But at the same time he felt no remorse. What should he regret? He had recognized no other virtue than intelligence, and had erected passions into duties. Both his intelligence and his passion were swallowed up easily in this great unbroken solitude of waiting without faith. Sleeplessness had robbed his will of all energy, for he had not slept seven hours in the seven days. His sadness was the sadness of a skeptical mind. He beheld the universe as a succession of incomprehensible images.

He commits suicide. "His last words are, 'It is done'—the very words in which Conrad had learned the death of his father, a significant verbal correspondence—and then waves cover 'the talker, the novio of Doña Antonia.' "

Lord Jim is the story of Decoud's opposite, of the man who erects duties into passions. This is the young man's burden, until his tragic end, when "He passes away under a cloud, inscrutable at heart, forgotten, unforgiven, and excessively romantic . . . an obscure conqueror of fame, tearing himself out of the arms of a jealous love at the call of his exalted egoism. He goes away from a living woman to celebrate his pitiless wedding with a shadowy ideal of conduct."

D. H. Lawrence thinks Conrad less sound than Melville, because Conrad sentimentalizes the ocean and the sea's unfortunates. "Snivel in a wet hanky like Lord Jim." He prefers Melville, because "Melville is like a Viking going home to the sea, encumbered with age and memories, and a sort of accomplished despair, almost madness. For he cannot accept humanity. He can't belong to humanity. Cannot." But perhaps Conrad is preferable for that very reason, because he comes from the sea, rather than returns to it, though encumbered too with age and memories; because he does not submit to despair, and finally because he can write to Edward Garnett, "The fact is that I have approached things human in a spirit of piety foreign to those lovers of humanity who would like to make of life a sort of Cook's Personally Conducted Tour—from the cradle to the grave. I have never debased that quasi-religious sentiment by tears and groans and sighs, I have neither grinned nor gnashed my teeth. In a word I have behaved decently—which, except in the gross conventional sense, is not so easy as it looks. Therefore there are those who reproach me with the pose of brutality—sentiment—idealism. . . ." Not sentimental, the author of *Lord Jim*, but rather one who earnestly quotes, "Something human is dearer to me than the wealth of all the world," and one who believed (to borrow from another letter) "Truth has not only been heard, it has even been chewed over and over again, and its true flavor has sunk into the very soul of the people. It is a bitter flavor but bitterness is the very condition of human existence"—how sentimental that is!—"and mankind generally is neither guilty nor innocent. It simply is. That is misfortune enough. Men die and suffer for their convictions and how those convictions are arrived at doesn't matter a bit. That's why, my dear fellow, satire seems to me a vain use of intelligence, and intelligence itself a thing of no great account except for us to torment ourselves with. For directly you begin to use it the questions of right and wrong arise and these are things of the air with no connection whatever with the fundamental realities of life. Whereas in the region of feeling there is nothing of the kind. Feelings *are,* and in submitting to them we can avoid neither death nor suffering which are our common lot, but we can bear them in peace." He was firm in his conviction that "When once the truth is grasped that one's personality is only a ridiculous and aimless masquerade of something hopelessly unknown the attainment of serenity is not very far off. Then there remains nothing but the surrender to one's impulses, the fidelity to passing emotions which is perhaps a nearer approach to truth than any other philosophy of life. And why not? If we are 'ever becoming—never being' then I would be a fool if I tried to become this thing rather than that; for I know well that I never will be anything. I would rather grasp the solid satisfaction of my wrong-headedness and shake my fist at the idiotic mystery of Heaven."

The fidelity to passing emotions, the grasping of the solid satisfaction of one's wrong-headedness, in answer to the logical Decoud, who saw himself "a victim of the disillusioned weariness which is the retribution meted out to intellectual audacity," and who had come to conviction of the "utter uselessness of all effort," this is the philosophical message personified in the young figure of Lord Jim. He is emotional, wrong-headed. He lives daringly. Like Heyst, he dies gloriously, triumphantly purified.

A romantic himself, the author of *Lord Jim* gives his hero a setting of mysterious grandeur. In a tropic sea, becalmed, under the "thin gold shaving of the moon," we first behold Jim, the parson's son, now chief mate of the pilgrim ship *Patna.* Early in Jim's tale, Conrad brings disaster on him, real yet poetic: the lives of the sleeping Arabs who are the *Patna's* cargo are endangered by the ship's impact with a submerged wreck. The crew fear an explosion when the in-rushing waters reach the boilers. Even more they fear panic when the pilgrims shall learn of what has happened. In a panic of their own, they abandon the sleeping Arabs to drowning. His participation in this desertion is to haunt and mark Jim the rest of his life. In his own eyes, and in the world's eyes, he is a coward and dishonored. (Conrad borrowed the outline of this incident from a true, scandalous event which had taken place twenty years earlier, the forsaking by her crew of the rusty, old S.S. *Jeddah,* in the Red Sea; these faithless seamen had heartlessly made off, without warning nine hundred fifty slumbering voyagers to Mecca, who did not even know that their ship was in peril.)

The book is long. Everything is shown in heroic proportions. In Conrad's telling, scene after scene of power and dramatic beauty follows: Jim's trial before the Court of Enquiry, his disgrace; the unexplained death of Captain Brierly, who has been head of the tribunal; then Jim's flight from himself, his adventurous pursuit of redemption through violence, in Eastern jungles, along Malayan rivers, in melodrama, in passionate love, in vivid physical danger. (There is also good evidence that much of the external detail of Jim's fabulous history is based upon that of the even more fabulous first "Rajah" Brooke of Sarawak.) He has now become *Tuan* Jim, the proud, inscrutable white "Lord Jim" of Patusan, master and counselor in dynastic warfare, feared, a legendary figure, invincible. An exultant man. . . .

Thus we see Jim, the self-designated fugitive from the *Patna,* as he recounts to Marlow, Conrad's narrator, a recent warlike exploit: " 'It was . . . it was immense! Immense!' he cried aloud, flinging his arms open. The sudden movement startled me as though I had seen him bare the secrets of his breast to the sunshine, to the brooding forests, to the steely sea. . . ." To which Marlow adds: "Immense! No doubt it was immense; the seal of success upon his words, the conquered ground for the soles of his feet, the blind trust of men, the belief in himself snatched from the fire, the solitude of his achievement. All this, as I've warned you, gets dwarfed in the telling. I can't with mere words convey to you the impression of his total and utter isolation. I know, of course, he was in every sense alone of his kind there. . . ."

In this aloneness, in this fame, *Tuan* Jim rises in power, in happiness and a strange kind of Eastern—Oriental—success.

The novel progresses in great pageantry, lavish with characters: Conrad is inexhaustible. We have Jim, his curious friend Stein, Doramin—the monstrous Malay—with his witch of a wife and his brilliant son Dain Waris; the vagabond Sherif Ali; Captain Brierly; the malevolent Cornelius, the girl's father; the girl herself; Tamb' Itam; Gentleman Brown and the "silly old" Rajah Allang; and Egström. These, and many others. In his oblique manner, Conrad uses them all to show us facets of *Tuan* Jim's developing personality, once a parson's son, now virtual ruler of a principality in the Malay archipelago.

But a second, a more crucial test of spirit awaits him. Conrad's novel mounts, surges on, a moral, a philosophical melodrama. *Tuan* Jim's end, his second fall, comes about through his faith in others, and—though to a lesser extent—his exaggerated faith in himself. " 'Nothing can touch me,' he said in a last flicker of superb egoism." He will not, in this second crisis, repeat his behaviour, his moral failure, of that fateful night on the *Patna.* He gives up everything, love, life, for his redeemed honor. It is the romantic's decision.

Marlow describes him: "I believe that in that very moment he had decided to defy the disaster in the only way it occurred to him such a disaster could be defied; but all I know is that, without a word, he came out of his room and sat before the long table, at the head of which he was accustomed to regulate the affairs of his world, proclaiming daily the truth that surely lived in his heart. The dark powers should not rob him twice of his peace. He sat like a stone figure."

The girl pleads. She sees hope that Jim and Tamb' Itam can escape. In any event, he should take action for his defense. Tamb' Itam too begs: "'Fight!'

"'What for?' he asked.

"'For our lives.'

"'I have no life,' he said."

The girl cannot accept this.

Her lover is adamant. "He was inflexible, and with the growing loneliness of his obstinacy his spirit seemed to rise above the ruins of his existence. She cried 'Fight!' into his ear. She could not understand. He was going to prove his power in another way and conquer the fatal destiny itself. He came out into the courtyard, and behind him, with streaming hair, wild of face, breathless, she staggered out and leaned on the side of the doorway. 'Open the gates,' he ordered. Afterwards, turning to those of his men who were inside, he gave them leave to depart to their homes. 'For how long, *Tuan?*' asked one of them timidly. 'For all life,' he said, in a sombre tone."

The final scene, with all its suspense, grows more sharp. "All at once Jim, who seemed to be lost in quiet thought, turned and said, 'Time to finish this.' "

He seeks to reconcile the girl to his decision.

"'Will you fight?' she cried. 'There is nothing to fight for,' he said; 'nothing is lost.' Saying this he made a step towards her. 'Will you fly?' she cried again. 'There is no escape,' he said, stopping short, and she stood still also, silent, devouring him with her eyes."

Her wildest pleas leave him unmoved. "'Enough, poor girl,' he said. 'I should not be worth having.' "

He is killed, unresisting, with an "unflinching" glance. His death is "the victory" again.

Marlow, the narrator, confesses: "Now he is no more, there are days when the reality of his existence comes to me with an immense, an overwhelming force; and yet upon my honour there are moments, too, when he passes from my eyes like a disembodied spirit astray amongst the passions of this earth, ready to surrender himself faithfully to the claim of his own world of shades."

Stein, the philosophical butterfly-collector, has said earlier of Jim, " 'I understand him very well. He is romantic.'

" 'What's good for it?'

"He lifted up a long forefinger.

" 'There is only one remedy! One thing alone can us from being ourselves cure!' "

Marlow wants something more. " '. . . The question is not how to get cured, but how to live.'

"He approved with his head, a little sadly as it seemed. 'Ja! Ja! In general, adapting the words of your great poet: "That is the question . . ." ' He went on nodding sympathetically. . . . 'How to be! Ach! How to be.' "

Stein puts the problem, in his German English: " 'We want in so many different ways to be. . . . This magnificent butterfly finds a little heap of dirt and sits still on it; but man he will never on his heap of mud keep still. He want to be so, and again he want to be so. . . .' He moves his hand up, then down. . . . 'He wants to be a saint, and he wants to be a devil —and every time he shuts his eyes he sees himself as a very fine fellow—so fine as he can never be. . . . In a dream . . .!' "

Marlow relates the old man's answer: " 'And because you not always can keep your eyes shut there comes the real trouble—the heart pain—the world pain. I tell you, my friend, it is not good for you to find you cannot make your dream come true, for the reason that you not strong enough are, or not clever enough. . . . Yes! Very funny this terrible thing is. A man that is born falls into a dream like a man who falls into the sea. If he tries to climb out into the air as inexperienced people endeavour to do, he drown—*nicht wahr* . . .? No! I tell you! The way is to the destructive element submit yourself, and with the exertions of your hands and feet in the water make the deep, deep sea keep you up. . . .'

"His voice leaped up extraordinarily strong, as though away there in the dusk he had been inspired by some whisper of knowledge. 'I will tell you! For that, too, there is only one way.' "

Marcel Proust prescribes this too: "If a little dreaming is

dangerous, the cure for it is not to dream less but to dream more, to dream all the time."

Stein—Conrad's voice—says it once again. " 'In the destructive element immerse. . . . To follow the dream, and again to follow the dream—and so—*ewig—usque ad finem*. . . .' "

Chapter 9

Good and Evil

"TO GRATIFY every desire, but not to buy at too dear a price. . . ." "To love a man who dives. . . ." "To make a philosophy for himself out of his own experience, unafraid of the truth, no matter how cruel that truth may be. . . ." Or else, "In the destructive element immerse. . . . To follow the dream, and again to follow the dream. . . ." These are the things our mythical young man, who all this while has been reading critically, has been telling himself. The adventures of our amateur critic, accompanying the adventures of these other young men, should have been vivid, many times brought up short by the likenesses the artists have presented. There has been something startlingly familiar about the open face of Tom Jones, the radiant face of Billy Budd, the melancholy face of Jude, the dreaming face of Jim—for not only have our own faces, and the features of our friends, been given back to us, but with bared intimacy. The novelist preserves no reticence. That is why, as that good critic and novelist E. M. Forster has truly observed, we feel that we know fictional characters—Becky Sharp, or Anna Karenina—even better than our closest flesh-and-blood acquaintances.

In a sense, what we have been studying in these books is the attempt of four authors to arrive at some morality that will have a relation both to their desires and the actual world. We have noted their picture of human desire and their description of the world. Now it will interest us to see how they have solved for themselves the problem of what is good and evil, since that answer must be the basis of any morality. Is there a good and evil? Does man have a choice between them?

To begin, we might refer to a fugitive essay of Fielding's, *On the Knowledge of the Characters of Men.* Fielding declares men to be naturally good or evil, denying that they become so through any volition of their own.

> Those who predicate of man in general, that he is an animal of this or that disposition, seem to me not suffici-

101

ently to have studied human nature; for that immense variety of characters, so apparent in men even of the same climate, religion, and education, which gives the poet a sufficient license, as I apprehend, for saying

"Man differs more from man, than man from beast"

could hardly exist, unless the distinction had some original foundation in nature itself. Nor is it perhaps a less proper predicament of the genius of a tree, that it will flourish so many years, loves such a soil, bears such a fruit, &c, than of man in general that he is good, bad, fierce, tame, honest, or cunning.

The evil that Tom Jones encounters is of this sort; Master Blifil, his ill-wisher, never once gives any sign of what Fielding calls Good-nature, "that benevolent and amiable temper of mind, which disposes us to feel the misfortunes and enjoy the happiness of others; and consequently, pushes us on to promote the latter, and prevent the former; and without any abstract contemplation on the beauty of virtue, and without the allure-ments or terrors of religion."

There is a curious, mystical or perhaps Freudian counterpart to this belief, in what Melville has to say of Claggart, the evil protagonist of *Billy Budd*:

But for the adequate comprehending of Claggart by a normal nature, these hints are insufficient. To pass from a normal nature to him one must cross "the deadly space between," and this is best done by indirection.

Long ago an honest scholar, my senior, said to me in reference to one who like himself is no more, a man so un-impeachably respectable that against him nothing was ever openly said, though among the few something was whis-pered, "Yes, X—— is a nut not to be cracked by a lady's fan. You are aware that I am the adherent of no organized religion, much less of any philosophy built into a system. Well, for all that, I think that to try and get into X——, enter his labyrinth and get out again, without a clue derived from source other than what is known as *knowledge of the world*—that were hardly possible, at least for me."

He says that at the time his "inexperience was such that I did not quite see the drift of all this. It may be I see it now."

He concludes: "In the list of definitions included in the authentic translation of Plato, a list attributed to him, occurs this: 'Natural Depravity: a depravity according to nature.'"

There is no doubt that Claggart is modeled on the real sailor Jackson, who accompanied Redburn—Melville—on his first voyage, and who is so remarkably a forerunner of Conrad's James Wait, the *Narcissus* Nigger. (But there is no suggestion that Conrad knew Melville's book.) Jackson was dying "for his sins" and had "the most deep, subtle, infernal-looking eye that I ever saw lodged in a human head." Redburn understands that it was "the consciousness of his miserable, broken-down condition, and the prospect of soon dying like a dog . . . that made this poor wretch always eye me with such malevolence as he did. For I was young and handsome, at least my mother so thought me, and as soon as I became a little used to the sea, and shook off my low spirits somewhat, I began to have my old colour in my cheeks, and, spite of misfortune, to appear well and hearty."

Redburn tells of "the shudder that would run through me when I caught this man gazing at me, as I often did; for he was apt to be dumb at times, and would sit with his eyes fixed, and his teeth set, like a man in the moody madness."

The malevolence of Moby Dick has something of this too, an evil that is largely beyond man's understanding.

Hardy, less mystic, sees an unconscious Nature as the cause for nearly all human trouble, and proclaims the "woeful fact —that the human race is too extremely developed for its corporeal conditions, the nerves being evolved to an activity abnormal in such an environment. Even the higher animals are in excess in this respect. It may be questioned if Nature, or what we call Nature, so far back as when she crossed the line from invertebrates to vertebrates, did not exceed her mission. This planet does not supply the materials for happiness to higher existences. Other planets may, though one can hardly see how." Hardy finds Tess and Jude helpless and pities them. What is evil is chance, whose victims they are. In sum, this differs little from Melville's view, or Fielding's. Each story absolves its protagonist of fundamental moral error.

Conrad, seemingly alone, believes that the fault lies not in men, for "mankind generally is neither guilty nor innocent. It simply is. That is misfortune enough"; nor in the natural world, which contains "enough marvels and mysteries acting upon emotions and intelligences in ways so inexplicable that it would almost justify the conception of life as an enchanted state." The fault, for Conrad, lies in the individual man. Mr. Jones and Ricardo, the villains of *Victory,* are embodied evil, just as Melville's twain—but Heyst's is the fatal flaw. One does not condemn the crew of the *Patna,* but accepts them for what they are—Jim alone must be convicted, for having betrayed himself. This is a romantic morality, based on the superior man's illusion of himself, the standard of conduct he sets for himself, without rigid reference to reality.

Thus we see that Tom Jones, no matter how much he might err, would still be good in Fielding's eyes; and similarly that the murderer Billy Budd could only be blameless to Melville; while Captain Ahab meets a violent end because he is pursuing what is in truth an incarnation of his own disparate qualities. Tom is naturally good; Blifil is naturally bad. Billy is naturally good; Claggart is naturally bad. Ahab cannot help himself; Moby Dick is supernatural evil. Mary Colum has denied that any artist can believe in determinism, but here obviously are two great authors who do. Hardy, of course, is not a determinist. His concept of fate is merely negative, since our fortunes are haphazard. Conrad alone believes in a measure of free will, and thinks that each man's choice is good or evil only if it fulfills or thwarts his dream of himself. Jude surrenders to chance. Jim challenges and conquers it, but at the cost of his life. Jim's decision to escape from the *Patna* is evil. His willingness to die for his honor is "good." Hardy and Conrad see the world as anarchy; but where Hardy, defeated by that view of anarchy, seeks to protect himself by indifference, Conrad still finds the spectacle of the universe a source of poetic astonishment.

Only Conrad demands of man a moral decision. It is a highly personal one. Fielding is actually amoral. He counsels prudence—that is his philosophical lesson. Melville is deeply moral, but the beauty and malignity of the universe overwhelm him. He is afraid of it and hates it—but at the end he affirms idealistic aspiration as the means to salvation. Hardy gazes on Melville's turbulent cosmos with ironic detachment. Yet he is not really detached. He suffers. He prefers to present what he sees and not to pass judgment. Intellectually he has the greatest fortitude—he does not delude himself or seek escape in ready dogma, cult, gesture, or helpful faith. He has heroic proportions that overtop Fielding, Melville, and Conrad. He would be the best of the four, if heroism were enough.

We know little now about good and evil. We have no single picture of it.

The disagreement here is only one of emphasis. The merit of the discussion, I think, is that if we have respect for the opinions of these four great and original thinkers, we shall ourselves be more hesitant in forming views of what is good and evil. That way we shall avoid the presumption of the young man in Shaw's *Major Barbara* who lectures his father severely on what is right and wrong; an exact knowledge of which the young man has obtained in two decades, as the Shavian father observes, although the problem has been bothering the world's wisest men for two millennia.

One way I had of entertaining myself, after having reached this point in my study, was to imagine how one of these four authors would have written the book of another: how Hardy would have told the history of Tom Jones, for example, or Billy Budd; or how Fielding would have related the adventures of Lord Jim. It showed me in some measure how important are personality and temperament, how varied is the world, if only because men are varied. Conrad, I fancy, given Jude, would have told him to immerse himself sufficiently in one element or another, as does Lord Jim; but never, as does Jude, try to walk on water. Fielding would quickly have forgiven Jim; Hardy could never have written *Billy Budd:* he would have depicted him as merely a boy whose personal beauty, for all its promise, proves to be bad rather than good fortune; a lad not divine, but one who stutters. Melville's Lord Jim would have struggled not with himself, not with his sense of honor, but with powers of darkness.

To that extent, the philosophy found in art is wholly temperamental. Art, properly seen, is a temperamental control of experience. Our lives, if we attempt to live them in the light of some philosophy, borrows from art in that it too is a temperamental discipline of daily events. The artist shows us the way.

There is yet another writer to whom our young reader should turn: a writer who, where these others have been looking up or about them, has been looking down. The proper element in which a man should immerse himself, he would say, should not be sea or air, but *man*. To recognize sensuality, and become conscious of the nature too long unconscious within us. . . .

Here once more we have something that is, if not philosophy, then prophecy, since Lawrence is the first to speak this way.

Chapter 10

Flesh: Lawrence

"A NEW artist is like a sort of first isolated individual of a species which does not yet exist but is going to multiply in the future, an individual endowed with a kind of *sense* which the human race of his generation does not possess," says Marcel Proust.

D. H. Lawrence has that *sense*. He is original. He is unique.

That Lawrence should be as original as he is seems almost incredible. Where else, though, do we have a celebration of sensuality like his?

He is sometimes considered merely a borrower of Freudian beliefs. His stress upon the importance of the sexual in daily thought and feeling is certainly akin to Freud's. Lawrence was indignant whenever this was suggested. He claimed that he had been thinking in the same direction quite in advance of Freud, and indeed that his own *Fantasia of the Unconscious* was published before any of Freud's monographs. This is inconsequential, save that we have the artist once more in the rôle of his own philosopher and psychologist.

Lawrence lived in a time of disintegration of social values, of transition, of moral anarchy. Beyond doubt the Freudian revelations, which had so startling an impact, contributed to that anarchy. Men and women, struggling in a loose and even turbulent society between the two World Wars, were forced to reëxamine all the moral standards and possible illusions by which they had been raised. In this later time of ours, when a new and liberalized mood, an emancipating psychology, surrounds and forms us from childhood, the difficulty of that preceding generation's adjustment to Freud's findings can hardly be appreciated.

"Ours is a tragic age . . ." wrote Lawrence, as we quoted him much earlier in this book. He speaks of the search for "new little habitations among the ruins."

Of this transitional period Lawrence is the conscious historian . . . a suffering, bitter, angry historian.

But he is something more than that. He is the prophet of the age to follow.

In prophecy there is originality, a new *sense,* as Proust says. Yet prophecy may also be merely a careful reading of what lies all about one. The future follows by a certain logic of events. Just as the present is to science the key to the past, so the present is the key to the future. Lawrence observes and interprets the events of his world, the temper of struggling men, their reproaches, hopes, demands.

His anger is prophetic. But his visions, though glorious, sometimes Blake-like, are the proof of intelligence. He has a terrifying intelligence.

We may question whether anyone is ever fully original or truly unique. Lawrence, like Hardy, is remarkably alive to the *zeitgeist,* the spirit of his day. His long, harried search in his last years that led him quite around the Equator, to Australia, Mexico, Sardinia, is but the outward wandering of a restless thinker and salvationist. He is more than a consumptive in search of the sun, which he so often allegorizes; he is a tortured seeker after the great truth of his age. He has an apostolic zeal. But he can never deceive himself, and it is not in him to deceive others.

What qualifies him for his rôle of historian and prophet?

Consider Lawrence's strange background and even stranger life! He was the son of a coal miner. He was born into poverty and surrounded with everything ugly. He has portrayed—particularly in *Sons and Lovers*—the dark, one might almost say the sooty, picture of his early days in the pits and collieries, a miner's child among other miners' children. He has portrayed there too his brooding and ambitious mother, a woman of education married to a brute miner, whose spell over her wild sensitive son was so great and lasting: an influence beneficent and scarring both. With his mother's help, he was properly schooled. He escaped from the drab village of coal mines and became a genteel school teacher. Then as a young painter and writer near London he mixed with artistic bohemians, particularly Katherine Mansfield and John Middleton Murry, and many foreign-born intelligentsia, Russians and Slavs. He finally married a German baroness, with whom he eloped while she was still the wife of a university professor. Through her he was allied with a proud Teutonic family and the Continental world in which they lived. He was now a polemic novelist of international reputation—rich and eccentric people flocked to him. He was almost the leader of a cult.

His health was broken, though. He began to travel. He lived in Italy. Then he came to the United States, to New Mexico. He became a weird, bearded man, who could shriek with feminine shrillness, who had bitter imaginings and quarrels with everyone around him, his followers. He hated them. He reviled them. He had visions of himself as a great leader, and he was surrounded by members of the lunatic fringe. He wrote tirelessly; he cursed, coughed out his lungs, spat blood.

In these people who surrounded him, the artists and would-be artists, the mystical *avant garde* Russians, Mansfield, Murry, this husband of the German baroness, this friend of rich eccentric Americans foresaw the collapse of his age. These frustrated, rich, brilliant people were the symbols—or perhaps better, the symptoms—of the sick civilization he lived in. His analysis led him to become a sort of later-day Thoreau, to a rather futile belief in an urgent doctrine of the de-mechanization of life, to a rediscovery of its sexual content. There is doubtless some personal reason for his taking up "sex" as a talisman. He "anticipated" the Freudians in recognizing and proclaiming that there is much more to the sexual determinants in personality than had as yet been realized. But like the Freudians he means much more than merely the sexual act when he speaks of "sex."

Fielding, the natural man, would probably not have known what Lawrence is talking about when he preaches of "sex." For Lawrence the very word has a mystical glow. He is writing of and for a new race of men and women, those with delicate nerves and over-refined feelings, inhibitions and neurotic impulses, who would have fazed the robust Fielding utterly. Yet in the centuries since Fielding's time, modern civilization had brought this troubled and unhappy new race into being. This was a corollary of the growth and spread of the middle class and its restrictive morality.

Lawrence sees in the sexual—in sexual awareness even more than in sexual experience—a flame, a warmth, a quickening of feeling and emotion that is regenerative, that will reawaken all men and women to complete living. To him the sexual is beautiful. He writes of it in terms of the highest and most vivid poetry. In his work is mysticism and evangelical lyricism. George Moore has spoken of passion as the "color of life." But Moore's "passion" is very pale beside that of Lawrence, that is so wonderfully stirring, so all-pervading, so nervous in the best sense of the word, and so fiery, exalted. His prose is incandescent; his sensuousness tender, ruthless, honest, invested with dignity. He is vulgar. His humor is scathing. Yet his mind is subtle, almost to the point of decadence.

E. M. Forster praises his bardic quality. Elizabeth Bowen, commenting on the requirements we set up for modern fiction, has said excellently: "We want the naturalistic surface, but with a kind of internal burning. In Lawrence every bush burns."

Lawrence parallels the Freudians too in the rediscovery of racial myth, in which most often he finds an energetic sexual expression as well as a cultural or social meaning. As we shall remark later, he gives us our first picture of fascism, the shape it is to assume, the use it is to make of racial and sexual myth, in his strange Mexican novel *The Plumed Serpent*, which at moments sounds as though it might have been produced by the Sigmund Freud who wrote *Totem and Taboo,* no less than by Pareto or Sorel. In his worship of and ecstatic description of Indian customs, of the inarticulate, the non-intellectual, the "dark blood," he is a forerunner of the contemporary widespread cult that prefers barbaric art and primitivism in all things. Barbaric here is not meant as a term of derogation. Such art, merely untutored, or else consciously adapted from that of earlier races, has the virtues of spontaneity, simplicity, strength, bright color. All these Lawrence himself acquires in his prosaic and poetic writing, intensely fluid, quick, striking.

It is only natural that an effete civilization should be attracted by the strength and mystery of a barbaric past, which in a few hidden places in the world persists into the present, as in the Taos and Mexico that Lawrence found and soon made famous. The rain dances, the fertility rites, the Aztec legends, become his ultimate theme. He offers them as lessons to his fellow-men, examples of how virile, pulsant, and alive their simple living can be. His universe becomes demonic. He is a Blake who believes in the Old Gods, the fierce supernal powers in man's own blood. His is an exalted animalism. Yet it is truly beautiful. No writer since Blake and Dante has ever revealed a divinity in man quite so palapable, so credible, so perfectly and intensely hymned, vehement, ardent. This is truly an Old Testament prophet!

His powers ebb with his illness. He becomes frantic.

II

In his books, Lawrence begins as an idealist, a most wrong-headed one. His fault is that, unlike Melville, he is not free of the defects of his own personality. Those are serious defects.

To me it seems that much of Lawrence—his earlier work especially, after *Sons and Lovers*—must be discredited. He was an unfortunate and oversensitive man, for whom the imagined world of his novels is not so much realization of his experience as wish-fulfillment. The Indian rain dances, the fertility rites, the reinterpreted Mayan myths are all very well: but they are not a solution to the ills of mankind—at least, not a practical solution. Especially in his own chaotic age. But then, that is the prophetic strain: those who love their country are not desirous of seeking other lands. And Lawrence's very sensitiveness equips him, almost too well, as an artist. Luke, in *Glad Ghosts*, says, "My spirit is like a naked nerve on the air." That describes Luke's author too. Who else has so tactile a sense of birds, beasts, and flowers—and people? Sometimes his communicated response is more sharp than we can bear.

The hysterical quality in him is easily explained. His almost intolerable sensitiveness, and the failure of his own life, set him apart from other men. He had to contend with too many things: that unnatural influence of his mother, then early poverty, ill health; and lastly, the hostility of critics—at least of the officiously over-righteous—and his sensitivity at the same time so unarmed him, what wonder he is strange and queerly irritable, and often hasty and too contemptuous. He himself is ashamed of the "cockney jeer" that is sometimes his answer to detractors.

The author of *Women in Love, The Rainbow, Aaron's Rod*, is a neurotic, struggling toward a vision clearly enough seen but unattainable in the person that he is. He himself declares: "One sheds one's sicknesses in books, repeats and presents again one's emotions to be master of them." He is, indeed, offering an apology for bad dreams.

His early vision is expressed in difficult allegory in *Twilight in Italy*: "It is past the time to cease seeking one Infinite," he proclaims fiercely, "ignoring, striving to eliminate the other." The Infinite, for him, is twofold, the Senses and the Mind. The consummation of man is twofold in the Body and mental Spirit.

What does this mean? I have simplified Lawrence's allegorical language. Perhaps I may simplify his fundamental idea. What he sees is a dualism, a conflict between sensuality and spirituality. He does not want them to merge; they should be bridged but not reconciled. Because either, with the other intermixed, is less than itself: spirituality that includes the sensual element; sensuality that is tinged or tainted with mind. He rails against this last particularly. Man should not seek a hyphenated sensuality-spirituality. He should instead have two goals. He should strive for two Infinites or two consummations, absolute sensuality and absolute spirituality, to use Lawrence's phrase.

By great retrogression back to the sources of darkness in us, the Self, deep in the senses, we arrive at the Original, Creative Infinite. By projection forth from ourself, by the elimination of our absolute sensual Self, we arrive at Oneness in the Spirit. These are two, And man must know both.

But he must never confuse them. They are eternally separate. The lion shall never lie down with the lamb. The lion eternally shall devour the lamb, the lamb eternally shall be devoured. Man knows the great consummation in the flesh, the sexual ecstasy, and that is eternal. Also the spiritual ecstasy of unanimity, that is eternal. But the two are separate and never to be confused. To neutralize the one with the other is unthinkable, an abomination.

Then not to neutralize, but to find some current or integrating force that flows from one to the other, "the rainbow that goes between, the iris of my very being" is the impulse of his early search. The novels following *Sons and Lovers*— and like it confessedly autobiographical—to the climactic *Plumed Serpent*, are a record of that search. By this time, in a fervent essay on Melville (*Studies in Classic American Literature*), he cries out:

"Melville was, at the core, a mystic and idealist.

"Perhaps, so am I.

"And he stuck to his ideal guns.

"*I abandon mine.*"

III

Melville stuck to his ideal guns. Lawrence almost shrilly abandons his. Henceforth in the dualism of Senses and Mind, Dark and Light, he chooses warm dark sensuality. He has struggled to attain an apotheosis of sensuality and an apotheosis of spirituality, but now sensuality becomes his only goal. He is no longer an "idealist." In that choice, I think, he owns himself a lesser man than Melville—yes, and a lesser man than Conrad. But he remains a great man even so.

As the amateur critic, I did not include Lawrence in my plan for any of his work leading up to the *Plumed Serpent*, but rather because—unlike most of his professional critics—I found his greatness better exemplified in works yet to come: *Sun, Glad Ghosts,* and *Lady Chatterley's Lover*. The charges brought against this later work, that he "allegorizes," that he shows no "new positive quality," no "implied conviction, as distinct from expressed asserveration," are assuredly just. Yet this later Lawrence, despite his polemicism, counts for more. For one thing, he objectifies—as the polemical, religious writer he thinks more of his audience, clarifies, re-identifies his life with theirs. For another—and this is a dangerous thesis, which I shall qualify later—as he narrows his search, surrendering the spiritual and accepting a "mindless sensuality" as sufficient, he comes to us at last with a single, quintessential doctrine which is truly original and valuable enough. He is finally sure of his ground. His friends judge him for himself, and love him for where he fails; for the moment, let us judge him for his readers, who will be grateful to him where he succeeds.

"Great men of letters have never created more than a single work, or rather have never done more than refract through various mediums an identical beauty which they bring into the world," observes Proust, who refers to Hardy, and Dostoevski, and Vermeer as examples of this. In the canvases of Vermeer, Proust continues, we find "fragments of an identical world, that is always, however great the genius with which they have been re-created, the same table, the same carpet, the same woman, the same novel and unique beauty, an enigma. . . ." Yes, the quality, the temperament, the compulsion of an artist are constants. He is very frequently magnetized by a single idea. It is, I think, especially true of Lawrence.

Sun—a vitally beautiful story—and *Glad Ghosts*—a mystically persuasive one—and *Lady Chatterley's Lover* are great statements of Lawrence's final vision, his revelation; his hypnotic prose here brings us, to borrow indirectly from Peter Monro Jack, to Lawrence's heart: "into his warm, sensuous nature, into his quick, vivid pictorialism, into his deep-flowing philosophy or metaphysic of the unconscious life." The early novels—*Women in Love, Kangaroo, Aaron's Rod*—represent a Lawrence who has not learned that it is better to "invent than suffer: imagine victims

> *Lest your own flesh be chosen the agonist . . ."*

(Robinson Jeffers wrote this to him, a chosen message on the flyleaf of a volume of his poems.) *Sun* and *Glad Ghosts* reveal a man nearer to inward peace.

IV

To Chénier we owe the formulated truth that "Heaven gives prophetic accents to the dying." There is, along with fear, a sweet release at the thought of death. The reader of Fielding's *Voyage to Lisbon* will have it evidenced to him; the reader of *Lady Chatterley's Lover* will see it too. The man is free of himself at last.

This may be too soon to judge—the prophet cannot be finally honored until his prophecies have had time to prove their worth, and who looks toward the future must wait upon the future for reward. Lawrence all his life denounces the world he finds and fights for another world to come: only that world can finally pronounce on him.

I do not believe that any but a dying man could have written a book so cruel—it tears away almost every intellectual and emotional pretense another might deem necessary to ordinary living—and yet so kind. A novel "frankly and faithfully phallic," he writes to a friend, "but tender and delicate, as I believe in it: and as I believe it is necessary for us to become. It'll infuriate *mean* people: but it will surely soothe decent ones."

His honesty is relentless. I emphasize this quality of honesty. A more honest man never lived.

And how decent is Lawrence's *Ästhetik* of the novel, contained in this paragraph:

She [Lady Chatterley] ought not to listen with this queer rabid curiosity. After all, one may hear the most private affairs of other people, but only in a spirit of respect for the struggling, battered thing which any human soul is, and in a spirit of fine, discriminating sympathy. For even satire is a form of sympathy. It is the way our sympathy flows or recoils that really determines our lives. And here lies the vast importance of the novel, properly handled. It can inform and lead into new places the flow of our sympathetic consciousness, and it can lead our sympathy away from things gone dead. Therefore, the novel, properly handled, can reveal the most secret places of life: for it is in the *passional* secret places of life, above all, that the tide of sensitive awareness needs to ebb and flow, cleansing and freshening.

That was hardly how the book was welcomed. Lawrence was immediately calumniated, as Fielding and Hardy had been before him. His nerves never let him withstand such attacks with calm. He was exasperated to new fury by them. He had printed the book himself, in Italy, and was selling the copies to friends, furtively, disguising the packages sent in the mails, like any peddler of obscene literature. It had become, most wrongly, a part of the world's erotica. *Lady Chatterley's Lover* is the dying Lawrence's selfless testament.

Some do not find release in the frankness of this book. But many do. It means less to those who have been inwardly frank and outspoken about the sexual all their lives, but for those who have been the victims of restraint fearfully self-imposed or imposed by family or social taboos, the effect of reading the book is often sharp, even crucial. Because *Lady Chatterley's Lover* is noble in every other respect, many who are profoundly troubled by deep conflicts reach through it a true catharsis. It is almost, for them, a confessional.

The novel is forthright in descriptions of the physical act, yet without grossness. No one ever calls it gross. Its language is blunt Anglo-Saxon. It is one of the evidences of Lawrence's genius that he has made this racy and shocking Anglo-Saxon the basis of the book's poetry, its most distinctive lyricism. What might otherwise be gross is here redeemed by the folk accent; though it is this very folk speech—the short Anglo-Saxon words now belonging to our gutter idiom—that the prurient and unco guid find too rude. The folk accent—so offensive to Lady Chatterley when she first encounters her gamekeeper, later her lover—catches in time the quality of their relationship, becomes for them the proper speech for the scented and vivid earthiness of their love, a sexual love that is natural, and being natural, a sexual love that is too fresh for the power of older, worn "poetic" words to describe. Lawrence finds a new vocabulary in the oldest English tongue of all, a higher language in the lowest speech, brighter, bolder, more real phrases in the "natural" words that Fielding might have used—though even the lusty Fielding dared not set them down in print. Here is a milestone, a touchstone, in literature.

We need make no other case for Lawrence. He has left impassioned essays—notably *Pornography and Obscenity* and *Apropos of Lady Chatterley's Lover*—in his own defense. Rebecca West answers the oft-quoted charge of obsession, in her reverence of him as one who sees more deeply than others and yet preserves his belief in the seriousness and beauty of life. Like Fielding, he stands forth all the more when seen against his contemporaries—Shaw, and the Aldous Huxley of *Antic Hay*—of whom it might be said with Hardy and Ruskin, that "the present cause of the want of imagination in works of the present age" is discovered "in the flippant sarcasm of our time. 'Men do not open their hearts to us if we are to broil them on a thorn fire.'" He is tender, for all his anger.

v

Sensuality is not a philosophy. Lawrence's place in our plan is complementary. He is wrong—as most prophets are likely to be—in his conviction that he has found the whole answer to the question we have been asking, but he is indubitably right in his courageous insistence that in the rediscovery of the phallic mystery he brings something that can be new and deeply important to our living.

Chapter 11

A Synthesis

OUR AMBITION, in this plan, was more than personal. We wanted to share in part the "spiritual development of the human race." While we cannot say that Fielding lived in a time wholly natural, Melville in a time altogether transcendental, Hardy in a time entirely skeptical, or Conrad in a romantic time—indeed, Hardy and Conrad were contemporaries—we may assume that our human history has followed in some measure the chronological order suggested by these men. Plato was an idealist two thousand years before Fielding was born: yet our concept of mankind begins with man as physical first, robust in appetite; then visited with those intuitions, those aspirations, which convince him of the supernatural and inspire him with a yearning known as idealism. As his knowledge of the world increases, and his physical desires rebel, he may fall prey to such pessimism and skepticism as Hardy describes. His inherent vigor, his idealism, may resist skepticism. His imagination may overcome it, as the romantic Conrad's imagination did. He may, in the face of such skepticism, acknowledge his yearning for idealism, yet hopelessly abandon it for a gross or mystical sensuality. Mankind does not progress evenly. Temperament dictates wide variations. Yet, over a broad front of centuries, men as a whole will trace this inevitable course; and each thinking man, in little, reproduces the history of our civilization in himself, as the fœtus repeats man's evolution in the womb. One thing is to be remarked: the "natural" man in us is not uninfluenced by our consequent idealism; we can never recapture our idealism as purely once we have attained to skepticism; once we have permitted ourselves to be romantic our skepticism can never again be as undeviating. Thus the "natural" man is not necessarily lower than the idealist; the idealist is not necessarily less intelligent than the skeptic. There is no longer any such thing, among those who think, as the simply "natural" man, the pure idealist, the whole skeptic. Through centuries of coexistence and exchange, those philosophies have interpenetrated. Today a

117

philosophy of robustness—in the light of one's temperament—may be as intelligent as one of pessimism; it will not be unmixed with skepticism, idealism. For each of us, the temperament dominates, but it is not exclusive. We are the sum of our civilization, we are acted upon by those around us, whatever may be our temperamental choice.

The purpose of our plan was to help us understand ourselves better, and to help us understand others. Those of us who are Jude, need to know more about those who are Tom Jones and Billy Budd; and Fielding and Melville can tell us more than anyone else. That justifies their being artists.

Several years ago, when the popularity of Hervey Allen's *Anthony Adverse* was at its greatest, someone asked its author what explanation he had for his book's fabulous success. The answer, which was seemingly meant seriously, amused some others.

"It shows that people are once more interested in spiritual things."

We know, however, as Hervey Allen too must have known, that not one of every ten of *Anthony Adverse's* million readers paid the slightest attention to the philosophical content of that rich, excellent book. Quite as little did they search for a definition of the chaste spirit in Santayana's *The Last Puritan* when that great proper philosopher finally turned to the novel to test the ideas he had been clarifying through so many brilliant volumes of formal thought.

Presumably our amateur critic is now able to read a novel and derive from it the ultimate enjoyment that comes from a fuller and matured comprehension of the author's intent. He can test his ability to do this by a reading or rereading of *Anthony Adverse*. When he does, he will find it more than a picaresque tale. He will discover in Anthony Adverse a young man who is by turns a "natural" man, the young Anthony, the Anthony in Africa; an idealist, the orphan Anthony of the convent, the conscience-stricken Anthony fallen to his knees before the martyred missionary; a skeptic, the Anthony in Cuba, the slave-trader; and an Anthony who is both romantic and deeply sensual. What Hervey Allen has sought to do is to create in one man, all men: his effort is prodigious, his success exceptional. Thus, in one book, the last on our list, the amateur critic will have summarized for him all those philosophies, those temperamental prejudices, he has been pursuing through his course of reading.

The scope of a book is not always synonymous with its accomplishment. Because *Anthony Adverse* embraces several philosophies, not one, it is not a better novel than the others we have read. It is not even as good. Some will feel that Anthony Adverse is veritably a synthetic figure, that he has not the vitality of Tom Jones, the clear identity of Billy Budd. In art, too, an author who accomplishes a number of things almost but not quite as well as others who have preceded him, may not be as highly prized as the master of a single style, the captor of a single quality, the unique giver of a certain illuminating mode of experience. But though *Anthony Adverse* is not a work of the highest art, it is still high art. It contains beautiful writing, a panoramic evocation of the past, a profundity, a seriousness, an excitement, none of them mitigated by the exuberance and humor with which the author flaunts coincidences in his long tale. This modern book has few equals.

The qualifications of the artist might be our final question, although it has already been answered many times by implication. Hardy warns us that "in the pursuance of his quest for a true exhibition of man, the reader will naturally consider whether he feels himself under the guidance of a mind who sees further into life than he himself has seen; or, at least, who can throw a stronger irradiation over subjects already within his ken than he has been able to do unaided." The writer of Genesis, says Hardy, is such a man.

The reader may ask himself whether Hardy is such a man, and whether Melville is such. Cervantes and Fielding and Conrad? Dickens and Tolstoi? Henry James or Thomas Mann or Proust? The reader may recognize, along with Anatole France, that failing the resolution to hold their peace, they can only talk of themselves. But can he think of another class of men as much worth listening to? Each gives himself to self-discipline for art; and through self-discipline finds truth. Lawrence has said of Dana, and Murry has said of Lawrence:

He lived through this experience for us; we owe him homage.

A LOOK AT TECHNIQUE

Chapter 12

A Look at Technique

A STUDY of the craft of the novel is chiefly important to the average reader as a way to increase his pleasure. Otherwise there are few reasons for him to spend time learning much about it. Primarily, technique is a writer's concern, and most of it should rightly remain his secret. But every reader should know about certain technical aspects of fiction, to add to his enjoyment of books.

Very much the same is true in other arts. What we learn of the subtleties of composition, how a sense of distance in one corner of a picture can balance a weighty shape in another, how warm colors offset cold hues of equal depth, how dimensionality and "tactile values"—the feeling of folded, glimmering silk in a Veronese, or fur in a Van Eyck—are caught, does much to heighten our awe and joy before a great painting. For us there is now an extra drama in appreciating the problem that the artist confronted, and in grasping how he overcame it; and we more fully measure his accomplishment. When listening to a sonata, if we recognize the form, we also perceive the invention the composer has shown in developing his themes to fulfil it: the architectonic qualities of the music become apparent to us. Similarly, the ballet-goer's experience is more rewarding if he is knowledgeable about the traditions and graceful requirements of that art. But surely the point does not have to be argued. An awareness of the formal demands of the novel, and an insight into how the author has met and triumphed over them, repays us by letting us share a small part of that triumph, and this is always a genuine source of esthetic delight.

Apart from this, today's novel is often cast in forms that are strange to us. When we read such novels, we may find their approach baffling and distracting. In the same way, certain types of abstract painting and constructivist sculpture elude us—what is the artist trying to say? When we go to a concert, music written in the twelve-tone system may sound exceedingly harsh. This could mean that we need more information about such new forms. Getting a clue to what the painter, composer or author is trying to do, technically, may open new vistas of enjoyment to us. Perhaps we will reject his vision and what at first appears to be his shocking method of achieving it, but in fairness to him and ourselves we must first comprehend them. Again, we may at last accept what he is attempting to express, by his unfamiliar devices, and by borrowing from him enrich our consciousness and insight. To do that is our aim in approaching art, and especially good fiction.

What is offered here about the technique of the novel is not confined to what I have discovered about it personally. I shall quote and paraphrase widely, for few critics are wise enough to embrace the whole broad subject; anyhow, I have always made it a practice to borrow the best ideas wherever I can. (This is a delicate yet respectable species of theft called "scholarship," and I expect not to be condemned but applauded for it. The scholar is a thief who puts down where he has stolen his ideas and calls it a "bibliography." I shall append one at the end of this essay, although that is a bit like going to the police station to leave a list of one's victims.)

II

When I was young and traveling in North Africa, I was much impressed by the sight of a public storyteller, cowled in a broad-striped *jellaba*, cross-legged on the ground in the marketplace of Tetuan, surrounded by fascinated listeners who at the end excitedly tossed coins to him to pay for the entertainment he had given them. I instantly recognized my vocation as being the same as his.

The very sophisticated novelist, Somerset Maugham, proudly describes himself as descending directly from the prehistoric tale-teller—Cro-Magnon man, it could be, chanting some anecdote to his fellow nomads around the flickering fire, while night darkened their cold shelter. Probably, though, the early stories to which aboriginal man listened were not always simple accounts of a clansman's savage prowess, but often a broader form of primitive history, the dimmed past of the tribe; and often, too, the tales were a kind of teaching, and an effort at religious and "scientific" interpretations of the daunting natural world, through an almost involuntary myth-making on the part of the fanciful shaman-narrators.

When written language supplants the spoken word, the same stories reappear, but they are much shortened—that is, less repetitive—and without detail; they are bald outlines. They are also increasingly humanized. The antics of gods, the bold deeds of ancient folk heroes, are now attributed to ordinary mortals. But almost identical deep mythic threads, archetypal themes, still run through them; and perhaps all our major "plots" can be traced back ultimately to those once ascribed by mankind's first poets to the conduct of supernatural or extraordinary beings.

With the early Greeks, storytelling has become a very high art, expressively stylized in the Homeric epic (or anthology) and the Sophoclean tragic drama; but we note that these are poetic forms. The prose tale, apart from the parable and the Aesopic fable, still lacks significance. In Roman times this is equally true. From Vergil we get the *Aeneid,* and from Seneca a new form of play, violent and rhetorical; but aside from the liveliness of the loosely connected anecdotes set down by Petronius and Apuleius, nothing comparable is brought forth in prose.

In the Middle Ages, something akin to the form created by Petronius is recaptured, the Medieval Romance, mostly episodes casually strung together. An Arabian princess, Scheherazade, tells thrilling stories to amuse a murderous king. The knights of King Arthur canter about slaying dragons and requiting wrongs. Aucassin indefatigably and exquisitely woos Nicolette. Much later comes Boccaccio's *Decameron,* in which noble refugees from the plague while away the long hours by exchanging bawdy stories, which are afterwards borrowed by Chaucer's pilgrims on their arduous journey to Canterbury.

It is said that the characters in the romance have no names and few specific traits of personality; but this is scarcely borne out by a reading, though it is true that usually the people in them do not grow or change. Also, the separate incidents follow without logic; any episode can just as well be the last or the first, for there is seldom a climax or goal. Nor are the happenings meant to prove a moral, unlike the earlier fable (and its medieval copy, the *fabliau*); they merely seek to stir a sense of marvel, evoke suspense, elicit a tear for tender lovers, or provide laughter by being ribald or telling of an act of cynical cunning. The best of the romances, too, are still mostly in verse.

The early seventeenth century brings the picaresque tale, which again repeats the meandering form employed by Petronius and Apuleius. The reader follows the fortunes of one character throughout a long succession of adventures that are connected only chronologically; yet they do have a token of unity by having a central figure or two. Most often the hero is a poor young man seeking his fortune, although this description does not fully apply to the most notable of all picaresque tales, Cervantes' *Don Quixote*.

In *Don Quixote*, indeed, is foreshadowed a major theme of the modern novel, for it incarnates poignantly the conflict between what is fantastic and ideal in life and what is disenchantingly real; from the profundity of its subject, and the brilliant originality of its gently grotesque characters and method, this classic work gains its unique eminence.

More typical of the picaresque tale is *Gil Blas* by Le Sage. A resourceful youth, hoping to rise above poverty, becomes the protégé of a series of patrons. He runs many risks and achieves many escapes, until he finally reaches a secure and respectable station in life. Here, as elsewhere, the picaresque novel has a satiric tone: surveying a wide variety of people and places, it looks at the world with amused cynicism, but hardly ever indignation. True, in *Gil Blas* the higher and more pleasant aspects of society are also shown; to this extent, Le Sage somewhat "refines" this genre of fiction.

Far more sordid are apt to be the panoramas offered us by Nashe, Smollett, Defoe, Sterne, and others. Notable examples of the picaresque tale in England, some of which we have referred to in an earlier chapter, are *The Unfortunate Traveller; Roderick Random* and *Peregrine Pickle; Moll Flanders* and *Roxana;* the rollicking *Tristram Shandy;* and, of course, in many aspects *Tom Jones* belongs to their company.

In some of these books a heroine takes over the center; and, if so, she is usually a young lady of light virtue. Her habitual companions are rogues, cutpurses, highwaymen; her lodgings are disreputable. Her motives are invariably mercenary, though she conveniently reforms at the end to placate the pious.

Since the hero or heroine of "the inn and road" is constantly traveling, the author has a pretext for picturing many kinds of places and all types of life. Consequently, these books were avidly read by stay-at-homes. In those times of difficult and hazardous journeying, the average person had little idea of the outside world. The picaresque adventurer, boldly questing, takes the reader everywhere: to prison, aboard ship; even to the far-off and little-known colony of America, where Moll Flanders is transported to close her days in an odor of unexpected sanctity. Today such stories are of keen interest as social history, yielding us—as they did their first readers—a lively cross-section of a turbulent century.

Generally, the hero is not drawn dimensionally; he is merely a peg, a device; he suffers an incredible number of vicissitudes, but is hardly real enough to engage our sympathies. Far more sharply etched and memorable is the odd collection of people he meets along his way. The author paints the mixed contemporary scene in colors as broad yet deft and strong as Hogarth's, his gestures savage and hilarious.

These two categories of stories, the romance and the picaresque tale, are prototypes of the modern novel. What is more, they still persist. In their present metamorphoses, many essential constituents of the earlier forms remain. A "romance," as the modern critic uses the term, is a story in which elements of the strange and marvellous predominate; as for example a historical romance that richly evokes the past while emphasizing deeds of derring-do by young guardsmen with cape and sword. Or, it may be, the romance is a skillfully contrived tale of contemporary espionage, or any other kind of breathless suspense story that involves the hero in physical danger. Another example is the mystery novel in which someone undertakes clever and daring detection. Hence, the romance appeals to our primitive love of being frightened, tantalized, excited. Its formula is that of the "and then . . . and then"; we ask, as might a child listening to a fairy tale, "What happens next?"

In fiction of this sort, characters and their motivations—and, often, even plausibility—are of secondary importance. What suffices is that the hero be bold and ingenious, the action fast, and that the good cause finally triumphs. The setting ought to be fresh, glamorous, perhaps exotic: it may even be placed, as are the fantastic romances of Jules Verne, under the ocean or on the cratered surface of the moon or the planet Venus. Such novels offer tired or bored readers "escape" and relaxation. Superficial though such fiction be, it nonetheless answers to a fundamental requirement, that the story be highly interesting—and serious novelists who overlook that demand do so at considerable risk. The superior author, disdainful of suspense, may never be read, or his books—though taken up—may be put down long before the reader has finished them.

The picaresque tale has also continued to flourish. A century later, even after Fielding lastingly revolutionized the novel's design, elements of the picaresque are found in the work of Scott and Thackeray; in Gogol's satiric *Dead Souls,* whose itinerant hero Chichikov encounters a fabulously odd collection of people on his travels across Russia; in Goethe's *Wilhelm Meister;* in Dickens, Robert Louis Stevenson. Ibsen adapts the picaresque form to the stage in *Peer Gynt,* Strindberg in *Lucky Pehr;* and Eugene O'Neill emulates them in *Marco Millions.* Recent American novelists who employ the picaresque hero are Hervey Allen (*Anthony Adverse*), Frederic Prokosch (*The Asiatics, The Seven Who Fled*), and Robert Lewis Taylor (*The Travels of Jaimie McPheeters,* a Pulitzer Prize book). Each writer infuses this form with a different spirit, peculiar to his own temperament; yet in each instance his story is loosely constructed, a mere linking of episodes that befall a restless young man on what is in essence his journey to maturity.

Edwin Muir discerns a more subtle equivalent to the picaresque theme in today's novels of humbly born young men and women who, talented and resourceful, climb to the top in the business and social scene. Such young "climbers" are later-day counterparts to the traveling hero of the seventeenth and eighteenth centuries. Just as going to London or abroad then was undertaken by only a small number, financial and social success today is attained by only a comparative few, and novelists lucky enough to observe it at firsthand pass on to their public the intimate details of accomplishing a rapid, even dizzying ascent to our century's higher circles. In handling this subject, modern authors also tend to be satirical and cynical. Yet, such stories of quick success have for many readers a fairy-tale quality that is quite engaging, too. The theme is very popular.

This fits well with Bernard De Voto's idea that many readers turn to fiction to prepare themselves for a possible change of social status. The young businessman is about to get a better job, with its concomitant privileges: entrance to the executive lunchroom and washroom, an extra window in a corner office; he will also face delicate problems of supervising the workers under him. Or the young wife is about to move to another community that spells for her a higher rung on the social ladder; perhaps membership in a nearby country club where many aspects of society are ritualistic. Both husband and wife will seek to learn about that new world in advance so as to be able to fit into it with less embarrassment. (I recall that as a stripling, before I went to college, I myself spent a summer eagerly reading novels about college life.) In treating with such material, informing us about other spheres in the contemporary world and simultaneously readying us for change, the novelist may decide that the freedom of the picaresque form serves him admirably.

III

In the chapter on Fielding, I remarked that the modern philosophical novel begins with him, but also that the picaresque vein is still robust in *Tom Jones* (as in the earlier *Joseph Andrews*). Here again is an account of the "inn and road" with a homeless, journeying hero—an average sensual young man—seeking his fortune and discovering the wicked world. We are offered a crowded, richly variegated survey of country and urban high and low life. A satirical quality is present, as in the chapters that set the pretentious Thwackum and Square before us, but now this negative quality is subordinate. In *Tom Jones* we have at last an author who embraces life with a manly shout of joy. In being affirmative Fielding's book differs from nearly all its predecessors.

From a technical point of view, however, what is most striking about *Tom Jones* is how it advances over the typical picaresque story in other ways: it has a firm plot; the action has a beginning, middle, and end, which Aristotle prescribed for a classic Greek drama. (Before taking up fiction, Fielding had begun his literary career as an able comic playwright and had worked in the theater as a producer. He had adapted *Don Quixote* for the stage with genuine success. And he had also derived some of his plays from those of Molière, who in turn had drawn on classical models, so we see where this young English author gathered his lessons.)

Here is amazing progress. The episodes are not strung together haphazardly: each follows logically from the one preceding it, and carries the story forward. One turn in the action leads to the next, with an element of surprise, yet with a sense of inevitability. The episodes cannot be arranged in any other order; few, if any, can be omitted, and the story cannot end and satisfy us until it reaches a "windup" foreseen by the author before he began to write, though admittedly he takes us on a long gallop before he arrives at it. Nor do we feel any need for the action to continue beyond the concluding page. The ending has been prepared for by deceptive, oblique hints—or, to borrow a theatrical phrase, "plants"—from the start. At last, the novel has attained a discernible pattern.

Consequently, we have an esthetically pleasing sense of a work that is an integrated whole. It has an overall plan and a goal; it is "constructed." It also has "variety in unity," which any major work of art must have. Our perception of this gives us an added joy in reading; it appeals to our innate delight in beholding and appreciating the skill and proportion that has gone into the shaping of anything, and especially a thing as intangible and difficult to handle as a fast-moving story that is thronged with people and several hundred pages long. No wonder that *Tom Jones*, with its clear outline and deftly interlaced lines of action, its headlong pace yet organic story, is afterwards hailed by Coleridge as having "one of the three best plots ever conceived." (The others, he says, are Sophocles' *Oedipus Rex* and Jonson's *The Alchemist*. Very likely we would not concur with that evaluation, but we can understand it as arising from that excellent critic's having considered the long history of formless romances and meandering picaresque tales that had appeared before Fielding's major work.)

Even more, the events in *Tom Jones* result from the dynamic interaction of the characters; once the people in it are established for us, which is quickly done, we have very little awareness of the author interfering or high-handedly contriving the incidents; the book rapidly assumes a life of its own. The people in it take over, and the book is theirs: *they* seem to create the plot. This is because they have impulses and conscious purposes, as human beings do; they are convincingly "motivated" as the figures in the Medieval and Renaissance tales are but vaguely and barely. The characters in romances and picaresque stories are moved by only the most elementary passions: each knight or wanderer or odd or grotesque person met upon the road is an oversimplified symbol of one emotion: love, loyalty, chivalric courage; or mercenary ambition, lust, or ferocity. Not so in Fielding's book. Tom has a wide range of impulses. He is generous, good-natured; he has sexual appetites, doubts, and feelings of guilt and dismay. He knows shame. He expresses sincere gratitude. He grows up before our eyes. Some of the characters in Fielding's prose epic still verge on being picaresque caricatures—Thwackum, Square, perhaps Blifil—but many of the others are nearly as real as Tom himself, as for instance Squire Western, Tom Nightingale, Partridge, and the gallery of ladies who engage Tom's affections. Much of this novel's enduring attraction to readers even after centuries is this vivid reality of the people in it.

True, this dimensional characterization places a limit on the author. Since the hero is real and rounded, things that happen to him must seem "probable." As a result, he cannot undergo as many wild and farfetched adventures as befall Gil Blas or Roderick Random or Moll Flanders. Because his people are more authentic, more flesh-and-blood, their conduct has to be credible at all times; and, amazingly, it is, and especially that of Tom. That the story is still as lively, varied, and captures so wide a sweep of eighteenth-century England, despite this self-imposed restriction on the author's part, is sure evidence of Fielding's virile, bounteous genius.

In some ways fiction had been approaching this kind of organic form slowly, tentatively, long before Fielding's advent. In *Don Quixote*, again, a moral—or moralizing—purpose is evident, so that it virtually qualifies as a philosophical novel despite its intrinsic formlessness. Though the story lacks cohesion, the tone itself, which carries out the author's intention, is not only unique, but consistent throughout and binds the whole together, a masterly achievement. Granted too that the incidents are without a logical narrative connection, each is in itself sustained and sharply dramatized, and the atmosphere of each scene is hauntingly realized. The characters are grotesque, often as fantastic as the humorous or nightmare images of Goya's later drawings, yet they are recognizable as belonging to the generality of mankind and symbolize something far more complex than the figures in most other picaresque tales.

Similarly, *Moll Flanders* and *Roderick Random* display advances toward a more coherent succession of events, and still more dramatization is brought into play to exploit the separate scenes in them, and they build up to conclusions that are adequate even if not quite as inevitable. We must also look upon Defoe and Smollett as having an earnest purpose; they are not, or at least purport not to be, mere spinners of idle tales; they belong by self-appointment in the ranks of theologians and moralists, who enthusiastically write of folly to demonstrate to their readers the ultimate cost of wrong conduct. But it remains for Fielding to fashion the standard form of the novel for once and all, and to make it the clear embodiment and dramatic test of a mature philosophy.

Perhaps mention should also be made of significant contributions to the technique of fiction by his singularly talented rivals, Richardson and Sterne. In works by them, plot is not as intricately conceived, story is not as smoothly unfolded, but there are other artistic innovations of great moment, which I shall discuss later.

In the romance and picaresque tale, as we have seen, the subject matter is usually the strange and marvelous. Certainly, an element of the "unusual" is never to vanish from fiction. But after Fielding and Richardson create the novel form, its divergence from the wild excesses of the romance begins and steadily widens. For now the novel has a new criterion. What is told to us must not only be exciting but believable. This is a rule which the novelist must obey. We might say that in serious modern fiction, as in classical drama, the author gives us a situation—sets in motion a suspenseful action—in which we behold ordinary people in somewhat exceptional circumstances; or else, a few extraordinary persons against an average social background; but never both, never an abnormal person or group of persons against a highly unusual setting, for this no longer meets the novel reader's demand for his own complete identification with the scene or the characters, the latter identification arising out of an invariable show of common sense on their part. The formula, henceforth, is that the novelist, as opposed to the romancer, permits himself to introduce no more of the "remarkable," the strange, than he needs as a good premise for a story; some degree of heightening of reality is always required of him, yes, even in the most Naturalistic work. But he is no longer free to indulge his fancy irresponsibly. He has a mature sobriety forced on him. In general, in a serious novel, only the premise of the story is a bit extraordinary; the working out of it, the solution of the moral or psychological problem set by the author, is as reasonable in terms of everyday behavior as he can render it. This requires of him intelligence, information, close observation of nature and human nature, of society and its deceptive conventions; he does not persuade us to go along with him unless he displays the utmost fidelity to physical fact and psychological truth. He must think logically and yet freshly. And, as we shall soon see, the development of the novel is to be toward ever straiter limitations, to satisfy the still more literal demands of readers who are growing more sophisticated. It is to move closer and closer to realism and seek new techniques for presenting the world to us as the author personally conceives it to be.

As a result, serious fiction becomes increasingly meaningful to readers. Soon people are seeking out novels not only to adjust to social change, but to inner change, too. Growing older brings to each human being new problems and experiences that he anticipates and fears. He turns to fiction and the presumable wisdom of authors to help prepare himself to meet these often shocking experiences. His parents die, his friends die. He himself faces new responsibilities and perspectives as he becomes a father, a grandfather. His children rebel against his authority, perhaps, and reject him; he is suddenly left alone, for one reason or another. He asks himself: "What do I feel about all this?" As Mr. De Voto puts it: "Every strong emotion is new and intolerable to the individual until it is fitted into a pattern of the familiar. Fiction, like the confessional and the conversation of old friends, is a ready means of such assimilation. Delivered over to emotions that exalt and crucify him, the individual is helpless to understand. All emotion happens to him for the first time. His paramount need is to know what it is, to give it contact and fixation in the known. Fiction provides a way of closing the circuit and bringing the known in."

Consequently, from Fielding's time on we shall see two

historical developments in the novel, for which suitable techniques must be found: one toward presenting us with a broader and yet more detailed social picture, and another toward bringing us the inner truth of living, a knowledge of our frighteningly complex minds and hearts.

Chapter 13

The Social Novel

THE POPULARITY of novel reading in the late-eighteenth and early-nineteenth centuries is chiefly accounted for by two new cultural factors: the rise and sway of the middle classes and their mode of life and, bringing many changes, widespread industrialization. People grow wealthier and better schooled; they have the money to buy books and the leisure to peruse them lovingly. Indeed, there is scarcely a better way for them to fill long, quiet evenings; for they have few of the distractions that now make our concentration on reading more difficult. Their world has also grown infinitely more varied, offering a rich field for the novelist, who can show his readers, still isolated in manor houses or vicarages or small towns, what other people somewhat like themselves are doing elsewhere in manor houses or vicarages, or in dazzling aristocratic circles in London, Paris, or Moscow; and also in the drab alleys and slums of those increasingly smoky cities. The average fictional hero now has a wider choice of careers, in realms partly beyond the reader's personal view; the hero has more social strata to explore than was possible in the earlier semifeudal and agrarian world that was Fielding's subject. At the same time, the caste system is still more or less fixed: genteel descent and good breeding are still all-important, so that the novelist can still delineate a scene that seems relatively stable, with manners, traditions, and values that do not alter too quickly. In such a society, surface behavior—conventional politeness—is apt to hide many hypocrisies, and hence it is ripe material for ironic portraiture, such as we see practiced by Thackeray (*Vanity Fair*) and Trollope (*Barchester Towers*) and Dickens (*Bleak House, Great Expectations*), and in kindred works by French novelists like Balzac, and Russians like Tolstoi. (An exception to this ironic approach is George Eliot, who deplores what she sees, and lectures us about it, rather than smiles at it with Olympian detachment.)

In all these books, the heroes and heroines go to the school of life to learn the truth about society. And we have them described to us almost entirely as social creatures, rising in the scale from one level to another; and, in the process, acquiring social skills and adjusting to new milieux; or, occasionally, losing out because of their lack of scrupulosity. Meanwhile, we learn little about their deeper personal lives. These novels are classified by Edwin Muir as "extensive," because their constant tendency is to broaden out, taking in more and more of the social world as their province, and to populate it with ever more persons who are "types" rather than individuals. In them we are given a full range of generalized characters: the ambitious and intriguing "climbers" (like Thackeray's Becky Sharp and Stendhal's Julien Sorel); the predators (like Dickens' Uriah Heep); the poor (Maggie Tulliver); the middle class (David Copperfield); the rich and noble (Lord Steyne and Prince Andreï); the clergy in Trollope and Stendhal again; the bankers and tradesmen in Balzac, the gentry in a host of fox-hunting stories.

All these, it should be repeated, give back to the middle-class reader a mirror image of the world he already knows something about; but he is also given clues by them as to how to advance himself in this increasingly diversified social realm. Another point about them is made by Henry Burrows Lathrop. Such novels do not provide "escape," as does the romance; hence, the social chronicle has never been very welcome amongst the very poor, who do need to be taken out of their miserable life by immersion in more fanciful tales. Nor do these novels greatly attract the idle rich, who are apt to spend their time in fashionable travel and sports to elude boredom. Social chronicles tend instead to depict average life and appeal to ordinary readers who identify themselves with the almost everyday characters presented in them.

In addition, this chronicle is—as Professor Lathrop has further observed—"a mundane form of literature and appeals to the mundane spirit." He attributes its rise in part to the decline of the religious spirit during these two centuries, the eighteenth and nineteenth; for the novels of that era are seldom, if ever, other-worldly. "The public must be capable of feeling an interest in the fictitious picture of life on this earth. Puritans and monks are not interested in novels." The comment strikes one as true; there are few if any effective religious novels written then (or since); the subject matter of novels continues to be very much this-worldly.

At first glance, a social chronicle seems to have little construction, to lack art. Later we shall learn that this is far from true. Its form might not be readily discernible, but it is nonetheless definite. Obviously, the sprawling chronicle does have a nucleus: the fortunes of a family, or several families, with anecdotes about the doings of their various members, of the elder and younger generations, all sketched in lightly. Usually, too, the chronicle has a narrowed yet vividly detailed background where the major portion of its action occurs: London, Paris, Moscow, it may again be; or a rural setting, such as Barchester or provincial Russia. The close-knit family, the interlinked social scenes, the limitation of historical period and place, lend a sense of unity lacking in the picaresque story which, in several other ways, the loosely spun chronicle resembles. These unifying factors provide a kind of elastic framework. But the chain of incidents, the dramatic events which involve each member of the family or families, follow one another casually, seemingly spontaneously. We may take for granted that we shall be treated to several love affairs, some happy, but more of them unhappy and for many pages frustrated. The scattered protagonists meet in a frequent round of tea parties, engagement parties, weddings, christenings, birthdays, funerals. The anticipation of what the reading of a will may reveal is a dependable theme. In addition to troubled love affairs and surprising legacies, there are appointments to higher positions, infidelities, elopements, scandals, financial disasters. Wars, panics, epidemics may at times provide a setting, and occasionally historical characters are introduced and play a minor rôle. Sometimes a single person is the focus of the whole action (as again is Julien Sorel, in *The Red and the Black*); sometimes two persons mainly hold our attention (as do Becky Sharp and Amelia Sedley in *Vanity Fair*); or as many as a half-dozen sharply outlined characters serve as leading figures (Prince Bezukhoï, Prince Andreï, Natasha, and others in *War and Peace;* and the large cast of clerics and politicians and their ladies in Trollope's pleasant works). We observe many of the people from birth or youth to age or death. A feeling of passing time, how it alters persons and fortunes and even physical environment, is an inevitable aspect of the chronicle.

The narrative pace is often leisurely. When we first dip into such a book, the story is shallow. The problem of exposition in the early pages is formidable, because so many characters have to be identified and then firmly established. Next we find ourselves engrossed in the increasing current of the plot more deeply than we expected, and before long are carried along by its strong flow, with incidents multiplying like whirlpools on every side. After a century of such social chronicles—more precisely, by the twenties of our century —authors are writing such lengthy histories of families and their descendants and their descendants' children (*Men of Good Will, The Thibaults, The Forsyte Saga*) that most appropriately such books are called by the French *romans fleuves;* that is, novels that continue on like swelling rivers, appearing as trilogies, tetralogies; some, actually, are six, eight, ten volumes long. Even then, the ending of these chronicles is seldom a true climax, but more often a mere stop, almost an arbitrary one: a pause, a temporary winding up, of the many crisscrossing story lines, a good number of which—as in life itself—are left unresolved. What we are given chiefly is an "image of a significant segment of our society."

The apparent ease and prodigality with which the author of a chronicle creates incidents for this interlocking chain of small conflicts, most of them arising out of ordinary and natural events (infatuations, schooling, rivalries, marriages, separations, family quarrels) is quite deceptive: we credit the author too little for his ingenuity and invention, and his careful planning before he dips his pen in his inkwell; though it *is* Thackeray's claim that he is simply making up his story as he goes along, with no forethought of what comes next. A contrasting example is Dickens, who runs a mystery plot or even several of them through many of his thronging books; this certainly calls for cunning foresight, since he has to plant clues and hints very early to carry out his design.

Inasmuch as many of these "extensive" novels, in the nineteenth century, first appeared in installments in the popular magazines, there was often pressure to compose them in haste—deadlines had to be met. Also, a crisis had to befall at regular intervals of so-and-so-many pages, to hold a reader's interest until the next issue. (As is well known, such installments of tales by Dickens were shipped by mail-boat to America, where anxious readers waited on the docks to buy up the next copies of the magazine.) All this imposes a measure of discipline on the writer, although it leads to carelessness as well.

The miracle is that our best chronicles are as fascinating and clever and lively and convincing as they still prove to be: and as crowded, as they are, with such delightful or lamentable yet always memorable characters as the luckless Sonya, the ever-hopeful Mr. Micawber, the fat and purse-proud Joe Sedley, the vivacious Mrs. Proudie and Mr. Arabin.

What is most important about these vast social chronicles, however, is their evocation of setting: the streets and houses and landscapes; the conveyances; the dinners; the fox-hunts; the vestry meetings, the elections; the duels, the court trials; all the mores and folk ways of the different classes depicted in them; indeed, in such later works of this ilk as *Buddenbrooks*, *The Forsyte Saga*, *Three Cities* and *Clayhanger*, the element of social history and its relentless documentation is at times paramount.

To understand the chronicle better, we ought to contrast it with another form, the dramatic novel.

Chapter 14

The Dramatic Novel

ALONG with the chronicle, a quite different kind of novel is developing; one that borrows much from the theater. Its prototype appears in France, in 1678, in *La Princesse de Clèves,* a delicate analysis of love by Madame de La Fayette (although that pious lady always denied authorship); and again, a half-century later, in *Le Paysan Parvenu,* by the famed playwright, Marivaux. In these novels, description is bare; we lack the piling up of detail that comprises the period piece. The characters are few, and nearly all have major rôles. The time lapse is comparatively short. The plot is sharply defined, and has a rising urgency, and the end seems not only inevitable but rounds off the story with a feeling of deep finality. Accordingly, the effect is highly unified. The essentials of the plot, and nothing more, are retained and highlighted.

Edwin Muir remarks that the "dramatic novel" is "intensive" in contrast to the "social chronicle," which he views as "extensive" or "spatial." Indeed, we have seen that historically the chronicle has grown ever broader and longer. All the while the dramatic novel has tended to be more condensed, until as put out by one of its latest and most honored practitioners, Albert Camus (*The Stranger, The Fall*), examples of this very compact genre fill scarcely one hundred small pages of large type. But compactness is the dramatic story's particular virtue.

As has been said, a novel of this kind resembles a play. The author must show a similar skill in distributing its exposition. Like a playwright, he chooses to portray only moments of crisis in the lives of his characters: actually, his "plot" consists of several minor crises within a major crisis, in ascending steps with growing tension, that lead to a well-placed climax. All the themes of the book must be adeptly externalized, for the author does not intervene in his own person to express his ideas, or to interpret the feelings of his characters, as do Fielding, Thackeray, and Tolstoi in their novels. He must remain tight-lipped, wholly silent, as does a dramatist. His characters must speak for themselves and carry the whole burden of the story, which has to be self-explanatory at every moment.

Significantly, *La Princesse de Clèves* was initially brought out by the seventeenth-century Parisian publisher, Claude Barbin, who only the year before had also introduced in print Racine's *Phèdre*, even today notable for its compression and elegant design. One of the tautest plays ever written, it has served as a criterion ever since. So we can observe that Madame de La Fayette, like Racine, reflects the concern of writers in that Neo-Classical Age to recapture the formal structure, balance, and economy of means of ancient Greek drama, choosing for their models the tragic Sophoclean plays that best embody Aristotle's enduring precepts. In that philosopher's *Poetics* those rules call for the strictest possible limitation of time and place, and always singleness of theme and focus. By having a small cast, an emphasis on action—as opposed to narration by the author and verbal digression by him—the dramatic novel, like a play, has a far sharper impact on the reader.

The social chronicle gives us far fewer scenes in which the characters have this autonomy. The author is apt to comment: "Edmund was angry," or "Jeanette was plunged into despair by this new turn of events." He is endlessly narrating, summarizing. This method yields far less vivid impressions of the people than when we are not *told* about them but *behold* them in action and catch their very words. In a dramatic novel we are allowed to hear Edmund's outburst, "I cannot tolerate your conduct any longer!" and infer for ourselves how wrathful he is; or we assume from Jeanette's air of depression—"She sat day long at the window, gazing at the gray sky and bleak landscape"—what is her state of mind. The dramatic novel is a quick succession of tense and pivotal scenes in which the people enact their story; they are presented to us objectively, and the author's narrative contribution is ideally no more than the equivalent of the barest stage directions. "She crossed the dimlit room to the writing-table, then turned to confront him challengingly." In the next sentence, she breaks into speech again, and the scene plays itself out before our mental gaze, quite as though it were taking place in a theater in the concentrated glare of footlights.

Such scenes do occur in social chronicles, too—in *The Newcomes*, in *War and Peace*—but only at lengthier intervals, perhaps at widely spaced peaks of intensity; and even then, usually, they are not as fully sustained nor as sharply realized. As a consequence, we have quite different kinds of esthetic experience when opening books of these two contrasting types.

Paradoxically, the shorter, more objective form of novel seems to be better suited for the exploration of character. In any event, it is the one chosen by authors whose chief interest is the inwardness of experience, and the nuances and depths of feeling. This is for reasons which I shall discuss later on.

II

In eighteenth-century England, Samuel Richardson—Marivaux's contemporary—shows a similar gift of theater in his work; as does Fielding who, like Marivaux, has a background of writing for the stage, as we have already noted. But the books of these great English novelists are still crowded and lengthy. Richardson's are also apt to be clumsy and prolix. It is really Jane Austen who shortens our novel, offers a smaller cast, neatly restricts the scope of her story; though her works are not always pure examples of the dramatic form. Still, they do mark an important progress toward it. A consciousness of some design is clearly inspired in her reader. One has only to compare the linear directness of *Pride and Prejudice* to a rambling, diffuse work like *Vanity Fair* or *David Copperfield* to appreciate the true difference. In her wittily perceptive work, too, character and plot are certainly one, the action springs logically from the charmingly high comedy characters, whose consistency is also in conformance with the best Classical principles. We have now the sense of what Galsworthy is later to say, that "character is plot." All this their feminine author seems to have arrived at by instinct, and by her native genius, rather than by a study of Aristotle. What the characters are determines the course of the action; what befalls them alters their nature in turn. That the people do change, not by merely aging—which is all that usually happens to them in the social chronicle—is yet another prominent trait of the dramatic novel.

Although narrower in scope, as we have observed, the dramatic novel possesses a more universal, timeless air. This is because the characters are far more vital; they are creatures of stronger emotions, those eternally forcible in human nature.

Hence, they belong to every age. The background is slightly out of focus, with the people themselves hotly highlighted in the foreground; and we follow the changes in them, as they struggle, suffer, and are transformed in a temporal flow; they are not "fixed" in one socially documented scene, one historical period. They are not mere typical figures of a cultural epoch. The dramatic novel is not a good form, then, for the discussion of topical ideas or for a broad social picture. It serves quite another purpose, which is to depict two or three intensely realized human beings at a crucial moment, in a desperate situation, one which will affect their lives forever.

Many critics, among them Mr. Muir, choose the works of the Brontë sisters as good examples of the dramatic novel, especially *Wuthering Heights* and *Jane Eyre*. Note how limited is the scene, how few persons are involved, how gripping and turbulent are the feelings, how much action of a theatrical kind occurs—and, most clearly in the instance of *Wuthering Heights,* how universal, how little bound to the manners of one period, these stormy and gloomy love stories are: they are perennially true, and their appeal to our imagination and sympathy is also everlasting. Perhaps by far the most effective author of dramatic novels is Dostoevski. His major works, *Crime and Punishment, The Possessed,* and *The Brothers Karamazov,* are apt to be thought of as panoramic because they are long and deeply significant. But Joseph Warren Beach has ably pointed out that in each instance their background is very narrow: a few desolate streets and dingy houses in Moscow, or a grimy small town in provincial Russia; and their characters comprise a mere handful of persons. The stories transpire within a very few days, in each book. There is "strict inner causation." The probing of character is deep and relentless, and the psychological changes wrought in the people are profound and in some instances fatal. Each person seems to move or be propelled inexorably toward a predestined end. (I shall return to Professor Beach's fine analysis of Dostoevski's novels.)

To our list of excellent practitioners of the dramatic story we might add almost capriciously Herman Melville, Guy de Maupassant, Somerset Maugham, Willa Cather, Ernest Hemingway, and André Malraux. That roster will suffice to show the odd variety of writers who use this dynamic formula. Along with Dostoevski, however, its greatest exemplars have been Gustave Flaubert, Ivan Turgenev, Henry James, and

Joseph Conrad, who have refined and perfected its technique. Their innovations are of great importance.

One of the pleasures of literature is that in it we see life freed of irrelevancies. The writer's task is to clear away the ordinary trivia and distractions of our existence and lay bare the core of meaning. In the social chronicle this is not as easily accomplished. But in the simplicity of outline of the dramatic novel, and its search in depth, this is far more likely to be done. Thus, although it is not a good vehicle for a bandying about of topical ideas, it is nevertheless the better form for the testing of philosophical concepts, as I have sought to define them.

III

The fact is, only a relatively few novels are purely dramatic or fit wholly into the category of the social chronicle. In most stories the techniques of the two forms are mixed, with good results. This is true in *Tom Jones*, where narrative bridges provide the exposition, rapidly summarizing or synopsizing whatever a reader needs to know, between those passages where the author turns on his stage lights. Now his characters play out a crucial encounter, a bold moment of confrontation; we are allowed to see and hear them in action; and next, the lights dim, and the narrator's voice resumes its task, leading us as rapidly and easily as possible to the next brightly staged scene. By combining these two methods, the narrative and the dramatic, a novel can cover more time, include many more incidents, than a play: and this is the unique advantage a dramatized chronicle has over a stage work; it can span many months and years, and be laid in as many places as necessary; and yet its highest moments of interest are presented to us with theatrical vividness. The bridge passages are like half-lit *entre-acts,* during which we peer at our programs to learn how much time is now supposed to elapse, and what is the setting of the scene that follows.

Fielding himself advises us: "When any extraordinary scene presents itself (as we trust will often be the case), we shall spare no pains nor paper to open it at large to the reader; but if whole years should pass without producing anything worthy of his notice, we shall not be afraid of a chasm in our history: but shall hasten on to matters of consequence, and leave such periods of time totally unobserved." He had enough experience and flair for theater to know precisely how to handle this, and his lively chronicle is both expansive in scope—as the purely dramatic novel is not—and yet is urgent and logical in structure—as the social chronicle tends not to be. He gives us a full, animated picture of the society of his day, at the same time that he brings his characters to life with an exuberance and bounce that only the immediacy of drama can lend them.

Another who blends both techniques with mastery is Charles Dickens, who was also fond of the stage. He did not write for it, but he himself had a highly theatrical personality; he liked to dress up and act in charades at home; in later life, moreover, he toured widely in England and America, giving extraordinarily dramatic readings of his books, to the excited acclaim of enrapt, even swooning audiences. In Dickens' novels the frequency of the enacted scenes is very great: the stage lights go on incessantly. He characterizes almost entirely by showing us his crotchety people in action, as a playwright must do. His penchant for stressing mostly their grotesque side, often in settings of cobwebbed dilapidation and fearsome shadows, and his fondness for having them commit acts of appalling violence and cruelty, are also indications of a theatrical imagination. Besides this, Dickens uses another technical device, that of alternation, which enables him to provide us with a broad social picture without loss of dramatic sharpness. We stay with a character for two or three chapters, then are switched abruptly to follow another focal character, on whom we fasten our attention for approximately the same length of time; but he is apt to be in a quite contrasting atmosphere and place: we are wafted from a cheerful, gay scene, maybe, to a darksome, eerie one, a dock-side slum or orphanage or garret. This effect has been compared by an astute critic to that of the vaudeville show. But it constantly piques the reader's fancy by giving him a fresh principal image to pursue, and also serves to illustrate how varied is life in Dickens' teeming, cold, foggy London.

By the same token, critics are forever finding fault with Thackeray for dramatizing so few incidents in his chronicles. He never outgrows his having been an essayist. He lacks Dickens' overcharged imagination and morbid gift for fantasy, which led the author of *Oliver Twist* and *Bleak House* to present so many thrillingly enacted moments of unreal melodrama (wild coincidences, discoveries of long-hidden crimes, recognition scenes of penniless changelings, and all the other claptrap that in less adept hands belongs to third-rate theater, so often offered by Dickens in his books in odd juxtaposition to fitful pictures of the grim truth of life). In Thackeray's defense, it has been said that his are not mere period pieces: it is not a specific society that is displayed to us in *Vanity Fair*, but "civilized life" itself: his "Vanity Fair" is indeed a symbol of the daily round of people in any society, at any age, in any wealthy city. This is due to the remarkable clarity of his observation. Hence, his work has an attribute of universality and timelessness, to a degree achieved by no other English chronicler. But Thackeray gives us mostly static characters; they do not change from the first chapter to the last of his long books; he endlessly generalizes; he creates his people by describing them to us rather than by letting us judge them for ourselves from what we are able to see of their behavior. We do not decide for ourselves that Becky Sharp is an adventuress; her author loses no time in telling us what the young lady is up to. He endlessly praises Amelia Sedley for her virtue, too. Both of his heroines are real to us, but not as real as they ought to be. There are climactic scenes in *Vanity Fair*, of course, but we come upon them too seldom, nor are they as powerfully evoked as they might be. For the most part, Thackeray diffuses our attention by unfolding before us too many petty incidents in a carelessly planned story. Galsworthy is charged with the same artistic error. "The large single occasion should stand for the mass of minor ones," suggests Professor Beach, who gives all writers a bit of practical advice. "Pay in large bills, and let the small change go." This latter, as Beach says, is the method of Tolstoi, whose energy at dramatization is unflagging and equal to all demands (as he later proved by his conquest of the stage).

Honoré de Balzac also uses these two techniques, and rather quaintly and candidly informs the reader, "Here ends the exposition," before proceeding to a dramatic scene. In Stendhal, again, we find Thackeray's fault, too much narrative, to the verge of the author becoming tiresome; although Stendhal too offers brilliant scenes at moments. As serious an error, though, might be to dramatize too much, particularly incidents of little importance; the reader's response is taxed and exhausted by this and, as in the instance of Hemingway, the practice can also cramp a book, enclosing it in too tight a form, one that allows no adumbrations of his theme. Especially when Hemingway deals with his one major subject, the behavior of men at war, his reliance on dramatic technique and nothing else limits him too severely; we fail to see his people in a large enough social setting; they are restricted to a world far too small and personal, and their talk is spent on matters too trivial to be worth our hearing. A tape recorder and a one-lens camera are not the best tools of literary art for material like this.

The most eminent theoretician of the novelist's craft, Percy Lubbock, warns the writer not to "squander" his dramatic scenes by having an excess of them. An author should save them for moments of true climax. They should also be prepared for carefully. To this view Frank O'Connor has added his dictum, that the dramatic handling belongs to the "development" of the story, seldom if ever to the mere exposition. The artistically successful author knows just how to apportion these two effects—the narrative, the dramatic.

The more sustained the dramatic scene, the more powerful can be its grip on the reader; depending, of course, on whether the characters and the conflict really interest us. Professor Beach, in his analysis of Dostoevski's work, shows that in the Russian master's immense novels some scenes stretch to hundreds of pages. As we noted above, Dostoevski's melodramatic plots are enacted within a chokingly small circle of houses and streets, and are also astonishingly compressed in time. *Crime and Punishment,* though over five hundred pages, relates events of barely two weeks' duration; and, even then, four days are skipped; so that in fact the violent doings of only nine days are touched on. *The Brothers Karamazov,* which runs nearly a thousand closely packed pages, has a time span of less than three months, of which again only seven days are actually detailed. To help the reader follow the story, Dostoevski gives brief prologues, epilogues, and narrative bridges. Much the same proportion is true of the *The Idiot* and *The Possessed.* Furthermore, there is a single center of interest, one person, on whom we are made to concentrate without respite. Thus, in *Crime and Punishment,* our attention is riveted on the harassed Raskolnikov for the first two hundred pages, which is more than the first third of the novel. Even when we are not looking at him, and sharing his pangs, we are forced to hear the other characters talk about him; he is never forgotten; the reader is also conscious of the hero's horrible dilemma. The same applies to the saintly Prince Myshkin, who is before the camera, so to speak, for the first two-thirds of *The Idiot*. Few novelists can keep one character so constantly in a close-up, and magnified, his every emotion bared excoriatingly before the reader's compulsively fascinated gaze. The effect of concentration is nightmarishly heightened because the events of each day, or a suite of days following without interval, are developed so fully. In *The Brothers Karamazov*, four such days are treated for six hundred some odd pages. Dostoevski's characters hardly sleep, they are so remorselessly in the grip of their emotions, the pressure is so strong upon them to reach a decision, to settle what is at issue. They take no time for food. Occasionally one does fall into the restless slumber of physical exhaustion, only to be visited by dreams that restore to him the urgent problems of his waking hours. Very often the haunted people keep going all night, "like eight-day clocks. . . ." In *The Possessed*, four successive days are linked by all-night talk and bitter debate. And no matter where they flee, these people carry with them the same passionate fevers, the same nagging questions. Yet, as Professor Beach points out, none of this seems too monotonous or lacks credibility. "An inexhaustible imagination enables Dostoevski to expand the occurrences of one day so as to fill the ordinary person's quota of drama for a lifetime." The consequence, of course, is an impact of tremendous force.

In this, Dostoevski is unrivaled, except later by the Joyce of *Ulysses*. To a lesser degree, some of the same gift is shared by Joseph Conrad, Marcel Proust, and Franz Kafka. (Kafka's innate sense of the dramatic in enigmatic fables like *The Trial, The Castle,* and *Metamorphosis* is very considerable, indeed.)

Chapter 15

The Disappearing Author

IN THE EARLY nineteenth century Ivan Turgenev and others bring a new kind of realism to the novel. In England, George Eliot is approaching it, earnestly, yet often clumsily. But in Russia and France a more sophisticated form is evolving. The effort is to present stories about normal events, that concern seemingly ordinary people.

The incontestable truth is that no one is ever quite ordinary or typical in fiction *or* life, and even less so when faced with a startling challenge such as the novel always sets before the hero. Everyone has quirks and individual qualities, and in a crisis is likely to display them more than ever.

Still, the highly successful and radical attempt is to dramatize logical and inevitable happenings with fateful outcomes, in what might be otherwise somewhat average personal histories. In every family is a "drama" of some sort: perhaps a tragic quarrel between a father and son; or the day-by-day course of an unhappy marriage between an incompatible husband and wife, both of whom are well-meaning; or another kind of daily defeat, the fruitless struggle to keep up appearances in genteel poverty. The whole "plot" might comprise the melancholy nuances of a broken liaison between lovers who for some reason cannot marry; or the hopeless attraction an indifferent young man holds for a bored, lonely older woman. In *Fathers and Sons, Smoke, Spring Freshets, The House of Gentlefolk,* Turgenev—George Eliot's and Dostoevski's contemporary—treats these viable new subjects with delicate art.

Such simple, sensitive pictures of life, matched by an uniquely haunting poetic simplicity of style, are markedly devoid of all the plot-trappings carried over from the romance, so effectively and liberally employed by Dickens, and even by Tolstoi and Dostoevski. Here we have no hungry and tattered waifs, surprisingly named as lost heirs; or satirically yet excitingly portrayed court trials that seek to establish to whom a fortune belongs; or lengthy descriptions of vast surging battles, and the burning of Moscow; or a calendar of hideous crimes, a bearded, tyrannical father slain by one of his sons, or an old woman pawnbroker's skull bashed in with an ax wielded by an ambitious but morally perverted student. Instead, in Turgenev's stories and even in his plays the plot is subdued, events flow along naturally, without salient intrigue or any incursion of violence.

To hold interest, in this new realism, the author must exercise a far more sure and responsible skill. He will probably have fewer characters, all closely related to the story; and he must externalize his theme in painstakingly chosen revelatory gestures and incidents. The plot is muted, at times almost indiscernible; the characters speak with restraint and tact. To give such elusive material a clear enough shape, so that the reader is always aware of a dramatic form and the tension it creates, several new techniques are required.

One means of simplifying the story, and thereby shortening the book and reducing the cast of characters, is to omit the subplot. As we have seen, the subplot, and even a multiplicity of them, is a device extremely popular with Thackeray, Dickens, Tolstoi, Trollope; indeed, it is a favorite with all writers of the social chronicle. It has been retained, and legitimately, by dramatic novelists such as Jane Austen. Much can be said on its behalf. A subplot, a minor motif running parallel to or alternating with the main story line, can add richness and complexity to a novel; it can heighten its colors by mild or striking contrast, or reënforce its tone and subject by a subtle repetition, like a musical variation, a theme transposed into a different key.

Used cleverly, the subplot can raise suspense by artful interruption, equivalent to the "cut-away" in films: we are watching a crucial struggle, and suddenly the scene is switched to another locale, to pick up a secondary story line, leaving us anxious to learn the outcome of the first. The Greek theater often allows the Chorus to break in to chant and moralize and hold up the tragic action at fateful moments, with the same result; accordingly, the device is age-old.

But the risk is that a parallel or subplot of this kind may merely distract us; it may contribute a sense of jerkiness, discontinuity. By braking the onward pace of the story, it may irritate the reader. This is certainly true in *Vanity Fair*, where Thackeray seeks—though he hardly succeeds—to divide our interest between his pair of heroines. Whenever the spotlight turns from the conniving Becky, who delights us, to the suffering Amelia, who is so dully virtuous, we are tempted to skip his recital of that paragon's woes. This is a major flaw in *Vanity Fair*. In novels aspiring to the new realism, the subplot, when it is used at all, is employed sparingly, indeed. In *Madame Bovary*, for example, we find none.

The method of Turgenev, Flaubert, and Henry James is scenic—that is to say, dramatic; yet, by comparison, *quietly* so. But now Flaubert lays down another cardinal rule. To achieve the highest dramatic effect within the limits fixed by this quiet realism the author must banish himself from his book: the story must seem "to write itself," be set down by no perceptible hand. Declares Flaubert: "The artist ought to be in his work like God in Creation, invisible but all powerful; let him be felt everywhere but not seen." Similar steps were being taken by Henrik Ibsen in the theater, where he was proscribing the "aside" and soliloquy, means by which the characters —and thereby the author—speak directly to the audience. Such devices disappear utterly from stage plays after Ibsen set the new fashion.

In the earlier chapter on Fielding I referred to the criticism directed at him for interspersing short personal essays throughout his story, and I quoted George Eliot's eloquent defense of his having done this. His voice is so good to hear, and he is such a fine, friendly person to meet intimately, that even the most modern reader is inclined to forgive his garrulity. But Fielding is exceptional, too, in that his private speculations are always set off from the main body of his narrative; he never actually intrudes on his story, but stays strictly within the confines of his chapter introductions.

This is not the practice of his successors. Sir Walter Scott, Victor Hugo, George Eliot, Thackeray, Trollope, Meredith, and others are forever entering their stories in person. They take us into their confidence and discuss their characters overtly with us, or pause to pass judgment on each turn of events. "Poor Maggie," laments Miss Eliot, tearfully expressing her sympathy for her heroine; and "Our gentle Amelia," exclaims Thackeray, who is so fond of that young lady he himself would like to beg a kiss, he tells us, "from such a dear creature." Even Henry James, in his early and middle works, speaks of "our friend," intending in one place the observant Strether in *The Ambassadors*, in a manner which joltingly reminds us that the novel is not happening spontaneously, but is being related to us by a professional storyteller. A decade or two after Flaubert, the license to do this is finally cancelled. The author gradually becomes, as Flaubert decrees, invisible, thereby encouraging in the reader the necessary "suspension of disbelief" that he must bring to fiction.

I have already ventured my opinion that, though we can well do without it, the author's intrusion is not really heinous, and that the reader is far less disturbed by it than some critics insist. But I am quite in the minority in holding this attitude. Loud and emphatic is the chorus of complaint about this Georgian and Victorian habit of the author presenting himself barefaced in his work and daring to voice his own views, avowedly moralizing. Says E. M. Forster, himself one of our foremost novelists:

> It is dangerous, it generally leads to a drop in the temperature, to intellectual and emotional laxity, and worse still to facetiousness, and to a friendly invitation to see how the figures hook up behind. . . . Intimacy is gained, but at the expense of illusion and nobility. It is like standing a man a drink so that he may not criticize your opinions. . . . It is bar-parlour chattiness, and nothing has been more harmful to the novels of the past. [Forster does qualify this a little:] To take your reader into your confidence about the universe is a different thing. . . . It is confidences about the individual people that do harm, and beckon the reader away from the people to an examination of the novelist's mind. Not much is ever found in it at such a moment, for it is never in the creative state: the mere process of saying, "Come along, let's have a chat," has cooled it down.

This is wittily put, and partly true, but perhaps an overstatement by Mr. Forster. Why does a novel lose "nobility" merely because the author makes a personal appearance in it?

To what extent is a suspension of disbelief forfeited in such enthralling books, which have now survived many decades, up to a century, as *The Mill on the Floss, Pendennis, The Warden,* and *The Ordeal of Richard Feverel*? The author's intrusion *can* be overdone, and perhaps Thackeray does break in too often. Of George Meredith, Professor Beach complains: "He doesn't stop talking when no commentary is necessary. He likes to furnish the commentary himself. He is forever *interfering* with the subject." Such loquaciousness can be boring, in fiction as in life. Yet there is much to be said, too, for the by now old-fashioned custom of the author occasionally and perhaps modestly making himself heard. It derives, as Dorothy Van Ghent has phrased it, from "an ancient oral convention of storytelling."

Admittedly, the novelist's "aside" is likely to fall quaintly and even jarringly on our ear today, but that is due chiefly to an always fickle critical norm of what is acceptable. During the past decade, the "aside"—and even the soliloquy—has returned to our ever more frankly artificial theater, where the search for photographic realism seems at last to have reached a too sterile end. Something of the same may well happen in the novel; we may have a splendid display of "literary artifice" for its own robust sake, as opposed to a relentless and futile effort to create only "the illusion of life."

This is not to be taken as a plea by anyone for precocity or self-conscious coyness. Professor Beach, for one, speaks cogently of "the losses suffered by the novel from the withdrawal of the author. With the effort to make the novel dramatic—that is, self-impelling—there was a notable tendency to do without that critical spirit which was furnished by the author's comments." But the chief reason he is ready to make allowances for the talkativeness of past fiction writers is that many of them really have something sound to say. "It is high time to acknowledge that few minds of equal solidity and critical power [that is, Fielding's and Thackeray's] have in our day occupied themselves with the English novel. Among the faculties associated with the English spirit everywhere is the burly male faculty of common sense, and whatever else we may boast of the spiritual achievements of the days since Thackeray, common sense is not what stands out as typical." Of modern novels, Professor Beach remarks: "They lack the geniality, humor, wit which were once the leading traits of English fiction. It is a general condition of the spirit of our bewildered, disillusioned times."

With this in mind, Professor Beach has elsewhere pronounced on the author's visibility: "There is something quaint about this Victorian manner . . . and yet . . . we are often apt to forget that we are dealing here with masterpieces of fictional art perhaps greater than any that have since been produced. It is so hard to retain one's perspective . . . in dealing with a school of art that has gone out of fashion. I am not even certain that the development I am tracing may not be a kind of degeneration—accompanying a gradual decline in vigor and spontaneity."

Percy Lubbock does not rule out, either, "the old, immemorial, unguarded, unsuspicious way of telling a story, where the author entertains the reader, the minstrel draws his audience round him, the listeners rely upon his word. The voice is then confessedly and alone the author's; he imposes no limitation upon his freedom to tell what he pleases and to regard his matter from a point of view that is solely his own."

Mr. Lubbock proceeds to show, with his usual sharp insight, that although Flaubert does not openly intrude himself in *Madame Bovary,* yet he actually does so—and extends the limited vision of Emma and the others in the book—by his personal ironic tone, which is all-pervasive and has "a distancing and widening effect." On the other hand, "The landscape that Thackeray controls is so much wider and fuller that even with all the tact of Flaubert . . . he could scarcely follow Flaubert's example. His book is not a portrait of character but a panorama of manners, and there is need for some detached spectator [Thackeray himself, in this instance] who looks on from without."

It behooves us, I think, to agree with Mr. Lubbock's judgment and not be too hasty in finding fault with novelists of the past who solve their artistic problems by devices no longer in fashion; and, since those technical devices work so admirably for them, we might hesitate before demanding that such inventions be discarded altogether. Much depends on the personality of the author who intrudes into a novel, and on what he has to say, and finally how amiably and adroitly he does it.

In any event, most distinguished writers have an individual style, and by virtue of it are markedly present in their works, however austere their method may be. Is this not true of Joseph Conrad, James Joyce, D. H. Lawrence, Ernest Hemingway, William Faulkner? Each leaves his fingerprints on every page he composes, however self-effacing he deems himself. The author has not really disappeared.

Chapter 16

The Point of View

IF THE WRITER is to stay out of sight and his voice no longer be heard, as Flaubert proclaims, some other means of commenting on the subject of a story must be found. A proxy for the author is needed. More than that, the story must be given a focus, a clear center of interest, so that it has dramatic shape; becoming ever more subtle and elusive, as it deals more and more with everyday happenings, it must have a boundary, a limit: a truly realistic picture of life would be boundless, limitless. This is the artistic problem to which novelists in Flaubert's day, and in the generation afterward, particularly address themselves. The problem becomes acute as fiction grows increasingly "subjective," and the novelist is ever more conscious of the "inside" instead of the "outside" of people and events; this has been the constant trend of fiction ever since the final decades of the nineteenth century. It is accompanied and abetted by the appearance and influence of Sigmund Freud and his followers, at the dawn of our twentieth century, when an interest in psychology spread among intelligent and educated readers; and it most certainly prevails unabated today.

Let us try to define "subjectivity" in fiction. It manifests itself most dramatically, a critic has said, when a story is built around a dilemma which the hero confronts indecisively. How is he to account to himself for the behavior of his beloved, or of a friend, of an enemy? What attitude shall he take? Human nature is enigmatic; the people we know best and care about most are also the ones we are apt to know least and be most puzzled by. How shall he interpret a sudden and fateful event? How is he to respond to it effectively, honestly? He must choose a "line of action." But the hero of the modern novel hesitates (as the uncomplicated hero of the old-fashioned romance never does). He is uncertain what is best, and a condition of emotional strain is started up in him. Very often, in our contemporary fiction, he is held back from action, hindered and crippled by some neurotic quality in himself. His indecision, his strain, is communicated to the reader who, by sympathy and a process of identification, shares it. This is the psychological, moral, and emotional suspense we derive from a thousand "subjective" stories; from, let us say, *Crime and Punishment* and *Lord Jim;* from *The Ambassadors* and *The Magic Mountain.* The deeper the hero's indecision, the more heartfelt and concerned is our response, providing that he conducts himself intelligently. This spiritual and cerebral drama is one which is better presented in the novel than in any other art form; it is the special property of the novel.

To get at this "subjective element," to penetrate more deeply, the novelist needs an angle of vision. From what vantage shall he tell the story? As seen by whom? His quest is for an effective point of view. In a picaresque tale like Cervantes' *Don Quixote,* the author is plainly omniscient. He gazes down like Jove at his characters, and is all-seeing, all-knowing. But this can tend to make the storyteller seem a bit removed and detached, unless he can break in from time to time and express his opinion; hence, he is forever tempted to resort to the "aside." But rule out the "aside," and the author again resumes his chilly Olympian detachment.

In *Moll Flanders,* however, the story is purportedly told by Moll herself, in the first person. We see events through her eyes, which involves us much more with the ups-and-downs of her fortunes, giving us a sense of participation; this makes the story far more vivid. What is more, the story is told in her picturesque argot, her own language, not Defoe's. To a considerable degree, the story is also more "subjective"; except that, of course, Moll is scarcely a deep or reflective person. But we do enter into her always mercenary thoughts with much more immediacy. In much of Thackeray's work, later, we are to have what is called the "generalized I," the author who is a Jovian and jovial onlooker and commentator; but in Defoe's "autobiographical tales" we already have the "specific I," because the incidents are supposedly related by a person who is an actor in them. Consequently, in *Moll Flanders* the events described are also given a boundary, a natural and logical limit: the story is confined to just those episodes seen or plausibly known to the "I" narrating the tale, our adventurous Moll herself; the author cannot go beyond that. A story needs a limit in order to have dramatic compression and shape, and here the writer provides it by adopting the first-person point of view of a character who is herself engaged in the events. This way of spinning a tale, through the eyes and in the very words of an actor in it, is to become a standard technique.

Sometimes the narrator, the "specific I," is a leading figure, as is Pip in Dickens' *Great Expectations,* or David in *David Copperfield;* or Henry in Thackeray's *Henry Esmond;* or Harry Richmond in Meredith's novel of that name; but just as often he is a minor actor, an onlooker, a proxy for the author, who studies the principals, analyzes them, and perhaps moralizes about them. Such a figure, though, must have a plausible access to the thoughts of the people he is observing; they must have a convincing reason to confide in him; and he must also have good reasons for being on hand wherever and whenever a significant incident occurs in the story. This can keep him very busy! And it can make a major demand upon the ingenuity of the author.

In Samuel Richardson's *Clarissa Harlowe,* for instance, the author is faced with a special difficulty: both his leading characters die before the novel's end. What is more, both have emotions they would never confess to the other, so neither would qualify as the "specific I." Nor would both pour out their thoughts fully to only one other person; that is, not to the same confidant. Not one but several "specific I's" are needed, and in *Clarissa Harlowe*—and also in his *Pamela*— Richardson cleverly solves his technical dilemma by having the story told in letters written by the hero and heroine, who thereby share their desires and disappointments with family and friends. These other persons also correspond with one another, passing along what they have heard, and adding their own comments to the news. By means of this round robin, a ceaseless exchange of letters, bearing anxious tattle and judgment, the plot is unfolded to us in tantalizing fragments, which sharply heightens the suspense; besides this, we have the fatal encounter of Clarissa and Lovelace viewed from all sides, by those surrounding them.

But this technique is not perfect; it slows the pace of the story too much for modern tastes; and it strains credibility. Indeed, as one critic has pointed out, Clarissa spends virtually her every spare moment sending out minute reports of the progress of her over-emotional affair. Her correspondents, in turn, also appear to be preoccupied with little else; and finally this device comes to seem too mechanical, too contrived, especially since Richardson is often hard put to move about his characters to places where it is natural that they would write letters, and where they desperately need to learn what has occurred during their absence. Too many letters have to cross before the reader discovers what has next befallen Clarissa, at any important stage in the story. But it does create an ambiguity and doubt about events and motives that is true to life. We are engaged in the story with the protagonists step by step, as it is taking place, inspecting and experiencing their every tortured feeling.

Another ruse of the first-person novel is the diary, which is really a letter written by the "specific I" to himself—and probably meant, as are most diaries, to be scanned some day by other eyes. The diary is merely a different form of the "epistolary" novel.

Later, Henry James looked upon the first person in telling a story as "a naïve and inferior medium," though he himself employs it in some passages in his chilling *The Turn of the Screw* and elsewhere. Marcel Proust adopts it for his great novel, though he does not always use it consistently or plausibly: he is apt to report scenes that the "I" could not possibly have witnessed. Throughout lengthy passages in Proust's book, too, the "I" is not even mentioned; although, as Mr. De Voto remarks, it is hardly necessary for us to be reminded on every page who the narrator is, for we have long since grasped from whose point of view the incidents are being described. Joseph Conrad often resorts to the "I," and very trickily and puzzlingly, in *The Nigger of the "Narcissus,"* where the "I" is sometimes the "we," and at the end is left wholly unidentified, the never-depicted narrator melting anonymously into the debarking crew and vanishing with them from our knowledge.

Among contemporary writers, Somerset Maugham is still a strong advocate of "first-person" storytelling. He feels that people's motivations are too elusive to be fully explained by an author; we can merely speculate about them, with the help of our intuition and experience of the world. For this, the more limited "I" is a natural and excellent device. His failure to know more is explicable. And even that eminent authority, Mr. Lubbock, finds cause to praise the use of the "characterized I," as he calls it; since, by narrowing the scope of a novel, confining the story to the vision of one onlooker only, it brings the scene into focus with more precision. "The picture now has an edge," Mr. Lubbock observes; and he stresses, too, that the story gains a "personal color, that of the narrator." Of course, a "generalized I" can lend his tone to a story, too, as Thackeray playfully does; and even the invisible and more objective author can do so, as has already been remarked about *Madame Bovary* and Flaubert.

Nevertheless, the first person has lost critical favor, for several reasons. Today it is wisely chosen by an author who has a romantic or highly fantastic tale to tell: a farfetched and fast-moving adventure, a journey into the supernatural, perhaps. Told by the "I," such a tale becomes more plausible, since the "I" is forever assuring us that all this did actually happen to *him*, and in exactly this way. A feeling that we are meeting the author face-to-face inspires in us the extra credence we grant in the presence of a raconteur who claims to be drawing on a personal past experience. He is there before us in the flesh; his voice and gestures help to convince us. Afterward we say, somewhat illogically: "I know it's true, because I heard it from the man himself." Some of this feeling of authenticity, by a very natural extension, carries over into the first-person narrative.

Besides this, use of the first person more effectively holds a reader in suspense in a tale of detection, for we can assume that the "I," a participant in the story, most likely the investigator himself, has not yet come upon the answer; he shares with us an exciting uncertainty as to the outcome. But if the tale is offered by an omniscient author, we feel that he is merely concealing information from us, and our interest is accordingly lessened. That is why the first-person narrative largely dominates this field of fiction.

II

Nearly always, when we meet a first-person narrator, it is the other characters in the book who seem most real to us. Mr. Lubbock asserts, and very rightly, that David Copperfield is a minor figure in the famous novel bearing his name: we know and see best the people whom David encounters; but the hero-narrator keeps his face turned away from us. We get to know little about him; his inner life is seldom disclosed; we have only a vague idea of the impression he makes on others, only that they like him. The one aspect of David that is vividly presented is his childhood, and there we have David looking back on his former self, already a different person. Of the mature David, the storyteller, we have only—as Mr. Lubbock insists—a silhouette or outline. We are always behind the hero as he looks out a window: he tells us all that he observes below, in the crowded world of the Micawbers' London; but we are gazing only at the back of his head. David himself is not a successful characterization. Indeed, wherever the first person is employed, a difficulty of this sort is likely to arise.

As we shall discuss later, even the characters whom David describes are not deep. The shortcoming of the "specific I" as a vantage for presenting a story is that the "I" hardly ever knows what is *really* going on in other people's minds; he can only speculate, which—as Somerset Maugham maintains— is "lifelike," but somewhat disappointing in a novel, where we want to learn far more about human nature than is possible elsewhere. Concerning fictional characterizations we usually desire more than mere guesswork: we hope to learn a great deal about ourselves and others from them.

In a first-person narrative, too, we see only as the "I" does, without being able to get an objective view of this perceiving "I." How competent is he to judge others? How much does he reveal about himself? It is important that we take his measure. But how can we? Is he a credible witness? An intelligent reader will ask that question.

Although the "I" may indulge in exhaustive self-analysis, still we are never sure that any person who talks about himself is telling the truth, whether he even knows himself well enough. Few people do. Even Proust's narcissistic "I" is confused about himself, his real nature. Sometimes, to the pleasure or consternation of the author, we are led to feel that the "I" is badly deceived; we form a quite different estimate, kinder or harsher, from that the "I" has of himself. He might also be talking of himself "tongue in cheek," as does the self-depreciating emperor whom we read about in *I, Claudius,* by Robert Graves: an "I" who constantly tells us that he is weak and stupid, when in fact we know him to be ruthless and cunning; but Mr. Graves's tactic is one that can be used only rarely, and even then it grows monotonous and results in far too broad a portrait. So, for the more subtle yet solid depiction of character, some other device is needed.

Several thoughtful novelists, among them Henry James and Joseph Conrad, answer this challenge. Henry James, in particular, is the most self-conscious of craftsmen. For a considerable time he had been striving to achieve a more dramatic shape for his novels; this search was greatly advanced by his attempt to write for the stage during an unhappy period in his mid-career. His efforts as a playwright failed disastrously, but like Fielding before him he learned much by having been forced to tighten his work to meet theatrical exigencies. A play must be taut. Thus James fully mastered the "scenic" way of staging a conflict, chiefly in action. But when he returns to the novel, he goes a step further. As we have noted, he had earlier experimented with narration in the first person, accepting the narrowed scope fixed by that limited "post of observation"—to use his own phrase; but finally, in novels like *The Ambassadors, The Spoils of Poynton,* and *What Maisie Knew,* he arrives at a method of telling a story from a still different point of view, one which strengthens its impact: the "third-person singular."

The plot is unfolded as observed by one person, who is himself a principal figure in the story; but we, in turn, have a direct insight into his thoughts. About one person in the story, but only that one person, the author is omniscient. He virtually trephines the hero's skull, lifts the lid from his brain. We see the other characters solely as the hero sees them, and from time to time he also turns his face to us, and we are allowed both to look at him and to read his busy, troubled mind. So we take two full measures of him.

The scope of the Jamesian novel is still strictly limited, as it must be for the best dramatic effect, having the intensity that can be produced by artistic economy and compression. The hero-observer, the one whose point of view we intimately share, is presented to us with the utmost objectivity. He is studied unceasingly. His most minute feelings are revealed to us. But everything is kept in precise focus. Thus, in *The Ambassadors,* events are shown to us only as Lambert Strether experiences them; we are given glimpses of him in a leading rôle in the subtle conflict that occurs during his visit to Paris; and we are also constantly privy to his thoughts. What is more to the point, he is a highly intellectual person, with fine ethical and moral sensibilities—James might be said to have set the fashion for such heroes as observers —so that his reflections of the people he watches and reacts to, and the painstaking picture given of him himself, result in extraordinarily complex characterizations. Here is a new means of storytelling that yields rich psychological portraits, with a truthful density, which is exactly what late nineteenth and early twentieth-century novelists were seeking. It might be called the "x-ray" method.

To say it once again, what happens is that we alternate between physical descriptions of Strether and beholding Strether in action, and Strether pondering and passing judgment on what he has just seen, or what he himself has recently done, or done in the further past. We are admitted into "the reverberating theater of his mind." The story, from this intimacy, conveys to the reader an acute sense of the "here" and "now"; it has an unwavering "center of interest," as Mr. Lubbock—a James advocate—argues: what we have, in fact, is a "directed suspense," just as in a play. Since one figure holds the center of the stage always, and we see only what he sees, and from his bias or perspective, we tend to identify strongly with him (as with Moll Flanders, speaking in the first person; but Moll is shallow, and scarcely truthful, and we hardly know whether to believe what she tells us; whereas, we have the truth about Strether). James is actually "dramatizing" the working of his hero's mind, and a new depth of subjectivity is reached. Mr. Lubbock finds fault with Dickens' first-person device, because—as we quoted him—we merely gaze at the back of David Copperfield's head as he looks out the window, reporting to us what is to be seen outside. With our x-ray method we might have stared right through David's head, as we do into Lambert Strether's thoughts, while at the same time we watch Strether play his part in the rarefied action of *The Ambassadors* (in James's novels the conflict is always one of ever-multiplying nuances).

So that the novel shall be consistent throughout, the point of view is never shifted; we stay with Strether always. Our understanding is matched to his, except that we are also permitted to know him far better than he knows himself, for we can peer into both his conscious and unconscious motivations. Although not for him, the invisible becomes visible for *us*, as always with an x-ray. We can also spy on Strether in the delicate process of absorbing the impressions he receives, which are colored by his own mental nature, and which in turn decisively affect and change his feeling about himself and life. Everything in the story is saturated with Strether's personality. His unique way of experiencing and thinking gives a tone to all that is described (a tone that is essentially

Jamesian, but need not have been). He matures psychologically and morally before our eyes; and, at significant moments we perhaps know what is happening to him even before he himself does. Or he may be unaware that, even in his responses and actions, he is giving himself away. The illumination of serious art is here.

In later and longer novels, notably *The Golden Bowl* and *The Wings of the Dove,* James does sometimes shift the point of view, and we behold the story from alternate vantages. Successively, we examine the minds of several characters, all of whom are involved in the dramatic issue, but each of whom adjudges it in the light of his own interest. This resembles Richardson's far earlier device of gathering the opinions of his gossipy circle of letter-writers. But James offers the differing points of view in the third person, and we enter into each character's reflections exactly as we probed Strether's, without hindrance. James does this much more deftly than Richardson, whose epistolary method is often awkward and long-winded. Also, in Richardson's handling the story is cut back and forth too frequently, too rapidly. This is distracting. In James, whole chapters or sections of considerable length of the book are assigned to one character and his "post of observation," which permits our sustained involvement with him, and a more sympathetic engagement with him. This technique has been appropriated from James by many other writers since he introduced it.

A highly interesting variation of James's method is to be found in John Galsworthy's *The Man of Property,* the first volume of his saga of the Forsytes. In this story we never enter into the consciousnesses of Irene and Bosinney, the lovers, whose adulterous affair causes so much scandal and distress. We see them only as do the other members of the Forsyte family, most of whom are disapproving. "The two lovers remain opaque," as Professor Beach phrases it. "The love affair is hinted at, rather than related. . . ." As a result, Irene and Bosinney remain, as Galsworthy wished them to be, "mysterious and disturbing persons." (A device akin to this is also used by Virginia Woolf in her mercurial book, *Jacob's Room.* The dead young man, Jacob, is also depicted only in the words and memories of others, some of whom loved him, or knew him well, or only casually. It is a very oblique but delicate means of characterization. No longer purely Jamesian in approach, it does have many echoes of James. This device too has been borrowed by a host of later writers.)

III

The vogue of the Jamesian technique—for a time any novelist who did not embrace it was deemed a naïve and elementary craftsman—owes much to its eloquent and persuasive advocacy by Percy Lubbock, who as a young man knew James personally, had a worshipful attitude toward him, and himself became an extraordinarily perceptive critic. Indeed, Mr. Lubbock's book-length essay is often called the first truly substantial study of the novelist's art, and perhaps the most important as yet published. If it is not that, it has been at least the most influential. Says Mr. Lubbock in it: "The whole intricate question of method, in the craft of fiction, I take to be governed by the question of the *point of view*—the question of the relation in which the narrator stands to the story." He goes on: "A story will never yield its best to a writer who takes the easiest way with it." In discussing the dramatic form of the novel, which his favorite James so ably handles, he remarks very justly: "The novelist, using this method, claims only one advantage over the playwright: it is the advantage of ensuring the best acting imaginable, a performance in which every actor is a perfect artist and not the least point is ever missed. The play is not handed over to the chances of interpretation—that is the difference; the author creates the manner in which the words are spoken, as well as the words themselves. . . ." But Lubbock asserts that James, with his third-person point of view, can go further than any playwright or any merely dramatic novelist before him could ever hope to do: "Strether's predicament, that is to say, could not be placed upon the stage; his outward behaviour, his conduct, his talk, do not express a tithe of it. Only the brain behind his eyes can be aware of the colour of his experience, as it passes through its innumerable gradations; and all understanding of his case depends upon seeing these." James does, indeed, help us to grasp the whole complex of Strether's personality. All that Mr. Lubbock claims for James is absolutely true.

But as the prestige of Henry James as a fictional craftsman

rose to dazzling heights in the literary world, at first a few and then many disparaging voices spoke up. Professor Beach, who as an analyst of novelistic technique ranks perhaps second only to Mr. Lubbock in the esteem of his fellow critics in the very recent past, has strong praise for James's concern with the niceties of storytelling: "The very assumption of a definite point of view implies an ideal of refinement in execution such as is prized in the arts of painting and engraving. . . . It implies a system of presentation. If the intention is successfully realized, that is an artistic merit." He enlarges upon this: "Critics of all schools agree that art involves a high degree of selection and elimination, of re-arrangement of the elements of the subject, of composition within the limits of the square on the canvas."

So far so good! Professor Beach continues: "If there is glamour in the fact that all art is at one remove from what we call reality, there will be an intensification of that glamour in an art that is at two removes from it." This is another way of saying that we have an enhanced esthetic pleasure in beholding carefully arranged material, selected by being presented consistently from a unique point of view. The one remove to which Professor Beach refers is the author's view of the world; the second remove is that of the character who is singled out. He is like a mirror that in turn is reflected in a mirror, which is a device resorted to in rear-projection cinema photography to obtain a sharper image.

Even further, in tribute to James, Beach acknowledges: "In fiction, facts are made important by being set in such a light that they become not facts but meanings." The Jamesian method is invaluable in attaining this. "In James, we often have a complete obliteration between the objective and the subjective." This is because all that is observed is, as I have remarked above, saturated by the values or interpretation of the character who serves as the onlooker.

But having said this much, Professor Beach confesses himself not too happy with a literature so addicted to "indirect presentation." Though such books yield esthetic pleasure, they are also likely to give no sense of direct contact with life; but, instead, only of life itself at one remove. Henry James and his disciples are too finicky for him, and their preoccupation with technique is seriously debilitating. The hypersensitive Strethers and the Newmans, who people such novels, "appreciate" situations rather than "participate" in them. A paradox results, in Beach's opinion: "The very tendency to dramatize the consciousness of characters has on the whole favored writers relatively weak in the power of dramatizing—of differentiating and projecting character. . . . Very often we get little more than a sort of spiritual autobiography." Too often, also, the people depicted in such subjective novels are very special, not typical of mankind at large. In them, we are apt to find only half-disguised profiles of the authors themselves, who may be neurotics. Fielding, Thackeray, and Dickens, and other social chroniclers like them, give us a vital picture of society, of mankind; today's authors, in an ever more warped Jamesian tradition, offer us only images of themselves, their inner torments.

A similar view is expressed by C. H. Rickword: "The much extolled purity of Henry James's plots is actually of less worth than the impurity of those of the 'great' Victorians, in which the presence of large masses of unassimilated matter is evidence of at least an attempt to be comprehensive." Surely, there is lacking in the novels of Henry James the "grosser appetites" that possess the characters of Henry Fielding.

Edwin Muir is equally belittling. He looks upon James's new form as a mere bud on the main stem of fiction, and not really an improvement on it. Says Muir, of the novelist using the form:

> He excludes three-quarters of life where another would make some effort to subdue it. His plots will no doubt be very neat; but they will not have the organic movement, the ebb and flow, of a plot in the main tradition. . . . Nevertheless, the novel is rich in offshoots, and these are of considerable secondary importance. They include some of the works of Flaubert and James. The fate of such novels follows a general course. At first they are accepted by the few as the last word in fiction, as the best and newest form. Then they fall into their place, and are absorbed into the tradition as minor elements. They add something to it which remains there for general use.

But perhaps the strongest dissenter of all is E. M. Forster. In answer to Percy Lubbock's statement, quoted at the beginning of this section, this world-famed author declares in his lectures on *Aspects of the Novel:* "For me the 'whole intricate question of method' resolves itself not into formulae but into the power of the writer to bounce the reader into accepting what he says—a power which Mr. Lubbock admits and admires, but locates at the edge of the problem instead of at the centre. I should put it plumb in the centre." Mr. Forster asserts that a writer can mix all the methods, and that some of the greatest novels, including those by Dickens, Tolstoi, and Proust, are very loose and untidy, but what matter?

Critics are more apt to object than readers. Zealous for the novel's eminence, they are a little too apt to look out for problems that shall be peculiar to it. . . . They feel it ought to have its own technical troubles before it can be accepted as an independent art; and since the problem of a point of view certainly is peculiar to the novel, they have rather overstressed it. . . . A novelist can shift his view-point if it comes off, and it came off with Dickens and Tolstoi. Indeed this power to expand and contract perception (of which the shifting view-point is a symptom), this right to intermittent knowledge:—I find it one of the great advantages of the novel-form, and it has a parallel in our perception of life. We are stupider at some times than others; we can enter into people's minds occasionally but not always, because our own minds get tired; and this intermittence lends in the long run variety and colour to the experiences we receive.

As for James's novels, they are far too narrow for Forster's taste, and he dismisses them with scathing contempt. James has too small a cast—the limitations of his form dictate that— and the same people appear under different names in every novel, and they are constructed "on very stingy lines."

They are incapable of fun, of rapid motion, of carnality, and of nine-tenths of heroism. Their clothes will not take off, the diseases that ravage them are anonymous, like the sources of their income, their servants are noiseless or resemble themselves, no social explanation of the world we know is possible for them, for there are no stupid people in their world, no barriers of language, and no poor. Even their sensations are limited. They can land in Europe

and look at works of art and at each other, but that is all.
Maimed creatures can alone breathe in Henry James's
pages—maimed but specialized. They remind one of the
exquisite deformities who haunted Egyptian art in the
reign of Akhenaton—huge heads and tiny legs, but nevertheless charming. In the following reign they disappear.

Now this drastic curtailment, both of the numbers of
human beings and of their attributes, is in the interests of
the pattern. . . . [Why is this?] A pattern must emerge, and
anything that emerged from the pattern must be pruned off
as wanton distraction. Who so wanton as human beings?

This brings Mr. Forster to only one conclusion: "That then
is the disadvantage of a rigid pattern . . . it shuts the doors on
life and leaves the novelist doing exercises, generally in the
drawing-room."

We might return for a moment to Professor Beach, who
enters a complaint on behalf of the average reader: "No one
thinks of taking Henry James as guide, philosopher, and
friend."

IV

I admire the credentials of all these critics, but I do think
their attacks are strangely misdirected. They are protesting
James's content, not his technical method. They are also
less than fair to Mr. Lubbock, who clearly and repeatedly
grants that all methods have their limits and none is perfect.
"A story is damaged by too much treatment as by too little."
After this, Mr. Lubbock goes on to say that if Dickens had
used James's devices in writing *David Copperfield*, he would
have had to make his hero much more complex than he
has, for a look into David's mind would have been dull and
thin. But *The Craft of Fiction* has much to say in favor of the
pictorial method, as opposed to the dramatic. . . . Though
it is also not my present subject, I would question whether
E. M. Forster and Edwin Muir—who, as we shall see, strongly
disagree about other things—do proper justice to James's
highly interesting characters. James could not exert the
hypnotic hold he has on an ever-growing public if his
figures are actually bloodless. They are typical of only a small
group of persons, but they are not at all untrue to life. It is

certain that we do not find in his novels much noise or robust vitality, no Dickensian clatter. But there is a delicate music in his work; it is well-composed and ordered, with baroque filigrees. Henry James has his own magic for some patient and attentive readers, and he does accurately present particular aspects of the world.

Concerning Henry James, a vitiating factor has been a mythical image of him; until recently it has been assumed that he was wealthy and more free than the rest of us from the pressure of necessity. But now we learn, from Professor Leon Edel's research, that James was far from rich. He was dependent upon the sale of his writings, which was one reason he worked so indefatigably and also aspired to a success in the theater. Many critics have pointed out that money is frequently the theme in his stories; his characters think, talk about it constantly; the tragedies in the lives of many of his people come about from their tireless efforts to obtain it. Indeed with them, as with us, it is the chief source of corruption, and varieties of moral corruption fascinate James. So his expertly drawn figures should not be considered as fleshless or removed from everyday concerns. Nor are they in the least without sexual promptings: their need for love and physical intimacy is often the driving force in them. And their social ambitions are such as many people share. (Frank O'Connor comments on what he thinks is an odd inversion in James: his poor people are corrupt and his rich people are innocent. The poor, or shabby genteel, scheme cruelly to get money from the rich, as in *The Portrait of a Lady* and *The Wings of the Dove*. To Mr. O'Connor this is a laughable contradiction. But he ignores the fact that most of the rich characters in James's stories have inherited money: they are intrinsically unworldly. In many ways, this is by no means a distortion of a truth in life.)

Professor Beach makes still another point: Maupassant achieves excellent characterizations by a means quite different from the one employed by James. Maupassant is totally objective. "In his tales the characters seem to have no existence except in the objective facts in which they are absorbed. It is the dominance of the objective." I take it that Beach is saying that we behold the characters, but the author—unlike James—never discusses them, nor explicitly reveals the values they attach to anything, and certainly we are never asked to bend forward to peer into their minds; instead, they are exposed by their behavior alone. Here, says Beach, "Men exist in the objective aims in which they are absorbed"; whereas in James, "men live mainly in reflection, perpetually conscious of their own reactions to the situations of which they form a part." This is a genuine distinction as to technical method, and it is one which Elizabeth Drew also draws, when discussing Willa Cather's lovely story, *A Lost Lady*. Miss Cather's procedure is identical to that of Maupassant. She does not analyze the changes occurring in the boy who is the onlooker in that story; she bares his feeling only by showing how he reacts to what he overhears or unwittingly glimpses. The reader can see for himself how the boy is affected by observing his conduct thereafter. The way in which this is done by Maupassant and Miss Cather is very artful, indeed. But in both instances these authors have written only short novels; neither ever worked on a major scale, and I question whether the "objective method" would succeed if one has a more ambitious goal.

The origin of James's device of the singular and consistent or shifting yet still consistent point of view has been traced back to the mystery and suspense tales of Poe—*The Gold Bug, The Cask of Amontillado, The Murders in the Rue Morgue*—and the fantastic tales of Robert Louis Stevenson—*Dr. Jekyll and Mr. Hyde, The Master of Ballantrae*. All these are "romances" in the first person. Henry James, and along with him, Joseph Conrad, grasped how this technique could be changed to the third person and adapted to the serious psychological novel, where the dramatic "mystery" to be solved is largely that of character: the true impulses and intentions, the hidden motivations, of people. Is Osmond really in love with Isabel Archer in *The Portrait of a Lady*? What is the actual relationship between Chad and Mme. de Vionnet in *The Ambassadors*? Those questions are meant to tantalize us. And, of course, *The Turn of the Screw* and *What Maisie Knew* fit even more into this new category of the mystery tale. The suspense that formerly belonged only to the melodramatic romance is now instilled into novels dealing very earnestly with real life.

But the best examples of this are in the powerful, intense fiction of Dostoevski, where we discover—possibly to our amazement—a design analogous to the Jamesian. *The Pos-*

sessed and *The Brothers Karamazov* are also filled with character-suspense and character-mystery. In both books we have an onlooker—in each he is a gossipy, anonymous "gentleman of our town"—who begins the story in the first person, but he is soon forgotten. Yet he is very useful. He is especially needed in *The Brothers Karamazov,* because an omniscient author would know from the beginning who killed the disgusting, profane old man; but a mere observer, contemporary with the events in the small town, would not. The reader, then, shares the narrator's perplexity. Also, in *The Brothers Karamazov,* there are two kinds of mystery: one is concerned with character, the other the elusive factual question of who is the murderer. Throughout the book, Dostoevski shifts to different points of view at strategic moments, to maintain and even raise both kinds of suspense; for if we stayed with one onlooker too long, we might prematurely learn the answers we eagerly seek. This is precisely what James does, too, in *The Golden Bowl* and *The Wings of the Dove.* It also clearly resembles Ibsen's theatrical method, when he ably makes a mystery of what has befallen his characters at a past hour of crisis: he allows each actor to recollect and recount the incident, but in such different and personal perspective that our puzzlement only deepens, and we hope for a final illumination. Dostoevski is not as careful or consistent as James, though by no means always a hurried craftsman—he falls back at times into the easier trick of old-fashioned exposition and a few "asides"; but in general his novels are triumphant proof that characters need not have their heads cut off or their twitching limbs lopped away to fit into the taut pattern that James prescribed. For where else in all literature are such vibrant people come upon as those in these immense Russian dramas? We must not confuse the content and the method. If we do not care for James's figures, that does not fault his technique. Despite Mr. Forster's disdain of it, I would say that the form sponsored by James is sound. Many novels profit richly by being cast in it.

v

Joseph Conrad avowed that he was not interested in problems of literary craftsmanship. On being asked about his

artistic method, his modest reply was: "I follow my nose."
On another occasion, he wrote to his friend and editor, Edward
Garnett, that theorizing about technique was "too difficult for
my brains"; accordingly, he had never formulated any rules
for himself. But this is only a pretense on Conrad's part. He
liked to pose as simpler than he was, and also to appear
enigmatic. Few writers have thought more about their art
or experimented more than Conrad; and his exalted *Preface*
to *The Nigger of the "Narcissus"* is one of the most quoted
and influential essays on it.

Conrad was not as lucky as James in finding a gifted and
early advocate like Percy Lubbock. Initially, he was much
criticized as an inept storyteller by those who did not
appreciate his originality and skill. Several decades passed
before the daring of his innovations were finally recognized.
Today he is acclaimed and studied everywhere for his many
contributions to the technique of the novel.

From the start of his belated career, Conrad's quest was
for a congenial method of presenting a story. He sought a
way of telling it that would be "perfectly devoid of familiarity
as between author and reader"—that is, the writer should be
invisible—yet "aimed essentially at the intimacy of personal
communication." At first, he fumbled. We have already noted,
however, that in *The Nigger of the "Narcissus"* his handling
of the point of view is strikingly unusual: he passes suddenly
from the Jamesian third person into the first person plural;
ten pages later, the narrator reverts to the third person; from
then on, the action on the ship is seen from one of these two
vantages. All this is smooth and acceptable; indeed, the
changes are almost imperceptible. At the very end, the "we"
abruptly becomes an "I," not one of the forecastle crew at
all, but presumably a ship's officer like Conrad himself. It
is a *tour de force* that comes off exceedingly well; but Conrad
never attempted it again, nor to my knowledge has any other
writer. The effect is one of welding the reader into the crew of
the *Narcissus*, so that he feels himself to be one of them.
At the finish of the haunted journey, looking on as the
intelligent and educated "I," he is given a superior and
detached view of the unlettered sailors, which is both needed
and effective.

Conrad often worked on several books at the same time.
As he once put it, when he tired of one task, he liked "to

pack [his] bag and travel to another." While he was composing *Youth, Heart of Darkness,* and *Lord Jim* simultaneously, he hit upon a new device which pleased him and helped him greatly: he would use a ship's captain, Marlow, who would both narrate the story—to listeners *within* the book—and be an actor in it. Marlow has the accent and cadence of a seafarer who is fond of spinning yarns, like Conrad himself; so it must have been easy for Conrad to identify himself with him. We must remember that Conrad was writing in a foreign language and agonized over his search for the proper English words, so he must have been grateful for a pretext like this to use a less formal style.

Yet Marlow is *never* wholly Conrad, nor was this device chosen for such a simple reason. Actually, Conrad was seeking a means for presenting characters much more fully than even James could hope to do with his limited third-person angle of vision. We have the story in *Lord Jim,* and in many other subsequent Conrad novels, related in Marlow's own words, and have Marlow shown in action, so that we can fairly appraise him as a person: we have an objective view of him who serves as the narrator, while we see and hear him reaching his subjective opinion of the unhappy Jim. We still have a license not to agree with Marlow. But in addition to sharing Marlow's vantage, we have—through Marlow, again —a host of other opinions about Jim, expressed by a succession of people whom Jim has encountered in his travels: the butterfly-collector, Stein; Egström; Captain Brierly; the scornful French lieutenant; the bitterly hostile Gentleman Brown. Each offers a different image of Jim; each judges him according to a personal moral code and temperament. They are a "relay of witnesses," or sub-narrators, whose conclusions Marlow collects and reports to his listeners, and at next remove to us. Their testimony presents a much more rounded, if usually contradictory, portrait of Jim than could Marlow's lone response. This device also works better than James's for the depiction of inarticulate people, which most of Conrad's figures tend to be: Far Eastern wanderers and adventurers, groping romantics, simple idealists of the sea. In each instance, too, Marlow judges the "witnesses": we see him arriving at his own evaluation of them, and we ourselves also have a chance to observe them objectively, while they are in action, playing their separate rôles in the intricately plotted story. Hence, we can form an opinion of them which is not bound to concur with Marlow's, though most likely it will. Here is a method which employs "parallax and refraction," with the honest-minded Marlow at hand to try and correct the distortion, if any; or, as Conrad himself puts it, his purpose is "by changing lights, to give varied effects of perspective."

Referring to William Faulkner, who later is to use a similar technique, Conrad Aiken and Robert Penn Warren term this "the spiral method, which takes the reader over and over the same event from a different altitude, as it were, and from a different angle. In relation to both character and event this . . . makes for a kind of realism and a kind of suspense (in the formal not the factual sense) not common in fiction."

The result is not a clear and focused picture of Jim, but an often confused and contradictory one. But this is just what Conrad has in mind, for he is fully aware of the irrational impulses that govern our minds and behavior, which any sharp and lucid characterization would belie: his method prevents his falling into any oversimplification of motive. He preserves, too, the inescapable ambiguity that is bound to bedevil any attempt to explain human conduct, why we act as we do: people are always partly opaque, beyond any logical explanation. Consequently, these simpler, inarticulate figures of Conrad appear far more complex and even more lifelike than James's brilliant, talkative players. Besides this, Conrad uses his technical device for yet another reason: his novels contain moral problems, which his characters—faced by a sudden crisis—must decide. But there are no clear answers to the great moral questions in life, and Conrad's "witnesses"—subnarrators—argue these controversial points and perhaps, in the end, leave them unresolved. The gain, at least, is that they have been thoroughly aired and forcibly expressed: this gives Conrad's fiction a philosophical depth which possibly only Dostoevski has surpassed. Each of the "witnesses," too, is dominated by a different personal passion that colors his attitude: love, in the instance of the girl; in other instances, anger, jealousy, inferiority feelings, pride, humaneness.

Thus Conrad has gone several steps beyond Henry James. He often uses a much larger cast than James does, and certainly a more varied one, for his people are drawn from all walks of life and all nationalities. (One of the rich and amazing features of Lord Jim is its cosmopolitanism: here we have, in one story, Jim judged by his fellow-Englishmen—Marlow, Brierly, Gentleman Brown; but also by a hard-headed French officer; by a kindly German, Stein; by a Dutchman, De Jongh; a Swede, Egström; by little Archie Ruthwell, a half-caste Portuguese; and last by the proud, hurt Malays. Each of them too seems to have a national or racial bias, derived from his opposing or contrasting culture, that helps him form his fragmentary estimate of Jim.) Conrad offers all these extra angles of vision, and yet does not pretend to bring his subject into any final clarity, for he has too much respect for the mystery of personality and admits to being daunted by its elusiveness.

I have already reported that Conrad's technique was at first belittled. Critics complained that a story lost vividness by being told at second and even third hand, as happens in Lord Jim and the other novels where Marlow appears. To the reviewers, it strained belief that anyone could talk as long on one occasion as does Marlow supposedly, with so much minute detail, while recounting Jim's legend; and it was equally improbable that Marlow could always have been on the spot along with Jim, at the right moment, to learn ever more about his history. To this, in an "Author's Note" to a later edition of Lord Jim, Conrad replies that the whole of the book can be read aloud in less than three hours (which to me is highly doubtful; I have never tried it, but I suspect that Conrad himself never did so, either). But is this of any consequence? Art has artificial conventions; every medium has them, and we accept them: we know that people do not sing at the top of their lungs while they are dying, but we do not cavil at their doing so in the opera—we appreciate that the musical accompaniment vastly deepens the emotion that is expressed; as part of an audience we do not object to many departures from the literal in a play being enacted before us; and we permit scale to vary from the actual in sculpture, and a third dimension to be suggested on a well-painted canvas. Similarly, in fiction, we can make quite as many allowances —providing our interest is held. Marlow is a fascinating teller of tales: he has an alert, sensitive, earnest mind and an eye for revelatory detail and a talent for creating a poetic scene: does it matter how long he talks?

Yet in many ways Marlow is a very credible figure. As a shipmaster, he travels incessantly in Eastern waters: it is quite convincing that he should meet up with Jim in many places. And meet up again with the sub-narrators, too. Furthermore, Marlow's peculiar interest in Jim is firmly motivated, for he not only likes him but also strongly identifies himself with this unhappy young man. We sense that the problem that confronts Jim is one that Marlow himself has often faced, in solitary contemplation, at least. Would he himself have stood up to the test of honor that Jim encountered on the *Patna*? In fact, other aspects of this theme of identification run throughout the book: Stein also recognizes an affinity with the hapless, romantic Jim; and so, apparently, does the ill-fated Captain Brierly, who in condemning Jim seems also to be passing a harsher judgment on himself; and even miserable Gentleman Brown claims there exists "a basic resemblance" between them, a challenge that when issued sickens Jim. All this helps to explain why the "witnesses" have such strong feelings, favorable or unfavorable, about Conrad's hero.

Another criticism voiced is that no sea-captain would be as intelligent and eloquent as Marlow; but the obvious reply to this is that Joseph Conrad was a shipmaster: he drew most of his stories from life, from his own experience; and so the verisimilitude of Marlow as a person is hardly to be questioned. He might be a rare figure, as is Conrad himself, but hardly an impossible one.

Conrad is not the first to line up a succession of witnesses who offer contradictory accounts of the same person or event: again, it is a technique borrowed from the tale of detection. (A somewhat earlier instance is found in Wilkie Collins's eerie *The Woman in White*.) But like James, Conrad applies the device to build up a psychological mystery, and to heighten suspense about the bewildering truth of human nature. He does this with an intensity that is, once more, second only to that achieved by Dostoevski (whom Conrad, as a Pole, vehemently professed to dislike; since the Slavophile author of *Crime and Punishment* patriotically defended Russia's foreign conquests, including the occupation of Poland). Whatever may have been Conrad's actual feelings about Dostoevski, one perceives that he consciously or elsewise borrows much from him, however different are their prose styles, the settings of their stories, the types of people they describe.

Conrad carries his experiments still further in novels that follow *Lord Jim*. Critics now study these variations closely. In *Nostromo* the story comes from the lips of Captain Mitchell, a naïve narrator who does not comprehend the full import of what he is relating. In *Under Western Eyes* the first half of the story is seen through the eyes of the hunted Razumov, in the third person; the second half purports to be a diary kept by Razumov, hence it might have been in the first person; but instead it has been transposed into the third person again by an English professor, who also knew Razumov and interpolates his *own* first-person comments, and the comments of others acquainted with the young man: this is a complicated procedure, indeed. But it does yield an "inside-outside" view of the tortured hero, a rare achievment. In *Chance* we get facts and slants on a character at fourth- and even fifth-hand, in an amazingly extended chain of rumors and impressions and assessments—but here, perhaps, Conrad pushes his device too far—or is it, merely, that in other ways this is one of his lesser works, although ironically it is the one that at long last brought him popular success.

After James and Conrad, other twentieth-century writers explored new forms based more or less on these bold experiments. Joseph Hergesheimer, in his exquisite, cameo-like *Java Head*, divides his novel into ten chapters; in nine of them the story unfolds progressively in time and each new advance in it is seen from the angle of vision of another onlooker. Each of these surrogates for the lapidarian author differs from the others in age, personality, and knowledge of the world. The result, in Professor Beach's words, is like the opening before us of "a beautiful fan of multi-colored leaves." Another variation of the Jamesian-Conradian technique is supplied by Wallace Irwin's *The Days of Her Life*. Sixteen chapters represent as many days in the history of the heroine, over a span from 1881 to 1899. The point of view is singular —hers—from start to finish, but her full life story to date is recreated in this mere sheaf of dramatically highlighted incidents. Even more ingenious is Rex Stout's *How Like a God*, where the tale is related by a man talking silently to himself, in the second person, as he walks up a flight of stairs. He is recollecting all the events that have led him to this fateful moment of climbing these steps. It might be called a cinematic device, with a suspenseful framework and explanatory flashbacks. Many modifications of it, not only in the second person, but in the more usual first and third, are readily encountered in the fiction of the past few decades. And this by no means exhausts all the possibilities—and clever variations—of the formal shape that James and Conrad brought to the psychological novel, to make it more subjective and to help it probe human nature ever more deeply.

Chapter 17

Into the Labyrinth

ALWAYS SEEKING WAYS to follow threads into the labyrinth of man's mind, the early twentieth-century novel also veers off from being tightly "well-made" toward an apparent looseness. This change in direction, quite the opposite of that taken by James and Conrad, results from the development of two other fictional techniques, of which Marcel Proust originates the first.

In Proust's vast, barely concealed autobiographical chronicle, *Remembrance of Things Past*, the hero-narrator dips a small piece of cake into a cup of tea, and the pleasurable savor of it suddenly brings back to him a flood of unsought memories, all lyrically detailed. Thereby the reader has created for him a huge panorama consisting of delicate impressions from the hero's childhood, touching and poignant, rendered with a deft pointillism: pictures of his strange adolescence, his busy life in Paris and the whole social scene of the higher reaches of society and its decadent nobility, critically and amusingly portrayed, over a span of decades to the turn of the century. The process by which this great novel unfurls—it runs to many volumes, adding up in some editions to seven thousand pages—is that of the free association of ideas, similar to that being used in psychoanalysis: one idea, one word, leads to another, in revelatory digressions.

I need hardly say, however, that in this novel the flow of images and recollections is far from uncontrolled. Such is Proust's guileful art that the lack of "discipline" is only seeming. Though the tendency of the book is quite centrifugal, and at first glance it impresses one as formless, even inchoate, it contains many passages, chapters, sections, that are carefully constructed along dramatic lines. At the same time, many themes and sharply evoked characters repeatedly play their parts throughout its length; in fact, there is very skillful interweaving—on which I shall expatiate later—to hold it together and to prevent it from disintegrating into anything like shapelessness. It has the very subtle form, real yet less

179

discernible than in works of classic temper, which Joseph Wood Krutch has attributed to the best Romantic art, of which I believe *Remembrance of Things Past* is incontestably the apotheosis in fiction. But digression, the privilege to wander to any subject brought up by a chance resemblance, is essential to its goal. Proust's aim is to "recapture the whole of experience," or at least a very considerable fragment of it; especially, he wishes to travel in the realms of dreams and the irrational. To do this he cannot stay within traditional limits.

He propounds, in a letter: "Voluntary memory, which is above all the memory of the intelligence and of the eyes, gives us only the surface of the past without the truth; but when an odor, a taste, rediscovered under entirely different circumstances evoke for us, in spite of ourselves, the past, we sense how different is the past from the one we remembered and which our voluntary memory was painting like a bad dauber using false colors." Of the involuntary memories to which Proust dedicates his art, Bernard De Voto writes paraphrastically: "They alone have the stamp of authenticity. They bring things back to us in an exact proportion of memory and forgetting. And finally, as they make us savor the same sensation under wholly different circumstances, they free it from all context, they give us the extra-temporal essence. . . ."

Thus a new subjective material enters the novel, of a sort to which James and Conrad pay scarcely any attention. Perhaps Proust had been distantly anticipated by Laurence Sterne, who also delightedly indulges in endless digressions, and who includes in his *Tristram Shandy* dissertations on an infinite number of topics (as does Proust himself, on music, politics, painting, topographical place names, psychology, even military tactics); and something akin to the Proustian manner is also come upon in Walter Pater and George Meredith, slightly in advance of Proust's day. Other writers, too—particularly Dostoevski, whom Proust had studied carefully—have brought in "dream material" and "irrational impulses" and stressed the force exerted by fancy, emotion, intuition, in fashioning a man's character, often at the expense of logical thought. But Proust goes much further than any of these vaguely similar predecessors.

His influence on writers following him is almost too important to calculate. To an extent not truly appreciated, he prepares the way for James Joyce and Virginia Woolf: first, by ignoring the strait jacket of the dramatic form, and all other restraints of conventional fiction; his spirit is independent and ready to break quite willfully from every established pattern of the novel. He also touches scandalously on sexual aberrations that have seldom if ever been brought into respectable fiction before now: this candor about forbidden topics is also to influence Joyce and his admirers. So too is Proust's addition to the novel of a more elaborate and self-consciously elegant prose style, and of a dazzling display of erudition. But most of all, his technique of the "association of ideas" is to be appropriated by hundreds of writers who succeed him; and its impact on Joyce and Woolf is exceedingly strong.

Proust, then, although he is almost inimitable, has probably left his mark on the novel of our time more perceptibly than anyone else, even more so than Joyce and his school. I am venturing to say that our fiction during the past three decades has taken advantage of Proustian devices far more often than Joycean ones, for a variety of reasons which we might examine.

II

James Joyce and Virginia Woolf are not the inventors of the "stream of consciousness" in the novel, but they popularized it, and employ it better than anyone else; consequently, their names are most often coupled with it.

The stream of consciousness technique is an even bolder twentieth-century approach to capturing the elusiveness of "subjectivity," though it has not yet been as richly productive as Proust's "association" in reaching that end.

By this device the unuttered thoughts of the characters are reported in their barely verbalized form, as if the author had lifted the lid of his peoples' skulls and attached a tape-recorder to the mysterious voice and noise within the brain and larynx: what is caught is incoherent at times, and discontinuous; but the report is also one of the most intense intimacy. It is as though the author—and the reader—were telepathists: but we do not read the character's thoughts as if clairvoyant; rather we *overhear* them, eavesdropping on them perpetually, by having an extraordinary aural gift. Flowing by, transferred onto the tape, is an intermittent river of words, exclamations, half-thoughts, repressed thoughts never spoken aloud to anyone, heard only by the thinker alone. The author is transferring to his manuscript—ultimately, to the printed page—not the formal rational conclusions of the character, but the very process of his thought, in which there are many irrational incursions and halts. So no Jamesian polish and clarity in the psychologizing is possible here.

Listen to an oft-quoted passage from *Ulysses,* by Mr. Joyce: "The man that was drowned nine days ago off Maiden's Rock. They are waiting for him now. The truth, spit it out. I would want to. I would try. I am not a strong swimmer. Water cold soft. When I put my face into it in the basin at Colongowes. Can't see! Who's behind me?"

What is happening here is that Stephen Daedalus is walking on the pebbled beach and observes some people wading in the surf, and suddenly we enter into his musing mind and share his very thoughts. Would he be brave enough to rescue a drowning man? What would it be like to drown?

He thinks again, and we—but no one else—can hear him: "I want his life still to be his, mine to be mine. A drowning man. His human eyes scream out to me of horror of his death. I . . . With him, together down."

And so on. His thoughts, by free association—in part, note, derived from Proust—forever digress, mingle with other images compelled by his deepest desires, hopes, fears, memories. At times we cannot quite make out what his thinking is; it is only half-formed, inchoate; at other times, his allusions are so vague or personal—references to past events unknown to us—that they escape us for a while or forever. And, of course, the trivial is mixed with the profound, the sacred with the profane, the decorous with the indecent, the lyrical with the repulsive, the playful and nonsensical with the serious and maturely perceptive: the very stuff of human personality and consciousness is set down here in startling juxtaposition. Furthermore, since Stephen's mind is not bound by time restrictions, he will be living mentally in the past, present, and future all at once: that is, in fugitive or persistent memories, present physical sensations and impressions, and imagined projections of things to come. He will be judging past incidents, reaching decisions about present affairs, and making plans for tomorrow and next year.

To find the source of this stream of consciousness technique we turn back once again to Laurence Sterne and his strikingly original *Tristram Shandy*. Dorothy Van Ghent summarizes it thusly: Sterne's subject is "the endlessly fertile rhythms of consciousness . . . exploring the comic ironies of a quest for order among the humdrum freaks of birth and paternity . . . and place and time and language. . . . Sterne himself puts the problem. . . . In setting up a certain body of human experience novelistically, what should come first? what last? what should follow or precede what? Should not everything appear at once and in fusion, inasmuch as this is the way the author's consciousness grasps it in its fullest truth?" But Sterne's work is offered to us as fantasy and humor, and we must remember that for centuries it has always been outside the main current of English fiction. Instead, it is in France, much later, with the Goncourts, that we find this device prefigured in novels that deal in true earnest with "reality." In their "slice of life" studies, which eliminate plot and present characters in passing and in flux only, something like the stream of consciousness appears; shortly it becomes part of the apparatus of Goncourtian Naturalism. Two other leaders of this literary movement, Zola (*L'Assommoir*) and Knut Hamsun (*Growth of the Soil*) have occasional passages in which the thoughts of their people are given with naked directness. Another French novelist, Edouard Dujardin, attempts the trick even more effectively thirty years before Joyce, and Joyce has duly acknowledged this debt. Any reader will also agree with Professor Beach, that Robert Browning incorporates it into some of his best-liked poetry, familiar to all students, and there are examples of it in Thomas Carlyle's dramatic forays into history.

But it is Dorothy Richardson, in her sequence of books about a drab, slightly less than ordinary girl, Miriam, who significantly introduced the method into twentieth-century fiction. Here there is no plot, no conventional story line, other than the day-to-day occurrences in Miriam's rather neutral life, not as viewed by the author—Miss Richardson— but as experienced directly by Miriam herself. Nor are the heroine's impressions and feelings probed in depth; that is left for the reader to do. The larger meaning of the story is only implied, never stated. We are given merely the data: what is "immediate in consciousness" for her, and perhaps— still more to be deduced by us—astir in her unconscious mind. Unlike the subsequent tack taken by Joyce and Woolf, past and future are not brought into her thoughts. Miriam is not involved with memories, or with visions of her future, except for some dull and moody daydreaming. Miriam is passive, apathetic, pathetically genteel. Her love affairs begin and lead nowhere. Her ambitions are nil. We are asked to grasp what is Miriam's "awareness," what for her is the "unanalyzed sensation of being alive." As such, this series of novels about a less than commonplace young girl is a remarkable achievement. All the same, the reader is apt to feel—with Elizabeth Drew—that the image of Miriam lacks proportion and perspective because her being flows on at an unvaried emotional level and pressure. This has the effect of making life too small. Her inner life is certainly too tenuous; too many phases of a normal existence are omitted. Nothing is ever at stake, and there are no dramatic moments.

Joyce and Virginia Woolf are to add much to their novelistic formula to overcome these lacks. For one thing, they are to choose more interesting heroes. For another, they are to adopt a far more poetic prose style. Finally, they are to select a much more colorful *mise en scène,* or a garish and picturesque variety of them; so that we will be excited not only by what is happening to their characters, but by the setting, too. In Joyce's book, Stephen Daedalus and Leopold Bloom are fascinating persons; and Mrs. Woolf's Clarissa Dalloway has extraordinary perception and sensitivity. What is more, both of these later authors have casts of several leading figures, and shift from one stream of consciousness to another in alternate chapters, thereby enriching their material: in the Richardson books, our insight is limited solely to Miriam's transparent thoughts. Past and future, as already suggested, coexist with the present in the consciousness of the characters with whom we travel in Joyce's *Ulysses* and Woolf's *Mrs. Dalloway* and *The Waves*. In addition, Joyce introduces a whole bag of other devices, borrowed from fads then contemporary: from Jungian psychology, from Greek mythology, from Symbolism, from Dada, Expressionism, and Irish political history, to enliven his story at every moment. We do not have to infer that *Ulysses* has a larger meaning than a mere presentation of three persons' minds: Joyce's intention is made abundantly obvious in every strangely fashioned sentence. (I will discuss his very odd prose style later.)

Even in Miss Richardson's books, which seek to give the

effect of realism, much skill and fashioning is called for. Actually, there is a painstaking choice of detail, and Miss Richardson very definitely sets up boundaries and peripheries beyond which her story does not wander. Such selection, and such confines, are even more apparent in the works by Joyce and Woolf: we have extremely narrow limits of time, of place. *Ulysses* comprises the events of only eighteen hours, all set in Dublin; and *Mrs. Dalloway*, a single day in the English capital. Indeed, one critic has defined the subject of *Mrs. Dalloway* as "what it is like to be alive on a fine day in London," not only for that lady, but for all the sharply contrasted characters whose feelings are presented to us in this short novel.

The stream of consciousness device, then, demands artificial shaping and handling to quite the same extent as the more traditional methods of storytelling: the illusion of spontaneity is as artfully contrived as any other effect in literature, and its claim to yield an ultimate realism is hardly to be allowed. More and more, indeed, as time goes by, the "thoughts" of Stephen Daedalus and Clarissa Dalloway sound less and less real to us. This may be because they are not at all ordinary persons. Perhaps young Joyce himself once had a flow of images and phrases through his mind like those of his hero, but surely few other living persons have ever had. Virginia Woolf too has an unique personality. But also it is the overembellished language in both these famed novels that causes them, after a few decades, to sound so overartificed. It is Leopold and Molly Bloom who come through to us with triumphant vulgarity and actuality; they are Joyce's daunting masterpieces of characterization.

In still other ways, artifice and discipline must accompany the author's resort to the stream of consciousness. We are lost, trying to follow the "stream," unless we are given objective "signposts." We must know who the character is, where he is, what he is doing, as well as what his helter-skelter thoughts are. This requires that the author must slip unobtrusively in and out of his hero's mind to show us the setting. Miss Richardson most often uses the imperfect tense for a transition from the scene observed to the recording mind. "The conversation was growing boisterous." "The men were smoking." "The sound of the piano was filling the room." From this we move smoothly back to Miriam's impressions and passive mood once more. But verbs and grammatical connectives are sometimes missing; and this, coupled with Miriam's own vagueness of feeling and thought, and allusions to which we have no key, frequently make for difficult reading, despite the very simple prose.

Joyce is a craftsman without equal. Consider another much-quoted passage in which Leopold Bloom is preparing breakfast for his wife: "Cup of tea soon. Good. Mouth dry." But these three phrases—his thoughts—are inserted in a flow that is less directly reported: "She didn't like her plate full. Right. He turned from the tray, lifted the kettle off the hob and set it sideways on the fire. It sat there, dull and squat, its spout stuck out. Cup of tea soon. Good. Mouth dry. The cat walked stiffly round a leg of the table with tail on high." We see vividly what Mr. Bloom sees—the cat, the kettle—and observe his actions, which are habitual; and hear his innermost thoughts, without the slightest jolt or realization that we are moving from one sphere to another and then yet another. This handling is repeated again and again throughout *Ulysses*. Only in the final section of the book, Molly Bloom's remarkable nighttime reverie, is the flow of thought unimpeded, the objective scene never referred to. But Joyce does not bring us to this crowning chapter until we have gone with him through hundreds of pages and have grown entirely accustomed to his method. The chapter opens, and we easily grasp that Mr. Bloom's sensual wife, Molly, is trying to fall asleep, while an endless gush of thoughts and images spring from her fading mind. She pictures herself a singer again—her former vocation—in a music hall. She recalls past loves, gifts she once received, a man she had been involved with who is long dead. Since there is no punctuation, it is not possible to excerpt a passage complete in itself, but a cluster of lines will suffice to show how Joyce presents her banal, tawdry musings:

more than anything else I wanted to give him a memento he gave me that clumsy Claddagh ring for luck that I gave Gardner going to South Africa where those Boers killed him with their war and fever but they were well beaten all the same as if it brought its bad luck with it like an opal or pearl must have been pure 16 carat gold because it was very heavy I can see his face clean shaven Frseeeeeeeeeeeeeeeeeeeeefrong that train again weeping tone

once in the dear deaead days beyond recall close my eyes
breath my lips forward kiss sad look eyes open piano ere
oer the world the mists began I hate that istsbeg comes loves
sweet ssoooooooong Ill let that out full when I get in front
of the footlights again Kathleen Kearney and her lot of
squealers. . . .

This is probably something closer to the matrix of real
thought than any novelist has ever yet attained, but we are
always aware while perusing it that the writer has arduously
selected every seemingly casual word, that it is all cleverly
arranged. Nor have Joyce or Mrs. Woolf ever written a whole
book in this vein; the reason being, I think, that a reader
would find it absolutely intolerable: it is far too hard going.

Virginia Woolf is much more concerned than Joyce with
helping the average reader to comprehend: her work always
has lucidity. She avoids many of Joyce's excesses. Their names
are so often linked that it is seldom recalled today that she
took up the stream of consciousness technique at a much later
date. Her first novels are quite conventional in form. She
wrote favorable reviews of Joyce's work, and finally followed
his lead, though she never lost her own very individual idiom.
Her style is precious, sensuous, lyrical. She has a feeling for
nuance even finer, because feminine, than Henry James had.
She announces her credo memorably in *The Common Reader,*
in a chapter entitled "Essay on Modern Fiction": "Life is not
a series of gig-lamps symmetrically arranged; life is a
luminous halo, a semi-transparent envelope surrounding us
from the beginning of consciousness to the end. Is it not the
task of the novelist to convey this varying, this unknown
and uncircumscribed spirit, whatever aberration or complexity it may display, with as little mixture of the alien and
external as possible?" She attempts to do this, but she never
does dispense with the "external," for she knows that we lose
orientation without an objective reference. Elsewhere she
writes: "What is meant by reality? It would seem to be something very erratic, very undependable—now to be found in a
dusty road, now in a scrap of newspaper in a street, now in a
daffodil in the sun. It lights up a group in a room and stamps
some casual saying. It overwhelms one walking home beneath
the stars and makes the silent world more real than the
world of speech—and then there it is again in an omnibus in

the roar of Piccadilly." (This is from *A Room of One's Own*.)
In her books we have the inner fountain of thought, but along
with it the crowded omnibus and the tumult of London traffic.

She plants her signposts before us clearly, so that the reader
is never in doubt about the external action. David Daiches has
even drawn a diagram of *Mrs. Dalloway*, to show how carefully that work is constructed: the passing of time is indicated
by the chiming of Big Ben or bells from Wren churches at
fifteen-minute intervals, which are heard by all the characters.
Also, a presumptive regal procession is en route to Bucking-
ham Palace, and a plane is crossing overhead, and they are
observed by one person after another: this places everyone at
an exact hour, a specific street corner. (A knowledge of
London's topography will assist the reader.) She uses fewer
characters than Joyce does, and their connection, if any, is
firmly established; one of the points of the story, of course,
is that some of the people are strangers. We are forever
partly in the characters' minds, partly outside. The author
frequently crosses over by using "one" transitionally: that is,
from the third person to the first person. "She knew . . .,"
then "One knew . . .," and "I knew." (Joyce employs these
and the second person, too: Stephen Daedalus often addresses
himself as "you.") The present participle is also a handy
bridge: "It is probably the Queen, thought Mrs. Dalloway,
coming out of Mulberry's with her flowers; the Queen." And
the following:

> Her only gift was knowing people almost by instinct, she
> thought, walking on. If you put her in a room with some
> one, up went her back like a cat's; or she purred. Devon-
> shire House, Bath House, the house with the china cockatoo,
> she had seen them all lit up at once; and remembered
> Sylvia, Fred, Sally Seton—such hosts of people; and dancing
> all night; and the waggons plodding past to market; and
> driving home across the Park. She remembered once throw-
> ing a shilling into the Serpentine. But every one remem-
> bered; what she loved was this, here, now, in front of her;
> the fat lady in the cab. Did it matter then, she asked herself,
> walking towards Bond Street, did it matter that she must
> inevitably cease completely; all this must go on without
> her. . . .

Both *Ulysses* and *Mrs. Dalloway* carry us backwards in
time. These books are the story of a whole lifetime, the full

history of several characters, told within the setting of a single day. This is accomplished by the magical act of memory. The stream of consciousness technique is also an excellent device for distributed exposition (a basic principle of dramaturgy): background material is brought in precisely when needed, in snippets, in flashes of recollection, rather than in formally and solidly fashioned flashbacks, which—inserted in most traditionally told novels—tend to slow the pace of the story and annoy us. In the majority of instances, the flashback is a tedious interruption: it serves only to flesh-out a past incident of which we already know the ending and consequence; hence it is largely devoid of suspense. But with stream of consciousness we constantly feel that what has occurred even long ago properly belongs to the present, because it is still alive and active in the mind; the effect is one of greater esthetic and psychological unity. "The realization, which this technique implies," observes David Daiches rightly, "is that a mood is never anything static but a fluid pattern 'mixing memory with desire.'" He has also remarked, as perceptively: "The significance of a novel like *Mrs. Dalloway* lies—to continue the metaphor—in the tributaries explored rather than the main stream."

Memory, then, dominates the feeling and thought of these people. In particular, Mrs. Woolf's characters "feel backwards along secret threads into the past of each." And this is quite as true of Joyce's figures. But in the work of both these modern masters, and in many of their later followers, the process of memory is not one of the Proustian "association of ideas" alone, but of what might be termed the "dissociation of ideas": the abrupt, odd, perhaps ugly juxtaposition of images and allusions that in practice derives from both Expressionism and Dada, and which is often a feature of Surrealism today. Here an object, a memory, does not inevitably conjure up another object or recollection that is similar, but often its incongruous opposite, and the result may be ludicrous, offensive, distressing. Joyce has a special fondness for historical contrasts of this sort: he presents, through Stephen's wanderings and erudite thoughts, mean and grotesque modern equivalents of past noble myths, taken perhaps from the classic age. This is meant to illustrate how much that is cheap, degenerate, and barbaric has entered our style of living today. A parallel to this is found in the poetry of Corbière and Laforgue, and T. S. Eliot's *The Waste Land*, where—as Professor Beach says—this burlesque distortion of an exalted or merely sentimental image from the past and presumably superior epoch has been elaborated into a system. Immediately after we hear "Time's winged chariot drawing near," as sensed by that great seventeenth-century poet Andrew Marvell, from whom Mr. Eliot quotes, we are told by the ironic Eliot with a false show of the same enthusiasm that, "Mrs. Porter and her daughter wash their feet in soda water." From the sublime we are rushed to the petty and cheap. The poet's intention is critical and antidemocratic: it stresses almost paranoiacally the vulgarity of our present mass culture.

Along with this, perhaps to gain the effect of a brain disturbed and whirling with sensations, may go much discontinuity, dissonance, and mixed syntax. Formal punctuation is often abandoned, and nouns become verbs, or the opposite. All this has been dubbed a kind of "imaginative shorthand." To give the wavering point of view of an anxious and troubled thinker, images are warped expressionistically: the size, direction, and duration of objects and experiences are slightly or grossly distorted, as in a hashish dream. Stephen Daedalus and Septimus Smith perceive events not as they are, but as they are colored and even nightmarishly disfigured by each man's state of mind; and the rapidity with which these moods can alter is also reflected, almost mockingly: it proves how insubstantial is personality.

In praise of the stream of consciousness novel, David Daiches declares that by its use Joyce is able "to make his hero perhaps the most complete and rounded character in all fiction." Virginia Woolf discovered in it a technique by which "she could evoke the disconnected, blurred, and shimmery experiences" that compose our minds. By summoning up "the past to illuminate the present," as Henry Levin puts it, we have the deepest and most intense subjectivity. Given to us, thus, is that "little world of confused sensation whirring or quiescent in the head of each character." Nonetheless, this complex form of novel has its detractors. Many complain that all this advance in psychology is too much at the expense of story *per se*. It is certainly not a form of fiction that unsophisticated readers can follow with ease. It also calls for filling many pages with irrelevancies, to achieve an effect of life's anarchy; but this is a tendency which I must cite as "anti-art," since I think literature should strive to bring us order and clarity, and ideas stripped of inessentials.

For whatever reason, each year we find fewer examples of the stream of consciousness in new novels. It is employed by many noted writers, however, including such Americans as William Faulkner, (*The Sound and the Fury*), Conrad Aiken (*The Blue Voyage*), and Theodore Dreiser (*An American Tragedy*); and Sherwood Anderson, John Dos Passos, Thomas Wolfe, and Evelyn Scott; and Europeans as well. But most of them resort to it sparingly and in restricted passages only, to depict moments of confusion or peaks of emotional stress in the career of their hero, not consistently throughout a book. It might be likened to the insertion of a montage in a film, to illustrate incoherence, an abnormal state of mind, for the most part, rather than a typical mood. In any event, the fight by Joyce and Woolf to depart from strict objective reality has long since been won, in a culture such as ours that now matter of factly accepts Munch's Expressionism, Picasso's Cubism, Dali's Surrealism, together with Abstract Expressionism and Action Painting.

Chapter 18

The Problem of Time

BESIDES THE QUESTION of the "angle of vision," a number of other problems confront the novelist. One of them concerns *time*. A cardinal difference between the short story and the novel is that the story is about a single happening, tinged by one mood, while it delves into some aspect of character; the novel describes the working out of a multiplicity of incidents, logically connected, in which the leading actors undergo a deeper change of personality or moral outlook as a consequence of their experience. Or else, if our novel is not primarily dramatic, but instead a social chronicle, it offers a broad view of the manners of society, also forever in process of change. To accomplish this, the novel must indicate gradually that time is passing: but, of course, time is intangible.

Obviously, a novelist can merely say "Six weeks went by" or "Two weeks later," but this is deemed artistically crude. The long effort has been to refine the craft of storytelling, and the responsible author seeks for ever more subtle devices, which delight the critics. He slips in unobtrusive references to a lapse of time, and he may leap over longer breaks by beginning his next section: "On David's eighth birthday . . ." or "One April day, when Alice was trimming the roses. . . ." Since the directly preceding scene showed David only six, or Alice housebound during a snowstorm, we grasp that two years or a few months have indeed gone past. (Notably careless about this, in one amusing instance, is Henry Fielding, who has Tom Jones enter a house for a short interview, and come out a while later to continue his journey in an entirely different season. The jump is from summer to winter in much less than a day.)

Customarily, a writer draws up a time scheme before he starts to work. He has to arrange his plot so that each incident fits in logically, fully motivated, and occurring at just the right time. A story will lack plausibility otherwise. He must also allow room enough for the emotions of his characters to develop. Some phases of a story cannot be rushed. A love affair needs time to grow and mature, if we are to believe in it. Jealousy and grief, which are ruling passions and have deep causes, must be established and explained; the course of rising ambition has to be followed through a credible and revelatory sequence of incidents, to convince us of its reality.

For centuries, a story was unfolded chronologically, the plot progressing from the first ingenious turn in it to the last. Even so, there are perceptible differences, which Edwin Muir analyzes, in how the effect of time is felt in novels arranged in that fashion. Mr. Muir declares that in the social chronicle time impresses us as an external force. It is not a subjective element that drives or obsesses the characters; indeed, they tend to be largely unaware of it. The reader beholds it measured by the author "as from a fixed Newtonian point outside." Though the people in the story steadily grow older, it is never at a pace much hastened by the intensity of their acts and emotions. Instead, time moves over and round them with a "cold and deadly regularity" that is unconnected to the plot. "It has one kind of necessity," writes Mr. Muir, "that of increasing the ages of all the characters arithmetically, at a uniform rate, without paying attention to their desires or their plans." Such time presents itself to us as having a quality that is "universal," "cosmic." Its progression through the chronicle lends an air of the "accidental" to everything that befalls its many figures: they are born and die; we seldom have a feeling of inevitability about their deaths; they seem merely to have been "snuffed out" at the whim of the author (who is substituting here for the Divine Author). Yet this "arbitrary and careless progression" is lifelike and gives the chronicle its particular reality. It is enriching because it offers the possibility of bringing everything. But again, a result of this looseness is that instead of tragedy we have pathos, and no catharsis is engendered; for we have no spectacle of a hero bravely challenging his partly self-created fate. A feeling of the pettily "accidental" effaces a conviction of the grandly "inevitable"; we do not grant that what has happened to him is unavoidable, that it has risen in the largest share from a *hubris,* a personal tragic flaw.

When the book ends, we do not feel that this is truly the finish, but that times goes on. (In Mr. Lubbock's summary: "The cycle of birth and growth, death and birth again.") Our sense that time is external to the story, too, accounts for the fact that "the conception of fate in the chronicle has often been religious." Mr. Muir cites this as being true of the ancient Homeric and Biblical chronicles, as in that of King David, for example; and of Tolstoi's great *War and Peace*. The characters are not responsible for their own destinies. An outside power is working on them, for better or worse. Thus we see man, and a degree of human accident, posed against supernal law. What happens to him transcends anything he makes happen to himself. This is certainly an idea that Tolstoi seeks to communicate to us.

Mr. Muir contends that quite the opposite impression is given by the dramatic novel. Time is mostly subjective, inward. Whereas in a social chronicle like *War and Peace*, time seems inexhaustible, Dostoevski's characters in *The Idiot*, and *Crime and Punishment* appear to be caught in a moment of time that is running out; they must desperately fight against this, and the action gains from it an air of compelling "nightmarish urgency." All this gives "the real edge of the dramatic emotion." In *Wuthering Heights*, the lovers—Catherine and Heathcliff—are aged by the fierceness of their passions. The effect in all these novels is of time flying by swiftly, and people swept along by it to their doom. Everything is inevitable, must be made to seem so. Muir borrows Nietzsche's dictum for this category of novel, that the characters "die at the right time." That is, their fatal ends are foreshadowed and are inescapable in a tightly and logically shaped story in which everything is cause and effect. We have a sense of finality which the social chronicle does not achieve. In Mr. Muir's view, both these presentations of time—the generalized and external, the particularized and subjective—are valid as pictures of life and as artistic methods.

Edward Bullough, in an essay on "Psychical Distance," makes a point that is relevant here: the foreshortening in a serious drama, as recommended by Aristotle, is an indispensable condition of tragedy. A man is allowed no time to be healed, or even to prepare himself to meet catastrophe: things happen to him too suddenly. Besides this, I should say, the story must permit him no chance to solve his dilemma by applying second thoughts or common sense. The situation demands that he make his decision quickly. Usually it is the fatally wrong one. This onrush of circumstance is a prime factor of tragedy.

II

The natural chronology of the novel—the straightforward telling of it—was finally altered, and radically, by Joseph Conrad and Marcel Proust. By changing the order in which the events in a story are arranged, Conrad again proved himself a major innovator of narrative technique. He shows that the best handling of a tale is not always from beginning to end; instead, in some books it is more suspenseful to shuttle back and forth in time, to take up later incidents first, and then go back to explain what has preceded and motivated or led up to them. Sometimes, the author adds to the effectiveness of a scene, too, if he refers to the future, telling what is to follow from the present action. All this can augment the reader's interest, deepen for him the color and significance of an episode, and—in terms of psychology— make the story appear more lifelike to him.

When we look at *Lord Jim*, where Conrad first adopts this technique, we see it opening not at the very start of Jim's unhappy history; but instead, like a play, in the middle of an action, which again is good Sophoclean dramaturgy. We are plunged into the very heart of a crisis, without knowing how it has come about, or exactly what is involved in it. By means of "distributed exposition" we learn those necessary facts later, bit by bit. What Conrad does is to take care first that he has caught our attention, stirred our curiosity; he wastes no words on providing the background until he feels sure that we are anxious to learn what it is. Think how many books we find hard to take up or, as we say, "get into." We are given too much factual information to start with, in a heavy initial chapter or two. The action begins somewhat later. But not so in *Lord Jim*. Conrad makes a "mystery" of Jim's past from the second page on; he raises tantalizing questions about him that are not answered for hundreds of pages. Jim lacks a last name, and his odd habit of quitting a job without notice and moving on causes him to seem enigmatic and leads us to wonder about him. When we are next told, in hints, passing references, that remarkable things are to befall him in the future, our interest is whetted still more. From time to time, Conrad opens up more of his hero's clouded past, documents it, relates it to Jim's current behavior, and to his inevitable destiny. This is a wonderful dramatic handling of the plot.

Granted that the opening *in medias res* is borrowed from the theater, the rest of Conrad's "mixed chronology" does not come from there, for no play has ever been as complicated in structure as is *Lord Jim*. But we do find its equivalent in the cinema, where a simple "dissolve" takes us back in time, and another brings us back to the present again, and so time shifts are fluid and easy. That probably explains why many stories by Conrad have lent themselves well to film adaptation, but none so far to the stage. But the motion picture as an art form had barely come into being when Conrad wrote this novel (1900); film-cutting was still very elementary. In large part the method is probably Conrad's own invention, but also to a degree once more a conscious or unconscious carrying over to serious fiction of the design of the novel of detection, the hyper-logical Poesque tale. The mystery plot usually departs from a normal forward progression of story line to look backward for an explanation of how and for what reason the crime has been committed. Conrad is concerned with the "mystery" of personality, the moral offenses people commit against themselves or others, and hence the same sort of commingled or suspended time sequence commended itself to him. To this author, nothing is so fugitive and hard to encompass as the mercurial truth of human nature; he wishes to view the possible intentions and desires and warring impulses of his hero from many angles, and so we not only see him from many conflicting points of view, as Jim has been glimpsed by Marlow and the chain of contradictory sub-narrators, but also from almost as many different vantages in time: at crucial moments he is observed and tentatively judged in the light of his past, his present conduct, and the next stage of spiritual development it is preordained he shall reach.

Consequently, in the first hundred or so pages of *Lord Jim*, we come upon eight major shifts, and additional minor ones beside, of both time and setting. If we have not met up with this device before, it may seem quite confusing to us; and that is how it struck the majority of Conrad's first readers, and the earliest book reviewers who ventured to appraise his work. They spoke of him as a clumsy storyteller because they did not appreciate what he was seeking to do. Today, this method of "dissolving" forward and backward in time is familiar and poses no problem to a sophisticated reader. Actually, it is the manner in which we ourselves often recount a story, picking out its highlight first, stopping to fill in the details, and then commenting on it as we go along with allusions to what follows. Part of the reason Conrad's method seems so natural is that Marlow is supposedly speaking aloud throughout, and he proceeds just as he would do in life. But also, by circling about certain all-important facts in the story, as if casually assuming that we know what he knows, although actually we do not, he keeps us in the dark about some surprising turns in the plot: the stunning reversals of fortune, which add dramatic emphasis at just the right moments; the foremost of these, of course, being the outcome of the desertion of the *Patna*, which we, like Jim himself, have had no reason to anticipate.

We must remember, too, that the story is being seen through Marlow's eyes. For him, who has knowledge of what lies in Jim's past and what is to be the final heroic gesture of his career, the facts exist with a simultaneity—drawn from the past, and for the reader the present and the future—which cannot be faithfully represented by a simple chronological sequence. Elsewhere I have written that the image of Jim as perceived by Marlow exists "in a busy cellular maze of impressions in which the three dimensions of time are dynamically intermingled, as are all the places in which the story occurs." The novel, in its temporal structure, reproduces that cellular maze. To use another simile, Marlow's mind, combining a questing intelligence and memory, is like a film montage, in which several visual images are superimposed one upon another. Filtered through these subtly blended images, the strong light of Marlow's intellect brings us a picture of Jim as brilliantly near to the truth as it is possible for this most sensitive and conscientious narrator ever to get.

A very similar approach is taken by Marcel Proust, as the first-person narrator of *Remembrance of Things Past*. References to the future are not intruded as often, but throughout this lengthy novel we coexist in the present and past, or move from one to the other very smoothly. A single word, a trivial image, can evoke a whole immense train of recollections. Proust was much influenced by Henri Bergson's philosophical speculations on the nature of Time, and the extent to which our perception of it is affected by subjective factors. (It happens that Bergson was married to Proust's cousin.) Bergson observes that the pace of Time depends on our state of mind. If we are impatient, it goes by leadenly; if we are deeply absorbed in a task, the hours can fly past us. Of course, this is not "clock time"—a limited mechanical attempt to measure "absolute time" or "cosmic" or "sidereal time"—but it is Time as we know it in daily life, and hence Time as it should be presented in a novel. In sleep and dreams, too, with which Proust is preoccupied in his book, Time has blurred edges, and is foreshortened or elongated fantastically.

The same thing is beheld in *Tristram Shandy,* where the prankish Sterne's treatment of Time is gaily accordion-like. The narrator has set out to write his autobiography; he finally becomes aware that his entire book covers no more than his very first day of life. Too much happens in those first twenty-four hours for him ever to proceed beyond that. He—Tristram, the presumed author—stops to calculate that he has used up a year writing about these few hours, and tells himself that to keep up-to-date with clock time he should live at least three hundred sixty-four times faster than his pen moves. (Is he not a bit confused here? Should he not, instead, write three hundred sixty-four times faster than he has been?) In an amusing passage of the book, too, four chapters are dedicated to one long conversation between Uncle Toby and the Doctor, as they descend a flight of stairs: they linger, argue, philosophize discursively. Dorothy Van Ghent is moved to say of Sterne's freakish masterpiece: "Obeying formal laws of its own, it is as skillfully and delicately constructed as *Tom Jones.* Having ruled out plot chronology as a model of the way experience presents itself, Sterne offers another model: that of the operation of consciousness, where time is exploded, where any time-past may be time-present, or several times-past be concurrently present at once, and where clock time appears only intermittently as a felt factor." Miss Van Ghent reminds us that this is foreshadowed in *Don Quixote,* too, when the Don goes into the cave of Montesinos, where past and present and dream experiences are mixed as one for him. But again, these are exceptions, even by-blows, in the long genealogy of literature; it is to be Joseph Conrad and Marcel Proust who establish such writing as legitimate and in the main line of the twentieth century.

David Daiches suggests that other influences than Bergson's metaphysics have been exerted here. Freud had won assent to his idea that people are far more complex psychologically than was generally realized. Carl Jung, pushing forward his much-debated but challenging theory of the "collective unconscious," has argued that all human beings have racial memories which make each individually the heir of the whole past, even of remote prehistory, from the very dawn of mankind. "The past exists always in the present, coloring and determining the nature of the present response." Such concepts find full-bodied expression in a play like Eugene O'Neill's *The Emperor Jones,* a powerful study of resurgent atavism; and in novels, in Joyce's never-sounded *Ulysses* and most notably in Virginia Woolf's *Orlando,* where the hero's life is traced for centuries, his many rebirths or reincarnations and changes of personality, status, and even sex, magically and vividly recalled. Daiches concludes that, to show the reader "the simultaneity of different levels of consciousness," an author must have command of new fictional techniques. "The whole truth about a mature person can be told by probing into his past through presenting the full texture of his present consciousness." Conrad and Proust do this within the scope of one character's life span; Joyce and Virginia Woolf, offering us Stephen Daedalus and Orlando, penetrate back through the ages and layers of racial experience.

Professor Beach has written discerningly about another cinematic device of Conrad's, the "close-up." But again, I doubt that Conrad took his "close-up" from the films; he used it at least a decade before Edwin S. Porter and D. W. Griffith and his cameraman, Billy Bitzer, "invented" it. Frequently Conrad has a character gaze through a porthole or transom, or keyhole, and behold some object or action, which is then minutely described: the effect is one of arrested time while this detail is set down, and the onlooker's reaction is painstakingly described; it does greatly resemble the filmic close-up because it has the attributes of a framework, slow-motion, and magnification. Examples of this are found in *Lord Jim, Victory, Chance,* and particularly in *The Arrow of Gold.* Professor Beach remarks that in this *ralenti,* an Italian term for the "slow-up," we share with the onlooker in the story the very sensation he is having of an impression sinking into his mind. This "especially appeals to the reader with a psychological bent," or one who enjoys catching the author's esthetic intent, for here the author is pursuing the most ephemeral shades of meaning, all the poetic nuances. But in Conrad this is a comparatively minor device. In Proust we have many such "close-ups" and "slow-ups" on a grand scale: time is forever being held in abeyance while the author-narrator tirelessly examines a response, an emotion; he is painstakingly seeking the significance of a character's tone of voice, or a flicker of his facial expression. "What exactly did he mean by *that*?" Indeed, time stands almost utterly still for a whole volume of Proust's novel, while the hero analyzes his grief over the loss of Albertine; until at last a large measure of tedium sets in for the reader. (I might add that schizophrenics often attach the same kind of exaggerated importance to a casually chosen word, a tone of voice, an actual or fancied change of facial mien. The artist's, of course, is a "controlled fantasy.")

In Joyce, too, we have a similar succession of close-ups and slow-ups, but Professor Beach feels that in *Ulysses* they lead perilously close to the disintegration of the story, a "divorce between motive and conduct." He grants that it was Joyce's intent to accomplish something like this. "The trinity of sensation-motive-conduct is broken down. Action is so slight and inconsecutive that it hardly counts, and we cannot have a proper behaviouristic reference of the subjective states. Motive, which is so largely judged by reference to action, appears in a weak and sickly condition. What dominates the landscape is sensation—actual and imaginary."

The slow descent of the stairs by Uncle Toby and the Doctor, which occupies four chapters in *Tristram Shandy,* is another good instance of the *ralenti*. It is "an infinite expansion of the moment." So the device can be used for many ends, and to fasten onto many moods. The bold and deft handling of time by a knowledgeable novelist is a means by which he adds subtler hues or stronger overtones to his story, but he runs many risks. He may sacrifice pace and clarity. Some authors lose more than they gain by tampering with straightforward chronology. They merely confuse the general reader, who by now has grown weary of the often over-used "flashback."

Chapter 19

Characterization

Someone has said that all of us, when meeting people, perform "a dimly artistic imaginative act," creating our picture of their character more or less in the image of ourselves. We project our self-knowledge into them. The novelist works in the same way, but "more intensely and more consecutively." (Perhaps the lover does it even more: he endlessly analyzes and creates the character of the beloved. Proust insists on this fact.)

Aristole gives primacy to plot-making over characterization, and rightly. He points out that a play can succeed if the action is interesting, even if the people involved in it are sketchily drawn; but a character study alone can seldom hold our attention for long. Most stage melodramas bear out Aristotle's contention. So, in books, does the romance, which emphasizes plot, conflict, and swift pace, but tends to have mere cut-out pasteboard heroes. The other attributes of a dramatic character, Aristotle stipulates, are that he should be plausible and consistent. The special requirements for a tragic and comic hero, as Aristotle, with keen sagacity, conceives them to be, I shall discuss later.

The idea that "plot" is more important than "characterization" in fiction has little critical favor just now. The fashion is to scorn "plot" and elevate "psychology." But it may prove a grave error for authors to court the attention of critics by following this latest trend. If the author's hope is to be read by a wide public, rather than a few critics, he had better hearken to Aristotelian counsel—a very respectable source, I might add, for Aristotle himself is a critic with the highest credentials. The novelist must first of all tell a story that readers will not want to put down, simply because the *plot* grips them.

But though secondary to plot-making, knowing how to fill a book with a truly sympathetic, interesting, and living cast is obviously of the utmost consequence. Very often the difference between what is deemed first-rate and second-rate in literature lies mainly in the achievement of better characterization. To become a classic, a novel must be about people portrayed with insight, who are always credible, and in some instances dynamic.

Not too much has been written about "characterization" as a technical problem, because it often seems that novelists create their most fascinating figures in the same way that legendary alchemists turned dull lead into pure gold. At any rate, it is largely a secret process with an aura of magic. Historic is the artist's dream of emulating Prometheus or Pygmalion, who in mankind's ancient myths breathe life into clay. The painter is often startled when by some apparently undirected impulse, his brush brings life to an eye or suddenly adds a true smile and expressivity to a face. It was doubtless from his own personal experience of this miracle, that Michelangelo was inspired to depict God the Father giving life to Adam by the mere vitalizing touch of His fingertip.

Yet any practicing novelist knows that he does employ certain devices that are not at all magical, in choosing and shaping his people. For example, he will tend to select *contrasting* characters when "casting" his story. That will help to make his book more lively and interesting. He may also borrow Turgenev's preparatory habit of compiling a thick dossier on all his people, even the most minor figures. In each dossier are many intimate facts that the author may never use, but this helps him to know his characters fully, before he even begins to write. The novelist will also be closely observing actual people at all times, making mental and written notes about their appearance, their speech quirks, their other revealing mannerisms. Henry James's term for this is "saturation." A novelist must first be saturated with his concept of the story, and particularly with the characters. He sees them clearly. In his mind his plot has "absolutely fulfilled itself to its uttermost consequence, not of detached arithmetical logic but of imagined vital inevitability," and "his characters are live beings . . . complete with hopes, and faces, and hands, and hatbands . . . and their world is complete." In their methods of approach, before setting down words, Turgenev and James follow a very similar course.

One of the most quoted comments on "characterization" is that by E. M. Forster in his *Aspects of the Novel*. He distinguishes between two types of characters, the "flat" and the "round." The flat character is unchanging, static; at the end of the novel he is essentially what he has been throughout. He performs by habit, like an automaton. He is identified with a speech tag of some sort, and a peculiarity of gesture, like Mr. Micawber in *David Copperfield,* who is always certain that something will providentially turn up; or Uriah Heep, in the same story, who is forever wringing his hands; or old Uncle James, in *The Forsyte Saga*, who perpetually complains that no one tells him anything. His every response is predictable: the reader can anticipate exactly how Mr. Micawber or James Forsyte will react to any turn.

Quite the opposite is the character portrayed in the round. He is profoundly altered by his experiences. Because he is at the mercy of his emotions and passions, his responses often take us by surprise. We do not have the same feeling about him, that he is oversimplified, verging on the caricature. He does not—like Mr. Micawber, Uriah Heep, or James Forsyte —embody a single idea or quality, but is much more complex. Perhaps a better word for him is that he is "dimensional."

This is a useful distinction, I believe. Flat characters are discovered in profuse numbers in the novels of Smollett, Sterne, Scott, Dickens, Thackeray, and Trollope. Mr. Forster pays high tribute to Jane Austen, who is not only one of the earliest to introduce the dramatic novel but to bring in rounded characters as well. In her neat comedies, the principal figures are dimensional, but the minor characters are flat, yet, says Mr. Forster, "they tend to curve into the round in moments of crisis," as does Mrs. Bennett in *Pride and Prejudice*. Excellent examples of full-fleshed figures are Catherine Earnshaw and her brooding, tempestuous lover, Heathcliff, in *Wuthering Heights,* although the people around them are mere sketches. Many other books show a similar mingling of rounded and flat characters, the latter playing the minor rôles, perhaps a little in the background; this is true in Fielding, and even in Proust's great work.

Mr. Forster looks with some disdain upon flat characterization; he consigns most of it to an earlier period, when novelists were less ambitious. He admits that a static figure may be memorable, but he hardly thinks flat characters populate the best books, and he remarks that they seldom if ever make their appearance in major Russian fiction.

Edwin Muir accepts Mr. Forster's two categories, but strongly takes issue with the values Forster places on them.

Muir, in my view one of our finest critics, asserts that flat characters are quite as true to life, hence as valid and important, as rounded ones. They have their rôle to play in the noblest fiction, and it is by no means an inferior part. He defends this rôle very shrewdly:

> The dramatic figure dramatizes his real nature, where the flat character dramatizes his second nature. . . . Since we are all creatures of habit, we are all potentially flat characters . . . especially when we go on doing things mechanically, saying things, gesturing half-mechanically, without feeling or any longer consciously meaning what we say and do.

He further points out that some of the most brilliant characterizations in all literature, Falstaff and Becky Sharp, for two, are "flat." Becky Sharp is still acting and talking much the same when we last see her in *Vanity Fair* as she is on the page where she first appears. The same is true of Shakespeare's gross but immortal clownish old man, until almost the final moment.

In general, Muir states, flat characters inhabit the social chronicle, and rounded characters the dramatic novel. In the chronicles these static figures "are to be met in thousands, and it is more reasonable to believe that there is method in their flatness than that they are mistakes which all great character novelists"—Muir's phrase for social chroniclers—"have had the misfortune to commit." And, again, "The unchangeability of the flat character is a quality rather than a fault." All that changes about these readily tagged figures is our knowledge of them; we merely get to know them better. In the unwinding chronicle, "they are gradually exposed to us, or we see them in different effects of light and shadow." What is more, insists Muir, disagreeing further with Forster, it is a mistake ever to round out a flat character in a moment of crisis: he should be consistent throughout; he should always behave as the reader expects him to do, for his very predictability is an element of his charm; it is what makes him amusing, familiar, endearing. The pathos of Falstaff's death scene, and the last-minute financial success enjoyed by Mr. Micawber, lack conviction and spoil their images. "Each is robbed of his eternal validity by this attempt to round them out."

One of the frequent features of these static figures is that they present one face to the world, another to themselves and us in more intimate moments of truth. The false face they wear in society, the duplicity they busily practice—from habit, a form of "second nature," indeed—is easily seen through by us if not always by their fellow-actors in the story. This unmasking involves for us no change in them, therefore. They are merely what they have been from the beginning. Dickens likes to lead up to a melodramatic exposure of his more hypocritical characters, which Muir deems an artistic error; since we have known the truth about them all along. "It makes a public announcement of an open secret." Thackeray, more intelligent, usually forbears doing this. He believes that the general reader can recognize the dissemblers without help from the author.

In the dramatic novel, however, appearance and reality are more often identical. "Character is plot," as Galsworthy once wrote. That is to say, in Muir's somewhat similar words: "Character is action, and action character." Change is wrought in the actors by their crucial experiences. Their moral outlook is likely to be utterly transformed. They are not so much aged by the years passing as by the intensity of their passions, which take a cruel toll of them. (Excellent examples are: the three people in *Ethan Frome*; or Raskolnikov, Dmitri Karamazov. All learn bitter lessons and are extraordinarily matured by them.) A sense of inevitability envelops all they are and do. Although the dramatic novel is most often shorter than the social chronicle, the leading characters are far more fully depicted. Since there are fewer actors, our gaze is steadily concentrated on them. Also, as in *Wuthering Heights* and *Crime and Punishment*, the hero and heroine are more emotional, caught in a more violent plot. Inasmuch as the presentation is more objective, the people have an air of ambiguity at first, which is more lifelike and interesting: they are not spelled out for us by a gossiping chatterbox, an omniscient author. We judge them for ourselves, without clues or whispered asides from him.

The ending of the dramatic novel is also of greater significance: it is not a mere tying up of the story as in *Vanity Fair*, says Mr. Muir, "but the final illumination. It is the end not only of the action, but of the characterization; the last touch which gives finality and completeness to the revelation of the figures." The people in the social chronicle, he goes on, "are not in need of this final touch, as they live in a state of perpetual completeness; such characters are complete in the beginning."

In the dramatic novel, then, the characters are sharply individualized, whereas in the chronicle they tend to be typical, generalized. But this does not make the "flat" characters less real; the social chronicle is simply another kind of vehicle for the truth about people, another mode of experience, another angle of vision in looking at the world.

II

I think we must distinguish between a "flat" character and a "stock" character, the latter term one which we often apply derogatorily. Since the days of Menander and Greek "New Comedy," the stock figure has been one whose traits are supposed to be generic to his occupation: the chicane lawyer, the gluttonous cook, the effete dancing-master, the quack doctor, the rascally servant. In every play he is satirically endowed with almost exactly the same qualities. Later, national "humors" add more actors to the roster of stock figures: the excitable Italian, amorous Frenchman, phlegmatic Englishman, canny Scot, pugnacious Irishman—and other unflattering stereotypes. The "flat" character does not belong with any of these, because he can and should be freshly conceived. He is merely a person who has dried up into habitual responses (which unhappily may be the destiny of many of us); but these do not necessarily derive from his profession or race. He may conform too closely to the society around him, and tend—like the Forsytes—to be typical of his class; but even that is a far wider category. Or he may be unique in some ways, yet hardened into a mold that is unyielding. But more often, as in Dickens and Thackeray, he fits into a universal pattern of human behavior, repeated and true from one generation to the next; hence, we recognize him at once, and he has about him an air of immortality. Falstaff is not merely Falstaff: he is all the fat, scheming braggarts who resemble him in all epochs: and the same is true of Becky Sharp, the imprudent Mr. Micawber, and the stingy Mr. Scrooge.

On the other hand, the dramatic character is *sui generis,* one of a kind: his like is not to be met again. He is hauntingly real for his personal combination of psychological qualities. He is seen as himself, apart from his class, time, and social background. In his very uniqueness he too may be eternal, lingering in the reader's memory, never to be confused there with anyone else: his inner life has been bared to us so intimately, and we have shared with him the experience of change brought about by his passionate and harrowing involvement in certain heightened hours of being.

Aristotle, it should be noted, prescribes the use of generalized characters for comedy. He also believes their names should be appropriate, to emphasize their having typical rather than unique traits, unless a lampoon of a specific person of prominence is intended. We find this still being practiced in the plays of that Neo-Classicist Ben Jonson, who names his principals Morose and Truewit and Sir Amorous La-Foole. The custom runs all through seventeenth- and eighteenth-century stage comedy, as witness Wycherly's heroic Manly and his loving follower Fidelia—and Sheridan's archly intriguing pair, Lady Sneerwell and Sir Joseph Surface. But it is also echoed in the comic novel: Fielding's Squire Allworthy, Thwackum, and Square. Such descriptive names do stress how broadly meant are these flat characters.

Ben Jonson's historic theory of comedy is that it deals with the "odd numbers" of mankind, each such ridiculous person dominated by an excessive "humor"—literally, each comic citizen having in his body too much choler, or melancholy, or phlegm, or blood, a regrettable fact which affects his disposition accordingly. This is only a slight modification of Aristotle's concept of burlesque and its use of generalized characterization; the Jonsonian theory was a pseudoscientific attempt to account for the oddity of such people. I would say that figures with such appellations, who are oversimplified representatives of common human frailties, belong to farce rather than high comedy, where the actor begins to round out and take on more individual attributes. Still, when such overt descriptions of people finally fall from fashion, more oblique and onomatopoetic names replace them, instances ranging from Arthur Miller's downtrodden Willy Loman (Low-man) in *Death of a Salesman*, to Aldous Huxley's bright but fading Mrs. Viveash and his Mr. Boldero in *Antic Hay;* and Wassermann's saintly hero Christian Wahnschaffe (whose name will carry adumbrations to any German-speaking reader) in *The World's Illusion*. We are still asked, by their very names, to take these characters as representing more than themselves. The point I chiefly want to make, however, is that flat figures appear mostly in farce and in the more obvious kinds of comedy; when they appear in serious plays and fiction we have —as has been remarked above—not tragedy but pathos. A good example of this, certainly, is Dickens, who often depicts the most miserable and drab aspects of life, and wrings our hearts; yet for this very reason, the flatness and predictability of his characters is seldom, if ever, tragic.

It has also been said of Dickens that he enlarges the oddity of his figures to the point of grotesquerie. He resembles Jonson and Hogarth in this respect. Professor Beach observes that although many droll people are met with any day, it is hardly likely to be within normal experience that as many as Dickens provides in his plots will be encountered within any other such narrow compass. To Professor Beach, however, this is all to the good: it explains why the novels of Dickens keep their lasting popularity: they are "a refreshment to the tired mind . . . fairy-stories for grown-up children." But Frank O'Connor reminds us that Dickens claims to be a complete realist, and then quotes Lord David Cecil's comment, that it would be "as sensible to criticize a Gothic gargoyle on the ground that it is an exaggerated representation of the human face." Lord David argues that this element of the grotesque adds greatly to the vitality of Dickens' characters. On the whole, though, I think that we do not wish to encounter too many such freaks and overcolored genre portraits in our fiction. They are acceptable mainly in Dickens' city of fogs, wharves; or on his bleak, lonely moors.

Apart from comedy, the flat figure plays a leading rôle in the romance, the fast-paced adventure story. Too often he is borrowed from the most shopworn "stock," but he need not be, as Conan Doyle and Dorothy Sayers and Agatha Christie have demonstrated. Sherlock Holmes and Dr. Watson, Lord Peter Whimsey, and Hercule Poirot are, while flat, nonetheless very real and lively creations. Muir says that, in the social chronicle the plot is loose enough to accommodate the characters; but in the novel of action, like *Treasure Island,* the characters are shaped to fit the plot. It is a salient rule of melodrama, as Arthur Miller has stipulated, that the action should not be stopped or even slowed down for "psychologizing." In plays and novels of suspense we are only concerned with what is to occur next: how will the hero escape, what fresh peril awaits him? The hero is always in flight or pursuit; he seldom pauses long enough for us to study him.

The historical novel, with only a few exceptions, also tends to revolve about generalized figures. Two very sound reasons have been proffered for this. Obviously the author whose attempt is to evoke a past age will wish to make his people typical of a social group of that period. But he will also try to avoid adding "strangeness" to what is already strange to us —that is, the background; he will not have odd or highly individual actors performing in front of the unfamiliar setting. He will prefer to make the picture more plausible and vivid to us, despite its distance in time, by choosing persons whom we can easily recognize, and with whom we can quickly identify ourselves.

Something similar is also found in a very different and perhaps superior kind of literature, the modern novel of ideas. Here the people too are simple in outline, for they tend to be intellectual at the expense of their emotional lives; indeed, they are not much troubled by their passions, and so seem less complex. They are like mermen on dry land. In the novel of ideas, especially of the sort that has long been produced in France, the figures are patterned "with a simplicity more intellectual, more analytic . . . in which the personages are more conscious of the problems of their lives and less completely the human expression of them," as Lathrop accurately puts it. If they talk about their emotional disturbances, they do so with detachment. Such intellectual simplification, Professor Lathrop continues, if carried to its extreme, results in allegorical figures, "incarnations of abstract ideas." They are not projected as living personalities. The allegorical tendency is not limited to the novel of ideas; it is also found in the weaker examples of romantic fiction, where too often we have the black-hearted villain, the overly frail and chaste maiden. To Lathrop, such allegory is "a waste of energy; it costs more and is less distinct than the direct communication of the idea."

Muir remarks, however, that there should be a touch of the abstract in every lifelike portrait of a man. "To meet the demands of a changing social order and of developing thought in the eighteenth century, the political economists invented the economic man. In the same way, and at about the same time, the novel of character popularized the social man. The economic man is a pure abstraction." The same thing is true of the social man, howbeit to a somewhat lesser degree. He is not only what he was born to be. Something else has been added. "He might be called the image which every man creates of himself, partly consciously, partly involuntarily, in adapting himself to society; the figure that he wants to make in the eyes of his circle, or the one that his character forces him to make, or partly the one and partly the other. Seen hastily, this social image might seem a façade merely; yet obviously it is an aspect of its possessor, even when it seems unlike him. It is not all of him, but it is true of him." This is the particular phase of a man which the social chronicle highlights and sets well in its foreground. At the same time, the author may show us that a man who wears a mask too long may have gradually grown to resemble it; and, when he is exposed, that important fact about him may be the chief thing discovered. He is like an actor who has played Hamlet so many times that something of Hamlet's nature, perhaps his mordant wit and irresolution, clings to him even offstage.

III

Another kind of oversimplification of character is found in all classical art: it is that which magnifies and thus idealizes. Sophocles is supposed to have said of his great rival and contemporary, "Euripides paints men as they are, while I portray them as they ought to be," by which Sophocles means that he himself depicts men, whether they be good or evil, as larger and more gifted and energetic than those merely life-sized. To this company of towering tragic heroes and heroines belong his Oedipus, Aeschylus's Clytemnestra, Marlowe's Dr. Faustus, Shakespeare's Othello, Macbeth and Lady Macbeth, Antony, Lear. To them we might add, from the dramatic novel, the sullen lover Heathcliff, the monomaniacal Captain Ahab, the guilt-ridden Ivan Karamazov; as well as such inspired leaders as Kutuzov in *War and Peace,* and Gabriel Bagradian in the *Forty Days of Musa Dagh*. The simplification here, with figures in the round, consists of heightening them wholly, or else a particular quality in them—pride in Oedipus and Ahab, jealousy in Othello, courage in Gabriel Bagradian—out of proportion to the rest of their being, and to the normal. Such simplification or idealization, says Lathrop, "emphasizes but does not distort the fundamental elements of human nature." He explains further:

The "betterness" or "exceptionality" of these ill-starred noble beings is not in the moral propriety of their behavior, which may be sinful, but in their great possibilities for good or evil, and especially in the impression they produce that from them some of the inhibitions or restrictions which thwart the full development of the ordinary man have been taken away. Commonly they *will* more ardently and more definitely than ordinary men, or if not they see life with more detached clearness. . . . The secret of their misfortune is that by the very necessity of the case their very largeness of nature makes demands upon life above the ordinary and therefore the less likely to be gratified.

The *pathetic* flat figure cannot respond other than he does; for this reason he is pitiable only. The *tragic* round character strikes us as "capable of change and growth"; hence, the possibility that he will by his own resources escape his doom is always dangled before us; but his rebellious spirit and passionate energy combine to hurl him at last to an unhappy fate. Here we are more deeply moved by the outcome. In tracing this short course to catastrophe, we are helped by Aristotle's concept of the "tragic flaw." That wise philosopher and critic tells us that the dramatic hero should be a man —"highly renowned and prosperous"—whose character lies between the extremes of complete virtuousness and complete villainy; he should be one "who is not eminently good and just, yet whose misfortune is brought about not by vice or depravity, but by some error or frailty." His *hubris*, the Greek term for the tragic flaw, might well be envy, rashness, vanity, lust. Or any of the human shortcomings ascribed above to Oedipus, Faustus, Othello; or the heroes of *Moby Dick*, *Wuthering Heights*, *The Possessed*.

Lathrop suggests that Aristotle's theory is not wholly sound, since neither Macbeth nor Lady Macbeth is "on the whole good" or "more good than bad." He admits that neither is entirely nor irretrievably wicked. ["They went wrong, but they might conceivably have gone very nobly right."] He also argues that Antigone has no flaw, and Othello really has none. He argues his own theory, that in some instances the hero is right but the world is wrong, and he is martyred. This would fit him to Nicholas Berdyaev's famous description of the tragic figure as the "unjust sufferer," the good and great man killed or punished through no fault of his own.

But the heroes and heroines Lathrop cites are far from blameless. In Antigone, I should say, there is a self-righteous pride coupled with a zeal almost masochistic; in Othello, a jealousy born of a fatal self-doubt—being foreign and black, he cannot quite believe that Desdemona loves him; while conversely, in Macbeth and his wife are qualities of resolution and wisdom (who has ever spoken more profoundly and poetically about the world of man than this same blood-smeared Thane?) that should have taken them to truly exalted peaks, had not their goading ambition misled them. Aristotle's description of the dramatic hero seems to me to suit them quite exactly.

I deem more valuable Lathrop's suggestion that change itself may be the trap that destroys the hero. "As the world is constantly changing, no man is fitted to it today, though he fitted it yesterday; and everything in the world is perpetually being adjusted anew. Indeed, the interest of the world is in its maladjustment. . . ." A failure to meet change is a major tragic flaw. How much ever-new tragedy results from it!

Thus the hero of the dramatic novel fits largely into the mold of Classic art, as defined by Aristotle and exemplified by Sophocles; but even so this dynamic hero is found as often in fiction of the Romantic Age: *Wuthering Heights, Moby Dick, Jane Eyre, The Brothers Karamazov, The Red and the Black.* It is here too that we have him guilty of what Lathrop calls the "interesting sin"; or, better, "the romantic paradox." He is the generous murderer, Raskolnikov, or the pure harlot, Sonya, in *Crime and Punishment;* or the good-hearted drunkard, Dmitri Karamazov, in Dostoevski's other dark epic. But it is not only in Russian works that he is so depicted: indeed, this theme of moral ambivalence runs through much of French and English fiction as well. Who is more innocent than Tom Jones, though outwardly he appears a wastrel and lecher? Or more kind than Mr. Rochester, in *Jane Eyre,* though when we first meet him he is sinister? What is accomplished here is another kind of exposure, of the true nature of figures in the round, rather than of flat characters; and also concerning tragic figures—Julien Sorel, Richard Feverel—rather than comic ones. Very often, in fact, what we are led to is the hero's final exposure to himself, his self-discovery of his true nature. It is one application, as I prefer to believe, of Aristotle's term *anagnôrisis,* here a climactic change from self-ignorance to self-knowledge. It is to just this moment of autorecognition that many major dramatic novels build, including *The Way of All Flesh, Victory, Of Human Bondage, Portrait of the Artist as a Young Man.*

IV

When portraying characters, some novelists introduce them to us with a preliminary sketch. Later we see the character in action, his behavior conforming to the premises our author has put down for him. This is Fielding's method, but he goes even further by having his hero illustrate the moral and psychological principles laid down in each brief preface. Much the same device is used by Trollope, whose people never depart from the outline provided for them. He merely fleshes out a black-and-white drawing prepared and offered in advance.

A very different approach is recommended by Aristotle. "It is by their choices that the characters of men are judged." If an author follows Aristotle's precept, he will not discuss his figures with the reader but present them objectively only. Hardy does this, showing his heroes and heroines solely in action, with no comment from him. Jane Austen is fond of combining both methods, as David Daiches observes; her preliminary sketch is only a partial one, and her characters are further portrayed by their conduct later. They do not change altogether, but do alter somewhat. This applies only to the principals; the minor figures in Austen, as already mentioned, are "flat" and delineated in short "set essays."

The flat characters will cause a writer little trouble, once they are established. He invents a succession of scenes to display them in diverse social settings; we already know what they are, but we do get to know them better; our first impression of them is confirmed by their being repeatedly shown against widely different backgrounds. More difficult is the task of the dramatic novelist, whose people must be caught in the process of growing to maturity and self-recognition, most often suddenly and in hurried hours of crisis. The urgent problem here is one of "psychological movement." Oscar Wilde testifies to it as the special challenge to the novel and play, in his *Intentions*:

The statue is concentrated to one moment of perfection. The image stained upon the canvas possesses no spiritual elements of growth and change. If they know nothing of death it is because they know little of life, for the secrets of life and death belong to those and those only whom the sequence of time affects and who possess not merely the present but the future and can rise or fall from a past of glory or of shame. Movement, that problem of the visible arts, can be truly recognized by literature alone. It is literature that shows us the body in its swiftness and the soul in its unrest.

We have observed that Fielding demonstrates change and growth in his hero by submitting him to a series of tests that temper him. The same formula is adopted by Conrad, but with two differences: Conrad's Jim is not shown to us in straightforward chronology from the first blush of his young manhood to his arrival at maturity, but midway, when he is in the heart of a crisis, after he has failed a very significant test—although the reader does not know it as yet. We are given a strong initial impression of him, and then Conrad moves by retrospection, together with hints about the already crystallized future, to modify the image: we learn more and more about Jim's past, which quite alters the figure he first presents; some of the enigma that envelops him is cleared up, while other puzzling aspects of his personality prove to be even more complex than we had supposed, which makes him completely rounded indeed. From beginning to end, the picture of him is a wavering one. Comparing Henry James's simpler time scheme to Conrad's, Professor Beach exclaims: "The method of James is to lay regular siege to Life; the method of Conrad is to lie in ambush for it." We see Jim as he is now, then we are shown him callow, as he was formerly; then we hear "asides" from Marlow about the remarkable figure this young man will become: again, our hero undergoes a series of harsh ordeals, but his change and growth are not put down in a straight line; they are, rather, "plotted" as a ship's master would fix his altered position on a navigational chart with a compass.

Along with this, Conrad has a predilection for having his hero face his tests in taxing solitude. His books are built around the dangers confronted by hermit figures: alone on the captain's bridge of a storm-tossed ship, as in *Youth, Typhoon;* or at a solitary jungle outpost or trading station, as in *Almayer's Folly, Heart of Darkness, Victory.* Here, after his ordeal, the hero discovers the truth about himself; or we, watching him—Lord Jim, Heyst—are led to revise our original impression of him: he is either better or worse, less courageous or far braver and more sentimental and idealistic than we expected him to be. Change has taken place, progressively, or suddenly, perhaps. That is, the hero has *actually* changed, or else our opinion of him changes: he is dramatically exposed for what he truly is, as opposed to the flattering illusion he has too long cherished about himself, or the mistaken conviction others have held about him. Perhaps his latent qualities have finally been brought out.

Such hermit figures are frequently come upon in French novels, and Conrad had read widely in that literature, for French was his second language. But doubtless, on his travels in Africa, the South Pacific, and the Far East, Conrad had encountered many such men who were living in self-chosen exile. They would interest him, and it was very natural for him to choose them as heroes for his tales; and I believe that this, rather than any merely literary influence, accounts for his adopting such principal figures. The problems of the lonely ship's master, bearing responsibilities that alter his character, Conrad plainly draws from his personal experience.

Change is depicted in quite a different fashion in Proust. In his very long novel, only the hero-narrator—the "I"—is followed continuously. The other persons appear only at intervals, sometimes after a span of years have elapsed. The hero-narrator remarks on how they have altered—physically, but also in character traits—since he (and through him, we) last saw them. Certainly this is true to life. We all have the identical experience of meeting people after months or years have gone by, and noting with shock and surprise how time has affected them. Proust stresses these changes by having his "I" recollect how these people looked and acted when he was last involved with them: his flashbacks summon up a host of vivid details about them as they were in the past. The toll that time takes, the gifts that time brings, are thus strikingly illustrated.

The stream of consciousness, having the most free and fluid time scheme of all, is another way to indicate psychological metamorphoses, *hidden* ones especially. This technique reveals not only what the thinker has been and is now, but his unspoken regrets, frustrated hopes, for what he might have

been; or, perhaps, the promises (made only to himself) of
what he might yet be, what he still feels himself capable
of becoming. When we are allowed to eavesdrop on his
innermost, hardly expressed thoughts, we have a sensitive
report of "change and growth" at work in character. It is like
overhearing the tick of a clock in a man's soul.

V

In some novels the minor figures confound the author by
becoming more interesting than the principals. When this
occurs, we say that so-and-so "runs away" with the book. To
prevent this, the writer must work the trick of properly sub-
ordinating his lesser people without having them appear pallid
or dull. He will not allow them to take over a scene, yet he
gives them some quirk which fixes them in our mind. We have
seen that Dickens is very fond of exaggerating the physical
oddities and compulsive mannerisms of minor members of his
cast: Uriah Heep, with his skeletonic "grisly" hands; Peggotty,
forever losing her buttons; Mr. Dick, acting out his obsession
about poor King Charles's head. To some critical tastes,
Dickens carries all these oddities to excess, over the verge of
caricature; but no one can deny that his minor figures are
remarkably animated: his supporting gallery of eccentrics is
perhaps the most picturesque in all literature.

Both for leading and lesser persons in a story, a bountiful
supply of "telling touches" is needed. A good instance of one
is found in Jean Stafford's *Boston Adventure,* where the
heroine falls in love with a young man whose face is disfigured
by a wide red-purple scar, resembling a burn, but actually a
birthmark. She is fascinated by this ugly welt on his youthful
features, and certainly the young man is made far more
physically real to us by this detail. In Arthur Koestler's
Arrival and Departure the hero is a prisoner being questioned
at Gestapo headquarters. While the interrogation proceeds,
he is peripherally aware of a Nazi official who stands by the
window, where the stronger light allows him to search through
his body hair for lice. Several references are made to this,
although the man at the window plays no other rôle in the
action. Yet the scene is powerfully established in the reader's
memory by this Nazi official's conduct. His casual hunting for
the nits symbolizes his indifference to the fate of the prisoner.
In *Lord Jim* Conrad implants an image of the philosophical

German trader, Stein, in our recollection by descriptions of the butterfly collection over which Stein hovers, marveling at his prized specimens, now and again exclaiming gutterally at their delicate splendor. In the same fashion, the brutal, vulgar German captain of the *Patna* is brought unforgettably to life for us by accounts of his girth, the ridiculous and monstrous clumsiness with which he waddles and climbs into the "ramshackle gharry" that flees around the corner "in a white smother of dust," as he makes his final escape from the Court of Inquiry. Lathrop picks out a particularly "telling touch" by which Dostoevski places Dmitri Karamazov before us and makes him palpably real. When the young roisterer is taken into custody, and accused of his father's murder, the police strip him of his blood-stained clothes. He is given a quilt to cover his nakedness, but is not at the moment "so much concerned with the charge against him 'as ashamed to have his feet seen,' 'especially the course, flat, crooked nail on his right great toe.'"

Effective characterization depends very much on the multiplication of fresh "telling touches" such as these. The reader takes them for granted, but they often impose a heavy task on the writer.

Chapter 20

The Setting

THE SETTING also presents a share of technical difficulties, but most novelists embrace them gladly. The novel is a prose form and emphasizes realism; its style ought to be, for the most part, terse and transparently plain. The speech of the characters must be simple, else it lacks credibility. Every effort is made to have the dialogue sound like Everyman's natural talk. Whatever poetic impulse the novelist may have is likely to be frustrated: only the *setting* provides him an outlet for it; for in his descriptive writing he is allowed to express his feeling for beauty and create a scene in lavish hues, if he wishes. Historians of the novel remark that "local color," in particular, is the equivalent in modern fiction of the poetry that infused Elizabethan tragedy: Christopher Marlowe's "mighty line"; Shakespeare's exalted lyricism and rhetoric; Webster's strange metaphysical and fascinating language.

This discovery that word-painting of the setting could be the prose writer's occasion for "poetry" was not come upon early. The eighteenth century, which saw the novel's beginning, had little appreciation of the charms of nature. For example, in Defoe there is hardly any sentiment of this kind; and in Smollett, not much more, though he does note with pleasure the rocky peaks and fir-girt mountain lakes of the Highlands, through which his picaresque heroes sometimes journey. Fielding's background is likely to be pastoral: "the gentle and proportioned beauty of an undulating landscape, softly touched by the hand of man—a lovely English park." Yet in Fielding the setting is quite distinct from the story; it is hardly integrated with the plot and characters, as we shall see it be later. In Jane Austen and Stendhal, any sensitivity to the natural scene or love for it is largely absent.

The Romantic Age brought in a passionate sense of identification with Nature, and an idealization of it. This is soon reflected in the novel, and especially in the "picturesque" works of Scott. In his fiction, as in the highly emotional stories of the Brontës and other prose writers of the Romantic Age, the wild landscape is more than a background for the characters; between them and nature springs up a "spiritual affinity," until, in a most intimate exchange, the moods of the people in the action are shared or governed by the climate of the day, or the changing aspect of the crags or moors. Each page tells us the time is stormy, gray, melancholy; or brightly vernal, leaves and brooks a-glitter, clouds white and fleecy. Scott's heroes and heroines, or Catherine and Heathcliff, respond to the weather, the scene.

With Scott, also the antiquarian, the "folk theme" enters the novel: the utmost "local color" and "regionalism." He took this from the ancient lore he collected, depictive of the habits and superstitions (many of them pagan in origin) that anachronistically hung on in his beloved, native Scotland. His neighbors there were still close to nature and stubbornly clung to old ways and beliefs. Scott, the ballader, recognized the poetic value of such legends and rituals, and brought a new kind of lyricism into what had hitherto been an eminently prosaic form of art.

Finally, it is Scott who excels in the historical novel, where obviously the setting is one of the author's primary concerns; he must bring back a vanished age, a past social order, in sufficient detail to have it vividly beheld by the reader. In the historical novel, the milieu counts for much and offers the imaginative prose writer a great challenge, to conjure up lost sights, noises, and smells, the brilliance and marvel of living in another day. So the meticulously researched background may take priority even over the plot and characters.

Some writers of this Romantic era discover cityscapes. Balzac and Dickens recognize and reflect the sinister beauty of metropolises like Paris and London, whose smoky splendor is a new phenomenon of the Industrial Revolution. If Balzac is not essentially a poet, he is nonetheless tireless in documenting his scene; his descriptions are so minute and exact, so thorough, that Daiches cleverly likens them to "an auctioneer's catalogue." To create such detailed environment an author has to be immensely knowledgeable about every crevice of city life, its many worlds within worlds. The encyclopedic Balzac is adequate to this task. His "saturation" is complete. He sets up a criterion for later "social" novelists, although it has become ever more difficult for them to measure up to it in our increasingly complex society. But if today's writer of city life lacks Balzac's zeal for description and his omniscience, he must nevertheless authenticate each minor fact in his scene. Readers now demand that kind of accuracy. That is why frequently novelists must travel abroad or spend tedious hours in a library, relying far less on their inventive fancy than could earlier authors.

Lathrop comments that all this zeal for documentation does not make Balzac (and I would say this also applies to Dickens) a truly realistic or naturalistic storyteller. He remains a Romantic, because his people pursue their ends, however small and mean, with a fanaticism, an ingenuity, that is hardly average; theirs is a furious purposiveness and dynamism borrowed from their author's own nature. He also dwells on what is evil in society and man personally, and adds to that something demonic; the shadow side of humankind deepens to the supernaturally dark in his work. From this arise elements of the strange, morbid, and abnormal that are characteristically Romantic, however drab the setting may be.

In Balzac's heir, Émile Zola, an intensity is reached that is also far above the level of realism, for in his books of protest "the factory becomes a living and terrible force, a monster; the city lives, the life of a smoke-breathing and filth-spitting dragon; evil powers reign, disgusting and obscene . . . but vastly and even magnificently dreadful." This is accomplished by the power with which the angry Zola constructs his Parisian panorama. I would venture that much the same feeling is imparted by Dickens, in his image of London slums: poorhouses; gas-lit, foggy docksides; dirty, snowy lanes, which often remind one of Gustave Doré's retort that he first conceived his vision of the "Inferno" while visiting the English capital, hearing its roar, and beholding the hellish traffic there. Such is the projection of a personal obsession or emotion in Romantic art.

Only in Maupassant, as Lathrop avers, is a factory "a dull pile of bricks with a smoke-stack. And men are what they are: one as good or bad as another, quite insignificant in themselves, facts of nature." In the keenness of Maupassant's observation, his social picture offered without the author's personal distortion, a detachment which soon sets a fashion for later writers, pessimistic realism is finally achieved. It lies in the dispassionateness with which the background is built up, each precisely realized external of the *mise en scène* added to another; as well as in the novelist's refusal to idealize his characters.

II

Thomas Hardy's approach is also uncompromisingly realistic, and proudly so; but he creates the settings for his pastoral allegories in a spirit quite different from that of Maupassant, and even from that of Maupassant's opposite, Scott; although Hardy returns to the regionalism and "local color" for which Scott had earlier established a popular vogue. Hardy's love of nature is ardent, but wholly without sentimentality. He looks upon Nature as an insensate and possibly hostile force; man's encounter with it is often cruel and costly to him. But Hardy also perceives its incredible beauty, to contemplate which humbles one; and he pictures his rural figures so joined in communion with it, that man and his natural environment are seen as inseparable.

In Balzac and Dickens, man placed against an urban background appears to be a figure more than himself, a representative or voice of the great, teeming City. Hardy's man also seems larger than himself, and so gains Classic stature: he is a child of Nature, a part of it; his union with it is absolute.

Furthermore, Hardy's loving sharpness of observation about natural details is quite the equal of Maupassant's about city life; but Hardy is a major poet, as the French novelists who were his compeers are not, and his descriptions of the Wessex landscape and the tiny creatures that inhabit it are often superbly lyrical. What he lacks in enthusiasm for living, for mankind, he more than makes up in his devotion to the natural spectacle, which he always portrays as though he were indeed pantheistic, which he steadfastly claims not to be. Yet he has an almost mystical affinity for his subject. Assuredly there is a Franciscan vein in this self-proclaimed agnostic.

His words soberly yet exquisitely conjure up the dip and flutter of small birds in flight; the busy, shy life and peculiar gait of little creatures in bog, shrubs, and grove. He shows us the huge-wheeled carts going to market along worn roads between stained rock and rut across the brown heath. His words bring the twilight mist and dawn fog settling over the crofts, hayricks, the thatched roofs of cottages. In a series of remarkably pictorial "set pieces" in *Far from the Madding Crowd*, *Tess of the D'Urbervilles*, and *Under the Greenwood Tree* are described the warm and fragrant scents and sights of a dairy with young milkmaids chatting and laughing, behind the manor house; and the songs and music and moving shadows of ancient festivals revived by torchlight, and the stamp and cries of morris dancers. In any other setting, we feel, these stories could not occur; this triumphantly rendered background is, as Professor Beach has said, "indispensable." The characters too are an outgrowth of it; in any other region of England or the world they would not be the same.

The "folk theme" fulfils still other aims for Hardy. The coincidences that feature his plots are made somewhat more believable by his use of omens: Tess's chin pricked by a thorn in the roses the aristocratic Alec has given her; or the gory butcher-paper that is wafted by the wind along the path ahead of Tess as she desperately approaches the vicarage. Elsewhere I have suggested that "chance" fits into Hardy's view of the cosmos, and hence is an appropriate factor in his fiction. Yet, art demands that the reader should feel each turn in the action of a novel to be plausible. Hardy's peasants are superstitious. Participating in their lives, we are shortly led to share their belief in supernatural portents, which cause "accidents" to seem preordained. We understand their submission to the workings of "fate," for this touches a chord in us, our own repressed awareness of and prayerful trust in the mysterious operation of "destiny." We are all, even the most sophisticated and rational, still filled with fears and awe, and still hesitant to dismiss the influence of "luck" in our daily life. Thus, by bringing in this note of the "supernatural," and his characters' primitive faith in it and hearkening to it, Hardy greatly deepens the substance of his books. Through them, as Dorothy Van Ghent shows, is carried an air of magic: the pagan folk rituals, the poetically conceived omens, the resignation of his people to a mute fatalism, all help to create this magical atmosphere.

Miss Van Ghent also points out that Hardy further enriches his work by weaving through it certain folk motifs of measureless age: for one, the "changeling theme," the ever-recurrent motif in fairy tale and myth of the "highborn hero or heroine in disguise." Such a heroine is Tess, who is distantly connected to a noble family, and places great stress on this relationship. (I might remark that the "changeling theme" is present in *Tom Jones*, too, where the bastard hero turns out to be of aristocratic origin. It is a theme which usually lends itself to comic treatment, for it permits the humorous premise of "mistaken identity.") When we encounter such motifs in literature they borrow "the deep-lying authority of our almost unconscious background of fairy tale and legend heard in child-hood."

By contrast to Hardy's work, most other "regional novels" seem thin and naïve. Their authors resort to dialect. This interposes a difficulty for the reader: while he struggles to translate the language, he is unable to respond spontaneously and enjoyably to the tale. It is usually best to capture a regional speech quality in idiom, rhythm, and sentence structure, rather than in phonetic spelling and local phrases that are not self-explanatory at a glance. In these novels, however, is sometimes found vigorous and compensatory humor, much of it arising from a peasant fondness for exaggeration in the "tall tale" and the preposterous boast. The characters are also apt to boast a flamboyant incongruity: they are often flat and yet highly individualistic. Eccentrics abound in these books.

The "local color" need not be that of a remote community: Ozark mountaineers, Pennsylvania Mennonites, French Canadian lumberjacks of the Gaspé. Some critics remind us that a novel dedicated to "local color," that exploits the idiosyncrasies and lingering provincialism of an enclave of people, can have its scene in a big city like New York or London; in its Harlem, Ghetto, Little Italy or *barrio*, its Soho or Whitechapel, where immigrants speak a foreign tongue and preserve their Deep South or Old World or West Indian family and ethnic customs. The regional novelist is primarily interested in whatever is romantic, picturesque or amusing about the life of these self-enisled communities, that still keep their narrow horizons and odd folkways.

Any social chronicle is also an exploration into "local color," into a kind of "regionalism." The shrewd and possibly ironic observation of the furnishings of homes, the manners, smart badinage, and clichés, the moral codes and customs of courtship, marriage (and, it may be, divorce) to which a particular circle of people conform, provide us with vital indices to them. Here the background is possibly as important as what happens to the characters. Everyone is strongly influenced by the fashions and tastes of the small world, within the larger world, he inhabits, and he can only be portrayed and judged by the ethical and social standards taken for granted by his little clique: these moral assumptions are often, again, a part of his second nature, and for that reason he is scarcely aware of them. The serious novelist is bound to establish them for us as being the automatic reflexes and the context of the character; that is, another less tangible sort of setting. How true this is in a period piece like *The Forsyte Saga*, and in the series of New York novels by Edith Wharton, or in Martin du Gard's great *roman fleuve*. This suggests that morality may be "local" too; and finally indicates that the "regional novel" may describe the life of the sophisticated upper classes in Kensington and Mayfair, as well as the daily round of tillers of the soil in Wessex.

III

Muir considers the social chronicle to be "spatial," distinguishing it from the dramatic novel, which is "temporal." In the social chronicle the people tend to be changeless, but the background is changing always. The chronicle is likely to offer a wide variety of settings for its incidents, many vistas of a crowded, larger world. The characters have fixed traits, but they are forever remarking on the disappearance of old, beloved landmarks, and the alteration (most often the "decay," I would say) of manners and customs. The dramatic novel has a far narrower setting, but a permanent one. The characters change, but not the scene. The fact is, they are hemmed in by it.

> Only in a completely shut-in arena can the conflicts which it [i.e., the dramatic novel] portrays arise, develop, and end inevitably. All the exits are closed. Or there are false exits bringing the protagonist back to the main stage again where he must await his destiny. . . . The world outside is ghostly and remote, and the countless figures peopling it are quite forgotten, wiped out. . . . We are conscious of England in *Tom Jones* and *Vanity Fair*; we are only aware of the Yorkshire moors and Egdon Heath in *Wuthering Heights* and *The Return of the Native*.

Since the chronicle depicts the society of a particular time and place, its background is very special. It may be the Five Towns of Arnold Bennett, or Anthony Trollope's manor houses in his green and gentle Barchester, or the elegant and snobbish Faubourg St. Germain of Marcel Proust. The people's costumes, the bibelots in their parlors, their means of conveyance, are peculiar to their epoch; by being so fixed in Time they make us conscious of how they will be altered, that change has already or is soon bound to affect them. But the setting of the dramatic novel is apt to have an aspect of universality. Usually, though not always, it is a natural scene: in *Moby Dick,* the eternal sea; in *Wuthering Heights,* the bleak and stormy moors; in Hardy's novels, the yellow rocks and heaths. Here the passing of the years is hardly perceptible: ocean, moor, and jutting rocks look today much as they have forever. Against such timeless backgrounds, the drama of "growth and change" is enacted. Muir makes much of this paradox: static characters are placed before a wide backdrop of change in the chronicle; changing characters are set before a narrow, almost changeless scene in the dramatic novel.

An exception is Tolstoi's *War and Peace,* which most nearly combines the attributes of the social chronicle and the dramatic novel. Percy Lubbock says that *War and Peace* has "no perceptible horizon, no hard line between the life in the book and the life beyond it. The communication between the men and women of the story and the rest of the world is unchecked. It is impossible to say of [the characters] that they inhabit a 'world of their own,' as the people in a storybook often appear to do; they inhabit *our* world, like everybody else." But it is Tolstoi's secret how he accomplishes this remarkable combination. Most other novels have the categorical differences which Muir has perceived for us.

In an earlier chapter, I cited Lathrop's argument for a similar kind of contrast between "strangeness" and "commonness." If the plot of a novel is farfetched, or the people in it are very strange, it is best that the background be highly familiar; then we are more likely to grant belief to the story. Lathrop offers as an example Defoe, who sets his "common folk" in such unusual surroundings as a desert isle and a city beset by plague. Contrary instances are provided by George Eliot, Balzac, Tolstoi, who select characters far above the average in energy or talent—Lathrop uses a fine phrase for Tolstoi's people, that they belong to the "aristocracy of passionate souls"; while the world painted by these major novelists is one that we quickly recognize as everyday in their time or even very much like our own today. Lathrop's rule, accordingly, is that if the character is superior in morality, immorality, brain, heart, he should be viewed against an ordinary backdrop; if he himself be ordinary, he is best shown in a striking or exotic scene. Robert Louis Stevenson—as quoted by Lubbock—notes that Dickens' trick in handling his implausible melodramatic intrigues is to lead gradually into them, "through well-populated scenes of character and humour; so that his world is actual, its air familiar, by the time that his plot begins to thicken."

I would say this method works well in the romance and adventure story. Alfred Hitchcock uses it in his notable and fantastic films in that genre. He introduces wild violence and danger in a most everyday milieu, where we least expect to encounter them.

Conrad might also be said to adopt this formula. His environment is splendidly colorful, but his heroes—like Jim and Heyst—tend to be rather typical: temporarily disenchanted young idealists. (Conrad vigorously insists that Jim is "one of us.") Perhaps one reason some of Henry James's *contes* seem unreal or remote for many readers is that he transplants his quite unusual cast of Americans into a foreign society, where —for those many—neither the physical and social setting nor the people are easily identified. For a smaller, cosmopolitan group of readers, however, both the setting and the characters are likely to be recognizable, though they do still have an air of the precious; and it is among these, the well-traveled, that James is apt to number his admirers.

The need for strangeness in one aspect or another of a novel—that is, in the characters or the background—is explained by Lathrop on the premise that for fiction to compete with life for our attention, it must have in it some element of the extraordinary. "It must be unlike life, must have a newness and energy such as to overcome the greater brightness and intensity of our own experience. At the same time, it must be familiar, capable of being assimilated into our own natures." So there must be a union of strangeness and probability in every novel; and to balance it between the background and the characters in some degree is an excellent way to attain this end. (Lathrop does lament that there are still no novelists who can show "the strangeness in common things," such as Wordsworth and other poets have sought to do. But this calls for a great artist.)

IV

It is interesting that Conrad deliberately keeps his backgrounds somewhat vague, to make them more symbolic. He describes them very specifically, telling us of every sight, sound, and odor, yet he prefers not to fix their exact place on a globe. He had Northwest Sumatra in mind as the scene of *Lord Jim*, but when his friend Richard Curle later made this fact public, Conrad wrote him an angry letter of rebuke. He wanted his story to be laid merely somewhere in that archipelago, but he did not ever wish the spot to be named. Similarly, when he finished *Youth*, he struck out of the manuscript all references to the actual shore his hero reaches and refers to it only as "the East." He was seeking the aura of universality which we are told all dramatic novelists should lend their work. Conrad also hoped to endow his stories with a mysterious air, which would illustrate the lure his heroes felt, that made them romantic journeyers. That was an indefinable feeling in them, and one not to be satisfied by their having finally visited one particular port of call. A certain vagueness in his backgrounds is integral to the effect for which Conrad is always in search.

We have noticed how the characters in Hardy's tales seem almost to grow out of and be a part of their natural setting. But in both Hardy and Conrad the opposite impression is often given, too: the natural world about them seems altered and lent new hues by the characters' moods. I have already referred to this in my earlier chapter on Conrad. He has an almost unequaled gift for viewing the physical scene as bright or dark, depending on the spiritual state of his hero. He seems to remake the world about his principal figure, to express how Jim or Heyst or Decoud is experiencing life at a moment of elation or distress. Hardy also selects just those natural details in the environment which reinforce the emotions of his people, or even serve as implicit critical comments by the author: the flower stained with the blood of the dog accidentally killed, while above it the birds sing in the dawn, can be taken as an ironic judgment; or the heavy udders of the cows in the dairy, are subliminally equated to the weight of a girl's pregnant desire. Another master of this art of matching a character's state of soul to significant and symbolic detail in the world about him is James Joyce. But I wish to discuss this subject more fully elsewhere.

Bernard De Voto, urging authors to capture more of the "illusion of movement" in their prose, says that not even the descriptive passages in a novel should be static. He expands Conrad's famous pronouncement, that his aim is to make his readers "see," to mean that they should behold the details of a scene in terms, perhaps, of a shadow flitting or leaping on a wall; that is, the images should not be "still shots," but "moving images." Besides this, the characters themselves should always be shown in motion: acting, gesturing, with the stage instructions frequently supplied by the writer. Action may also be created in the dialogue, by commands uttered by other characters: "Come up." "Watch out!" "Jump across!" All these cause the deed to be visualized far more effectively by the reader than if it is merely described: "Jules invited him to come up." "John warned her to be careful." Still another kind of "motion" in a scene may be created by rising emotional tension. These devices, taken together, can add to the vivacity of every paragraph.

v

Most authors delight in turning out lengthy passages of description, "set pieces," with lavish strings of adjectives. But by now that belongs to a past fashion. Today's reader is impatient and skips solid pages or even paragraphs that do not advance the story. It is best to insert description as unobtrusively as possible, an image here, and the next—after dialogue, or a bit of action—a few lines later. The novelist should "distribute" or scatter his pictures of the physical background, just as a dramatist artfully handles his "exposition."

In recent years two famed and highly gifted women novelists, Virginia Woolf and Willa Cather, have asserted that fiction is better for having far less description in it. In an essay Mrs. Woolf criticizes her contemporaries, notably H. G. Wells, Arnold Bennett, and John Galsworthy, for their almost scientific thoroughness in cataloguing the milieu. "Novels are in the first place about people and only in the second place about the houses they live in." Miss Cather calls for the "unfurnished novel"—she borrows a French phrase, demeublé—and declares that too many scenes in novels are encumbered with a litter of irrelevant facts. This recalls an earlier statement by Hazlitt, who wrote of Samuel Richardson's Clarissa Harlowe: "She is interesting in her ruffles, in her gloves, in her samplers, her aunts and uncles—she is interesting in all that is uninteresting." And Professor Lathrop is led to say, in assent: "The glitter of small points, the vibratory scintillation of lively detail, involves the danger of triviality, superficiality, restlessness."

The opposite, of course, would be an uncluttered novel, stripped of all meaningless detail. Percy Lubbock observes that such fiction has existed, and could exist again. "It is possible to imagine a novel as bare of all background as a play of Racine. . . . One thinks of the story of the Princesse de Clèves, floating serenely in the void, without a sign of any visible support from a furnished world." Indeed, we do again have fiction closely approaching that ideal in the works of Ivy Compton-Burnett and Henry Green. They consist largely, in fact almost wholly, of dialogue; and Mr. Green is so sparing of words that he also prefers to give his books extremely brief titles: *Living, Back,* and *Loving.*

The trouble with such fiction as Mrs. Woolf and Miss Cather sought for, is that it can impress us as more than a bit vague. Elizabeth Drew finds the tendency merely to present an outline results in Mrs. Woolf's work "seeming to the reader a little wavering and misty." Can it be, she asks, that the houses which people live in tell us more about them than Mrs. Woolf thinks? "It may be that . . . if we have not so spiritual a sense of life as Mrs. Woolf, we cannot apprehend life in any completeness when it is presented to us so immaterially. . . . Life is not only inner life. Wraithlike humanity inevitably leaves the impression of anemic humanity." David Daiches feels much the same. Commenting on Balzac's love of piling up physical data for our scrutiny, he says that such background "gives the novel a sensual impact, a physical body lacking in the work of Jane Austen and Stendhal." Bernard De Voto also disagrees with Miss Cather. Although she is partly right, in his opinion, he also believes that a novel reduced to little more than the essential dialogue often lacks substance and color for the reader: "He must have some way of visualizing the characters against a background. . . . A scene can't be only dialogue for him." De Voto remarks that the artist should be highly selective in choosing the details of his setting; they should not distract or bore the reader by being too numerous or intrusive; they should, if possible, be "inside the scene" by affecting the characters, as they frequently do in the novels of Hardy and Conrad. Another good example of this fine selectivity, cited by De Voto, is Crane's simple yet visually written *Red Badge of Courage.*

Percy Lubbock observes that paring a novel bare of most detail is occasionally good, but not very often. The consensus is that the factual inventory can be carried too far, as it is by

Hugh Walpole and Theodore Dreiser, who compile altogether too much insignificant data; but that is merely abuse of a method. Too few externals can also be an error. To most of us, clothes and houses are telling clues, and the novelist owes it to us to report how his characters dress, and vividly where and how they live. At the same time, he fulfils his rôle in a larger degree as a social historian. But besides this, as Professor Lathrop suggests, the setting has become ever more important in contemporary fiction, because we increasingly recognize a man's background as one of the factors that has shaped him. The active pressure of environment in forming personality is widely acknowledged now. "The setting is seen as a 'force'. . . . The plot is often presented not as a thing in itself, but as something caused and conditional, possible and characteristic only in its own milieu. Hence the greater demand to have the setting authentic, realistic. A thin or inadequately studied setting is not acceptable today."

Ultimately, the kind and amount of background detail one likes in a book depends on its subject and aim, and no less on the temperament of the author and each reader.

Chapter 21

Style

So MUCH HAS been written about "style" that I prefer to say little here. Such discretion is the better part of wisdom. But certainly the affair of his prose, how well or badly he writes, is a major problem for the novelist. Every time he puts down a sentence and reads it over to be sure of his having expressed himself exactly, he must be as alert as a man crossing in heavy traffic.

With very few exceptions, a novel not couched in good prose has little chance for survival. But too many contemporary books that ask to be taken seriously are pretentiously overwritten. An assured, first-rate writer resists the temptation to indulge himself in "poetic" prose. Unless he does, he will seem to his readers either very young, which offers some excuse, or else still enamored of his own skill with words and immaturely eager to show off. Every author needs to be an ascetic and work next to a capacious wastebasket. He must also master the mechanical rules for writing properly; a surprising number of authors depend on editors to correct their prose.

Books in a racy style, marked by current slang and allusions, sound more alive and timely; but with their air of having been written in journalistic haste, they "date" quickly and grow pale on the page. Glanced at after a few years, they seem very old-fashioned. Still, our most carefully chosen words inevitably if slowly alter their meanings; the plainest allusions gradually become difficult for readers in later periods; it is impossible for even the sturdiest prose to withstand wholly the advances of age. Think how much of Shakespeare is now unintelligible; we need a scholar's footnotes to grasp him fully. That fate awaits us all.

Ford Maddox Ford tells how he and Conrad determined to improve their prose by avoiding clichés and replacing each familiar adjective with a fresh one. In the instance of Ford Maddox Ford himself, the result of this mechanical process of "brightening" his sentences is often deplorable. His English is no longer idiomatic; it sounds highly artificial and stilted. Luckily Conrad's genius was strong enough for him to escape this fault. A writer cannot divorce himself from the inflections and ready phrases of everyday speech; if he does, what he puts down will seem to have scant connection with his native language.

Perhaps the most famous comment on this subject is Buffon's: "Style is the man." This is true in every art; one has only to hear Mozart being played, to recognize the music as his. Every great composer has his personal idiom that stamps him. One can also identify a painting by Botticelli, Rembrandt, or Velásquez at a glance; the characteristic arrangement, the line, the color harmony, the lighting or chiaroscuro, the visible brushwork or lack of it, are uniquely theirs. Similarly, a well-read person can open an untitled book by a major prose artist and, scanning only a few paragraphs, name the author. The grandeur of Melville's descriptive style is his only—who else attains such an exalted pitch? —and D. H. Lawrence's electrically charged prose is *sui generis*. Henry James's well-termed "Mandarin style" is also quite his own, his odd, onflowing sentence structure simply inimitable. Who is as exuberant as William Saroyan? Nor can a personal style of this sort be deliberately cultivated; that only results in a second-rate mannerism, an easily discernible affectation.

Style has something to do with a writer's nervous system and his psychological traits: he is influenced by his ear for the music of words; and is guided despite himself by conscious or unconscious predilections in his habitual choice of adjectives. (Havelock Ellis has made an interesting study of this factor.) Together with these, a writer draws from somewhere within himself his intuitive feeling for rhythm. From the peculiarities of his senses, his inherent quirks of mind, he shapes the particular kind of metaphor that tells us much about him. Perhaps his hearing is abnormally acute: his descriptions soon reveal this. Or his response is sharper than average to the dazzle of light on a variety of surfaces: he constantly mentions such effects. Or his sense of smell is extraordinary: his book reeks with his references to this or that subtle fragrance.

What is his temperamental bias? What are his preoccupations? If he is a sensualist, he is forever rhapsodizing about the physical: he describes with greater keenness the loveliness of women; he reports with mouth-watering savor a delight in food and ascribes it to his characters, but we suspect that it is his own pleasure that inspires him to discourse on this; he makes us share with him the feel of sunlight on flesh, the warmth and sweetness of wind crossing a field on a June day. His love for every such experience is involuntarily exposed.

If he is coldly intellectual, his sentences are neat and logical; he is always trying to express himself with precision and clarity. If he is witty and fond of paradox and word-play, his tone is whimsical. In all these and other ways, style is definitely the man. No two personal styles are alike, any more than any two men have the same fingerprints. (George Moore, in an amusing essay, claims there is also a relationship between an author's name and his prose: that Hardy has a "hardy" style, and Trollope a "trollopy" one, and so on.)

Style is also affected by the sex of the writer. One can usually remark at once whether the author of a book is masculine (and even boldly and robustly so, as is Fielding), or feminine, with the exquisitely keen sensibiltiy and lyricism of Isak Dinesen or Edith Sitwell or Virginia Woolf. Sex is as recognizable in prose as in the quality of a voice or the fall of a footstep; we can tell even from a voice heard afar, or from the light or heavy click of a heel, which sex is approaching us.

II

"One should correct Buffon and say that style is the subject." This epigram comes from Mark Schorer.

The point is well taken. A skillful writer clearly adapts his style to match a new theme. Perhaps the best example of this is provided by Flaubert, who turns to the romantically lush prose of *Salammbô* and the *Temptation of St. Anthony* from the wholly matter-of-fact manner he uses in his scrupulously realistic account of the daily life of an unhappy middle-class woman in *Madame Bovary*.

Still another instance is offered by Conrad. Few writers were as self-conscious about their prose. He was forced to be. After a few years during his youth in Marseilles, he gave up his native Polish tongue. He habitually thought in French, but wrote even the first draft of his stories in English; yet he spoke English badly—with an accent. He is one of the greatest prose writers in our language. But his feat cost him dearly: his correspondence and recollections of him by others are filled with reports of the anguish he suffered in trying to express himself.

Conrad sets down his artistic goals in a preface to *The Nigger of the "Narcissus,"* to which I have made some partial references. He wants his effects to rise to "the plasticity of sculpture, to the colour of painting, and to the magic suggestiveness of music." His creed is further summed up: "My purpose is by the power of the written word to make you hear, to make you feel—it is, before all, to make you *see*." (The italics are his.) In consequence, he amasses for us a huge amount of vivid detail, most of it rendered poetically: every physical impression of the scene is presented with all its sensory nuances. If there is any fault in Conrad's style, perhaps it is that he makes us see too much; a better aim might be to have us *remember,* by choosing fewer physical details and stressing them by repetition, to fix them in our memory. But Conrad's success is undeniable: his books are almost tangible and tactile experiences for his reader. That his sentences are long, even to the brink of verbosity, is true. But Thomas Moser finds merit in this, too, arguing that this wordiness "dramatizes the overflow of human emotion." Besides, this "Oriental style," as Professor Beach calls it, is admirably suited to Conrad's earlier Malayan novels, with their colorful and exotic backgrounds; although Professor Beach holds that Conrad might have trimmed his outpouring considerably. He suggests that Conrad's method is to hunt for *le mot juste,* the right word, but never quite make up his mind what it is; instead, he puts down several alternatives and leaves them there. A scrutiny of a typical Conradian sentence bears this out.

But in *Lord Jim* and the other novels narrated by Marlow, Conrad shifts to a different prose, a "natural, anecdotal manner," in the rhythm of a man speaking aloud. Marlow has his own pattern of speech, which replaces the author's former tone. Our sea captain is a yarn-spinner; he is authoritative, yet questions much, betraying his many inner doubts. He is anxious to convert his listeners to agreement with his opinion of Jim, or whatever else may be his topic of discourse. As Professor Beach says, all this lends Marlow's narrative a striking air of authenticity: we can always *hear* him talking. Even though his hypothetical listeners—our proxies—are barely if ever named or described, we are conscious of them too, because Marlow is always referring to them.

Joyce is selected by Mark Schorer to illustrate the point he makes in the epigram I have just repeated. In *Portrait of the Artist as a Young Man* Joyce progressively alters the "texture of his style." The novel is in three sections, each covering a different period in Stephen Daedalus's life; as the hero matures, the prose in each section changes with him. His childhood is reported to us in a stream of consciousness. His boyhood is pictured in sentences that have an increasingly heavier rhythm, coupled with an ever-growing body of physical sensation that reflects his expanding awareness of himself and his world. Stephen, the serious university student, exposed to much theology, is finally shown to us in a style that is severe, almost bare, matching his frequent ventures into abstract thought.

In his stories of incidents painfully recalled by a first-person narrator in *Dubliners,* Joyce uses what David Daiches describes as a "jagged line" opening: the fateful facts are introduced "waveringly," in mixed tenses, present, past, past perfect, as if to capture the difficulty of bringing back any lost event to conscious memory; the effect to which this alternation of tenses contributes is like that of an uncertain witness beginning his testimony at a court trial. The mind of the narrator is searching, groping, for what is a proper beginning. In no time, however, the full recollection comes rushing in, the style firms and becomes sharp and sure, and the story continues in a direct line to its emotional climax.

Frank O'Connor asserts that a characteristic of modern prose is a deeper contradiction between style and material, though they match on the surface: ugly stories like *Madame Bovary* and *Ulysses* are "beautifully" written, however realistic their tone and detail. He believes that this results from the detachment, almost scientific and clinical, with which the authors of both these books approach their subjects. (I have already quoted Flaubert's creed that the novelist should be invisible though as omnipresent as God in his work . . . "let him be felt everywhere but not seen." Joyce issued a similar pronouncement, however, typically a bit more sardonic: "the artist should be an onlooker, standing off, gazing down, 'like God, paring his nails.'") This implies that their "control" is almost inhuman. They never become personally involved with the life they are portraying, and get just the results they wish. Besides, neither of these men is a complete realist or naturalist; they still belong in some degree to the more poetic Symbolist school. Combining the temperamental traits of writers in these supposedly opposed movements, they can go even farther stylistically than an obvious "naturalism"; possessing subtler artistic sensibilities than the average realist, they use them to obtain effects in ways that are over and beyond direct and simple communication.

Such effects may have, again, a subliminal influence on us; we are acted upon without our being aware of it. In Joyce, and in his disciple Faulkner, too, O'Connor says, "style ceases to represent a relationship between the author and the reader and becomes a relationship between the author and the object. . . . It is what Flaubert meant by *le mot juste,* and the right word applied to the object is frequently neither the word required by the nature of the object nor the word that conveys that meaning to the reader. Instead, it is a glorified form of onomatopaeia, like the sound of the falling stream in *Ulysses* or the idiot's monologue in *The Sound and the Fury*, where the timelessness of the idiot's world is supposed to be conveyed in a timeless prose that has neither past, present, nor future." Such subliminal effects, if I may presume to call them that, may lead to a "higher realism" through an artful prose style.

III

Style is more than personal, however, and is determined in still other ways than by adaptation to the subject. The prose of almost any writer is influenced by the time in which he lives. What we term the style of an epoch arises from a great many factors; we have no space here for a philosophical discussion of them. The many explanations have long stirred esthetic controversy. But as students, we soon become aware of a distinct and prevalent tone in all the arts of each past epoch; although on better acquaintance we may discover that within a period several styles really overlap in time, one declining as another takes over; and, as civilization grows more complex, so too a phalanx of minor schools seem to flourish competitively in them. Yet even these rival schools, purportedly marked by sharp differences at the time, reveal surprising likenesses and affinities not hitherto noticed, when

critics of a later age look back at them; the critics then un-
obligingly group them together and lend them a single and not
too discerning name: Elizabethan, Jacobean, Georgian, perhaps. These, in turn, belong within larger groupings: Renaissance, Baroque, Neo-Classic, and so on.

A "period style" is reflected not only in formal literature,
but even in the letters, diaries, and journalism of the people
of a particular time. It affects the cadence, sentence structure,
and vocabulary of their prose, to say nothing of the letter
writer's or journalist's turn of mind and critical standards.
Accordingly, we speak of an eighteenth-century prose style,
and we think of such models as Addison and Steele, Dryden,
Dr. Johnson and his eager friend, Boswell, all of whom express
themselves with polish, clarity, and balance. In the early nineteenth century, a romantic excess of feeling and a love for
the picturesque and macabre is echoed in the prose of Scott,
the sisters Brontë, De Quincey, Dickens. Or, if we refer to the
prose style of the late nineteenth century, the English *fin de
siècle,* we have thoughts of the overly elegant and even
recherché phraseology and tinting of Cardinal Newman,
Ruskin, Carlyle, Pater, and Wilde. Something makes the
artists of an era consciously and unconsciously akin; the
Germans call it *Zeitgeist,* the climate of ideas. For writers, and
other artists, it also goes far to influence their choice of
subject and fixes their attitude toward it. One should appreciate that, as a result of the all-pervasive *Zeitgeist,* no novelist
writes in a manner that is wholly his own; and it can add to
our pleasure in reading, to note the extent to which our
author is unwittingly a spokesman for his time, or perhaps
is merely a child of it. Some writers fulfil a dynamic rôle,
some a lesser one, in this regard.

The English novel, mainly originating in the eighteenth
century, shows in its earliest prose that it has a background
of the Baroque. Thus, Dorothy Van Ghent has very perceptively compared the style and design of Samuel Richardson's
and Henry Fielding's novels to the characteristic buildings
of that period. *"Clarissa* makes a simple figure of a circle,
a circle of fatality." The rounded line, the circle, is
everywhere the chief glory and mark of swirling Baroque art.
"Tom Jones is a complex architectural figure, a Palladian
palace perhaps; immensely variegated, as Fortune throws out
its surprising encounters; elegant and suavely intelligent in
its details (many of Fielding's sentences are little complex

'plots' in themselves, where the reader must follow a suspended subject through a functional ornament of complications—qualifying dependent clauses and prepositional phrases and eloquent pauses—to the dramatic predication or denouement. . . .)" This is period art, truly.

In the recent past, the second and third decades of the twentieth century, James Joyce and Ernest Hemingway set the most imitated fashions of prose in fiction. Perhaps Hemingway has had even more followers than Joyce, but I suspect that is largely because his manner is far easier to copy; the trick is to write with a limited vocabulary and staccato rhythm. Perhaps Marcel Proust and Thomas Mann offered better models at that time for neophyte authors to play the "sedulous ape" in the hope of forming their own eventual styles; but to equal the poetic beauty and precision of prose by Proust and Mann takes more doing; most minor or still youthful writers had not the ambition or talent for it.

Hemingway's lean, terse style is not wholly his own creation. Stendhal, Maupassant, Sherwood Anderson, and Gertrude Stein—Hemingway's somewhat eccentric mentor during his Parisian days—served him as examples, as might have the Joyce of *Dubliners*; and amongst his other contemporaries, James Cain and Dashiell Hammett also plied their trade in a similar manner, but they had less serious pretensions. In any event, this almost monosyllabic prose quickly became identified with Hemingway, who is undoubtedly the best practitioner of it. Besides, this style has the virtue of expressing his personality and suiting his subject very well.

In Hemingway's stories and novels we have a sharp turning away from the gentility of Meredith and Galsworthy and Henry James and Edith Wharton; we no longer read of tea parties in Mayfair or weekend gatherings on the manor's well-tended lawn, where croquet is being played; nor do we listen to talk of art and family gossip in Parisian salons and Fifth Avenue drawing rooms. The new subject matter is a celebration of simple people in a very different milieu: prize-fighters training in smelly gymnasiums, and countermen in roadside diners; and soldiers caked by Italian and Spanish mud, in long retreats; and toreadors dying in the hot, dusty bull ring, and hunters seized by blood-lust in the African bush. The tone of these books is, as Douglas Bush puts it, "toughness plus sentimentality," though the sentimentality is Hemingway's unconscious weakness and he never intends it to be there. His

characters are inarticulate, or nearly so. Their speech, therefore, as Hemingway writes it, consists of "plain thoughts in
plain words." The plots are minimal, very simple. The action
is rapid, and often suspenseful. Although the author does not
philosophize or moralize ever, his personal values are very
strongly implied: his love of an active, vigorous life, and his
admiration for simple, virile adventurers; and especially those
men—athletes in their souls—who can bear the trials of living—
being knocked about in the boxing ring, or facing up to certain death from gangsters, or suffering the loss of loved ones—
with "grace under pressure." The clipped dialogue suggests
"the stiff upper lip" one would expect from such men. As
Mark Schorer says, "the effect of verbal economy as mute
suffering" is most applicable. The descriptive passages, though
laconic, are always adequate.

Professor Beach sums up the total effect better than I could.
(I must confess that I have always lacked a personal affinity
for Hemingway's work.) "On the surface the talk is trivial
. . . but somehow conjures up, by repetition of apparently insignificant remarks, a feeling of tension and emotion which is
both dramatic and satisfying to the esthetic sense. . . . Mere
simplicity, when it is deliberate and artful can be a most
telling feature of 'style,' whether in dress or in the fine
arts. . . . It is a deliberate conventionalization, as much so as
any other style." For some readers, in some moods, Professor Beach concedes, all this works excellently. Along with
this, Hemingway dramatizes every situation, externalizes every
mood, with a zest that springs from his sheer love of physical
conflict and violence. I find it surprising that he was not more
successful in his efforts to be a playwright, for many incidents
in his novels show his true flair for theater.

The rash of imitators who soon arose have formed a very
large school of writers dedicated to the *faux-naif*, as synthetic—in my view—as Picasso's similar and more sophisticated effort to recapture a primitivism in painting. In
Hemingway's later work, too, when he approaches themes on
a larger scale—as, for instance, the behavior of men in the
Spanish Civil War in *For Whom the Bell Tolls*—the style
fails to measure up to the task imposed on it. He fills his
longer books with rich and footloose intellectuals, who travel
without money worries, and who are deeply disenchanted
by everything except uncivilized living. Sport is their principal
diversion: deep-sea fishing, swimming, hunting, fighting; and

the simple folk engaged in these sports and occupations are the only ones with whom they feel any rapport. They drink hard, play hard; and, being completely amoral, are always busy with promiscuous sex. It is difficult for some readers to grant that these "intellectuals" are either worldly or intelligent: upper-class bohemians they doubtless are, and their like is met in many fashionable "out of the way" places: little French villages on the Italian and French Riviera, or the Costa Brava in Spain, or Key West and Cuba and Mexico; but they strike one as empty and dull people, without serious tasks in the world; and their often vulgar speech, their callow values, which Hemingway seems to admire greatly, often makes one lay down the book, finding it tiresome. His terseness is an excellent device for presenting the extraverted folk whose courage he so enthusiastically wishes us to emulate: his bull-fighters, his guerrilla warriors, his lonely fishermen. We are forced by it to analyze for ourselves the motives of these wordless people whose inner lives are never translated for us. But his advanced intellectuals are supposedly far more complex, and therefore their speech should be fuller and richer; a revelation of their thoughts and emotions calls for a more probing and intricate style.

By now most of his critics agree that Hemingway excels in the short story, where his subject—elementary characters hardly given to introspection—is certainly more within his grasp. He deserves much praise, moreover, for bringing a very fresh subject matter into literature, and for his conscious effort to "purify" the novel's prose. Before he appeared and became influential, too much fiction was composed in an overblown and fussy style. One might cite Meredith as a horrible example of it, and even Henry James offers us some very bad pages. Hemingway has done much to correct that. And, even though he is easy to imitate, he himself is never a careless craftsman. He rigorously selects every detail of what his people do and say and evokes their background with rare economy, in well-chosen pictorial images. That is why his prose has, ultimately, a muscularity that none of his followers ever attain.

Others who have written effectively in this lean style, however, include John O'Hara, John Steinbeck, and Albert Camus, the latter two—like Hemingway himself—destined to be awarded Nobel Prizes. But I would hazard that the most distinguished authors today using this plain and natural prose are Christopher Isherwood (*The Berlin Stories, Prater Violet*) and Graham Greene (*The Heart of the Matter*). Their characters and themes, of course, are far more subtle and ambitious than Hemingway's; but for the moment I am paying tribute only to their remarkably simple and rhythmic language.

Meanwhile, James Joyce was taking style in quite a different direction, that of overcomplexity. In *Dubliners* and *Portrait of the Artist as a Young Man* Joyce early demonstrated that as a master of prose he was gifted far beyond most other writers; he had also established himself as a youthful lyric poet in *Chamber Music*. But in both *Ulysses* and *Finnegan's Wake,* his major works, he betrays a preoccupation with words carried to an extreme not seen since the Elizabethan days of Lyly and his absurd Euphuism. He also sets out to create new words, a special vocabulary, wholly his own invention; the number of such words in Joyce's prose is beyond count; he might be said to write in a private language. In minting these fresh hybrids, morover, he takes an odd delight in giving them roots and connotations that display his great erudition.

Many of these words are complicated puns, as well; but one would have to share Joyce's knowledge of Sanskrit or Irish history or Classical mythology to appreciate it. Considering how many words already exist in English—excellent words that appear hardly anywhere but in the dictionary, because the general public is not familiar enough with them to make their use feasible in fiction—what accounts for Joyce's tireless and immense labor in coining hosts of new ones? Why does he waste his time and great talent—and the reader's time—at such a sterile game? Is it only a pedant's humor? At all odds, the average reader is not a cabbalist or Rosicrucian, seeking magical and arcane meanings in words.

One answer might be found in Joyce's near-blindness. John Updike, discussing James Thurber, who is also something of a playful word-monger, remarks: "The puns are understandable. Blindness, in severing language from the seen world of designated things, gives words a tyrannical independence." Both Thurber and Joyce take a strange joy in verbal virtuosity for its own sake, and in puns especially; possibly this is because their sense of hearing grew abnormally acute, and a similarity of sounds became perversely important.

Frank O'Connor, who is of the opinion that much of Joyce's prose belongs in the realm of the "crossword puzzle," tells of going to Joyce's Dublin home. At the end of his visit, a sketch on the wall caught his eye, and he praised it. Joyce was gratified. "It's a view of Cork. But look at the frame, too—I had it especially made of cork to match." Mr. O'Connor says that this correspondence, a picture of the city of Cork, placed in a frame made of "cork," apparently gave Joyce much pleasure. It suggests that in Joyce's instance, as in that of Gertrude Stein, words had an autonomous and special significance that only abnormal psychology might explain.

The erudite puns were seldom taken up by Joyce's disciples, but the less difficult word-coinings were for a time. Thus we had a rain of equivalents to "snotgreen" and "Nilebank babemaries." But fortunately this vogue is ending, before our language falls into chaos. I do not believe literature prospers if every author brings to it a personal vocabulary, requiring that the reader pause to examine and grasp each new-formed noun, verb, and adjective. In the best writing, the reader is not aware of the words, they so quickly become images, ideas, or emotions for him. Between the excesses of Hemingway and Joyce, most novelists readily find a middle way, one that recognizes—to an extent the "Anglo-Saxon, monosyllabic" school does not—the traditional resources and beauty of language; yet without the "purpling" and fustian of Meredith, let us say; or a Joycean lack of clarity.

IV

Some time ago, a young writer of my acquaintance sent me a manuscript, to ask my opinion of it. In the first minute's perusal, I saw that he had invented a considerable glossary of his own, as had Joyce; and he had also followed Joyce's practice in the "Molly Bloom soliloquy" and omitted all punctuation. My friend's novel ran for several hundred pages of unindented type.

In my reply I pointed out that typographical errors were bound to occur at the print shop, and it would be very costly to correct them; a mistake in only two or three lines, at intervals throughout the book, might mean that the compositor would have to reset many pages of it. If for no other reason, I ventured, paragraphing has its virtues. Most publishers would hesitate to buy a manuscript that offered such an expensive printing risk. The young writer heeded my warning and, despite his artistic qualms, he inserted punctuation and broke up his text into paragraphs. But doubtless he thought me old-fashioned and a Philistine.

This brings me to an idea advocated by Professor Beach, who greatly favors having novelists divide each chapter into smaller sections, set off by double spacing, Roman or Arabic numerals, or a row of asterisks. This way, each chapter will appear to be built up of short incidents. At present, says Beach, "writers who use this method are likely to be such as deal in the 'extrovert' type of characters, characters who live greatly in the fact. . . ." In novels about these out-going people, "each section brings its neat and definite increment of objective incident or drama."

But Professor Beach feels that other types of novelists should form the very same habit. Galsworthy is lacking for not doing this, and Beach complains that Proust is difficult to go through for the same cause. In Proust, one meets "a certain Teutonic solidity of page after page of unbroken prose, which frightens the most enterprising reader." (Is this true? Possibly. But is not "Teutonic" a very odd word to apply to Proust?) To break up a narrative into short segments is, Beach feels, "indicative of a certain fastidiousness of taste which makes for neatness and order; it often implies a superior concern for the niceties of classification and arrangement, and, further still, a sensibility to the attraction of the perfectly finished phrase. . . . The asterisks are like points of contact between musical phrases . . . indicating clearly the pauses in a piece of music, and rendering with exact finish the effects of staccato and legato."

Professor Beach further believes that the novelist should be careful to end each section with a telling phrase. He commends Sigrid Undset for consistently doing this. Lastly, he says, the author can place at the end of the final sentence of each brief, separate part some word he would like to have sink deeply into the reader's consciousness.

I must agree with Professor Beach that a delicate emphasis can be gained in certain instances by the device he recommends. Particularly, it is often good to drop the curtain or momentarily dim the lights on a scene of light comedy, for a joke cannot be long sustained. But I would favor it less in a serious work, where too frequent interruptions and breaks might cause the story itself to appear too episodic. A dramatic scene often requires a long, slow build-up; a novelist might feel that he should let nothing stop the rising tension of his chapter, which is like an act in a play. One should not be dropping the curtain in it every few minutes. The more prolonged the slowly mounting and sharpening conflict, the stronger its hold on the attention. An ability to keep a scene going, with the drama in it climbing to new peaks of intensity with no let-up, is the mark of a truly first-rate storyteller.

In addition, I doubt that a reader is daunted by a lack of white space on a page, if, as in Proust at his best, what the page contains is sufficiently absorbing.

Chapter 22

Unity

WE DO NOT often feel that real life has "unity," but we do insist that a work of art shall have it. Whether it is a vase, a picture, a statue, or a novel, the art object must seem to be complete in itself, and its design integrated throughout. We ask, has it symmetry, ideal order, logical coherence?

By "order" in a novel is meant that each element of it must enter at precisely the right place and in an exactly due proportion to attain symmetry, and be clearly or subtly related to all the other parts. By "logical coherence" is intended that all the incidents in the story must strike us as "probable" or, better, "necessary," one leading inevitably to the next, and even being the cause of it. In sum, the novel must appear to have a pattern that life itself probably does not have, a pattern of "diversity within unity" that pleases an esthetic sense in the reader. Why we make this demand of art is still rather mysterious. But perhaps the answer will one day be found by researchers in the field of *Gestalt*, a school of psychology dedicated to learning more about our inherent sense of pattern and our ever-present need to have it fulfilled.

In the short story "unity" may be achieved more easily, for the short story usually concerns a single event, has one mood and few characters. In longer fiction, the task is far different. Since the novel began as a mere series of loosely connected episodes, often sprawling and digressive, its integration came somewhat late in its history, only with Fielding and Richardson; and even today it presents to an author a problem that he may reasonably deem the most difficult and elusive of all.

Obviously, the dramatic novel can more readily be made to seem organic, since it has a strong plot situation at its center, from which every incident springs, and to which it is bound; each episode develops within the framework of that single crisis, and the episodes have a causative linking. What is more, the story is limited in time lapse, in place—as in *Wuthering Heights, Moby Dick, Ethan Frome*—and has a small cast of actors. The mere fact that the hero meets a dilemma which must be solved, and everything revolves about his dynamic effort to do this, relates the ending—the resolution—to the beginning, the statement of his dilemma.

But in the social chronicle, and especially the *roman fleuve*, the story elements are not always as helpful. The time lapses may be very long, the setting broad, the cast multitudinous and ever-changing: new figures introduced, earlier ones vanishing, as the decades pass. At its heart is no single, crucial event about which all the action moves. How shall this shapeless world be given an appearance of form? Let us take up, one by one, some of the methods by which a real or illusive unity, at least, is created, even in books like these, which too often defy it.

In *Clarissa* Richardson is not too greatly taxed. His circle of letter writers is concerned with only one subject, the seduction of the heroine; and the novel simply wheels about that hub, that unifying theme, to which the episodes are attached like the discrete spokes of an eighteenth-century post chaise.

In *Tom Jones* Fielding is more ambitious. His novel is half dramatic, half a social chronicle. Tom does have a goal to reach; his birth is obscure, and he must learn his true identity. So the final revelation does refer us back to the opening chapters, and rounds out the story. But, before then, he travels widely, across the English countryside to London; and, once in that metropolis, in many spheres of life. He is surrounded by a host of other characters who are vividly drawn and hence divert us and hold our attention, as those in *Clarissa* do not. All this is necessary if Fielding is to carry out his announced purpose, which is to paint a broad picture of the life in England of his time.

Does *Tom Jones* have unity? Decidedly, yes. Aurelien Digeon points out that the book is held together by a very ingenious crisscrossing of the people in motion, all of whom "take to the road" in frantic pursuit: Sophia following her beloved Tom; then, in a typical comic reversal, Tom seeking to follow her; while Squire Western tries to overtake his fugitive daughter, and Mr. Allworthy and the villainous Blifil also join the merry chase. This is not all. Partridge and Jenny Jones are also on the go, and their paths are destined to cross Tom's; and Mr. Fitzpatrick is *en route*, searching for his wife, and they also become mingled with the fortunes of Tom and Sophia in London. All this movement, pursuit, confusion, is part of any comic effect, as is the unifying concept of "the chase"—which appears in hundreds of later adventure and suspense stories. (One might remark that "the chase" is standard in the films of Alfred Hitchcock, as earlier—and for a different reason—in the classic Mack Sennett farces.) At the same time, the ever more rapid pace, the sense of headlong motion—blurred and almost out of control—is also unifying in its effect, and is also a requisite of comedy. Admittedly, many coincidences are called for here; but this does not bother Fielding, and probably few readers are bothered by them, either (any more than they are by the profusion of them in *Anthony Adverse*). At the conclusion the charge of murder against Tom, and his horrified worry lest he has been guilty of incest, brings together all the loose ends of the story in a climax of unexpected power. In retrospect the novel seems to have been all of a piece.

In addition, Fielding's head chapters help much to hold the story together: they do this by setting a consistent tone of "moral comedy." Consistency of tone, like consistency of character, solidifies a work and makes it seem all one. The reader is reassured by these regular interruptions, the appearance of the narrator, Fielding himself, who casts a philosophical light over all these wild goings-on. We feel that the omnipresent author has a firm rein on the story, the illusion of frenzied complication to the contrary—and this reassurance, too, lends an aspect of unity to the book. He makes each separate part of his story seem significant, by showing that he deems it worthy of his comment or analysis; and, of course, he subtly establishes many interconnections in passing.

Here, then, unity is attained by a plot that calls for a solution, that ties in the end with the beginning; and by an exciting "pursuit" or "chase," and by a headlong pace; and by consistency of tone, to which is added an infusion of the author's strong personality. Many writers have used these devices in the same or, more likely, in different combinations since Henry Fielding's day.

II

The point of view is another way of holding a story firmly together. Percy Lubbock says, "The use of the first person, no doubt, is a source of relief to a novelist in the matter of composition. . . . It composes of its own accord, or so he may feel; for the hero gives the story an indefeasible unity by the mere act of telling it." But perhaps Mr. Lubbock should have added that the author is likely to be self-deceived about this. Because a string of episodes is observed by the "I," dramatic unity does not necessarily result. It is, at best, a thin and brittle unity that the "I"—by itself—lends any work of fiction.

But the singular point of view, first person or third person, does help, of course. By limiting the scope of the story to what one character knows and perceives, a narrowed post of observation shared by the reader, the action is given a definite edge, a sharp outline. Then, too, the story is strained through one consciousness, the onlooker's, which again gives it a consistent set of values—his—and perhaps a uniformity of tone borrowed from his personality, if not the author's; or from both. This happens not only in the works of Henry James, where we watch events through Strether's eyes and participate in his thoughts about them; but also in those novels of Conrad wherein Marlow's voice continues throughout, lending every paragraph his accent, while the facts are filtered through his beholding mind. Even greater unity is reached, for we not only gaze solely into one mind, but Marlow's is above all a synthesizing one. Also, in some books, of which Hardy's *Jude the Obscure* might serve as an example, the effect of design is enhanced by our attention being directed to a single figure, Jude, and fixed there. And in *Lord Jim*, again, by means of the "parallax and refraction" to which we referred earlier, the portrait of the hero is not only sharpened but made the ineluctable focus on every page, by being viewed from so many reflective angles.

In talking about how the post of observation contributes to shaping a book we are back with the dramatic novel, however. We must still touch on the more acute task that daunts the author of the social chronicle, who must discover other cohesive principles for his story.

III

To begin, the chronicle is often a "period" work, a circumstance from which a kind of unity accrues to it almost unbidden. Especially if it deals with a past decade or two we find that by the very virtue of its belonging to a specific and circumscribed point in history, it is encircled in time and place, a particular city, a social circle, like a mirror in a frame. This is true of *Vanity Fair* and *The Forsyte Saga*. The costumes, the manners and special language of a period, give everything in it an air of relatedness.

Besides this, some historical novels revolve about a great event; an instance is Tolstoi's *War and Peace*, with Napoleon's invasion of Russia and the burning of Moscow. As a consequence of all the stories of the various people being linked to the invasion and conflagration, the novel has a nexus, a center.

The *roman fleuve* has neither of these advantages, a fixed period or a magnetic great event. It flows on through many generations, many decades, past many interesting historical occasions; but always the doings of one family or closely allied group of families act as a binding force for the story: blood-lines are shared, and the characters are akin by descent or marriage. This impresses on a loosely connected narrative some stamp of form. The fact is, this theme of consanguinity, of close family ties, runs through period and historical fiction as well; as a result, they cohere even more.

It has been remarked that in *The Forsyte Saga* another pair of devices is used: contrast and parallelism. The follies, intrigues, deeds of the principal figures are repeated, possibly in a subplot, by the minor characters at much the same time or a few decades later; or else we behold the very opposite behavior in a contrasting set of people, perhaps also of a succeeding generation. Two of the younger Forsytes fall in love, just as had formerly Soames and Irene, their divorced parents who are now married to other persons. Equally clear is the parallelism in the moral and psychological attitudes taken by the people in the *Saga*: Soames, the "man of property," looks upon his wife, Irene, as another possession, much as he considers himself the undisputed owner of his beautiful house and valuable paintings. Indeed, all the Forsytes have monotonously similar opinions about money, politics, society, typical of their class and period. But we have salient contrasts, too: Irene and her second husband, Bosinney, and the others who are on the periphery of the Forsytes' world, hold alien values and offer wholly different opinions as a consequence. In such likeness and opposition a novelist has a chance for bold or delicate plays of light and shade, for strident emphasis or ironic nuance. The contrast between the lives and characters of Becky Sharp and Amelia Sedley in *Vanity Fair* is divisive, as we have observed, because it splits our interest between two heroines; but in another way, by its very interweaving, it binds that sprawling book together.

Parallelism and contrast are also employed in the dramatic novel. In *Pride and Prejudice* we follow the stories of the Bennett sisters, particularly those of Elizabeth and Jane, which move in the same direction, toward matrimony; yet have significant differences, highlighted by their always being compared. Here the subplots also contribute to the major one, by interposing obstacles or aiding it. Charlotte's marriage to Collins is responsible for Elizabeth's going to Pemberton, and Lydia's elopement with Wickham allows the arrogant Darcy to display his true generous nature, whereupon Elizabeth's prejudice against him is happily vanquished. More examples of the same kind of parallelism and contrast are evident in novels as distinct from each other as *The Three Musketeers* and *The Brothers Karamazov*. The leading figures in these unlike stories are joined by friendship or blood, and so their lives have natural points of contact, but their personalities differ greatly. We might sum up the point by imagining a novel of three men climbing together up a glacial mountain, heading for the peak. They are united by having a single goal; yet any novelist who knows his craft will insist on showing each man of the three as quite individualistic, and each one temperamentally different from his fellow-climbers. Contrast is best illustrated when it is based, in this fashion, on a parallelism of some kind, and further heightened when the separate persons in a group are held together by a common purpose. To this might be added a build-up of suspense, by frequent and ever more rapid reversals of fortune, which also makes the fragmented elements of a book adhere.

IV

Joseph Conrad began *Lord Jim* as a short story. As it grew under his hands into a lengthy novel he was deeply concerned about how to give it unity. He talks about this in his letters at the time. He felt that it tended to break into two parts, the first centering about Jim's desertion of the *Patna*, and his trial (which was originally to have been the sole subject of the story); and the second about Jim's subsequent adventures in Patusan. Conrad calls on his every artistic resource, bringing to bear all his invention, to solder these two sections into one. As has already been seen, he partly succeeds in doing this by having Marlow as his narrator; Marlow's voice is heard always. From this the story has a unity of tone, a unity that only a personal style bestows. (I even wonder if Conrad did not deliberately name the ship the S.S. *Patna* and Jim's final refuge "Patusan," so that the two widely distant settings of the story would have a similar ring, causing the reader to link them subliminally.) Besides this, Conrad has the events in *Lord Jim* limited to and filtered through Marlow's mind, by restricting the point of view. Finally, the problem of his redemption that Jim has to solve for himself ties the ending to the opening.

Yet there is another skillful ruse Conrad uses to give his book organic form, and that is his mixed chronology. By going forward and backward alternately, with hints of the future and with very frequent flashbacks, Conrad weaves the separate parts together. This may be still another reason, in addition to its psychological advantages, for his having adopted his "eccentric" time scheme.

Even before we hear of Jim's cowardly act, and the ensuing trial, we have intimations of events that will occur in Patusan. The result is, the sudden shift of the story to that place—in the middle of the book—does not disconcert us at all, nor do we feel that the story is abruptly moving to a new locale, that the former thread has been broken and almost arbitrarily a new narrative line taken up: we are so well prepared for the change-over that it seems an inevitable development, and the book has an appearance of real unity.

The same method is adopted by Proust, of course, in his vast and digressive *Remembrance of Things Past*. What gives this labyrinthine book a shape is that it echoes one voice, Proust's own, a very strange one, in every beautifully shaped sentence, and that theoretically, or at least by implication, it is told from a limited point of view and passed on to us after being tinged in the "I's" very distinctive kind of awareness; and that it circles endlessly in time, with each dip of the *madeleine* into the scented tea, or other stimulant to memory, from the present to the past, back to the vibrant "now," with inevitable forecasts or anyhow a prescience of events to come.

A mixed chronology also contributes a semblance of unity to wildly disconnected facts and impressions in the vortex that is James Joyce's *Ulysses*. In Virginia Woolf's more orderly explorations of memory and present sensation, too, we shuttle back and forth in time, and the effect is much the same: the books of these two writers strike us as exceptionally controlled. Both *Ulysses* and *Mrs. Dalloway* have a Neo-Classical time limit imposed on them, as well, a span of less than twenty-four hours, which acts as a framework.

In Conrad, Proust, Joyce, Woolf, a consistency of atmosphere—by which I intend something slightly different from tone—is also a unifying factor. The stories have an ambience: every carefully chosen sensory detail in a scene contributes to it, from the color or scent of physical objects that are referred to, the very arrangement of vowels and consonants in a sentence, so that they give off a particular sound, to create and sustain an aura throughout a chapter or incident. A pastoral setting, the hue of the hills, the noise of sheep or goats; the lavish décor of a room, the glitter of a gilded frame, the flash of a crystal chandelier. Such poetic images add up to an ambience. Some of this is accomplished by a harmonious linking of metaphors, too. A good example of this is observed in Stephen Vincent Benét's *The Devil and Daniel Webster*, wherein everything is likened to an aspect of the forested, mountainous New England landscape against which the momentous conflict takes place; "he turned to Jabez Stone and a smile broke over his face like the sunrise over Monadnock." (Note that one of the characters is even named "Stone," and that in this simile a specific local mountain is cited.) Or, "his eyes glowing like a fox's deep in the woods." And, "his hands came down like a bear trap on the stranger's arm." Again, "his black eyes burning like anthracite." Still again, "he drew back his foot for a kick that would have stunned a horse." In each instance the simile is strikingly consonant with the rural setting, the nineteenth-century period, the hardy folk. Turning to the very sophisticated stories of Henry James, such as *The Beast in the Jungle, The Figure in the Carpet*, or *The Golden Bowl*, we have a similar conjuring up of a prevalent mood or unifying atmosphere, this time evoked and sustained not by linked or consonant similes and metaphors, but by each story having at its heart a central symbol, from which rays out some light or hue that infuses the action, and which also integrates it.

Proust provides us with examples of another sort of device that unifies, the repetition of motifs. In all other arts—music, painting, sculpture—repetition is a means of gaining an esthetic unity. A phrase, a line or form, a color, a texture appears again and again, often varied a little in rhythm or size or tone to avoid monotony; and just as often altering in intensity to lead excitingly—it may be—to a climax somewhere.

Minor variations notwithstanding, an overall symmetry is still perceptible, as in the harmonious design of a rug, a tapestry, a border on an illuminated page, a balanced architectural façade. In *Remembrance of Things Past,* as in Wagner's music dramas, certain motifs reappear at intervals, to carry us back to earlier occasions and bring always the same feelings and remembered images with ever-heightened intensity. One is the musical phrase of Vinteuil that the lovers consider to be particularly theirs; their "signature," we might say today. Another is the secret word which for them connotes their act of sexual union. But also there is the reëntrance, at logical but surprising turns in the story, of characters we have met earlier, whom we have hardly expected to see again, but whose reappearance gives the book an additional touch of unity by a hint of predestination.

In Joyce's *Ulysses,* the vice-regal procession is such a motif. It has another function in the story, to connect the characters as they go about their separate errands, but also bestows a sense of pattern. The chiming of the bells in *Mrs. Dalloway* and the passage of the royal limousine not only orient us to the slow progress of time and change of place, but carry us along with them in London's swirl from one group of people there to another. From this a feeling of form arises. The story is never diffuse. At the dinner party the doctor speaks of one of his patients who pathetically killed himself that day, and Mrs. Dalloway thus hears a fugitive reference to Septimus Smith, who shares the novel with her, though they have never met. This is an even more delicate motif, but is exactly what the story needs to make it "organic" before its ending.

The more complex the subject material to be reduced to unity, the more unexpected and diversified the contrasting elements within it, the more subtle and interesting the means, the higher is our pleasure in it; and the more we pay tribute to the storyteller's artistry. Mr. Forster suggests that the patterning of a novel depends on the author's intuition and that much of what he does cannot be planned in advance. It must be left to improvisation as he goes along. But I think this is only partly true. The author must have an intensely clear concept of his theme and story to start with, together with an extraordinary gift for synthesis. From that comes a firm design that completely fills his mind before he begins to write. Some degree of improvisation may follow, in the working out, to inspire those "local impulses when the right interval is reached," which Mr. Forster so much admires, and which he avers gives a book a "rhythmic structuring." Let me quote from him: "The effect can be exquisite, it can be obtained without mutilating the characters, and it lessens our need of an external form." Exquisite such touches may be, but I doubt that they will ever be enough.

Mr. Forster refers specifically to Proust's long novel, and we have already seen that other factors than "recurrent motifs" contribute to its effect of pattern. Along with its "mixed chronology," it too is a "search"—as Muir points out —and it has unity because we share the mind engaged in carrying out the search. This rounds out the book and takes us back from the end to the beginning. It is, again, like a detective story; it has an inherent design because we participate in the detective's problem and follow through with him, our suspense increasing along with his to the conclusion. Proust's hero wishes to learn the truth about his past; and that whole past, viewed from the present, is "given unity by the perspective . . . which composes it into a picture." I feel Muir's explanation to be more nearly adequate.

Unity in a story may arise from the consistency of a principal character, a howling Ahab, whose wooden leg loudly stamps its pages throughout. This is notably true of *Moby Dick*, where an obsessive search and chase also holds together a long book. But the pursuit is of more than the White Whale: the goal is a metaphysical truth, an answer to the profound mystery of the universe.

Sometimes an author, when his novel is being conceived, has an almost mystical vision of it, in which he sees its design as analogous to a specific physical object. A famous instance is Anatole France's *Thaïs*. M. France asserts, without his usual tongue in cheek, that, from the first moment the idea of it came to him, he had a clear image of his story being shaped like an hourglass. An even hurried examination of the novel shows how well it fits this description. The ascetic Paphnuce is losing his heart and mind to a courtesan. He leaves his chaste life and yields himself to sensual impulses, while she turns from her licentious ways and enters a nunnery. The reversal is complete, and the moment of decision for both occurs about midway in the book.

In Henry James's *The Ambassadors* we have a reversal similar to that in *Thaïs*. The older man and the younger, Strether and Chad, gradually change their attitudes and even their rôles; until Chad goes back to a Puritan America, and Strether accepts the more hedonistic Parisian approach to life. Chad will marry the girl his mother has chosen for him, but Strether will not marry the mother. Everyone is partly successful; at the same time, everyone is partly defeated. All this gives us a beautiful feeling of symmetry. Why it appeals to us so strongly is, again, a question for Gestalt psychology to learn and tell us.

Earlier we remarked on Joseph Hergesheimer's *Java Head* and how it resembles a slowly and gracefully opening fan, one leaf after another in the life of the principal figure being exposed to us.

Tom Jones shows the hero's luck going from bad to worse, whilst his foes prosper; but in the end the weight shifts, as is typical of comedy. Tom rides high while his foes plunge downward. Dorothy Van Ghent perceives in this the traditional "Wheel of Fortune," a design shared since by scores of other novelists.

v

In another class of books "unity" is sought by imposing an extrinsic device: a framework is laid over the events, although it is not truly part of them. We have seen that Joyce gives his *Ulysses* many aspects of genuine unity: he limits its time span and locale; he brilliantly mixes the tenses of his characters' thoughts so that they live in past, present, and future simultaneously; he introduces parallelism, contrast, and repetition and variation of motifs; he sets up "signposts," and his unique style and personality are present in every paragraph. But even this does not suffice to bring form to his chaotic work. Consequently, he looks desperately for other ways to strengthen an inadequate design. To an extent these come off very well, which is a tribute to the power of his mind and very original craftsmanship; but elsewhere they are too artificial and fail.

Joyce's first resort is to give his story a mythical parallel, as the title of his book suggests. Bloom is Ulysses, and Stephen Daedalus is his son, Telemachus, in search of his father and his own identity. (Bloom is not an actual father, of course, but a Freudian father-image.) Throughout the book, and often in the gnomic self-coined language, these mythical parallels are indicated and subtly developed. Many critics are excited by Joyce's playing and doubling on a mythical theme and feel that by his doing so he deepens and enriches his work. But does he? The truth is, the significance and applicability of this are largely lost on a reader who does not share Joyce's immense (and largely sterile) erudition, his special knowledge of philology, obscure Classical mythology, Vico's theories of history, Jungian psychology. (I speak of Joyce's erudition as "sterile" because he used none of it to illuminate the truly crucial problems of his time, but mostly for what seems to me vain pedantic display.) The "unity" of *Ulysses*, so far as these Homeric parallels go, is perceptible mostly only to a handful of scholars; the average reader needs an exegesis in order to have much insight into it. No other writer makes such demands on us, and I doubt that Joyce repays the extra effort he requires if we are to comprehend him fully.

In his defense, it is said that Joyce introduces the epic theme to "mock" by sordid contrast the petty life of Dublin as he knew it; always looming behind his contemporary scene is the noble Greek past. The mean figure that is Bloom is by implication cruelly compared to the hero Ulysses and his legendary feats, and Stephen and Dublin's other denizens are also viewed in the same harsh light. But Homer's crafty, dishonest Ulysses is a strange figure to have chosen for this purpose, for in the ancient epic he is neither so idealistic nor admirable that an ironic contrast is achieved. Nor is the' analogy too well drawn. Do we really feel that the intellectually proud Irish-Catholic Stephen considers the miserable Levantine Bloom a father-substitute? The point is never made explicit, for of course Joyce determinedly and properly avoids any overt statement in his book. But to me, at least, the mythical parallel is too weak to give the novel a firm structure.

Quite absurd, going further, is Joyce's delighted ordering of his book so that the various sections of it symbolize parts of the human body: the head, arms, torso, legs, and so forth. Here he allows his inventive faculty to run riot, and comes up with a principle of organization that is patently nonsensical. What is the value of giving a book this design? It has no vital connection with his story.

Joyce was applauded for his extrinsic devices by T. S. Eliot, who made the Joycean approach popular. Today we have much talk about "myth" in fiction, and a self-conscious quest for it by many young writers, who feel it will allow their work to be read on two levels. Thus a Classical parallel is implied in their books in hopes of having it give off adumbrations of a more universal meaning. But I fail to see how it has much if any relevance. Literature should be drawn from life, not from Bulfinch's mythology; and the pattern of a book should develop from something in the story itself, and by virtue of that alone be integral.

VI

Other kinds of extrinsic devices are used by John Dos Passos. In *Manhattan Transfer, The 42nd Parallel*, and *1919* many chapters have introductory prose poems. Typical ones are titled *Metropolis, Nicolodeon, Rollercoaster, Skyscraper, Revolving Doors*. Like Fielding in his essays, Dos Passos voices in his prose poems his personal feelings, his angry protest or sympathy, about the city he describes. How cheap are its pleasures, how drab or garish its life, how wild and jazzy its pulse, and how hopelessly chaotic its pattern! Consequently, his novels consist only of heaped-up, broken segments: yet the stony beauty and grandeur of Manhattan are also captured, along with the grim side and the dross. In addition to these prose poems, Dos Passos inserts in his text newspaper headlines in large, screaming type, reporting historical events and fugitive and trivial happenings. These headlines run on without punctuation, juxtaposed as in a collage. Like Joyce's "mythical parallel," they are meant to be an ironic comment on the drama of small people, which takes place against the large-scaled documentary background the "banners" provide. One newspaper is announcing the outbreak of a local war or uprising somewhere, another an exposure of graft in New York's municipal bureaucracy, another the sensational killing of a foreign statesman, another a flood or train wreck, or the opening of a new Broadway play or film, or the speech of a hypocritical political candidate. And snatches of popular songs are put in at random. All these help to fix the stories very definitely in their time and specific place.

Encouraged by the success of *Manhattan Transfer*, Dos Passos goes even further with his experiments in *The 42nd Parallel* and *1919*. He includes capsule biographies of noted persons of the decade: Woodrow Wilson, Thomas Edison, William Jennings Bryan, Luther Burbank, Eugene Debs, among others. The only connection of these short nonfictional essays with his story is that the real people they portray would have been contemporaries of his imagined characters. To heighten the effect of discontinuity, his cutting from scene to scene is staccato (a method later borrowed by Malraux); there are very abrupt leaps of time in the careers of his figures. These sudden transitions are like cinematic "wipes." The final impression is compared by some critics to looking at a Cubist painting, each block of narrative a different size, shape, and tone.

The purpose is to give a panoramic view, much as a newspaper does, if one quickly scans its separate and unlinked accounts; or, better, it is like the mosaic report of a newsreel: indeed, Dos Passos calls one of his devices the "Camera Eye": in *The 42nd Parallel* and *1919* it comprises forty brief pieces depicting episodes in the life of a young man as he passes from childhood to Red Cross service in World War I. The stream of consciousness is also widely used, but inconsistently.

Only slowly and belatedly do Dos Passos' leading characters become clear to us; for a long while we cannot pick them out from the generally middle-class masses inhabiting roaring Manhattan in his crowded pages. Many of the other figures to whom snapshot paragraphs are given are merely transients who never reappear, like all those people we glimpse in street traffic or during subway rides who go on to destinies we cannot begin to imagine.

Dos Passos' very original tricks do give us a vivid cross-section of a restless, rootless society. He has also a remarkable talent for sensory description: he enters intimately into the nervous and physical experiences of his people, the momentary impact on them of soft sounds and loud dins, the feel of humid heat and windy cold; the tickle of odors, sour and sweet tastes, in daily existence. For the most part, their lives seem disordered, and this anarchy, heightened by the jumble of their sense impressions, is reflected in the prose style and preconceived design of the books. By juxtaposing what are at first glance the incongruous elements in society, he builds up a many-faceted and "extensive" image of it. This is done, ultimately, by what might be called the "dissociation of ideas," a combining of startlingly disparate scenes and allusions to attain a fresh insight, a device also found in T. S. Eliot and Joyce, and derived by them from French *fin de siècle* poetry, as has already been noted.

A similar repertory of extrinsic tricks is taken up by the German novelist, Alfred Döblin, in his *Alexanderplatz Berlin*. He too employs a newsreel, excerpts from hit ballads and songs; he pursues a trolley car on its rounds to link his otherwise unrelated characters. Döblin introduces Biblical quotations and even a number of supernatural motifs, including visits of angels. His picture of the swarming Prussian capital is eventually much like that of Dos Passos' clangorous New York.

The symbolic chapter titles, prose poems, collages of songs, headlines, biographies, obituaries, do lend these books importance. They portray more than the mere highlighted crises of the two or three persons on whom the conventional novel usually focuses. How people in a large city have their lives touched by others whom they do not even know is boldly established, and this is a facet of modern living that deserves to be demonstrated in fiction. Joyce and Woolf have also sought to do this, but in *Manhattan Transfer* and *Alexanderplatz Berlin*, the scale is broader.

Dos Passos' literary influence was great for a time, and many other novelists adopted some if not all of his audacious devices. The "composite novel" has had a considerable vogue: that is, a story which has no clear or single dramatic issue, but is compiled of fractional accounts of a number or even host of people, the whole of the novel being hopefully more than the sum of its many separate parts. In *Street Scene* Elmer Rice transferred this design to the stage.

Henri Peyre has said, in another context, that "the novel is probably a better document when it is one without the author's being aware of the fact." Is he right? Are all of Dos Passos' extrinsic aids necessary? Or is the traditional novel form used by Dickens and Thackeray and Tolstoi good enough to frame a truly dynamic portrait of modern city life?

VII

Two noted writers of our time, André Gide and Aldous Huxley, have developed still other extrinsic means for achieving unity.

Gide, who is the elder, wanted to break completely with all "well-made" types of fiction. He was convinced that they distort truth. He wished to place more emphasis on pure improvisation. No fixed plan should guide him. Was such a novel possible?

He had been studying Bach's *The Art of the Fugue*. He decided to shape his novel along musical lines. It would be fugal, having several contrapuntal themes. Thus he conceived *The Counterfeiters*. He would ignore any *a priori* idea of where his story should start or how it should conclude. (In point of fact, *The Counterfeiters* does not end . . . it simply trails off indeterminately, as often happens in real life.) Gide trusted that his work would grow organically, if he let his instinct lead him.

He became fascinated by the thought of a novel that would be musical in form. "I am like a composer who seeks to juxtapose and overlap, in the manner of César Franck, an andante motif with an allegro," he declared.

The same goal is embodied in Huxley's clearly derivative English novel, *Point Counter Point,* as its very title indicates. One of the leading characters in this story is a novelist, Philip Quarles, who is likewise interested in attempting "the musicalization of fiction." To do this, Quarles suggests, an author requires a goodly number of characters and "parallel, contrapuntal plots." In both novels, Gide's and Huxley's, there is much talk by the people in them about fugal arrangements of material, variations, shifts in mood, modulations, abrupt transitions. Certainly, neither of these authors makes any secret about what he is trying to do; the reader is kept fully informed.

Gide had been reading *Tom Jones* for a second time and admiring it. He envied Fielding's freedom and felt that he too would like to intrude himself into his story, to offer comment on his characters and their foibles; but he saw that it had to be done more obliquely than by Fielding and Thackeray. He rejected the "I," the first-person point of view, because he agreed with Henry James that the third-person technique allows the author to probe more deeply.

Conrad was another of Gide's favorites. He was struck by the multiplicity of angles from which a Conradian character is seen and judged. "Multiplicity," then, became another of Gide's aims, and also Huxley's. Both men were basically interested in writing "novels of ideas," a form which is more Gallic than Anglo-Saxon. To Huxley, indeed, the contrapuntal "novel of ideas" was now badly needed because the whole twentieth-century "way of looking is multiplicity." In the fullness and handling of ideas in fiction, the then young English disciple was destined to surpass by far his master.

Gide hit upon another device, which Huxley also borrows. In both stories, a principal character is a writer at work on a novel: Quarles, in *Point Counter Point*, as we know; but also Edouard, in *The Counterfeiters*. Both discourse about their artistic problems and voice their theories about what a new form of novel might be. Much dialogue in both books is taken up with this. Edouard is a wealthy amateur. The title of his novel-in-process is also *The Counterfeiters*. By calling it that, Edouard is suggesting that the well-made fiction of his time is largely a false image of life.

Edouard, the dilettante, draws much of his material from himself, and from those around him; but alas, he is not able to transmute much of this into "fiction." He cannot shake off the claims of the form of the traditional novel, to which he— like every other reader—has been exposed so long; and, struggle as he may, he cannot bring any sort of order, even a musical structure, out of the inchoate facts of life. He cannot get far enough outside himself to view the world objectively.

Edouard's young secretary tells him that his difficulty arises because he is beginning his book with an "idea" and cannot fit the facts to it; he should, instead, start with a magnetic "fact" and the right ideas will follow or be attracted to it like steel filings.

Ironically, a great deal of drama is occurring around the preoccupied but ineffectual Edouard: his rival heads a ring that circulates false coins—a more practical kind of "counterfeiting"—and hires schoolboys to pass them. One of the boys corrupted by this ring is Edouard's own nephew, Georges Molinier. But Edouard is not aware of this until too late.

Many other themes run through the book. The characters are perverse and often paradoxical. Each person gives a somewhat "deformed" report of the happenings in which he is involved, and Gide himself never corrects the distortion. He wishes the reader to do this for himself, thus becoming a collaborator of the author. Consequently, a haze of ambiguity hangs over each character and incident. The values are shifting, never resolved.

The action does not go forward so much as sideways. The reader gets a picture of life as highly ramified, of many people acting simultaneously in different places without anyone knowing what all the others are up to; and of the same events being viewed by people of different temperaments, with varied values and desires. The attempt, then, is to cut across a broad section of society; but inevitably—owing to Gide's limitations —only a small and special circle is portrayed. He falls far short of the breadth attained by Dos Passos and Döblin, by Joyce and Mrs. Woolf. Or, we might say, by Jakob Wassermann in *The World's Illusion*; or by Waldo Frank.

Still, the effort is made. Edouard discusses it, and qualifies it. " 'A slice of life,' said the naturalist school. The great mistake of this school is cutting its slice always in the same direction: in the direction of time, lengthwise. Why not breadthwise, depthwise? As for me, I prefer not to cut at all. Understand me: I should like to get everything into this novel." His project is so ambitious, that explicably it never gets written.

About one-fourth of *The Counterfeiters* is devoted to Edouard's notebook, in which he confides his hopes for his unrealized novel, and the frustrations and difficulties he meets. Meanwhile, Gide himself was keeping a journal of his own progress, an account of his actual hopes and setbacks while composing his book. Later he published this, too, though separately. So that we have a journal in which a novelist has a day-to-day report of his writing a "musical" novel *about* a novelist trying to write a "musical" novel. One can only compare this to a set of Chinese boxes, one box within a slightly larger box, and that box within a somewhat larger one, and so on. (Gide was an inveterate journal-keeper, and something of an exhibitionist: he issued these descriptions of his most intimate thoughts annually, and they add up to many volumes.)

In general, where Edouard fails to compose his dreamed-of book, Gide himself does bring off at least a part of his experiment successfully. Certainly, *The Counterfeiters* is interesting; and particularly to critics and students of the many metamorphoses of the novel form, or in this instance, a species of little form or no form at all.

Yet this major novel has many faults. In his early venture, *Fruits of Earth*, Gide wrote prose marked by a ripe and pagan sensuality; but his subsequent writing is pale, and this anemic quality is evident in *The Counterfeiters*. He explains that he is seeking to do away not only with plot and form in the novel, but also with description of the physical background and the outward appearance of his people, to center his gaze on their inner life. He feels that the still camera and motion-picture camera record the "material clutter" of a scene better than words can aspire to do, and hence the novelist should no longer bother with naturalistic details which are now extraneous. He fancies a future technique of prose fiction that might be approximate to abstract painting: his term for it is the *roman pur*. An ingenious rationalization? The criticism brought against those authors who have advocated the *novel demeublé* might be applied to Gide as well. His works often lack tangibility and impact. We do not experience them with our senses. What is more, the abrupt transitions make his narrative line too discontinuous: he scorns to sustain his dramatic scenes and conflicts, and to develop his characters. The reader views them with detachment: the constant talk about the esthetics of the novel prevents one from becoming involved in the story itself or having an emotional response to it. The musical analogy is hardly valid, either: the final impression of the book is one of formlessness, not of any kind of integration. Edouard, like Gide himself, never commits himself to a theory or technique.

Huxley's *Point Counter Point* is livelier by far, filled with vivacious wit and attractive erudition. He is a learned writer whose intellectual characters discourse on a large number of esoteric subjects without ever becoming boring or pedantic. He creates them as genuinely brilliant conversationalists, and their ideas seem spontaneous. So, his novel is packed with dazzling talk. The people, though odd, are much more normal than Gide's; and, besides, this is obviously a *roman à clef*—critics and readers lost no time identifying the leading figures with prominent persons in London's literary world—and this adds to the book's considerable interest, as well as to its value as social history. As always, Huxley writes with remarkable grace, in a highly personal style rich with physical imagery, and with exuberant humor. In describing the painful death of a child from meningitis, he shows himself fully capable of creating a tragic mood that deeply moves the reader. Though not as effective a work as his earlier *Antic Hay*, perhaps, *Point Counter Point* still proves Huxley a novelist of rare distinction.

The contrapuntality is here, as well as ironic contrast. In alternating scenes, each person in this striking group vies for our attention, our sympathy or perhaps our loathing. Their ideas are strongly at variance; each tends to view the world in terms of his own profession or scholarly specialty (which causes them to differ among themselves as much as do their temperaments, which are also quite opposite); everything bespeaks "relativity," everything is—indeed—"multiplicity"; life also seems, most of the time, ridiculous, or at least exceedingly odd. Huxley looks at the twentieth century with the "innocent eye" of a Mrs. Woolf, to whom he also owes a considerable literary debt (as he does to such earlier English novelists of ideas as Peacock and Norman Douglas, who present talkative characters quite as eccentric, though they are perhaps not quite as much spokesmen for the warring philosophies of their time.) By violent juxtapositions, by witty debates, by ironic high comedy—sometimes with frightening overtones—the novel is a perfect mirror of its decade, or at least of the London *intelligentsia* of that day.

A novel of ideas runs the great risk that its figures may seem to be mere mouthpieces for a scolding author. To avoid this, the characters must first be established as interesting in their own right, as flesh-and-blood persons. In Thomas Mann's *Dr. Faustus,* for instance, this is not done. We are plunged immediately into intellectual and esthetic controversy, without having had time to learn much if anything about the disputants. The result is deadly. Is there a duller work of fiction than *Dr. Faustus*? Huxley does not make this mistake. It is objected that his people talk too much, but of course they do, and that is just as it should be. It is one of the characteristics of intellectuals that they talk incessantly. That is both their virtue and fault. A point is also made that Huxley's people are too "odd," too "grotesque"; but anyone who knows the upper- and lower-class bohemians who chatter away and write in the Bloomsburys and Greenwich Villages of our Western culture can testify to the accuracy of these portraits; Huxley's figures are not caricatures at all, or barely so.

One able but momentarily confused critic argues that Huxley's people do not embody in their lives and personalities the ideas they propound. Yet, a paragraph earlier, the same critic says that "the real nature of intellectuals can seldom be judged by the ideas they spout. They tend to throw up smoke screens between themselves and the world, and between their real selves and their imaginary selves with which it is their pleasure to live." I find this observation truly astute, but it can hardly be reconciled with the critic's own objection that the conduct of Huxley's people does not always jibe with their ideologies. Huxley's point, if anything, is precisely that: men's professions and their deeds are often sharply at variance. Indeed, in the very untenability of the "ideas men live by" there is an element of comedy that Huxley exploits.

The "musical pattern" is far more apparent in *Point Coun-*

ter Point than in its model, *The Counterfeiters*. But this seems to me of less consequence. I do not believe that the fugal form of the novel, the repetition and variation of motifs, the sprightly changes of tempo, account at all for its popular success, which has been much greater—at least in the English-speaking world—than Gide's. More likely the acclaim it has won is due to the loquacious vitality of its characters, the freshness of its erudition, and the relevance of the topics the book discusses. It ranges far beyond the narrow themes that preoccupy Gide's principal figures, and shows us a far broader and more significant segment of twentieth-century society.

Artistically, too, Huxley's book is the more effective. The aims that André Gide set himself are essentially contradictory. He attempts to be "anti-realistic"; he wants to bring the author back into the story, in a transparent disguise; and also to do away with formal plot, physical description. At the same time, he seeks for a higher "psychological realism" in his work, which he hopes to achieve by not "reshaping" his characters to fit into a story line, and by not making them too consistent, or too clearly or plausibly motivated. Are not most of these negative goals? He wants to write a book that shall be mostly unwritten. But then again, he seeks to give his work a "musical structure"; he wishes to produce a novel which shall be formless and yet have form. It must strike us that he is trying to accomplish too many things at once, and also to attain ends which are completely antithetical.

In recent years I have met and talked to many writers who tell me that they construct novels along musical lines: one informs that his latest book is in essence "symphonic," another proudly likens the design of his work to a "suite." Much as I respect Huxley's achievement, I do not believe it should be attempted again. To me it seems that each of the arts has its own forms, proper to its own medium. I cannot imagine why anyone should want to transplant an alien form into literature, which has its own natural ways of shaping itself. To organize a novel as though it were a musical work, an affair of horns, trumpets, strings and cymbals, is preposterous. One might just as well try to impose the principles of sculpture onto fiction. In any event, having been undertaken twice by two renowned novelists, is this truly vain experiment worth repeating?

The Chinese-box novel—that is, the novel within the novel —has also been copied many times since Gide and Huxley tried it. Another example of it is provided by a Polish author,

Ferdynand Goetel, in his *From Day to Day;* still another is Doris Lessing's *The Golden Notebook.* In both these books a writer is keeping a diary while composing a novel. When done the first or second time, it is a *tour de force,* but surely its freshness as a theme has been exhausted by now. It also has an unpleasant quality of narcissism. It is all too self-conscious. Aside from this, the device is self-defeating: it hardly allows the reader to lose himself in the story; he is always being reminded of its fictional aspects. This is not the art that conceals art. The writer is best not portrayed in his shirtsleeves, unshaven, with his collar open, and ink smudged on his fingers. The image is a distracting one. All works of art should keep their invaluable aura of mystery. The reader should wonder: "How was this created?" He should not be told by an indiscreet novelist, whose only excuse is that he is a chatterbox by nature.

Chapter 23

Other Directions

IN SOME WAYS *The Counterfeiters* has been the harbinger of a newer movement in French letters, whose members are variously called the objectivists, the Neo-Realists, or *L'école du regard* (The School of Viewers). For some time there had been French writers (most artistic "isms" are born in Paris) who were dissatisfied with traditional fiction. More and more in their books appeared the "anti-hero," a principal figure without heroic qualities of any sort, often a man lost and purposeless. He is found, particularly, in novels like Gide's *Lafcadio's Adventures*, Sartre's *Nausea*, and Camus's *The Stranger*. Gide's anti-hero Lafcadio and Camus's anti-hero Mersault commit murders quite casually, for hardly any reason. Life has little meaning and no restraints. The leading characters are, in the purest sense of the phrase, atheistic existentialists. In Sartre's book, Roquentin is a portrait of the disintegration of a personality. Yet, in form, these are still somewhat conventional novels. But now a group of new authors, Alain Robbe-Grillet, Nathalie Sarraute, Michel Butor, Claude Simon, Marguerite Duras, Claude Ollier, Marc Saporta, revolt against all previous ways of writing fiction: they seek only the barest semblance of a plot, or no plot at all; hardly any characterization; and, certainly, no hint of ideas or philosophizing in their books. Hence, what they turn out is sometimes known as the "anti-novel." They feel that all conventions of fiction are worn out, that all novelistic attempts at psychologizing—even Proust's—are obvious and cliché, and should either be omitted altogether or else infinitely refined. Nathalie Sarraute is quoted as saying: "'Psychology' is one word that no author today can hear mentioned in connection with himself without lowering his eyes and blushing!"

Each of the writers in this school has a somewhat different aim and method: generalizations about them are not easy. At present the best known, except possibly for Miss Sarraute, is Alain Robbe-Grillet (*In the Labyrinth, The Voyeur,*

Jealousy). He often acts as spokesman for the group. His work has fairly definite traces of plot, sometimes even the outline of a story of suspense or detection; but his whole emphasis is upon capturing the "thingness" of physical objects, which are to be seen for themselves, as if sharply recorded and slightly magnified by an all-revealing slow-motion camera. Since he is forever pausing to do this, the narrative tempo is agonizingly slow and demands much patience from the reader. Robbe-Grillet was formerly an engineer and has a fondness for describing everything with geometrical exactitude. He has a vision of nature rather like that of Cézanne; he perceives inherent shapes in things: rectangles, circles, squares. But his point is that no human value or association should be attached to the worldly objects: they exist apart from man, have their own attributes, and now for the first time—he believes—are being seen in fiction for what they are. It is impossible and absurd to suppose there can be any communion or exchange between man and his physical environment: it is neither hostile nor friendly to him, but wholly apart. It is to be studied coldly and "with no softness." Some French critics dub this approach *choisisme*. Robbe-Grillet ends the "pathetic fallacy" of poets, who endow Nature with spirits, and renounces Balzac's technique of imagining and writing about the world that encircles man as though it is an extension of his own qualities, and in turn a palpable force acting upon him.

This is a rigid objectivity which even Maupassant never approximated. Robbe-Grillet's characters too exist purely in physical sensation: their author offers no interpretation of them, and ignores any complex thoughts or involved feelings they might have; he reports only their nervous awareness and most basic perceptions.

Here is an excerpt from *In the Labyrinth*:

The man looks down at the smooth snow, where the newly made footprints turn at right angles just in front of him. In the section parallel to the sidewalk the footprints are wide apart and smudged by running, a tiny heap of snow having been thrown up behind each one by the movement of the shoes; on the other hand, the few steps leading to the path show the pattern of the soles very clearly: a series of chevrons across the width of the sole and, beneath the heel, a cross inscribed in a circle—that is, on

the heel itself, a cross incribed in a circular depression in
the rubber (a second round hole, much shallower and of
extremely small diameter, may indicate the center of the
cross, with the shoe size shown by figures in relief: thirty-
two, perhaps thirty-three or thirty-four).

The soldier, who had bent over slightly to examine the
details of the footprints, then walks to the path. As he
passes it he tries to push open the apartment-house door,
but the latter resists: it is shut tight. It is a wooden door
with ornamental moldings, with extremely narrow jambs on
either side. The man continues walking toward the corner
of the building and turns down the cross street, which is
as empty as the one he has just left.

The cross street, like the other, leads to a right-angle
crossroads with a final street lamp set some ten yards before
the end of the sidewalk and identical façades on each
side. The base of the cast-iron lamp post is a truncated
cone embossed with a strand of ivy, with the same curves,
the same leaves growing at the same places on the same
stems, the same faults in the casting. The entire design is
accentuated by the same borders of snow. Perhaps the
meeting was supposed to be at this crossroads.

The soldier raises his eyes to look for the enamel plaques
which should show the names of these streets. There is
nothing visible on one of the stone walls at the corner. On
the other, about three yards above the ground, is attached
the standard blue plaque from which the enamel has chipped
off in large flakes, as if boys had taken it as a target for
throwing pebbles; only the word "Rue" is still legible and,
further on, the two letters ". . . na . . ." followed by a down-
stroke interrupted by the concentric rings of the next chip.
The name must have been an extremely short one. The dep-
redations are quite old, for the exposed metal is already
badly rusted.

In Robbe-Grillet's novels there is much repetition: the
same "things" are seen over and over from slightly different
angles. Space and time are not formally organized but "dis-
mantled" and sometimes take on a nightmarish aspect, they
metamorphose into new combinations so rapidly and endlessly. Past and present events are put down exactly as they
occur in consciousness; no "values" are intruded. Again, a film
seems to be unwinding before our gaze, but it is an uncut

film: it has no dramatic arrangement or even lucid order. All experiences are given exactly the same weight by the perceiver, the anti-hero (as, for instance, the footsteps in the snow, the eroded street sign, in the excerpt I have quoted above, are equated with his unexpressed motive in going to the house). It then remains for the reader to complete the story, to find in it and add to it the significance of the events. If Robbe-Grillet presents terrifying mysteries in his anti-novels (in *Jealousy*, is the wife an adultress? in *The Voyeur*, is Mathias a compulsive murderer of little girls?), the reader must determine the answers to them too for himself; M. Robbe-Grillet never tells us. Surprisingly, by the compilation of so many isolated and uninterpreted facts, offered dispassionately, without comment, without apparent "organization," portraits of amazing sharpness do evolve: seldom have the emotions of jealousy, its insane depths and suspicions, or the minute-by-minute life of a thoughtless and obsessed child-murderer, been so tangibly realized. These "unwritten" novels have a tremendous cumulative impact.

Obviously, despite all the disclaimers, there *is* much planning here, much painstaking selectivity; and, too, M. Robbe-Grillet attaches much human significance (at least, of a geometric character) to physical objects, whether or not he admits it. But he does see the world with startling newness. He says: "We ascertain from day to day, in those who are most conscious, an increasing repugnance for words of a visceral, analogical, or magical character. Meanwhile, the optical, descriptive adjective, the one that is content to measure, situate, limit, define, is probably showing the difficult path to a new fictional art." It is too early to predict, but perhaps this French Neo-Realist will prove to be a major innovator.

On the other hand, some critics complain that this heavy-footed narrative pace, this insistence on reproducing page after page of factual minutiae, are deadening. We are shown so much that very soon it is tiresome and confusing, and we see less clearly. Furthermore, the author is making such a strenuous effort to notice each tiny facet that his descriptions seem distortions from the unnatural strain of his looking so hard, so closely, and so long. A close-up on film may give us the same sense of unreality as a result of its gross exaggeration. The critics also say that M. Robbe-Grillet makes an impossible demand on any novelist, by urging that he see things as they *are*, not as people take them to be, since we can never apprehend objective reality. To assert that the truth about the physical world can be obtained by the eye is a hopeless pretension; and it is quite unlikely that even such man-made instruments as calipers and rules can give us an actual measure of *things*. But this leads us into metaphysical problems that are rather outside a literary discussion.

Close in spirit to Robbe-Grillet are Claude Ollier and Claude Simon. Both also produce with scientific fervor the most exact possible approximations of the physical world. Significantly, Simon is a former botanist; his precise catalogues of objects and sensations sometimes run on in sentences a thousand words or more in length, with involved parentheses within parentheses. He exclaims, "To know is to possess!" His most admired work to date is *The Wind,* and his purpose is to do away with the story element *per se.* He supports his esthetic aim with a statement from Boris Pasternak, "One does not see the story any more than one sees the grass growing," but this overlooks that Pasternak constructs elaborate plots in his own novels, to judge by his acclaimed *Dr. Zhivago.* It is generally conceded that Simon writes with power. Of Claude Ollier (*The Setting*), François Mauriac exclaims:

What an eye! Every particle of the desert sand, of the barren cliffs, of the hardy tufts of grass, every line along a track or shade of a teapot is patiently described. . . . The theme is that of a mystery story laid in the desert. But all the talent, which is rich, is lavished on the inventory of objects. Man is relegated where he belongs: he is a being without communion with things. . . . Human beings themselves yearn only for geometric soullessness.

Michel Butor is another gifted and successful member of this school. His *A Change of Heart,* winning the Prix Renaudot, has already sold over one hundred thousand copies, most unusual in France. His book is about a French typewriter company executive, Delmont, on a train from Paris to Rome, and is written in the second person. The first words of it are, "You put your left foot forward." Butor hoped that by this technique the reader would identify himself much more closely with the anti-hero Delmont: both would be "you." The traveler from Rome is planning to leave his wife and four children and join his mistress, Cécile. On the long journey he debates with himself. His torment, like that of the principal in Robbe-Grillet's *Jealousy*, is portrayed by letting us peer into his mind, which shuttles back and forth between past, present, and the projected future; and between images of the two cities that represent his divided allegiance. Sensations are fragmented. Butor terms his technique "methodical experience," and confesses his debt to mathematicians, engineers, and botanists. The emphasis throughout is on innumerable physical details, yet Butor is not as fanatical as other writers of this group about excluding all psychologizing or dispensing with all symbolic connotations in his factual descriptions of the environment.

In a later book, *Degrés*, the second person is used again, but not as consistently, the time is once more mixed and often confused. Butor holds that each new book calls for a change in technique, and on occasion indulges in eccentric punctuation, frequently omitting capital letters from the start of sentences, though quite as often he employs them elsewhere. His other works include *Passing Time*, which features a diary in which the leading figure simultaneously records happenings of the present moment and of several months earlier; and *Mobile*, a survey of the United States that borrows many tricks of style from Dos Passos.

As has already been remarked, Nathalie Sarraute disdains Proustian—and Joycean—characterizations as too obvious. She believes that for too long the novel has been populated with "defined types": the jealous husband or lover, the careerist, the cynical man of the world, the lady social-climber, the sensitive and rebellious youth, it may be; and many others, all of whose contours are quickly recognizable to the reader. In this respect, Proust and Joyce arrive at portraits that, however more complex and "tedious" their methods, give us people little different in outline from those offered boldly and directly by a Hemingway. What is more, Joyce's characters live too much in the past, seldom in past and present at exactly the same moment. Proust is also forever calling upon the "intellect" of the reader to help him, instead of providing the very feel of "reliving an experience"; so that the reader, "without knowing too well what he is doing, or where he is going, will accomplish actions himself—which has always been and still is the proper function of every work in the novel form."

Accordingly, Miss Sarraute herself, in *Portrait of a Man Unknown*, *The Planetarium*, and other books, plunges into psychology to a depth not hitherto reached in fiction; so far below the surface of consciousness that many of the manifestations she seeks to describe are nameless. She has borrowed a phrase for them, *tropisms*, from biologists who apply that term to microscopic, formless, nascent organisms. It is our elementary, wordless emotional disturbances that she wishes to depict: feelings and responses of which we are not normally aware, for which we have hardly any words; it is as though Miss Sarraute says that the age of "molecular psychology" is ended: within the molecule revolves its atoms, within the atoms their protons, and within the protons their mesons, and so on—and it is this ultimate "mesonic psychology" that she will give us. Beneath the level of the most commonplace conversation, which may outwardly concern only a small domestic crisis, the emotions, reactions, hidden and protean fears, the angers, the hopes of her characters are raging, thrusting, withdrawing; all this she will try to indicate to us, although these elementary movements within us never reach the stage of even half-conscious formulation in the characters' minds. This does make for fascinating reading for her clique of admirers, but others are apt to find Miss Sarraute's novels difficult and boring. Joyce's inner monologues, chaotic though they be, are nothing like this.

Many of Miss Sarraute's figures have no names: they are "he," "she," "you," "I." She often writes in the first person. In *The Planetarium*, too, there is no hero at all. As for secondary characters, they may be very abstract: they are more or less distorted projections of the "I" who views others in terms of himself, who finds in others only the qualities that interest him. "In the same way," Miss Sarraute propounds, "modern painting plucks the object from the universe of the spectator and deforms it in order to segregate the pictorial element." To highlight conversation, since the characters' almost imperceptible responses to words are all-important, the books are often bare of physical description. In this, they resemble the works of Ivy Compton-Burnett, which also consist mostly of dialogue—Miss Sarraute has expressed her high esteem for this English writer whose style is so unconventional. But what Miss Sarraute herself is seeking to present is the subconscious element in seemingly ordinary dialogue: the "conversation" and the "sub-conversation" that are being voiced together, but saying different things at the same time. The contradiction between our words and what we really mean without our realizing it is the drama she stages for us. This is often a highly elusive task, for an appropriate vocabulary is still lacking. In *The Planetarium,* one of the characters tells himself: "The language had not yet been discovered that can explain at a single stroke what one perceives in the flick of the eye: a whole being, and his myriads of little movements surging forth in a few words, a gesture, a sneer. . . ." But Miss Sarraute has probably come nearer to creating this language than any writer thus far. Her imagery is often violent, and always startling, drawn from unexpected sources.

All this, Miss Sarraute avers, leads to the "New Realism." Much of it may impress us as not completely original, but with Miss Sarraute (as with Alain Robbe-Grillet) it is the extreme or excess to which the theory and practice are pushed that is new in fiction. In any event, its value is yet to be determined. One question is whether the world of the microscope *is* the real world for us? Whether the world of quantum physics and discontinuities, of the proton and meson, *is* the one that we experience? If these subliminal responses are so imperceptible, is it of consequence to us that we have a literature emphatically and wearisomely devoted to them? Is Miss Sarraute leading novelists into a new, broad domain, or only into a *cul de sac*, an extremely narrow and personal byway of her own, that ends only a short distance from where it begins?

At all odds, if literature does gain by these new principles, it will also have lost much. Story, characterization, social concerns, and philosophical themes, all these are renounced by this French school. And background, in which lies much of the poetry of the novel, is either largely dispensed with (as in the work of Miss Sarraute and Miss Duras) or else offered impersonally in such overwhelming detail that it exhausts us (as with Alain Robbe-Grillet, Claude Simon, Claude Ollier). What is present, for certain, is a fresh and often striking *concreteness* in physical imagery, and a spirit of exploration and innovation, without which the novel as an art form would petrify or wither away. Apart from this, it would be wise to wait and see what future direction may develop from these curious experiments.

II

Over the past seventy-five years, and at an ever accelerating pace, then, the importance of form in the novel has steadily grown. Some types of modern fiction now make extraordinary demands upon the reader, and when approaching *Finnegan's Wake* or *The Counterfeiters* or *Portrait of a Man Unknown* he must know something about the theory that dictated their technique, in order to cope with them. From this tendency has come "a specialization of audiences," an appeal to cliques of connoisseurs and experts. The works of Dickens or Trollope can be enjoyed by all fiction readers, and no one pretends to be so sophisticated as not to admire them. But Proust, Gide, Joyce, Woolf, or Robbe-Grillet and Butor are destined to please much smaller audiences, perhaps a self-constituted élite. To say this is not to find fault with these later writers, nor—I hasten to add—is it to praise them. Their limited appeal is simply a fact. It is not of great consequence, nor should it be a deterrent to them. Their new techniques are meant to bring into "modern fiction" the whole of consciousness, and even what lies buried far under in the busy and resonant mind; and hence to some critics—Mark Schorer, Bernard De Voto, Elizabeth Drew—technique is not a secondary affair, a merely mechanical one, but "a deep and primary operation." If these new methods bring hitherto neglected subject matter into fiction, exploring with them might well yield original insights. The twentieth-century novel, by its "advanced" technical means—it is now claimed—has opened uncharted regions of experience, unsounded mental depths, that many authors evaded or did not even guess at in pre-Freudian days.

Good! But, I suppose, the argument might run the other way, that a spate of new material has itself called for finer instruments of presentation, always more precise. The novelist's experimentation has not really led to psychological discoveries, so much as that fresh psychological concepts invoke bold and ingenious new tools. The fastidious thoroughness of a James or a Conrad, the fantastic dissections-in-depth of a Sarraute, are a response to, not a merely personal attack on, an ever-changing world.

Still another question is whether there *is* anything new, whether artists have not always known the facts and sub-facts of life, and whether the Greeks—Euripides, perhaps—were not as cognizant of them as are novelists of the latest school. Do we learn more about the world from new writers and their modern craft than we are taught by Fielding, Samuel Butler, George Meredith, Dostoevski, Tolstoi? Certainly those masters tell us what people were like in past days. Have people really changed much, or is human nature more or less a constant, and are the old techniques still competent to lead us to an understanding of what is at the core of personality? I, for one, would not venture an answer. But even if this *is* so, even if one might find in essence in Euripides or Shakespeare everything that one is likely to come upon in Joyce or Sarraute, this does not imply that the technique of these later writers has to be the same, that there is only one valid way to tell a story.

I am convinced that technique has a value in and for itself, not because it is a means to new truth—if there is any such thing, which there possibly is not—but simply for the charm and beauty technique possesses as an aspect of art, its esthetic appeal. At very least, a personally evolved technique allows an author to tell the same old story in a rather fresh way, and that is a blessing! It will make the oldest tales, the reincarnated myths, look momentarily new. The art of fiction needs that, if it is to survive.

But to be acceptable, a fresh technique must seem to have a logical necessity. The author must make us feel that he needs to tell his story in this manner only; and, since this is a bit of sleight of hand, for any subject can be treated in a wide variety of ways, this does impose a severe task on him. His form must appear to match his subject so closely that we feel them inseparable; they look integral, even if to some degree they are not. (Actually, the subject *is* changed, if it is handled differently: to this extent, subject and manner do interact; a shaping, dynamic exchange takes place between them.) The style of treatment chosen must also do the job of telling the story with the utmost dramatic effectiveness, which in my view calls for lucidity. So a new technique, a new form, cannot be capriciously attached to a story. The author must see in his project an opportunity to compose it in a rather new fashion—there are, unhappily, limits to originality—and still do justice to his theme.

Accordingly, the critics should not make false claims for technique by insisting that the latest device is the best, merely because it *is* the latest, or by inflating the importance of any new approach. Percy Lubbock, the first to investigate technique as an aspect of novelistic art, is properly modest about it. "We know of novels which everybody admits to be badly constructed, but which are so full of life that it does not appear to matter." This should certainly not be overlooked. Professor Lathrop makes much the same point. He agrees with Aristotle, who calls the plot the *soul* of the drama; but Lathrop feels that a close-knit plot is not as necessary in a novel. "Certainly the greatest English novelists are not great draughtsmen, or skillful finishers of plots. . . . The plot-makers are the smaller figures." He concludes that methodological skill is seldom found in English fiction, at least, in union with the greater imaginative qualities.

De Voto also holds this view. "We will always choose the novelist who is a superior person but a second-rate technician over the one who is a first-rate technician but a second-rate person." It might have helped if Mr. De Voto had defined what he means by a "superior person" and a "second-rate person," but his sentiment is clear. Elsewhere he writes: "Preoccupation with technique usually indicates weak creativeness, the slighting of it weak intelligence." He also warns his contemporaries, most of whom were highly enthusiastic about all the then current innovations: "Some experiments have been at the expense of real characterization and story. . . . Sometimes in devising instruments with which to explore recesses of personality ignored by earlier novelists, the novel of our day has come out with phantoms that might have been characters. . . . And often it has refined its substance so much that it has refined it away."

All of this is true! De Voto sums up the misguided enthusiasm of his time as follows: "When *Ulysses* appeared . . . critics told us that Joyce had made the writing of any other kind of novel impossible, or at least absurd. A smaller number now assert that, at any rate, he did so with *Finnegan's Wake*, which would appear to have made novels like *Ulysses* absurd, or at least rudimentary. Following the publication of *Ulysses* many imitations and modulations of it were written. . . . It did not last long and one concludes that Joyce has given instruments to the art of fiction, not limits or necessary conditions. Though many novelists use those instruments for brief passages and occasional effects, few now care to use them for Joyce's purposes or to the exclusion of other instruments." At the same time, Hemingway's *The Sun Also*

Rises had made popular an exactly opposite approach. "Whereas Joyce was as subjective as possible, Hemingway was as objective as possible. The greater part of the characters' behavior in *Ulysses* consisted of thought-processes, and all of it governed by energies and patterns of the unconscious mind. That of the characters of *The Sun Also Rises* neither exhibited nor implied any thought-processes whatsoever but appeared to be a form of conditioned reflex." Obviously, neither technique —if it is effective—can be exclusively right; both can be used. Mr. De Voto reminds us that the "group-novel" of Dos Passos was also acclaimed by critics as destined to make all other kinds of novels obsolete, but this has hardly come to pass.

E. M. Forster, commenting on Gide's *The Counterfeiters,* says: "The novelist who betrays too much interest in his own method can never be more than interesting." Professor Beach is moved to declare: "The discovery of a new device does not necessarily mean a technical improvement, since it is possible for the discoverer, and still more his imitators, to exaggerate it, to misapply it, and to produce an ingenious technical monstrosity rather than a work of art." (He was writing in the days before the appearance of Neo-Realism and *choisisme.*)

Professor Beach expresses himself further: "The well-made novel need not be the great novel, any more than the well-dressed man need be the great man; nor need the great novel be the well-made novel. Many of the novels that best deserve the adjective 'well-made' are the products of weak imaginations or flimsy brains; and it may turn out that extreme preoccupation with technique has been the accompaniment of a decadent tendency in art." This drift, I might suggest, has been greatly aided by scholastic critics. "The emphasis on form may be carried too far, with a corresponding loss of vitality." James Joyce, in particular, with his love of riddles, his literary virtuosity, is described by Beach to be "a classic example of that disposition amongst modernists to pursue technique beyond the point where it can serve the end of art. The whole trend is, in many ways, a continuation of the nineteenth-century movement of 'art for art's sake.'"

But it is H. G. Wells who has written most scathingly about all this. He had begun as a personal friend and protégé of Henry James, but when the ever-fussy James found fault in print with Wells's careless writing, the younger man turned on him and published a bitter counterattack.

Literature is not jewelery, it has quite other aims than perfection, and the more one thinks of "how it is done" the less one gets it done. These critical indulgences lead one along a fatal path, away from every natural interest towards a preposterous emptiness of technical effort, a monstrous egotism of artistry, of which the later work of Henry James is the monumental warning. . . . The subject has long since disappeared in these amazing works; nothing remains but the way it has been manipulated.

Granted that Wells overstates his case, what he says does convince many readers. Later, in a note of apology to the offended James, Wells points out "a real and very fundamental difference in our innate and developed attitudes towards life and literature. To you literature like painting is an end, to me literature like architecture is a means, it has a use. Your view was, I felt, altogether too dominant in the world of criticism, and I assailed it in tones of harsh antagonism." (Henry James modestly replied that he had no such literary influence as Wells imputed to him, and also denied any distinction between art for its own sake, and art for use. "It is art that *makes* life, makes interest, makes importance, for our consideration and application of these things, and I know of no substitute whatsoever for the force and beauty of its process." But that famous dispute is not our affair now.)

This is sampling enough of the strong reaction against the major stress on technique in the recent past and at present. I have already intimated that academic critics like to lecture about novelistic devices, for want of something else to talk about in their classes and in their essays in literary magazines. If the author has been clear as to his meaning, he requires no interpreter—as I have said in an earlier chapter; but his method, if successful, is properly almost invisible to the average reader, who may need the critic—a frequent re-reader—to analyze and perhaps explain it. Consequently, it gives the critic and teacher legitimate employment to dwell on this phase of fiction, although I fear they do it far too much. Similarly, critics place a disproportionate emphasis upon innovation and innovators, for historical minutiae lends itself to scholarly display. Shakespeare is not a creator of new forms. Often the true innovator is, in other ways, an inferior writer. The important thing is, not who does it first, but who —like Shakespeare—does it best.

To speak candidly, much criticism has a very snobbish side. The discoverers of the latest technique are apt to look down their noses at all earlier methods. They are in possession of (or have knowledge of) whatever is the last word, the *dernier cri*. The intolerant snobbishness of the *avant garde*, and especially of its fringe hangers-on, hardly calls for description. My readers will probably be acquainted with it at firsthand, for one has never to go far to encounter it. It is found particularly among college intellectuals. One should be open-minded about new ideas, but not welcome them simply because they are the newest direction and one fears to be not slightly ahead of the fashion.

Plot and suspense remain the *sine qua non* of the novel. I can think of no permanently successful fiction that lacks them. Proust's *Remembrance of Things Past* contains an amazing amount of plot; in that respect, as has been pointed out, it is not outstripped by the adventure tales of Jules Verne. Since the end of World War II the great popularity of mediocre fiction has been a phenomenon, especially in the field of historical romance. This might well be a sign, as Mr. De Voto believes, of a revolt against the novel as a vehicle for ideas and "psychology," and against the difficulty of trying to cope with the deliberate obscurantism of advanced writers and their strange new narrative devices. Even the "specialized audience," Mr. De Voto argues, "reverts explosively" to story for its own sake. Since major authors no longer have stirring and dramatic plots, the public is forced to turn to lesser writers for the pleasure we all take in an easy-to-read, well-told tale.

No longer have we leisurely books, such as those of Dickens and Thackeray. This too is regrettable. After World War II, Trollope was re-issued and widely read (although he is still ignored by the snobbish critics, who do not recognize his truly great gifts). The delights to be found in his books were chiefly reported by word of mouth; people "discovered" him for themselves—I can recall no articles about this or appreciations of him in the literary magazines. I think his appeal is largely his emphasis upon story, his boundless invention, and his unhurried pace. He is a shrewd and genial person one is happy to come upon in tense days like ours.

Has not the amount of "psychology" in fiction become excessive? I am persuaded that Mr. De Voto is sound when he asks if a novelist should be a psychiatrist, and answers no. "You will lose everything we have found, for which the right name may be warmth. A novelist works not to cure a patient but . . . to persuade a reader that for a moment he is not alone. . . . Fiction is to let him know that someone is swimming by his side." When a new edition of Dumas's *The Three Musketeers* was issued in France not long ago, Jean Grenier hailed it in these words: "Here at last is a superficial writer!" This anti-intellectual reaction, long overdue, has been brought about by too much loss of story, too much concern with technique, abnormal psychology, sociology, and abstract philosophy. "Characters in contemporary fiction can no longer drink a glass of whisky or vodka without making definitive pronouncements on life, death, destiny, freedom, Man and Nature!" But the average reader continues to be interested in learning only "what is going to happen next."

This much said, however, I would repeat that form and technique are sources of genuine esthetic pleasure. Naturally, Lubbock is wholeheartedly of this opinion. "We are inclined to forget, if we can, that the book is an object of art, and to treat it as a piece of the life around us. . . ." This is true, and a tribute to the power of fiction that leads us to suspend disbelief. "Does the fact that a novel is well designed, well proportioned, really make a very great difference in its power to please?" Lubbock asks. "In the other arts . . . a lopsided statue or ill-composed painting is a plain offense to the eye, however skillfully it may copy life." And the same, he believes, applies to the novel, although the disproportion there is apt to be far less apparent, owing to the length of the form and the elusive nature—verbal—of the artistic medium. Says Beach, after uttering his strictures against too much critical attention to technique, "Still, the preoccupation with form will certainly tend to good art, if it is not allowed to occupy the whole field. It is not the cause of decadence, nor even the symptom of it, except in so far as it is exaggerated and exclusive."

Furthermore, the author who comes latest on the scene has a fuller bag of tricks to use, as a result of the experimentation of those ahead of him. He might not be as good as some masters of the past, yet excel beyond what he might otherwise have been, because any novelist today has sharpened devices available to him. He can select, among many technical resources, those that best serve his purpose. Literary history since the close of the nineteenth century has seen the development of ever more subtle means of exposing "the intricacies of human relationships, of accenting the element of the unseen and the unexpressed in the affairs of life." The artist appropriately combines all these devices, as his book may demand; but he should take care not to overstep the reader's tolerance and patience.

One complaint against the "well-made" novel, as we have seen, is that it sacrifices too much of life to fit a preordained pattern. This charge is repeatedly (and perhaps quite unfairly) brought against Henry James. In the work of D. H. Lawrence and other of his contemporaries—including Conrad, Proust, Joyce, Malraux—we observe the novel going off in another direction, away from a single, spotlighted central issue or character, to diffuse its action and subject matter in partial shadows. A sense of discontinuity, of fragmentation, and even chiaroscuro, is frequently present in these books, to make them more lifelike. What are touched on are highlights in a crisis, or in experience; the reader relies on his own imagination to fill in the dim gaps and twilit peripheries. Professor Beach says of novelists using this impressionistic technique: "They feel that the imagination is actually exhilarated by broken bits of information, stimulated and rendered more active by it, as the nerves are stimulated by the discontinuity of an electric current." This works somewhat against the too tight and logical shaping of a book, a feeling that it has been too rigidly planned.

In every story, as in life, an element of chance should also be allowed to play its part in the plot. Otherwise the story will not seem real, for luck and coincidence are everyday occurrences: indeed, even science admits of their presence and makes use of "laws of chance" and a "calculus of probability." A work in which *all* events follow by logical necessity in sequence, and *all* characters are unfailingly consistent, has an air of the mechanical. The story seems oversimplified. Muir remarks that this is true of Prosper Merimée's otherwise fine tales; the characters are well drawn, but they are too transparent and closely chained to overplotted situations, and exist only to fulfill the author's too clever contrivance. Here again form and technique are carried too far. Even in the dramatic novel, Muir asserts, although categorically it depends on logic, the characters must progress and change, and sometimes "spontaneously." There is always an element of the unforeseen in them, although the best novelists will try to foreshadow what at the first moment appears to have been the "unforeseen." On second thought, after our surprise, we realize that this development too in the character was inevitable.

In dividing the novel into two categories, the social chronicle and the dramatic novel, Lubbock and Muir insist that a principle of exclusion is all-important. In the social chronicle, some facets of life—change, subjective Time—are omitted; and in the dramatic novel, the broad spatial facets of existence are left out. But it is essential that we have only a partial picture of life in order to see more. If we try to take in the whole of the world at a glance, we are bound to grasp little. But a partial view lifts us out of the confusing flux either of Time or Space. It is a moment of abnormal vision, then, when by being shown less than the entire scene of life we do see an aspect of it more intensely, and hence have a memorable and even haunting vision of some phase of living. The novel, by limiting itself, gives us a larger picture of life than if it mistakenly sought to embrace the whole world at once, which no novel can ever actually do and should never attempt.

Consequently, the novel needs form and freedom, but not too much of either. The novelist himself must draw the fine line between them. In doing so, I suspect, he will be guided by his temperament. If his bent is classical, he will be inclined to seek for clarity, simplicity, and a beautiful formality. His impulse is to impress a sense of order on life. Again, if he is romantic, he will soon grow impatient of restraint, as did Lawrence and Proust and Joyce, and all the others who share their emotional and exuberant nature: in their hands, the novel loses its shapeliness, reserve, and definition. It becomes diverse, complex, and even expressionistic, which means that it may be wildly distorted to express subjective disturbances and dreams.

In summary, knowing a little about technique is like visiting the author in his bestrewn study, the sculptor in his dusty workshop, or the artist in his turpentine-scented studio. Afterwards, we have a sense of having been "in" at the creation of his work; we have a keener personal interest in it, and somehow we even seem to have had a part in producing it. That is only an illusion, of course, but a flattering one; and, like most illusions, it often helps to make life more interesting.

SOME FURTHER ASPECTS OF THE NOVEL

A Note

The three essays that follow were not part of my reading plan but instead were orphan essays. They were too short to appear alone, and I doubted that I should write very much more that pretended to be critical, so I asked hospitality for them between the same two covers of this book.

They were afterthoughts about critics. They were inspired by questions that came up with my reading plan. Whenever I read another novel, I feel there are a host of things that should be said that have not even been touched on here. Anatole France's "adventure" is not a brief one but lifelong. A symbolic work of art—*Oedipus Rex* or *Moby Dick*—is never exhausted of suggestion. This tantalizes the would-be critic. If I were to wait many years more, I would write a book twice as long as this one, but it is just as well that I do not.

Chapter 24

Lawrence and Koestler:
The Novel Reconsidered

IN THE ERA of the Second World War, there appeared a new novelist on the world's horizon. His name is Arthur Koestler. His novels, such as *Darkness at Noon* and *Arrival and Departure,* stirred much comment.

I feel if we were to look about for a predecessor with whom to compare Mr. Koestler, we would very quickly think of D. H. Lawrence. His novels, like those of Lawrence, might be called "thought-adventures." They have vivid characters, but they are primarily concerned with ideas.

This phrase for the novel, a "thought-adventure," was formulated some years ago by J. Middleton Murry, in his book on Lawrence, and I think his point is worth considering.

Much better "art" has been produced by Lawrence's contemporaries; books better shaped, novels more objectively conceived, poems more concentrated. Beside Lawrence's work they seem frigid and futile. It is simply that they are not commensurate with our deep needs of today. Our modern art is all obviously, irremediably minor. And it must necessarily be minor, so long as its aim is to be art. There is, and always will be, a place for minor art; but to produce it is not the function of a major soul. Lawrence was a major soul.

The polemical plays an undeniable part in Lawrence's success as an artist, but I wonder whether Mr. Middleton Murry is right in seizing on this and turning it into an attack on the modern novel when it is anything less than polemical. Indeed, I have wanted to take this up, for I may have seemed to have set myself an inimical paradox when I also expressed belief earlier that Lawrence, at the time the polemical entered his work, emerged in his final greatness.

Let us follow Mr. Murry somewhat further:

Unless society is an organic unity, in which the artist feels and knows himself spiritually secure, the undisturbed concentration of his artistic faculty upon the created object is impossible. The necessary condition of great art is that the artist should be able to take elemental things for granted. The artist needs to serve an authority which he acknowledges to be greater than himself, whether it be God or King, or both together; he does not question the powers that be. . . . The artist today finds no spiritual authority which he instinctively acknowledges. If he acknowledges any it is the authority of Art itself, which is mere wordy nonsense. Art is not authority, it is the means by which authority may be revealed and expressed. So that the artist who is conscious enough to be capable of great art is inevitably involved in the endeavor to discover or to create the authority without which his activity as artist is either trivial or anarchic.

[For this reason Mr. Murry admires Lawrence as one who] intuitively grasped the situation; he understood it better than any other artist of his time. He gave up, deliberately, the pretense of being an artist. The novel became for him simply a means by which he could make explicit his own "thought-adventure," a poem a means of uttering immediate experience. His aim was to discover authority, not to create art. Therefore to criticize him for not doing what he never intended to do is stupid; and it implies an inability to rise to the level of Lawrence's own comprehension.

A similar point has since been made by other critics. Francis Fergusson remarks: "There is no use trying to appreciate [Lawrence] solely as an artist; he was himself too impatient of the demands of art, which seemed to him trivial compared with the quest he followed." The noted poet, Stephen Spender, has put it this way: "What interested [Lawrence] was the tension between art and life, not the complete resolution of the problems of life within the illusion of art. . . . For him literature is a kind of pointer to what is outside literature. . . . This outsideness of reality is for Lawrence the waters of baptism in which man can be reborn." Dorothy Van Ghent, however, is less forgiving than Mr. Murry on this score: "Lawrence's sensitivity to twentieth-century chaos was peculiarly intense, and his passion for order was similarly intense; but this sensitivity and this passion did not lead him to concentrate on refinements and subtleties of novelistic technique in the direction laid out, for instance, by James and Conrad. Hence, as readers first approaching his work, almost inevitably we feel disappointment and even perhaps shock, that writing so often 'loose' and repetitious and such unrestrained emotionalism . . . should appear in the work of a novelist who is assumed to have an important place in the literary canon."

II

Mr. Murry was writing almost four decades ago, when the traditional philosophic effort to determine what is truth had been more or less discredited by the advent of physical science. He mentions too the moral devastation of the First World War, and of the disturbing new psychology whose Gabriel was Freud. Today, after World War II, the moral devastation is even greater; for we are finding that science, including psychology, can also be our enemy. Fission can destroy our universe, and psychology—in the wrong hands—can be an evil magic. Over the air, and on the television screen, it can lead the world to madness, even to suicide.

Newton having given way to Einstein, whose relativity spreads to all things, nothing remains wholly reliable save relativity itself; our intellectual and moral structure—and the spirit of man housed in that structure—is discovered based upon the shifting sands of desire and satiety.

We were mistaken, indeed, ever to put our faith in science. We know now that it too, with its "method," must accept the limits of mere subjective intellectuality. Indeed, science has been subjective at all times. The ear of Kepler was attuned to what he described as the "music of the spheres"; Newton himself nourished the theory of gravitation at the breast of medieval metaphysics. The claims of science to complete objectivity have been presumptuous and misleading. Then if we cannot trust science, what is to be our "authority"? Shall it be religion again? Shall we escape into Vedanta or Zen, and reconcile ourselves with the absolute Nothing?

The climate of the hour is not much changed: unrest and chaos are the only words that can describe today's scene.

Mr. Murry referred to a similar questioning which held all

things suspect, even science—the questioner. The world we inherited from Queen Victoria had already been blown apart before the atom took over. The true explosion of our age has been a moral one, otherwise the atom would present us with no problem. Lenin, rather than the scientists at Los Alamos, is perhaps responsible for our perplexity. He preached that morality took a second place to expediency, and in this won the concurrence of too many of the intelligentsia. Before now, the intelligentsia had been the upholders of public and personal morality. Mr. Murry wrote about the time that Lenin was in power. So nothing Mr. Murry said then does not still apply to us.

I hardly intend to discuss this thoroughly, but only to consider whether it means that the novel, if it becomes a "thought-adventure," must change its form. That is a very deep question, though on the surface it may not seem so.

One thing we might do is to look at Mr. Koestler.

III

I think nearly anyone may declare himself in agreement with most of Mr. Murry's statement, and also with what the other critics have said. That books better shaped have been produced in recent times, that yet seem "frigid and futile" beside Lawrence's loosely constructed novels, must be readily acknowledged. But then, it would be difficult, perhaps impossible, for even a major artist twice as profound as Lawrence to oppose him with works of equal warmth and color: not because the first man's writings were less relevant to our times, but because Lawrence, a painter at the start of his career, possessing a painter's eye and sensitivity in his style, chose sensuality for his exclusive subject. The very subject enlivens his work. Then "frigid and futile" might not be just words.

Mr. Koestler too has chosen a theme of great inherent melodrama. What other contemporary artist, writing of man's more familiar concerns, can hope to compete with him? The revolutionary background of his stories is ominous, bitter. His characters are always in momentary danger of torture and death. Mr. Koestler needs great courage to attempt such subjects, but he has enough boldness to do so, and he brings to them remarkable intellect.

I think there are other subjects, though, that demand equal courage. They deal with the intimate and personal life of man, his private hopes and desperations. The success of novelists undertaking to study them subtly and honestly may not be as apparent, but should they not be respected?

That our modern art is generally "obviously, irremediably minor" is probably so. It has probably been so in every age. That "there is, and always will be, a place for minor art; but to produce it is not the function of a major soul" sounds tolerant and true. And that Lawrence was a major soul, I wholeheartedly assent.

But the rest of Mr. Murry's statement lies open to contradiction. To me it seems he has been trying to make virtues of Lawrence's faults. And to condemn other artists for not sharing Lawrence's faults is amazing folly.

I feel that Mr. Koestler has escaped Lawrence's fault, though he is not Lawrence's equal in any other respect. But that is why I chose to borrow him for this essay. For Mr. Koestler is a writer of stature, he has undertaken "thought-adventures," and yet he is not polemical in the short novels that have won him eminence.

Presumably Mr. Murry's "spiritual authority" is the equivalent of what I have called philosophy elsewhere. I think he makes his first mistake when he looks upon art as a subject endeavor, slave to the philosopher.

That is another thing about Mr. Koestler: he does not borrow his personal philosophy from anyone. Certainly not from Marx, though he is a Marxist. We find that he is an independent thinker, whose views of the world's politics have been formed by his own harsh experience, in prison, in concentration camps. Koestler was once sentenced to death during the Civil War in Spain. Then what is the authority, in our chaotic world, that lets him write strong novels? He bases it on his own temperamental and intellectual response to experience. That suffices.

But to return to Mr. Murry, does he not err when he even says that Lawrence gave up the pretense of being an artist? Lawrence never gave up the pretense; his posthumous works—*The Escaped Cock,* and the stories in *The Lovely Lady,* for two examples—show him deeply interested to the last in the symbolic articulation of his ideas. True, he struggled with "form" until in exasperation he tried to cast it away as an "empty classical husk."

He was of two minds, or perhaps—better—of two wills. He was torn ceaselessly between his desire to be an artist, and his restlessness at accepting the discipline necessary to being one. When Arnold Bennett pointed out his shortcomings as a craftsman, Lawrence dashed off a contemptuous letter to his literary agent: "Tell Arnold Bennett that all the rules of construction hold good only for novels that are copies of other novels. A book which is not a copy of other books has its own construction, and what he calls faults, he being an old imitator, is what I call characteristics." An able rationalization! But on another occasion he wrote: "Art speech is the only speech." Still again: "Being a novelist, I consider myself superior to the saint, the scientist, the philosopher and the poet. The novel is the one bright book of life." Finally, in tribute to the novel form, he says elsewhere with passion: "Morality is that delicate, forever trembling and changing balance between me and my circumambient universe, which precedes and accompanies a true relatedness. . . . The novel is the highest example of subtle interrelatedness that man has discovered. Everything is true in its own time, place, circumstance, and untrue outside of its own place, time, circumstance. If you try to nail anything down in the novel, either it kills the novel or the novel gets up and walks away with the tale." So he did aspire, not primarily to bare and explicit "thought-adventures," not to polemics, but to the novel *sui generis*.

The fact is, Lawrence could not attain "form" in his longer works. His short stories are beautifully shaped—take *Smile* or *The Fox*. Perhaps the fault was that in his earlier novels he was not yet ready. He was not clear in his mind. *Lady Chatterley's Lover* is shapely enough—and here Lawrence was expressing his simple, sure quintessential doctrine.

In much of his other work, haste and carelessness can be sighted everywhere. The unhappy result is that he frequently contradicts himself. Analyzing many of these full-length works, David Daiches is led to comment that Lawrence never seems quite sure what he wanted to say; and, to hide his self-doubts, he protests too much and too loudly. In the short stories, Lawrence is apt to be more precise and offer us the right embodiment of a limited idea. Much the same view is held by Mark Schorer, who suggests that Lawrence, too often scorning a technical approach, failed to objectify his material properly, and hence often sounds badly confused.

Yet, the mere fact that Lawrence turned away from the objective and formal at times, hardly means that he was not an artist. It takes more than devotion to "form" to establish an artist as we have defined him. Though "form" is something more than an "empty classical husk," of course: I like to think of it enclosing a segment of life in an esthetically pleasing pattern that helps us to understand the world and see its implicit beauty. Henry James said something like this about "form": "Really, universally, relations stop nowhere, and the exquisite problem is eternally but to draw, by a geometry of his own, the circle within which they shall happily *appear* to do so." Or we might compare "form" to the deep quiet of a well, where ripples from a dropped stone are forever circumscribed.

To go back to Mr. Murry's premise: "Unless society is an organic unity, in which the artist feels and knows himself spiritually secure, the undisturbed concentration of his artistic faculty upon the created object is impossible." That must be admitted, but we might ask whether the greatest art results from the undisturbed concentration of the artistic faculty upon the created object. The obverse might easily have as much of the argument. The Renaissance, the Elizabethan Age, save that they are now seen in the unified past, presumably had no such organic unity as Mr. Murry asks; yet their yield was rich. Beethoven lived in a time of transition. Or look back at the sentence: "The artist today finds no spiritual authority which he instinctively acknowledges. If he acknowledges any it is the authority of Art itself, which is mere wordy nonsense." (Joseph Wood Krutch has said as much when he declares that great tragedy is lost to the modern dramatist, because we no longer believe in the existence of those spiritual kings among men before whose blindness the Greeks sat deeply moved.) But why is the authority of art mere wordy nonsense? It is only so if Mr. Murry considers art a word and nothing more. Define art as the artist's self-discipline, his control over his medium and over those who are his audience, his projection of a deep personal insight, and it is palpably something more than wordy nonsense.

Conrad said that art is "a single-minded attempt to render

the highest kind of justice to the visible universe, by bringing to light the truth, manifold and one, underlying its every aspect. It is an attempt to find in its forms, in its colors, in its lights, in its shadows, in the aspects of matter and in the facts of life what of each is fundamental, what is enduring and essential—their one illuminating and convincing quality—the very truth of their existence."

Is that mere wordy nonsense? To my mind, art so conceived is both an authority and the means by which authority may be revealed and expressed, as we are both the lighters of our torch and the grateful recipients of its flame. The artist finds his authority in fidelity to his temperament.

Says Thomas Hardy in *The Profitable Reading of Fiction*:

> It may seem something of a paradox, to assert that the novels . . . which most conduce to moral profit are likely to be among those written without a moral purpose. But the truth of the statement may be realized if we consider that the didactic novel is so generally devoid of *vraisemblance* as to teach nothing but the impossibility of tampering with the natural truth to avoid dogmatic opinions. Those, on the other hand, which impress the reader with the inevitableness of character and environment in working out destiny, whether that destiny be just or unjust, enviable or cruel, must have a sound effect, if not what is called a good effect, upon a healthy mind.

How may Mr. Murry presume that Lawrence has made of the novel for the first time in its history a "thought-adventure"? Are the novels of Lawrence "thought-adventures" more profound, more quick with life, than the novels of Fielding, Melville, Hardy, Conrad?

Somewhat less profound, somewhat less quick with life, I think, to the extent that they are occasionally polemical. For in art a man *proves* his philosophical ideas, as Mr. Koestler so earnestly tries to do. He does not merely preach shrilly.

As yet, there has been very little written in our time that has the moral depth, the persuasion, of Arthur Koestler's *Darkness at Noon*. It has had more force, and cast more light, than has any other explanation of its most important subject, and largely that is because it is a respectable work of art. He writes of life in flux, of society in chaos, yet needs no other authority than human experience and his own conviction. He has lived in the world that Lenin has helped to make, but he does not find art inadequate to describe it, and this, I think, is very significant indeed.

Chapter 25

Bread: The Social Novel

DURING MY SHORT stay in Russia some years ago, I went to the theater with a young woman of Moscow, who asked me at the first intermission what I thought of the play.

"Don't you grow weary of propaganda?" I wondered.

"This is not propaganda," the young woman answered. "Why do you and all other foreigners call it that? This is a picture of our life."

That was true. All art, if it has a moral purpose, is propaganda. The artist is seeking to convince us. He demands that we accept his vision of life. He wants us to acknowledge the verity of his people. Conrad pleads for Lord Jim. Lawrence becomes Lady Chatterley's proponent.

In Russia then, the last strenuous year of the Five Year Plan, men and women were seeking their individual salvation by immersion not in cults of mystical sensuality or in personal dream but in a tremendous mass social action. In the philosophical art, the plays and novels of these people, one could not rule out the social idea as a quintessential impulse. It was a mistake on my part to think that I dismissed such works by calling them propaganda. The crudely satiric comedy I was seeing was bad art. For that reason it was bad propaganda. But art and propaganda are the same. The challenging question was how would I know good social art when I saw it.

What were the rules I had set for myself as an amateur critic? Excitement. Yes, the excitement of my superior faculties, my deepest emotions. Proof. But that is what social art must have in equal measure, along with excitement. Here again I was meeting the polemical, but I would also demand a *vital* demonstration of the author's ideas. I would challenge his authority. In all fields, none should have higher requirements than those set for social art. For many reasons, this is imperative.

II

What is social art in one generation is not in the next.

If social art is that whose quintessential idea is the contemplation of society, then we might go back to Cervantes' *Don Quixote*: it satirizes the dying society of feudal Europe. One might also choose the novels of Defoe and say that the social novel in English literature, far from being a new phenomenon, actually precedes the philosophical novel of Fielding.

But the novel of Cervantes and Defoe had not coalesced to where it demanded an organic whole. When that came about, the novelist began to struggle to keep the social idea within the bounds of art. He found it difficult to do this because of a strange misconception as to the nature of art. This is that social ideas are topical, and what is topical has little chance for survival, and survival is the ultimate test of artistic worth.

On the one hand, the artist has always felt social problems crowding in on him. But he is so envious of immortality that he wishes to write only of the universal and enduring. He may justify this by saying that he is taking "the long view," that he is keeping an Olympian perspective. He wants to work with what is eternal.

This conflict, in the conscious or unconscious minds of novelists, brings in the early nineteenth century a stirring new form, the historical-social novel. Scott, and more particularly Victor Hugo, evoke the past and study it in terms of religious and social forces, portraying crusades and revolts on vast, Gothic canvases. We should not think of Scott and Hugo as mere romancers; to their contemporaries, they were great social philosophers. Of Scott, so learned and intellectual a man as Ruskin said admiringly that he was "the truest philosopher of his time." He further calls him, "the writer who has given the broadest view of ordinary modern thought." Cardinal Newman pays him similar high praise as a font of religious inspiration. In point of fact, Scott is a conservative aristocrat and believer in caste, and much of his antiquarianism derives from his love of tradition and his dedication to its preservation as a source of "social strength and beauty."

But social problems of any time are too pressing to be treated by the expedient of historical precedent and allegory. Dickens and Tolstoi recognized this and embraced the topical more openly, as had Cervantes and Defoe before them. But where the writings of Cervantes and Defoe have a simple thesis, implicit in *Don Quixote*, explicit in *Moll Flanders*, the novels of Dickens and Tolstoi are complex and the social theme, while obtrusive, is relegated to a very secondary place. It is digressive. It is more direct, more pertinent, than in Scott or Hugo, but social art, as art, has lost rather than gained in its struggle to achieve an organic form of its own. One comes upon social ideas in *Hard Times*; there are passages about agrarian experiments in *Anna Karenina*, but they are so little integral to the plot that the reader can skip them without loss to the story. By this device, this compromise, a book gains contemporaneity without serious prejudice to its chances for survival.

This method has been most popular. It is still used. It allows the novelist to be polemical at will, by simply choosing a mouthpiece in the story for his ideas. He may even, by doing this, escape responsibility for his character's opinions, if he so wishes. He explains, "That is the point of view natural to my character. It is not necessarily my own." In many ways, this is admirable. All ideas profit by having more than one side exposed. Art becomes a clearing house for opinions rather than a pulpit. And art most fully plays its rôle as history in this manner.

But does the novel itself, with all it might mean to us, profit from the social digression? It suffers. One has only to compare, for example, the part played by the Chatterley mines in Lawrence's book with that of the silver mines in Conrad's *Nostromo* to see the loss. The Chatterleys constantly discuss the coal mining problem, but the matter is remote from the novel's central thesis. The rich burrow of San Tomé, on the other hand, is veritably a protagonist of Conrad's romantic story. The latter is the way of art.

Indeed, we find almost with surprise on later readings that Conrad was a clear-sighted critic of his social scene, although he was hardly recognized as one in his own day. In *Heart of Darkness* he records with horror his experiences in the Belgian Congo and, giving us unforgettable pictures, condemns the brutal and merciless exploitation of hapless natives there. In *Nostromo* there is a superb examination of how modern commerce, an aspect of the ever-encroaching industrial revolution, contaminates the souls of well-meaning men. Yet never once in these books does Conrad raise his voice in open personal protest, nor does he nominate a proxy to express his thoughts; he wishes to let his stories speak their message for themselves; and, alas, the public was slow to hear what he was saying. Consequently, his novels of social comment were not as effectual as those by Dickens, Tolstoi, and Lawrence, who were even more determined, as men of social responsibility, to contribute practically to the advance and amelioration of their times, and so turned from pure artistry and chose the digressive method.

The way of art is always the better way. But how can art be reconciled to the social theme?

The error may lie in the vain and snobbish belief that art does not treat with the transitory. That to include the topical, a compromise is necessary . . . that immortality is one of the tests of great art. . . . This presupposes that a book read and liked by twenty thousand persons over five decades must be a better work than one read and liked by a hundred thousand persons in a single decade and then forgotten. But is that so?

In Eckermann's *Conversations with Goethe,* we read of the astonishing significance many contemporary books have for that master: Byron's *Manfred,* for example, and what seem to us the lesser works of Scott. Byron, to Goethe, is a character of such "eminence as had never existed before and probably would never come again." We can hardly agree with the Socrates of Weimar. But is Goethe wrong in his contemporary judgment of men and their works, or is his contemporary judgment a better one, since it measures personality and artistic accomplishment more exactly in their setting, along with their impact on the times? Goethe's own *Werther,* one of the most influential books ever written, seems wan and exhausted today and survives, as does Byron's *Manfred,* only because of the more timeless merits of the author's other productions. We behold how, in period after period, books die forever or are surprisingly reborn, often without explicable logic.

Proust suggests that the "neurasthenia" of people of taste is responsible for the death of books. He tells of having seen men of talent "take the place of men of genius who were called 'worn out,' simply because they had worn out the lazy minds of the intellectuals, as neurasthenics are always worn out and always changing."

But Proust has not the full explanation, either. Is there any? Survival is an accident demonstrably beyond the artist's design. He must work with the materials of his age and even of his moment. The longevity of his book may not be a just appraisal of his distinction, his originality, his intrinsic success.

Then the compromise between story and digression, art and the polemical, if born of this vain aspiration for survival, is obviously a wrong one. Social art, though destined to be dated, can have an organic greatness of its own. Matthew Arnold speaks of books of the times and books of the ages. I doubt whether any inherent superiority distinguishes them.

What deceives us is perfection of form, which does endure. The subject-matter of Byron's *Don Juan* is trivial and flippant, but his great skill continues to delight. *Manfred* is a more serious work.

What would Byron say? Which, to his eyes, would be the greater success: that, in his own times, his *Manfred* moved Goethe; or that now, when *Manfred* is no longer read, thousands of adolescents scan *Don Juan* with eager pleasure? Or let us ask another question: Would a Goethe of our day like *Manfred*? Probably not. Then how well does survival serve us as a measure of artistic achievement?

III

The result of their oblique solutions and compromises is that scarcely anyone today thinks of Scott, Hugo, Dickens as social novelists, or *Barnaby Rudge* or *Nicholas Nickleby* as social art. True, Bernard Shaw attests that he was converted to Socialism by having read *Little Dorritt*! But most of us conceive of the social novel as being made of sterner stuff. We speak of it as born in France with Balzac, a Romantic, certainly, but also a tireless documentarian of the social and economic *milieu* in which his characters live, and which shapes them. Indeed, the French social novel might be said to date back even earlier to Rousseau and *La Nouvelle Héloïse*. But it really becomes a force with the Goncourts and Zola, henceforth to be identified with Naturalism. Naturalism is a salutary move forward, for it brings into modern literature a rich new material. A *fin de siècle* art experiences a needed invigoration; the world of Defoe, the crowded world of the poor, the oppressed, the victimized, is rediscovered. Simultaneously the novel is given a new method, real people, and vital subject matter. The processes of science are borrowed, and under the missionary pens of the Goncourts and their French, Russian, and belated American followers, the social novel becomes the sociological novel.

We too seldom think of George Eliot as belonging to this movement, yet essentially she does. She was prominent in Herbert Spencer's circle and shared his then radical and sacrilegious Evolutionary views. She is a scientific determinist. Her people are thwarted and doomed by their heredity, moral weakness, and poverty; theirs is the "tragedy of attrition" that later becomes the standard theme of Naturalism. Even the best and noblest of them, like rebellious Maggie Tulliver, are in conflict with the dull and commonplace in their environment; and the blighted background, again, is that of the Industrial Revolution. In George Eliot's work, cause leads to consequence inexorably. As an artist, she is one of the pioneer sociologists, always zealous for moral reform. She is a brilliant and serious woman. It is only her tearful, hand-wringing quality that we dislike, but this too is surprisingly characteristic of Naturalists, who tend to be sentimental.

Yet it is the French, Russian, and American Naturalists who excel. Some say the work of Zola, Maxim Gorky, Frank Norris, and Theodore Dreiser is sociology, not art at all. The heaping up of commonplaces, by which these novelists achieve their impressive effects, is considered too unselective; the brutality of the subject matter is repulsive, especially when unrelieved by such earthy humor as is Defoe's. The patience required for scientific exposition becomes tedious. It is too easy to write a Naturalistic novel: there have been too many mediocre imitators. The social novel, as a consequence, even as it attempts to gain greater integrity, has fallen into disrepute and is described as writing without style, poetry, or spiritual content.

This reputation persists, and not without cause. Naturalism is still with us. What began as an influx of new blood into the realm of art, still threatens to become a barbarian invasion.

IV

Meanwhile, social art begins a new phase. In books and drama a group of great artists take the material made available by the frankness of Naturalism and transform it into a more subtle, more organic art by abandoning the Naturalistic method. The poets return. Their names are Ibsen, Hauptmann, and Shaw; Anatole France, Romain Rolland; Galsworthy and Wassermann, Thomas Mann, Franz Werfel, and —I would include him again—D. H. Lawrence. Arnold Bennett writes stories of The Five Towns. Jules Romains begins to write *Men of Good Will*. In Scandinavia, England, France, Central Europe, America, the best artists are social artists whose approach is poetic and individual.

Earlier, Flaubert and Turgenev had set a fine example. Flaubert's provincial, middle-class world of the Bovarys is created in authentic detail, with an exactness of observation still unequaled. His dull, unhappy Emma frets and dreams of a richer, fuller life than that which has been meted out to her. Whether it is true or not, as Henry James asserts, that Flaubert's characters are too insignificant to bear the weight of all the meaning with which their author wishes to burden them, the fact remains that their foolish, even cheap and desperate aspirations are signs of inner revolt against too much mediocrity and conformity. What Flaubert brings home to the reader is a realization of how much a restrictive environment of this sort counts in the life of an ordinary person, a factor that had been too little emphasized in preceding fiction. The whole point of *Madame Bovary* is that Emma is the victim of the society in which she finds herself; there is scarcely need for a critic to say this again.

Flaubert's contemporary, the superb artist Turgenev, always makes a considerable ado about shunning social topics. He even declares: "To a man of letters, politics is poison." Perhaps expediency had something to do with this, since the Tsarist censorship was strict. Yet histories of Russian literature tell us that *A Sportsman's Sketches* helped measurably in creating a favorable opinion in that benighted country that led to the emancipation of the serfs; and few novels are intrinsically as "political" as *Fathers and Sons*. It is Turgenev, I believe, who coins the term "nihilist" to describe a certain by now universal type of young radical. He does not propagandize overtly, but his work nearly always deals with a social subject, and the best commentators assure us that Turgenev has written hardly any major story in which there is not a political overtone of some kind. To us, at this much later day, some of this might not be readily apparent; and this is all the more true since his tone is both skeptical and pessimistic. Unconsciously, we feel that social reformers are optimists. Like Dostoevski, whom he detested, Turgenev has no admiration for revolutionists, and views the future with the same misgivings. It is very interesting, indeed, to compare *Fathers and Sons* and *The Possessed*. In both novels, by authors of very different temperaments, we have portrayed archetypes of the schemers and Utopians who, torn and warped by self-conflicts, shall a half-century later rise to dominate and plague our present world.

But Flaubert and Turgenev, and their modern successors, do not take in the whole field of social art, but only a part of it, and in consequence their unprecedented success is a narrowed one. They avoid economics. Hauptmann shows in *The Weavers* and Galsworthy in *Strife* that there is a cathartic poetry in the violence of class struggle. But on the whole, the theme of these early twentieth-century playwrights and novelists is not economics, and they do not join Zola in leaning toward an economic interpretation of history. Thomas Mann, in *The Magic Mountain,* reads modern Europe's story in utterly different terms. Galsworthy, striking out for social reform with rapier-like realism in *The Silver Box* and *Justice,* fights for jurisprudential changes; when he discusses rents and food, as in novels like *The Freelands,* his ineffectuality betrays him as a romantic in the poorest sense of the word. Werfel celebrates man's redemption through racial unity. Lawrence, quite the most original and personal of them all, writes *The Plumed Serpent* to dissent acridly, as Lawrence always dissents, with the doctrine that social salvation lies in economics or technology. And so *The Plumed Serpent* does not pass for a social novel, or even for what might be called a political one, although Lawrence foretells the shape and spirit of Fascism with an uncanny exactness. He does much the same in his Australian novel, *Kangaroo.* Sometimes artists do possess clairvoyance.

The social art produced by these superior and subtle minds has been virtually absorbed in the wider stream of the philosophical novel, which in its reflection of life has become encouragingly aware of the individual seen in his environment. Since 1914 the world's history has been so much one of mass movements that men can scarcely be portrayed indifferent to them, or isolated from them, and still have verisimilitude.

Lastly, before the Second World War comes a group of writers so imbued with social feeling that they barely stop to weigh their chances for artistic survival. They are above all determined to bring economics into the scope of literature. Their attempt is the proletarian novel. The proletarian novel is the social art of the decades between the wars. It was proletarian drama I saw on the stage of that crowded Moscow theater, a drama concerned almost solely with men and women reduced to caricatures, puppets of economic forces. The method is not that of Naturalism, but of Constructivism. It impressed me as being, as I said, very bad art. But that does not mean that in the hands of other artists, the same materials and the same method—or an even newer one—might not be used for very great art. Could it? That, since the problem attacked by the proletarian novel is so urgent, is what we should ponder.

V

Thus far the proletarian novel has compromised the least, has come the nearest to achieving a kind of organic wholeness, but none can deny that its popular reception has disappointed its proponents. By readers and fellow-artists alike, it is most often dismissed as mere propaganda, but that, as I told myself in Moscow, is a lamentably wrong view.

Good proletarian art would be good propaganda, yes. But in three ways, thus far, the proletarian novel has failed to become good art. Thus, it is disappointing propaganda.

The first reason is that its authors have not been able to inform their work with the necessary ingredient of personality. Perhaps the one exception up till now has been André Malraux, whose *Man's Fate* and other works have earned a just renown for their power, horror, and savage truth, but no less because of their individuality, because the strange character of the author interests us. He keeps us curious about the man, the poet, the adventurer, behind the books.

The most objective of writers nonetheless show themselves in their work. Henry James might seek to make his work utterly independent of its creator, but we never turn a page of James without being conscious of his unique mind and style, if only through the peculiar conformation of his endless, delicate words; he is as much present as is Fielding in every sentence he writes.

Why is this quality of uniqueness so lacking in practically all the proletarian writers? Proust remarks succinctly, "A mediocre writer living in an epic period will remain just as mediocre." It may be that when men immerse themselves in idealism, or intellectuality, or dreams, they are still themselves —or more themselves than ever before—but when they immerse themselves in other people, in mass action, they forfeit whatever makes them distinct. Or does the impulse to join such movements arise from an original want of self-sufficiency?

Does this apply to Malraux too? One never felt that he was deeply involved in the Communist movement. He was certainly not caught up by its mass fervor. He was at all times self-conscious, mentally detached. His approach was personal. This does not impute his sincerity or the depth of his conviction at that time; but the people of his novels, the amoralists, the opium smokers, the terrorists, are not the men and women who make up the rank and file of a great reform movement. They are extraordinary characters, and we felt that Malraux himself must be very unusual. His ultimate desertion of Communism, his subsequent espousal of De Gaullism, though a *volte-face* to antithetical concepts, must have come as no great surprise, even to his ex-comrades in the Party.

The proletarian novel has also been handicapped by its authors' refusal to compete with literary tradition, with the great writers and works of the past. Goethe speaks of himself as lucky that he is not an Englishman—he does not have to stand against Shakespeare in the surpassing current of English literature. He says of himself that he bulks large in German letters only because the scene was so barren before he came. Actually, of course, he did measure himself against Shakespeare in his own mind and was so ranked by the public, because the Shakespearean plays were known in Germany. All great writers compete with the accomplishments of the past, model their prose—as obviously Malraux has done—on the rich styles of tradition, scan previous works for what they can teach of the craft of literature, with the result that standards of literary composition steadily rise. The proletarian writers have been too busy with innovation to discipline themselves properly, to attain a sure eloquence. They mistake vulgarity for realism and violence for strength. Only Malraux dares to be subtle. . . . And where subtlety is lacking, the rewarding depths of literature that bring us back to a book more than once, for the finer shades of analysis, for esthetic pleasure, are attendantly absent.

Finally, the proletarian novel, because it undeviatingly expounds a single point of view, the Marxist one, has little element of surprise or suspense. The patness, the fervor of that view, becomes painfully monotonous to the unconverted reader. Its facility seemingly prevents the proletarian authors from investigating their social problems with any profundity; they make no personal contribution; they borrow their explanation of all phenomena and share it in common. Similarly, they share their plots with a spirit that is amiably Communistic. Strikes are one subject. The lynching, that cruel, vicious melodrama of our Southern states, is another much favored; but while at that period there were actually six or seven lynchings every year, there were surely, in each twelve months, five or ten times as many earnest stories describing them. The proletarian novelists may not be charged with indifference to a humane cause, but they have neglected to examine the rest of our economic life. They make little or nothing of the richest new material claimed by any group of writers in literary history.

Malraux, brilliantly, has not missed the opportunity. He has made himself the sympathetic historian of the Communist movement in our time. He writes of those who risk their life in a selfless, dangerous cause. If the Marxist interpretation is implicit in his work, it is never discussed overtly. All that is shallow, jejune, facile, unrealistically optimistic is missing from his books. He pictures the world as a Communist sees it, remorselessly, horribly. It is perhaps only logical that, having explored that world so thoroughly, he himself should finally have been repelled by it.

Malraux's attraction to Marxism came about because, like Conrad, he had observed at firsthand the horrors of a corrupt and oppressive colonialism: this time, not Belgian but French; and not in Africa, but in Indo-China, where his father was an official serving in the French colonial service. Young Malraux began his career as an archaeologist: his researches in the Far East soon put him at odds with an interfering bureaucracy.

From that field he shortly switched into one of direct political action, and to literature, which in the 1930's won him world renown as a leader of the Communist intelligentsia. Later, like Koestler, he participated on the Republican side in the Spanish Civil War; and there, apparently, his first disenchantment with the Stalinists set in. Next, he was engaged in the Partisan movement during the German occupation of France. Both his liking for Communism, and his disillusion with it, are based on his actual experience with it; he was no closet radical. Interestingly, his novels record only the lure that Communist political activity had for him. Since he left the Party, he has written no fiction, but instead turned to art criticism. Whether he will write any more novels is not yet known.

Most proletarian authors are Marxists. Should Marxist logic prevail in the future, its pioneer literature will gain a special importance. If Communist and Socialist doctrine should be disproved, its literature will be judged precisely for its artistic virtues. Dante's astronomy, Shakespeare's geography are weak, yet their works have not died. But why should we concern ourselves with future judgments? That is an error we should avoid.

VI

The distinguishing method of proletarian art has been Constructivism, although to my knowledge this phrase has not been used of literature. I think it may be so used, particularly in describing Malraux's work, the plays of the proletarian stage, and the often strange poems of the proletarian school. In stage design, Constructivism embodies two seemingly contradictory theories, the Presentationalism of Craig and Evreinov, who want art to forswear reality, and the "modernism" or Functionalism expounded by visionary architects such as Louis Sullivan, who think a structure should not look like anything but what it actually is. The union of these theories in Constructivism is by virtue of their inner consistency, for to Craig and Evreinov the theater is the world of illusion: they think it should aspire to be that and no more. They draw on the theater of China, Persia, the Orient, for telling examples of what they believe is man's instinctive delight in the theatrical, the symbolic, as opposed to the real.

Evreinov insists that men want to indulge their fancy when they go to the theater: they do not wish crudely painted scenery substituted for what their own imaginations can supply. Craig, we remember, even suggests the use of puppets instead of living actors. These theories seem absurd, at first blush, but in a few years they bear richly: Appia begins dressing his vast, dark stage with columns of living light instead of paint; Formalism makes its appearance and Hamlet's Elsinor becomes a breathtaking sweep of steps diminishing skyward; Symbolism, Impressionism, Expressionism all flourish with this return to theatrical illusion. Finally comes functional Constructivism, which is neither formalized nor expressionistic, but exploits the naked stage, the bare brick walls, the mechanical appurtenances of the stage itself. In architecture, Sullivan preaches that the skyscraper should proudly show its steel skeleton. The Constructivist stage designers too show the skeleton of whatever properties they need for their set, and soon, at Meyerhold's and Tereshkovitch's theaters in Moscow, the actors are emulating them, are—by the violence of their gestures, the excess of their make-up—betraying the raw materials of acting. This is considered by them a dynamic exchange of acting theory and stage design theory.

In Russia at that time, and on proletarian stages everywhere, there can be no doubt that Constructivism had validity. To begin, the plays of this proletarian theater were intentionally crude and over-simple; the plays were meant for boorish minds, and to hold the attention of illiterate audiences, such bare, violent acting served admirably. But more important, I suspect, was the physical economy of this stage design. The Communists of Russia, intent on the tremendous five-year task of national industrialization, had little money to spare for elaborate theatrical sets. A play could be shown anywhere, in hall, barn, or dispossessed church, without equipment but also without apology, by Constructivistic doctrine. Tereshkovitch's group, for example, traveled thousands of miles every year, bearing the gospel of Marxism to the remotest Volga villages. Then, the bare use of stage machinery appealed to the Russians; they were deeply devoted to the cult of the machine: it was the symbol of the industrialization that was to lead them to Utopia.

What is the equivalent of Constructivism in literature? The exploitation of the raw materials of authorship . . . the proletarian poem that is really the notation for a poem, the novel that is actually the unfleshed bones of a novel. The mechanics of literature exposed. . . . Skeletonic grammar: sentences without verbs . . . shifts of scenes without transitions. . . . And, characteristically, caricature, puppetry, instead of careful portraiture. Not even Malraux's *Man's Fate* is exempt from the criticism that it does not develop clearly, from episode to episode; any reader of the book will admit that it is not easy to follow; the author plunges us into action without first letting us orient ourselves; the streams of consciousness of his people are often difficult to disentangle. What we have are fully matured passages of analysis and plot piled together like huge uncemented blocks. The novel is not really finished. Elsewhere, Malraux himself has stated: "All art rests on a series of ellipses," and adds that this is a premise of the utmost consequence to him personally. In prose, the "ellipse" is an omission. (Henri Peyre offers an ingenious and sensitive defense of Malraux's abrupt transitions, and even daunting lack of transitions, in these words: "It would have been an artistic fault of the author to weld the varied scenes and episodes of his book into an organic whole at the expense of the impressions of jerky, scattered, and futile truth, which he wanted to produce. The real unity of the novel lies in the parallel but always separate preoccupations of the characters. More than any other motive, the consciousness of their implacable solitude drives them to common action.") But in any event, and for whatever conscious reasons, Malraux avoids the polished organization that gives the works of more conventional artists their fine clarity. We are reminded of the practice of the stone-cutters who followed Rodin, their massive granite chipped to reveal the grain of the rock; in them we find again a motive akin to that of Functionalism and Constructivism.

The strange consequence has been that whereas Presentationalism in the theater, Post-Impressionism in the plastic arts, and Constructivism in literature are supposed to appeal to what is primitive and instinctive in us, only the most sophisticated observers seem able to understand or appreciate them. That the proletariat cannot understand proletarian poetry is an oft-cited complaint.

Let us stop and consider this paradox.

I might demand of myself why I should stare at a roughly timbered runway on the stage and think of it as a wooded

path through a forest. In these matters I am not entirely
Philistine or unimaginative, and I do not ask that the whole
forest be planted for me. Two trees modestly suggested, two
sprigs even, would suffice. . . . But let the stage design have
some relation to a forest path: at least, do not insist upon
showing me the very opposite—brick walls, radiators, and
scaffolding. The novelty of that soon passes.

Burke has pointed out that one of our primary esthetic
pleasures comes from the observance of fidelity to nature.
And, since the technique of Constructivism is patently so
much easier in its demands on the artist, we also forego the
pleasure Gautier describes us as having when we observe the
triumph of skill in a difficult medium.

Simplicity? Practicality? Immediacy? Sullivan did much for
American architecture by helping to realize the possibilities of
a new form, by teaching his fellow architects to be unafraid
in their search for height, but is the steel skeleton the most
beautiful part of a skyscraper? In remaining content with the
skeleton or glass wall, does the artist indicate enough of his
creative resources? An art given to decoration is usually a
decadent one. The rococo in architecture is decadent. Decadent writers embellish their sentences with pretty phrases. Yet
in the hands of Keats, the decorated line becomes the apotheosis of poetry. Let us take the evidence of the eye: the neo-
Gothic pinnacles of Cass Gilbert soar with sunlit beauty
upward. There is no need to confound physical evidence by
intellectual theory: the fallacy of Evreinov, possibly, is that
he insists his audience must have time to *learn* acceptance of
what he has claimed rises from unsatisfied instinct. This, too,
the proletarian poets demand. They, like Evreinov and Craig,
fail to consult the full number of our instincts. Poetic experience must have immediacy, but mere immediacy does not give
us poetry. Pure illusion is as unselective as Naturalism. Not
only must art awaken the imagination, but it must startle us
by its representational skill.

There is wisdom in the belief that proletarian literature
should have a new method, and many reasons why what is
stark, pointed, and physically economical, by the tenets of
Constructivism, should attract Communist artists. But in its
every aspect it requires a knowledge for its enjoyment that is
foreign to the audience they seek. (The Chinese, after all, are
not a primitive people: their "theatrical" theater is like our

ballet, designed for a culture of the ultimate refinement.) The average reader can no more decipher Malraux, his broken narrative manner, than the average man can find beauty in the harshly colored daubs that pass for proletarian graphic art.

VII

These are some of the counts against proletarian art; they vary in pertinence as proletarian artists as different as Nexø and Malraux vary among themselves. This newest social novel is generally lacking in the excitant warmth of an artistic personality; its craftsmen have not properly prepared themselves, and they neither seek deeply nor range widely. And because of its Marxist prejudice, proletarian literature has inadequate suspense, surprise, originality. It has hobbled itself with a method whose nakedness, like that of the king in the fairy tale, is ultimately a most unroyal lack of costume. But what is more important is to ask, as I did in Tereshkovitch's theater, what warrant these novelists have when they turn to explore and report on the world of economics. Are they economists? Whence do they draw their authority? From the world of everyday experience, where Fielding, Melville, or Conrad acquired the practical knowledge that helped them to determine ethical values? Do they stand superior to the theoretical economist as the philosophical novelist does to the proper philosopher?

Plato says, on behalf of the artist, that he can describe a table better than a carpenter. He argues truly that Homer's descriptions of battles are more vivid than any a general could set down. He would probably have said the same of economics in art, had Athens produced a proletarian novelist. But the economics of Athens must have been a relatively simple subject, well within the artist's mental grasp. Our modern economics? That is something more complex than a Platonic table or even a Homeric battle.

An artist lives in the world of fish and fowl the same as any other man. Because he is a sensitive observer, he may have much to tell us of the psychological and emotional truths of men at work. But of the workings of the economic system itself, how much does he know? How much does he know of political science, which is so closely related to economics? He has the same opportunities to learn of them, of course, as the academic theorists. A man who shares the knowledge of

Veblen or Keynes and is a novelist besides, might be well-equipped to write a social novel. There, if his work is pervaded by honesty, would be the place for an empirical trial of his ideas: we have something of that sort, in a different field, when Santayana turns novelist. Still another instance of it is provided by C. P. Snow, who is both novelist and physical scientist. In his *Strangers and Brothers* series, Snow is hoping to bridge the gap between the widely disparate worlds of art and politics and the academic life and physics. He feels, and rightly, that the average person knows too little of the impact of modern science on everyday life, and that artists in particular are too uninformed about such things.

But usually the artist does not acquire his ideas by reading books, or by scientific thinking. The men who pore for years over abstractions, delighted with logic for its own sake, are seldom artists. The physical researcher is even less apt to be. The artist is intuitive. When he is not intuitive, impatient, poetic, he is a Naturalist: he writes long, tedious, factual novels. Zola and the Goncourts seek to weld science and art. But generally we concede that theirs is a mistaken effort.

Of course, a qualified economist might write a social novel, but we can doubt that it would be a great one. Great writing demands a lifetime to learn the craft. Our concern, always, is with major literature. We already have a competent but still not satisfying contemporary social art, at its best in the relentless and brave reporting of Steinbeck and the cinematic panoramas of Dos Passos. In Steinbeck, especially, there are the sentimentality and false heroics, the faults and timely virtues of good journalism, of which *The Grapes of Wrath* and *The Moon Is Down* are excellent examples. But we are looking for more than this.

Oddly, the proletarian theme—which flourished in the United States during the Depression years, the hungry and grim 1930's—is now, three decades later, having a recrudescence in England, in the lively novels of Alan Sillitoe, Kingsley Amis, John Braine, and others, with an even more powerful expression of protest in the plays of John Osborne, Arnold Wesker, and—in part—Harold Pinter, all belonging in some degree to the so-called School of Angry Young Men. Some years ago, Joseph Warren Beach stated that English writers were too class-conscious and hence could not portray working-class people as well as American authors do; they tried, but betrayed their condescension; they looked down at the lower classes and pitied them, or thought them quaint. (Arnold Bennett and D. H. Lawrence were certainly exceptions.) Obviously, this has changed. It is interesting that this new school of novelists has as yet won little attention over here, where their subject is something which the American fiction reader experienced and grew weary of a long while ago. Years of steady prosperity since the almost forgotten Depression doubtless account for some of this difference in attitude. Also, there is no deep feeling of resentment in America against an Establishment such as apparently exists in England, where militant social change among the working classes is still in process. In any event, none of these "proletarian" writers—they are mostly Socialistic—has as yet been attributed major stature, though all are still too young to have their future clearly foretold.

What are our chances for art dealing with economics that shall be exciting, compelling, "hypnotic," as is other art? We find such hypnotism only in Malraux, among our present day advanced social writers; and Malraux, as we have said, qualifies as such only because he records the violent proletarian movement of which he was for a time a participant, and not because he makes any pretense to being an economist. He sympathized with certain economic ideas, but that was not to him sufficient authority for his outright espousal of the logic of Communism in a novel. He simply tried to make us sympathetic to Marxists, rather than to Marxist dogma.

Ethical theories are centuries old; economic theories are most of them new. All ethical ideas have many times been put to proof of both experience and probing art, but many economic ideas are still untried (among them, Communism). We may even wonder whether there is yet a science of economics. There exists such disagreement among economists themselves that some onlookers suspect that the formulation of their "science" is still in the stage of medicine before Harvey and psychology before Freud.

The fundamental fault, then, may not lie with the proletarians or their method, but with their subject. Economics is not yet malleable material for art. Most of the proletarian writers, of course, would not agree. They accept Marx. But they are weak novelists. They lampoon, distort, protest. They too seldom convince.

Like the proletarian authors, I would like to see the social novel enlarge its field, but I question the novelist's authority—lacking a blind faith in Marx—to sift economic problems and propound solutions. Perhaps the artist's rôle remains one of sharpening the social conscience. It continues the failure of Dickens and Tolstoi to attain an organic wholeness for their social themes, of Galsworthy to include a personal, realistic, profound presentation of economics in his socially crusading works. But to sharpen the ethical-social conscience of the reader, to tell him vividly of misery, poverty, and distress, to predispose his attitude toward reform, is a good part of society's battle.

At the same time, this task implies that the novelist must concern himself with what Lionel Trilling has called "moral realism." The novelist must ask what, in each specific instance, might lie behind a seemingly good or altruistic impulse. He must examine the true reasons for people taking up a social cause, it may be. Are they doing it for disguised motives? Are they, perhaps, psychologically compensating thereby for some other want or desire in their lives? "Moral indignation," as Mr. Trilling astutely observes, "may be in itself an exquisite pleasure. This does not invalidate moral indignation . . . but only says when it is legitimate and when not." For, as he elaborates, "The moral passions are even more wilful and imperious and impatient than the self-seeking passions. All history is at one in telling us that their tendency is to be not only liberating but restrictive. . . . Some paradox of our natures leads us, when once we have made our fellow men the objects of our enlightened interest, to go on to make them the objects of our pity, then of our superior wisdom, ultimately of our coercion." The novelist must, by his tireless investigation of human nature, help to "prevent this corruption, the most ironic and tragic man knows." Indeed, this has been the catastrophic story of our age, this very corruption of our best-intentioned people, many of whom have become the unwitting yet self-willed dupes and agents of tyranny. Finally, as Mr. Trilling also warns, "To act against social injustice is right and noble, but to choose to act so does not settle all moral problems, but on the contrary, generates new ones of an especially difficult sort." This is a plain fact which our social novelists too often have not recognized or have failed to point out to their readers. Much more needs to be contributed along these several lines by the novelists of the future.

What we really await is economics, that unshaped science. When it appears, if it ever does, the novel will be able to cope with it, to illuminate and test it. By then, I predict, it will have been assimilated into the philosophical novel as have all other phases of social art before it.

Chapter 26

The Changing Novel

Two DECADES ago there was an amazing renascence of interest in Henry James. Even while the Second World War was on, books about James began to pour from the press, and new editions of his works became highly popular. Frankly this is hard to explain. None of James's critics of an earlier decade had expected it. They prophesied that James was virtually through. He was too refined, too aristocratic, to have any mid-century appeal. But now they are confounded, for James has continued into the day of the atom and the space race with startling success. In one recent year, I counted four new critical studies of James. Has as much been written about any other author in so short a time?

I confess that when I was younger, I expected to see a return of pleasure in writing like James's, but then I gave up hope. So I was confounded too, but more pleasantly, by the James revival. He repays anyone's reading of him, for he was keen in every way, and he was a wonderful maker of plots. So much else is said about James's gifts, and so little is remarked about his creative imagination. He saw the drama in very small things, the crises of tact, where very often the world's greatest drama lies. His mind was so alive. He was an artist in his own living, because every word had meaning for him. Those who make fun of his preoccupation with words, those who grow impatient with him, are missing the point. They miss a good deal of the point in life too, only they do not know it.

But I was speaking enviously of James's creative imagination. His fertility is breathtaking. (Edmund Wilson says that James is short on invention!) I wonder if any other writer has invented as many plots that are at the same time capable of allegory, or as revealing of states of consciousness, of character? His people all belong to the same world, true. But what is the harm in that? Every novelist has his own cosmos. James's world is a rich one in terms of personality. His people are worthy of our attention, because they can teach us much about possibilities of living. They set us a goal. His brother William James wrote a book about *Varieties of Religious Experience*. Henry James's work, his whole Human Comedy, is about "Varieties of Romantic Experience," and I thought he struck a prophetic note in this.

II

I do not know whether André Malraux has ever read James, but it does not matter. I have never read St. Thomas Aquinas, but I live in a mental world that Thomism helped to shape, and I am different because of that, whether I know it or not. I confess to not knowing much about the physics of Maxwell, either, but I guess that many of my daily actions, the switches I click, result from Maxwell's genius. These men have made us. So it must be with Malraux. He is a child of James, because James and Joyce were the novelists preëminent of our time, and no worker in the craft has gone uninfluenced. I would only like to say, if there had never been a Henry James, there would never have been a *Man's Fate*. Malraux is different in many ways, but his analyses of consciousnesses are so much like James, that they astonish me every time I look at his novel.

Of course, Malraux owes other debts: to Dostoevski and Conrad. They too probe the conspiratorial mind. In *The Secret Agent* and *Under Western Eyes,* Conrad gives us notable studies of revolutionary zealots. I mention this only to stress how close our most modern writers are to those they have supposedly outdistanced.

The point I want to make is that the novel of the future may not be too much different from the novel of the past. One reason for this may be that literature reflects life, and human nature probably does not greatly change, despite revolutions. Hitler and fission, Stalin and sociology, come and go, and we are still the same. One thing we see is cycles. I think James began a literary cycle which is still far from ended.

III

Some years ago there was a book on James, C. Hartley Grattan's study, *The Three Jameses,* which concludes this way:

It would seem logical to suppose that the passion for analysis and discrimination and logic by which those contemporary critics not affected particularly by economics are beset, should have its creative counterpart in fiction of the structural sort. The great danger is that it will be, if it comes, fiction definitely set apart from life which is, today, so immediately conditioned by economic influences expressing themselves through science and technology. In the light of the social forces at work in the world I cannot help agreeing with Edmund Wilson that the next period in fiction will be characterized by the social novel, the pre-War development of which Henry James so thoroughly ignored.

Mr. Grattan is writing as an advocate of the proletarian novel. But whatever his critical leaning, he should be grateful that Henry James did ignore the social novel for the good reason that this "historian of fine consciences" knew little or nothing about politics and economics. Henry James stays faithfully at the task of writing consummately well about the people his nature and experience had allowed him to observe with individual penetration. Those people were innocents who were politically naïve. That he is the historian of a dying class, as Malraux is the historian of a rising one, does not make him less important than Malraux. The artist's virtues, says Goethe, are his own; his faults are the failings of his time. In his own day, James was a revolutionary. He was even considered daring, immoral. *Daisy Miller* was deemed an outrageous tale, as was *The Ambassadors*. When one realizes how far James went, to accuse him of not having gone further —with the perspective of an additional twenty years—is hardly appreciative.

But what of Mr. Grattan's statement that literature in the tradition of James—that is to say the philosophical novel at its finest, most subtle—is destined to become an art "set apart from life" by its very fineness and subtlety? There did seem reason for thinking so, in that world of great violence.

Yet Henry James was never as removed from life as his later-day critics seem to think. He could not have been and have achieved his rank as a novelist. It is only that Mr. Grattan, like the rest of us, is far removed from the life that was Henry James's. But though the world has changed, the literary tradition that Henry James found and improved continues the same. André Malraux is really in that tradition. His writing betrays him an artist as deeply concerned as ever James was with subtle motivation, with words—words are little traps set to catch the heels of sensory experience—and form and poetry. Malraux is James's inheritor, as are other modern artists. This is part of James's greatness.

My belief, expressed in another essay, is that the philosophical novel by an inevitable osmosis continuously absorbs the social problem; for where the social novel becomes art it is philosophy. Its aim is ethical; it guides the reader by helping him to determine what is good and evil in the social scene. Through the osmosis of art, this social philosophy becomes part of our personal heritage. If James were writing of fine consciences today, he could not omit a political awareness. He actually takes up the theme in his *Princess Casamassima,* a revealing study of a woman who embraces radical social causes from guilt feelings at having sold herself into loveless marriage to get wealth and a title. Anyone who reads this very original novel will discover for himself that James is adequate to his subject.

IV

Quite a different opinion of contemporary art is found in Mary Colum's *From These Roots,* a book to which I have referred before. Mrs. Colum looks at modern writing and finds it to be chiefly "decadent realism," still dominated by the once invigorating but long-since exhausted ideas of Sainte-Beuve and Flaubert. She believes that in *Madame Bovary* Flaubert himself has quite the last word. All realistic writing since has had declining force.

But I do not agree with Mrs. Colum either, for it seems to me that in gazing at modern literature she has overlooked our greatest writers. "In the highest realism there has to be romanticism," says Mrs. Colum, "for that is natural to human life and human imagination." That is very true. But after Flaubert, starting with James and continuing to the present, have we not had an ever richer literature expressive of this highest realism, that is romanticism? By and large, it has been the significant literature of our time, and I believe the novel of the immediate future will be even more romantic. What we may expect, what we already have, is a "New Romanticism."

James, Conrad, Galsworthy, Lawrence—are they "decadent realists"? Mann, Werfel, Rolland, Gide, Undset?

It is important to define our words. This New Romanticism needs to be separated from the French and English Romantic movements of the early nineteenth century.

Those movements in French and English literary history, deriving from the ideas of Rousseau and Godwin, and beautifully expounded by Hugo and Shelley and Keats, are characterized by a sentimental emotionalism. They also represent a mere revolt from a narrowing Classical tradition, and actually serve as an approach to Realism, and finally the Naturalism of the Goncourts and Zola.

By Realism here we do not mean the "primitivism" of Fielding, or even Flaubert's careful study (the author of *Salammbô* was never a Realist at heart), but what is substantially the equivalent of a skeptical materialism, sometimes hedonistic, sometimes fatalistic, apotheosized in the works of Anatole France, Thomas Hardy, and A. E. Housman. Flaubert evolved the method; he never possessed the philosophy. The philosophy itself was called into being by the rising materialism of the eighteenth and nineteenth centuries, that soon crushed Romanticism. Winter came to those exuberant Romantics, but Spring was very far behind. A comparison of Hugo's *Les Misérables,* so full of faith, and Zola's sociological *Nana* tells us the story. Lately the materialistic discoveries of Behaviorism, so emphatically environmental, have sustained the sociological novel's progress.

The New Romanticism has been a shift in emphasis from the objective, the environmental, to the subjective and instinctive. Realism made gains for art. The New Romanticism has preserved but modified the observant method of Realism, without relapsing to the old emotionalism of Chateaubriand, Hugo. The greatest of the new realistic Romantics, Conrad, declared himself "mindful of that sobriety of interior life, that asceticism of sentiment, in which alone the naked forms of truth, such as one conceives it, such as one feels it, can be rendered without shame." He pledged himself to avoid, we recall, the "maudlin and indecent verity that comes out through the strength of wine."

Particularly the New Romanticism has derived from the psychological realism of Henry James, who opened a whole new subjective world to the novel. Henry James was perhaps the first "New Romantic."

The true study of any movement disclaims the notion that

it begins at a single point in time, and seldom if ever does it find a wholly satisfactory exponent in one man. Besides, were I to attempt that, I should be repeating the error of the professional critics, of whom I have sometimes complained. I do not even believe that literary movements have any but a general existence; they cannot be established by specific examples without resort to half-truths about the men chosen to prove a point. Thus I dare not oppose James to Anatole France and say that while James was starting a Romantic resurgence, France in turn was bringing Realism to its full and final glory. The opposition is doubly perilous. It refers to Realism only in the narrowest sense. And outwardly France, the wonderful colorist, the inspired sensualist, shows many more signs than James of the traits conventionally termed romantic, an unfavorable contrast that would seem to spill any such argument from the lap of fact.

The contrast results from James's fading sensory equipment, which was unequal to his later task of subtler investigation. The famous difficulty of his style, in this period, comes from a lack of visual images that reduces his ideas to mere words printed on a page. The reader is so infrequently given a picture, that he must stop to translate the meaning of every word, and even a novel as rich and witty as *The Ambassadors* grows dull from this effort.

But glance back at France, satyr and philosopher. We shall never see his like again, for he was the product of an age that is gone. It was an age of Realism, of satire, in which skepticism came into its own as a means to the discovery of new truth. Oscar Wilde too belongs to that age.

Even in America, it was around the satiric, decadent banner of James Branch Cabell that the standards of youthful revolt gathered only a few decades ago. And this very skepticism, which soon devolved into a pagan cynicism, spelled, in literary form, the "Renaissance of American free thought, vital art, and native letters."

Victorianism was responsible; it was something grand to revolt against. Today the problem has become more difficult: the cause of future revolt, always against established authority, must be against skepticism itself. Americans linger far behind Continental writers in this.

I wished, in speaking of the New Romanticism, merely to illustrate this assured truth that the task of the artist has become once more creative, rather than predominantly critical. And that is where Henry James and France part company; for there is a skeptical spirit running through France's realism that at last narrows his appeal. Henry James is realistic too, but his mood is anything but skeptical. *The Ambassadors* affirms life in terms as glowing as he could muster.

And Joseph Conrad's affirmation is infinitely more resounding, in proportion as his humanity is greater, his experience broader, and his senses more alive. He does not use his intellect and his sensory equipment—one of the richest given to any man—to celebrate skepticism, as does Anatole France, but triumphantly to overcome it. *Victory,* he calls his great novel.

Then the New Romanticism could be defined as a movement of creative affirmation, originating in James and Conrad and flowing contrary to the continuing Naturalism and Skeptical Realism that marks much of the literature of our day, especially here in America, descending from Norris and Dreiser to undecided and unhappy realists like Sinclair Lewis, Hemingway, and Faulkner. Some of these last are nostalgic, but nostalgia alone is not a creative offering.

v

By what authority could these Realists turn Romantic? It may have been by the authority of temperament, by acknowledgment of that truth aphorized by Mrs. Colum that romanticism is "natural to human life and human imagination." But there was also appearing in the world's intellectual atmosphere a new conviction. Science, that was supposed to have destroyed poetry, suddenly admits that it is itself but another kind of poetry. The great astronomers and mathematicians, Eddington, Sullivan, Jeans, confess that the "truths" of science can lay no greater claims to objective validity than those of mystical art. They paraphrase, in a sense, all that Conrad bespeaks in his vision of the "spectatorial universe." They give imaginative literature that philosophical warrant of which we have so insistently spoken. Eddington, in particular, declares that man's sense of humor is as mystically born, as physically real, as any other force in our world: for the disciples of these scientists, a strange, unexpected dignity now attends Fielding's expressed endeavor "to laugh mankind out of their favorite follies and vices." The poet's vision is as important as the astronomers'. "Confronted by the same enigmatical spectacle," Conrad writes, "the artist descends within himself, and in that lonely region of stress and strife, if he be deserving and fortunate, he finds the terms of his appeal."

Thus Conrad, the spectator, the poet, renders the "wonders of the visible universe"; while we have had concomitant in Lawrence and James separate explorations of the worlds of "sense and sensibility." In every field of human experience, these creative workers have been busy. Feuchtwanger and Allen study the past—are these "decadent realists"? Edith Wharton and Willa Cather search for the romantic beliefs that women cherish and live by: "decadent realists!" Proust opens to us the resources of memory. The puritan Gide is led by inversion to attack the very morality by which he was formed, that gave fire to his mind, to attain a new physical freedom: a liberty, perhaps a license, won only by mental emancipation. Bunin records man's brutal new idealism, contrasting it with the old. Schnitzler gently mourns and memorializes; Thomas Mann tells us of the artist himself. These are some of the men we might call the New Romantics. . . . They are the important writers of our era.

"The changing wisdom of successive generations discards ideas, questions facts, demolishes theories," observed Conrad. "But the artist appeals to that part of our being which is not dependent on wisdom; to that in us which is a gift and not an acquisition—and, therefore, more permanently enduring. He speaks to our capacity for delight and wonder, to the sense of mystery surrounding our lives; to our sense of pity, and beauty, and pain; to the latent feeling of fellowship with all creation—and to the subtle but invincible conviction of solidarity that knits together the loneliness of innumerable hearts, to the solidarity in dreams, in joy, in sorrow, in aspirations, in illusions, in hope, in fear, which binds men to each other, which binds together all humanity—the dead to the living, and the living to the unborn."

VI

Is such later-day Romanticism a "literature of escape"? There are some who think so, who would even welcome it as such. They see no reason why modern writers should not embrace Matthew Arnold's prophecy that as machines occupy the world, men will turn to poetry for refuge. They foresee that the Romantic artists are an answer to Ortega's cry in *The Revolt of the Masses* for those who shall preserve from the mass-mind and the mass-emotions what is tender, nostalgic, hallowed, breathlessly delicate and true. They would have them a consecrated band, who like the medieval monks in their cloisters should tend in private adoration the precious relics of civilization, all that is proud, all that is rare, persistently unflinching, beautiful, too fine for common use, evolved by a chosen few through long generations.

But we should rather think of the New Romanticism as a "literature of expression," defining man's subjective contribution to the universe, not a refuge at all, but a *fountainhead* of what is rightfully romantic in life. It is William James's contention that man is not only affected by the real world, but that he himself *adds* on to "reality" by his concepts of it. The romantic artist is one who formulates the universe in poetic, musical terms—but remembering always, that as he is an artist, his terms must be honest, not self-blinding, like those of the early nineteenth-century Romantics. For that other is false romanticism.

This is one form of the serious novel of the present and near future, as I see it.

VII

In general the literary method of Romanticism is impressionistic. It not only centers on the significant detail, the memorable picture, but like that movement in French painting —Impressionism—which was born in the lifetime of James and Conrad, it spiritualizes, realizing atmospheric qualities not apparent to the naked eye.

Impressionism in literature is not new. Sterne is an Impressionist. Yet its general acceptance, I think, has been only recent, and in particular the use to which it has been put. For with Impressionism our artists have been able to achieve something new, a literary accomplishment more purely exemplified in the short stories of Chekov and his followers than in the novel. In the short story, the "impression" remains both the means and the end. In the novel, it can by virtue of its effluent nature be but a means to a larger end.

Chekov is the first among moderns to write a form of story that many readers still protest is not a story at all. It pays little attention to plot but places emphasis upon physical scenes and characters in a deliberate search for *qualities* of experience. Just as the French Impressionist painters seek to *realize* light, so the practitioners of this type of story seek for a higher awareness of mental and physical phenomena. They attempt in words what Debussy and Ravel attempt in music, to capture moods. Katherine Mansfield and Lawrence write stories of this sort. Kay Boyle, Sherwood Anderson, and William Saroyan are later workers.

A deft economy of means is also a feature of the impressionistic technique. Chekov himself puts it thusly: "To do something with the least possible number of movements is the definition of grace."

Elizabeth Drew summarizes the functioning of this "graceful" and "spiritualizing" method: "Chekov illustrated something of the impulses, desires, instincts and emotions which can be released into consciousness in an instant of time. . . . The artists who feel everything in flashes which sting the nerves and senses, who can convey a whole situation by a gesture. . . . Sometimes 'existence' becomes like a drop of water seen under a microscope, a substance teeming with unsuspected activity, where the reader lives in a tensity of feeling, a keenness of perception and a pitch of sensitiveness —a complete heightened reality—which makes normal life seem nothing but a shapeless blur." As further exposited by Miss Drew, the impressionistic writer seeks to catch "what Montaigne calls 'the many little nimble motions of the soul.' "

This *realization* of emotional mood, of mental state and physical atmosphere, is what we observe illuminating the pages of James, Conrad, Lawrence, and Mann. Through significant detail, through painstaking choice of words—indeed, through nervous attention to the very sound of words, their every connotation—the author works as does a painter. Hardy knew this; Egdon Heath is bathed in bleak light. There is scarcely a scene in Conrad in which the environment is not truthfully shown as a reflection of the characters' states of mind; and those states of mind, as a reflection of the evanescent environment. "All my moral and intellectual being is penetrated by an invincible conviction," said Conrad, "that whatever falls under the dominion of our senses must in nature and, however exceptional, cannot differ in its essence from all the other effects of the visible and tangible world of which we are a self-conscious part." Description, then, becomes not an ornament to a story, but almost the story itself. What is sometimes called "fine writing" becomes the very means of art. All the feeling of Lawrence, that master of electric prose, is implicit in what he tells of the luminous color, the caressing softness, of the cold, moist flowers he holds in his hand, his nervous eyes examining the shaking stamen and stem as Monet or Renoir would gaze upon them. But no one has so well symbolized his scene as Conrad; every hue of the sunset is a metaphor of his characters' anxious states of soul. That is why *Nostromo, Heart of Darkness, Lord Jim* are transcendental works.

"The romantic," says James, "stands for things that, with all the facilities in the world, all the wealth and all the courage and all the wit and all the adventure, we never *can* directly know; the things that can reach us only through the beautiful circuit and subterfuge of our thought and our desire."

Where the impressionistic short story concentrates on the heightened experience itself, the novel is a compilation of such experiences that illuminate some central and major problem. Impressionism has been rightly defined as a refined realism. It may, inexpertly handled, result in art that is sketchy, tenuous. Perhaps that is one reason why cautious Romantic novelists, while impressionistic, have also been very formal in structure, harking back to James, whose preoccupation with "form"—the singular point-of-view, the well-placed climax—has made him best known; indeed, emulating Degas and Cézanne, who are insistently formal, as is Ravel in music.

The analogy to painting and the other arts, and the problem of "form" which arises, is also skillfully illustrated by Professor Beach:

> The impressionist painter saw his subject less in terms of the outline which is known to be there and more in terms of the mass which strikes the eye. And his technique was to build up an impression of the mass by laying spots of color side by side. James is pre-impressionist in the novel by virtue of the precision with which his issue is defined by the tight little line of his plot, the steadiness with which he maintains a chosen point-of-view—what

may be called the exact fixation of each element in the narrative. Lawrence, in poetry and the novel, is an impressionist because he is not concerned with the dramatic shape of the thing but with the living "feel" of it. He has a character—Paul—say, that he seeks, in his sketches, not the stiffness of the shape but "the shimmering protoplasm in the leaves and everywhere." . . . It is this shimmeriness which is the chief contribution of D. H. Lawrence to novelistic technique . . . in reaction to the well-made novel. He is, in the novel, very little of the dramatist and very much of the poet.

In Conrad is present, as Professor Beach remarks, a better balance between an acutely and poetically reported "feeling" and again the more formal elements of "drama" and "shape."

From a delicate prose Impressionism of this sort to forthright poetry seemed to me but one step.

VIII

I am indebted to Henri Peyre for his comment that the rôle of a minor prophet is a safe one. "No one takes the trouble to read his prophecies and, if he knows his part at all, he makes them ambiguous and contradictory enough so as never to be without honor."

In my earlier version of this book, more than two decades ago, I went on from my discussion of Impressionism and bravely wrote: "We can no more prophesy the novel of the distant future than we can prophesy the world's far-off political and economic future. The two are inexorably one. But the highest art has always been poetic art. The novel derived from the epic: Fielding sought for the epic in prose. I wonder if the novel will not eventually return to poetry."

I said further: "Scott was the last important poet to turn to the novel. After him, only Byron successfully writes verse in extended form. But fifty years ago the tired novelist Hardy wrote *The Dynasts* and again gave English literature great poetry in epic form. Since then, in the works of Robinson Jeffers, Archibald MacLeish, Mark Van Doren, and other good modern poets we have been having novels in verse. If I am not mistaken, Jeffers' *Cawdor*, E. Arlington Robinson's *Tris-*

tram, MacLeish's *Conquistador* are new epics. There is already a public for them. Of what are they a forerunner?"

Alas, for my honor as a prophet: they proved to be the forerunner of nothing. Novels in epical verse have not continued to appear; they have almost vanished as a genre. Furthermore, if the "Neo-Realist School" is to be taken as an indication, the novel is presently moving away from Impressionism and poetry, not toward it.

But I am far from convinced that this is so. Actually, the poetic novel has been very much in evidence and highly influential during the past two decades since I set down my risky prediction, but in a different guise from the one I then appreciated or foresaw. Its prevalent new form is the Symbolist novel, and its most important exponents have been Franz Kafka and Albert Camus. (Kafka wrote before World War II, of course, but was published and became a vogue only posthumously.) But Symbolism is another topic, too complex for brief discussion, and I prefer to touch on it separately.

A Reading List

Here are the titles of some notable books on the technique of the novel. In particular, those by Professor Beach, Professor Lathrop, and Mr. Muir are most rewarding.

The English Novel, by Walter Allen

The Twentieth-Century Novel, Studies in Technique, by Joseph Warren Beach

The Intellectual Hero, by Victor Brombert

The Novel and the Modern World, by David Daiches

The World of Fiction, by Bernard De Voto

The Modern Novel, by Elizabeth Drew

Aspects of the Novel, by E. M. Forster

Art of the Novel, by Henry James

The Art of the Novelist, by Henry Burrowes Lathrop

The Great Tradition, by F. R. Leavis

The Craft of Fiction, by Percy Lubbock

The Structure of the Novel, by Edwin Muir

New French Writing, by Claude Mauriac

The Mirror in the Roadway, by Frank O'Connor

Forms of Fiction, edited by William Van O'Connor

The Contemporary French Novel, by Henri Peyre
Society and Self in the Novel, by Mark Schorer
The English Novel, Form and Function, by Dorothy Van Ghent
The Common Reader, by Virginia Woolf
Craft and Character, by Morton Dauwen Zabel

Chapter 27

Albert Camus and Symbolism

THE VERY term "Symbolism" is elusive and difficult to define. Usually, one begins by differentiating between what is "symbolic" and what is "allegorical." In an allegorical work, we clearly perceive the author's intention: "x" equals this, and "y" equals that. We know exactly, as in Aesop's *Fables*, what is the moral, although it is presented a bit obliquely. It is easy to guess the point of the story about the fox and the sour grapes, or about the race between the tortoise and the hare. The same is true of such classic allegories as *Pilgrim's Progress* and *Gulliver's Travels*. But a work of art that is symbolic is much less specific: it has a vague or multiple meaning or reference. The author's point is ambiguous, often deliberately so, because he wishes to suggest infinitely more than he states. To an extent much greater than in the allegory, the Symbolist writer requires that readers make a large personal contribution to the significance at which he is hinting. Indeed, each reader may interpret the story for himself and attach to it his own meaning.

Stéphane Mallarmé, leader of the nineteenth-century French Symbolist school, puts it this way: "The symbol contains the idea as the seed contains the flower." We ourselves, as readers, must imagine what form the flower shall later take, and our guesses about it may vary. Mallarmé also sought for poetic symbols that would have the effect of "pure" or "abstract" music, whose suggestion stirs amorphous, drifting images in the mind and soul of the listener. But when I speak of the Symbolist novel, I am not referring to any work of Mallarmé's *fin de siècle* school, in which he was joined or followed by Verlaine, Maeterlinck, Stefan George, Gerhart Hauptmann, Hugo von Hofmannsthal, Leonid Andreyev. All these artists practiced mostly in poetry and drama and the short story: what applies to those art forms does not apply to the novel. For one thing, the novel is much longer than any of these other literary genres and therefore requires more unity and a more definite sense of structure; nor can it remain "vague" too repeatedly, or for too many pages, lest the reader become too confused or find it too tiresome.

Symbolism of a very minor sort appears in all fiction. Indeed, in essence language itself is symbolic, each word representing a physical object or intellectual concept. Keep in mind, however, that a writer usually tries to have his language be not vague but as plain and concrete as possible. But the symbolic nature of language is too elementary a question for us to stop and examine now. To proceed to another point, even the most realistic story may and in fact should contain what might be termed "symbolic business" or "symbolic detail." In Joyce's *Ivy Day in the Committee Room,* as David Daiches remarks, one of the characters pauses at just a certain moment to put a match to the candles; this lights up the bareness of the room and stresses its denuded aspect. Dorothy Van Ghent singles out a similar symbolic touch in *Lord Jim.* The S.S. *Jeddah,* the actual ship whose fate had inspired Conrad's tale, had been in danger of foundering in a storm. Conrad alters this, and has the *Patna's* hull ripped by a submerged reef instead, which could be an allusion to the young man's equally hidden cowardice. But symbolic touches or details like this, although they enrich a story, do not put a novel into a Symbolist category; for they are too superficial or peripheral.

The true Symbolist novel is one in which the central idea is capable of limitless interpretation: it is built around a "multiple image" that has not merely two planes of meaning, as in an allegory, but a boundless number of them. The foremost example is *Moby Dick.* When first published, Melville's tale of Captain Ahab's world-wide pursuit of his nemesis was looked upon as merely a long-winded story about whalers, and later it was recognized as an allegory; but in both forms it was quite neglected. Only when Symbolism came into fashion, many years later, was Melville's novel "discovered" and revived and wildly, even worshipfully acclaimed: it is now found to be crowded with meanings and mythical adumbrations without count. Hundreds of doctoral theses and books by critics seek to unravel its mysteries: their titles fill scores of index cards in library trays. (A ten-year halt to them might prove a blessing to subsequent scholars who must attempt to read them all!) Much the same has happened to Melville's shorter, later work, *Billy Budd,* which was once a simple tragic drama of an innocent stammerer mistaken for a rebel, and then an allegory of the moral intricacies and dilemmas of a human struggle between good and evil. *Billy Budd* is now rumored to hold many more layers of meaning, many ambiguities and paradoxes, and to call for ever new readings in search of them.

Some critics aver that Henry James flirted with Symbolism in at least one of his widely read *contes*, *The Turn of the Screw*. Since critical probing-in-depth is currently in vogue, *The Turn of the Screw* is no longer taken to be merely a ghost story, or nothing more than a virtuoso's venture into the realm of the supernatural: instead, it is variously said to have a host of concealed meanings, ranging from its being a Freudian fantasy (as Edmund Wilson argues persuasively), to its very opposite, a theological parable. (The claim that the central theme of *The Turn of the Screw* is a dramatic conflict between the forces of divine Good and demonic Evil for possession of the children's souls is interestingly supported by the recent revelation that no less a person than the Archbishop of Canterbury gave Henry James the basic idea for this story.) Actually, the whole tendency of James's artistic nature is against mystification of motive: he explores human nature to *reveal* it; but this carries no weight with the critics. Still, I do not rule out the possibility that *The Turn of the Screw* invited a different handling by him, and that this one work by James is an exception to his habitual approach to ideas that fascinated him.

Joseph Conrad too is supposed to have written a Symbolist tale in *The Secret Sharer*, although no strain of ambiguity of this kind appears elsewhere in his work. Who is the secret sharer of the hero's cabin? He is not simply a fugitive, a young man seeking to escape punishment for a murder he has just committed. That answer is too plain, too unambitious. He *must* be the hero's other self, his *alter ego*? Even his *doppelgänger* (double)? The guilty and repressed side of his nature? The hidden, dark aspect of Conrad's own enigmatic personality?

Here is an analysis of Conrad's story by a professor at a New England university, who learnedly writes of it as "a double allegory."

It is an allegory of man's moral conscience, and an allegory of man's esthetic conscience. The form of *The Secret Sharer*, to diagram it, is the form of the capital letter

L—the very form of the captain's room. (It is hinted at, again, in the initial letter of Leggatt's name.) One part of the letter L diagrams the allegory of the Captain's divided soul, man in moral isolation and spiritual disunity. The other part of the letter represents the allegory of the artist's split soul ("the man who suffers and the man who creates"). The angle stands at the angle of the two isolations and the two searches for selfhood.

For myself, I doubt that Conrad had the time or the desire to indulge in abracadabra of this sort. I question whether any serious writer is interested in refining his work that far. But this does illustrate the excesses to which the quest for meanings-in-depth is carried by academic critics, who do have the time and patience for fanciful research and theorizing.

In any event, *Moby Dick* in its time was a lonely and unrecognized forerunner of a novel of this type. The work that finally launched the Symbolist fashion is Joyce's *Ulysses*, with the help of T. S. Eliot's authoritarian comments on it. In 1923, Mr. Eliot announced that the novel as previously formulated was dead.

Mr. Joyce has written one novel—the *Portrait;* Mr. Wyndham Lewis has written one novel—*Tarr*. I do not suppose that either of them will ever write another "novel." The novel ended with Flaubert and with James. It is, I think, because Mr. Joyce and Mr. Lewis, being "in advance" of their time, felt a conscious or probably unconscious dissastisfaction with the form, that their novels are more formless than those of a dozen clever writers who are unaware of its obsolescence.

In using the myth, in manipulating a continuous parallel between contemporaneity and antiquity, Mr. Joyce is pursuing a method which others must pursue after him. . . . It is simply a way of controlling, of ordering, of giving a shape and a significance to the immense panorama of futility and anarchy which is contemporary history. It is a method already adumbrated by Mr. Yeats. . . . Instead of narrative method, we may now use the mythical method.

It is from this dictate by Mr. Eliot that so much of the critical talk about "myth" has come, and deluged us for the past several decades.

Although the "mythical" method does not by itself create a Symbolist novel, it soon becomes the most popular tool for fiction of this kind. Small wonder, for witness how large a rôle it plays in *Ulysses*: as we have already noted, a major theme running through the book is that of ironic contrast to matching incidents in Homer's *Odyssey*, the search of Telemachus (Stephen) for his father (Bloom), and the parodied adventures of Ulysses himself on his long homeward journey. Then there are the implied correspondences between each section of the book and the organs of the human body. Besides these, there are also parallels in many of the same episodes not only to Homer's epic but also to Shakespeare's *Hamlet*; and each section also refers simultaneously to a different fine art, as well as the human organs. Add to this the very language, the portmanteau words Joyce tirelessly coins, in which an inherent linguistic symbolism is deliberately and immeasurably heightened. The attempt is, as Mr. Eliot says, to achieve unity and suggest universality, but at the same time it does offer a happy field day for critics. They can search and revel in this maze of analogies and "multiple images," and certainly have done so.

The action of *Ulysses* is handled fugally, musically. The characters change their sex and identities, while we share their hallucinatory experiences in realms of personal and collective dreams and drunkenness. The map of Dublin becomes a chart in sharp relief, garishly highlighted, of the agonized human mind. In both *Ulysses* and *Finnegan's Wake,* as Daiches remarks, there are at least three levels: actual, symbolic, esoteric. In *Ulysses* these three are somewhat distinguishable; but in *Finnegan's Wake* they fuse and can hardly be told apart. In *Finnegan's Wake* also, as Daiches states, each word has simultaneously many meanings, "like chords struck all at once, leaving an infinity of connotations reverberating and mingling in the mind." (The latest scholarship has established that many details in both books to which critics have fastened deep intentions were actually put in by Joyce carelessly or accidentally, but no matter about that.) All this makes for extremely difficult reading and interpretation, Daiches admits, but he pays tribute to *Finnegan's Wake* as a "stupendous achievement in pure art." Granted that Joyce had prodigious talent and dedication, *Finnegan's Wake* might also be called an achievement in pure nonsense. What value has it? But

Ulysses is another affair; though frequently obscure, it does remain readable, and it has moments as well of intensely clear communication.

The work of *Ulysses* has naturally been a subject of controversy. E. M. Forster describes it bitterly, as follows: "A dogged attempt to cover the universe with mud, it is an inverted Victorianism, an attempt to make grossness and dirt succeed where sweetness and light failed." He deplores its aim "to degrade all things and particularly civilization and art, by turning them inside out and upside down." Yet high praise of Joyce's masterwork is offered by C. H. Rickword (*A Note on Fiction*):

> Everything in *Ulysses* is reported; everything is shown or dramatized . . . not only the discrepancy between actuality and individual values, between things as they are and as they appear modified by sensibility; his irony springs from a more profound opposition—that within the subject, the contrast between actual impulse and the appearance that, too, assumes in consciousness. . . . He [Joyce] is able to exteriorize and objectify vast psychological tracts that as a rule lurk shapelessly outside the action of a novel, perceptible only as unaccountable influences that distort and hinder its progress. And regarding with an equal eye the response both to external and internal stresses, attributing no more value to the one than to the other, he is able to compel both into the same perspective and so set in motion events that, occurring simultaneously on both planes, are in themselves adequate and self-sufficient. Thus the authority and directness of objective presentation is secured for the subjective narrative, Joyce's unit being the consciousness, not its social crystallization, the character. Daedalus and Bloom are but symbols of disintegration. . . .

On the other hand, the noted poet and novelist Richard Aldington rejects *Ulysses* with vehemence. "I say that when Mr. Joyce, with his marvellous gifts, uses them to disgust us with mankind, he is doing something which is false and a libel on mankind." This provokes T. S. Eliot, as Joyce's defender, to reply in these words: "Mr. Aldington treated Mr. Joyce as a prophet of chaos; and wailed at the flood of Dadaism which his prescient eye saw bursting forth at the

tap of the magician's rod. Of course, the influence which
Mr. Joyce's book may have is from my point of view an
irrelevance. A very great book may have a very bad influence
indeed; and a mediocre book may be in the event most
salutary. The next generation is responsible for its own soul;
a man of genius is responsible to his peers, not a studio-full
of uneducated and undisciplined coxcombs." After which, Mr.
Eliot contemptuously dismisses Richard Aldington's "pathetic
solicitude for the half-witted," which apparently includes all
who lack his admiration for James Joyce.

What strikes me most forcibly in this last exchange of
opinions is the snobbery of Eliot's position, his appeal again
to an élite cult. In my own view, to overlook the content
of a novel because the method of telling it is clever (if not
overclever) is to prove oneself a very poor literary critic
indeed. The technique in and for itself is valueless. But one
must observe in Mr. Rickword's truly perceptive analysis the
"expertise" that is now needed to appreciate a Symbolist
book like *Ulysses,* and the special glossary now employed in
discussing such works, a tendency also apparent in other
fields of criticism today, especially in essays on abstract
painting, atonal music—not only is art becoming unintelligible
to the layman, but so too is the language used in critical talk
about it. Criticism itself is becoming as obscurant as the art it
sets out to dissect.

It is possible to see Virginia Woolf's *Orlando* as belonging to
the Symbolist category. Sometimes it is called "expressionistic." Professor Beach considers it a study of "multiple
personality" and a protest by Mrs. Woolf against the "stigma
of her sex," a revolt against forever being pigeonholed as a
"woman author" and nothing more. She shows in this character how intertwined our sexual natures and inheritances are;
her tone is quietly satirical. Orlando finally chooses to be a
woman, because that rôle grants her certain privileges and permits her to play a superior part in life. But *Orlando* qualifies as
a Jungian portrait as well; or it might be looked upon as
simply a colorful fantasy, a *jeu d'esprit,* a poetic and good-
humored flight by the gifted Mrs. Woolf; or even a history
of English literature, "virile in Elizabethan times, effeminate
under Victoria." Whatever its purport, its merits as a work
of art can hardly be disputed, and its likely meanings are
easily discerned; it does not tax the reader beyond the point
where pleasure ends.

II

Symbolism is one facet of a larger Romantic reaction to Victorian Philistinism; to Darwinian scientism and its concomitant Spencerian materialism; to the Industrial Revolution, Marxism, Zola's Naturalism—all that was too crass, brutal, coldly overlogical, factual, and ugly. It is a flight from these into subjectivism, fancy, even into supernaturalism. Whether those protesting became Pre-Raphaelites, Symbolists, Expressionists, their attempt was to get away from literalness. In France, especially, some of this reaction went to extremes, into black magic, decadence, and ultimately pseudo-Primitivism, Dadaism, Cubism, Surrealism, Abstractionism, the emerging Theater of the Absurd. The real or at least "realistic" image of human nature had to be destroyed, along with the traditional concept of God and society, and a wholly man-made representation, defiantly and willfully distorted, was set up to replace it. Part of the movement, therefore, is a destructive orgy, nihilistic; and part of it oddly constructive, humanistic. Symbolist artists were not without a critical and satiric spirit, nor unaware of the nightmarish aspects of life in our century and the torment that sensitive persons have suffered while trying to adjust to it. At the same time, some Symbolist artists have also been affirmative and compassionate.

A certain amount of experimentation in fiction has no other prompting than the perpetual desire of restless artists to find new forms. But in recent years some of it has resulted from an urgent need for devices to handle fresh material: Freudian and Jungian concepts, let us say; and to cope with a breakdown in the armature of society: religious disillusionments and loss of faith, moral revolts, a pragmatic relativism leading to a collapse of fixed standards. To some writers it seemed that realism and naturalism were inadequate to meet this challenge, for presumptively they deal only with the surface of people and events, not with what lies beneath, which had now become many readers' main concern.

Symbolism often brings the resources of poetry—"a highly charged language"—into prose fiction, and employs complex "multiple images" to suggest or express what had heretofore been the inapprehensible or inexpressible. The "multiple images," or symbols, are appropriate, for the Freudians and Jungians had demonstrated how dreams and neuroses use just such symbolic disguises for our real motivations. The consequence is that the Symbolist novel becomes a more difficult form to write and read; it grapples with far more intricate themes. Ineluctably, such a novel is more subtle and elusive, for its matter is often subtle and elusive too: intensely subjective, amorphous, fugitive, ambivalent; yes, the very stuff of dreams. But there is a limit of difficulty to which fiction of any kind can go and still have readers willingly follow it; some Symbolist novels, like *Finnegan's Wake,* overstep that line.

By no means all the Romantic protest in the novel took a Symbolist form. Some found an outlet in simpler fantasy. Among the writers who turned to this genre are W. H. Hudson (*Green Mansions*), H. G. Wells (*The Shape of Things to Come*), G. K. Chesterton (*The Man Who Was Thursday*). One thinks also of Luigi Pirandello (*The Late Mattia Pascal*), Sir James Barrie (his rueful plays especially, like *Peter Pan* and *Dear Brutus*), Walter de la Mare (*The Memoirs of a Midget*), Aldous Huxley (*Crome Yellow, Brave New World*), David Garnett (*Lady into Fox*), Richard Hughes (*High Wind in Jamaica*), William Golding (*Lord of the Flies*); and several books by Sylvia Townsend Warner, James Stephens, James Branch Cabell, Rebecca West, Elinor Wylie, and George Orwell. Nearly all of these fantasies have a sinister side; some, if their implications are grasped, are quite frightening. As the age grew darker, so did they. If this is a flight from reality, into dream, it is too often into a dream tinctured by nightmare.

Mark Schorer points out, very interestingly, that even some realistic writers, who did not turn to Symbolism or Fantasy, were forced "to press naturalism far beyond itself, into positively Gothic distortions." He cites Sherwood Anderson, William Carlos Williams, Ira Wolfert, Nathaniel West, and Erskine Caldwell as such would-be realists who often present us with grotesquely warped or exaggerated people and situations in their fiction. "The structural machinations of Dos Passos and the lyrical interruptions of Steinbeck are the desperate maneuvers of men committed to a method of whose limitations they despair. They are our symbolists *manqué,* who end as allegorists." The somewhat Gothic excess of violence in works by William Faulkner (*Sanctuary, The Sound and the Fury*) and Graham Greene (*Brighton Rock,*

The Ministry of Fear) may also have this source, and that theme of violence too may be an allegorical comment by these authors on our fearsome time.

III

Franz Kafka takes his place along with Melville as one of the incontestably major prose Symbolists. His work, after Joyce's, is responsible for the vogue of this kind of writing; it is tragic and ironic that his popularity followed only after his early death. At first glance, Kafka seems to be far easier reading than Joyce; his style is beautifully simple. His story outlines are clear, firm, always suspenseful. Walter Kerr has said, speaking of certain Symbolist plays, that before one can have an *overtone,* one must first have a *tone.* Much of the writing of this school has been soft and pretentious, with no bony structure to support it: the reader is given no plot, no definite story line. In the best Symbolist work there is a bold plot or situation on which changes can be rung: the exciting chase by Ahab of the White Whale, in *Moby Dick;* the perpetual and finally frantic conflict in which K engages, in *The Trial,* as he tries to fight the unspecified charges brought against him. Neither Melville nor Kafka ever shirk their obligation to tell a story first and foremost, to hold the reader's attention by making him anxious to learn what next befalls the hero. *The Castle* keeps us on tenterhooks: will the visitor gain entrance to that inaccessible citadel? This basic need for an engendering suspense should never be overlooked. Franz Kafka is a master at skillfully weaving a tale.

But Kafka's meaning proves to be as opaque as his prose is plain. The very simplicity of his style and storytelling method teases us: all seems so clear that the author's intent should also be clear. It is not. Kafka is baffling beyond words. He tantalizes us to the point of vexation. I have perused as many as twenty or twenty-five well-reasoned interpretations of *The Trial* and *The Castle,* none of which agrees or even resembles any other. What is the charge against the hapless K, and who has arrested him? Is this a political satire? Has he offended the rulers of a totalitarian state? Or is this, instead, a comment on the proliferating complexity and confusion of twentieth-century life? Is he merely caught in a headless maze of bureaucracy (Kafka himself was the employee of a state insurance office)? Or is the symbolism larger? Is K a dying man (as the tubercular Kafka knew himself to be), taken into custody by Death? Facing a Last Judgment? Is K an atheist, ordered held by God? Or is this a Freudian fantasy, as many critics claim? Or is it Marxist propaganda, as has also been asserted? Does it have, as stated by Kafka's literary executor—Max Brod, now living in Israel—a pro-Zionist message? We can read *The Trial* over and over, and never be sure. What is the significance of the hero's growingly frenzied attempt, in *The Castle,* to get admittance at his destination? Who is lodged in that hilltop citadel? Why is it so important that the hero be allowed into its remote fastness? Who is listening, at the other end of the telephone? We may guess, but we shall never know. We are left forever unanswered, perplexed. Sometimes our suspicion grows that Kafka is playing a sly game with us, that he has no meaning at all at the heart of his Symbolist tale. Reading him is like sharing a frustration dream, wherein we never attain our goal, whatever it may be.

The reader has been asked to make a larger contribution, once again, but here the contribution is wholly in vain. Kafka's novels and many of his short stories elude any final comprehension. But there is a limit to the guessing games that readers want to play, and I believe that one Franz Kafka suffices . . . a whole school of him would reduce literature to a collection of runes, Rosetta stones, mere intimations.

Melville's *Moby Dick* and *Billy Budd* are built around cosmic symbols: we admire them, but they leave us somewhat detached. The symbolism in Joyce is contrived and artificial, too unrelated to our lives: *Ulysses* is overloaded with "multiple images"; it lacks a story, and it is also overencrusted by Joyce's pedantry and his fondness for logographs, anagrams, his odd and perhaps pathological infatuation with words. Kafka is by far the best of recent Symbolists; he fascinates us, and he grips our attention by his ironic melodrama; but if he has anything to communicate, he never quite does so. We do not even know at times whether he is writing in a humorous or tragic vein; he overtantalizes us. That is why I am tempted to turn to Albert Camus, who is a lesser author than any of these, and say that artistically he is the most successful Symbolist writer thus far. In *The Plague* and *The Fall* he does use "multiple imagery," and yet he communicates meaningfully. What he has to say is also of serious concern to the reader; his themes are of personal importance to us.

IV

Almost the first thing remarked about M. Camus is the smallness of his fictional output; only three novels, two of them scarcely long enough to earn that description; and a single book of short stories, *The Exile and the Kingdom*. Indeed, Camus himself never referred to any of his books of fiction as a "novel"; he called the two shorter pieces *récits*, a term borrowed from André Gide; and *The Plague* he designated as a *chronique*. Besides these, he wrote two book-length quasi-philosophical essays, *The Myth of Sisyphus* and *The Rebel;* some shorter prose sketches, consisting of travel notes and ruminations; and four plays, almost all adaptations—only one of them, *Caligula,* is wholly original. He did a fair amount of journalistic work, especially during the period of the Resistance. Yet, when he was only in his forties, he was awarded the Nobel Prize for literature.

Most major writers are prolific. Their output is often uneven, but they are prodigal at tossing off work of all kinds. One reason for Camus's sparse flow may have been his engagement in political causes, especially his journalistic tasks during the Nazi occupation of France. (But Sartre and Malraux were even more deeply involved in such activities, without loss of literary vigor.) Another may have been his ill-health; he was tubercular. (But Chekov, D. H. Lawrence, Somerset Maugham, Kafka, suffered from that dread illness, and they wrote endlessly.) To judge from Camus's completed work, he does not have a strong inventive faculty. His *récits* and short stories are almost plotless. He cannot sustain a fictional idea for long, in any event. He is weak at creating characters. He is repetitive and has no sense of narrative pace: in consequence, though they are very short, his books are always a bit tedious. They could have been told even more economically. He writes beautifully, but in a derivative style—or variety of styles—and his sources are obvious and strangely mixed. He aspires to be an intellectual writer, but he is hardly a clear thinker. He is sentimental and naïve, and he is surprisingly unoriginal. Yet he is one of the most important writers of our time.

He offered books on most unattractive themes, and yet his popularity is immense. One of his books, describing a whole city isolated by an epidemic and its people dying of a loathesome disease, minutely detailed, sold 120,000 copies immediately after its publication. His appeal is also to the most intelligent, the most critical. Clearly, something in Camus's work has profound significance to twentieth-century readers.

Is there a clue to this in the Nobel Prize citation, which extolls him for being "the moral conscience of our time"? But even his high-mindedness is not special to him. Sartre, Malraux, and Mauriac, amongst his talented contemporaries, are equally high-minded; indeed, French literature has a long tradition of moral earnestness amongst its novelists, which goes back to Rousseau, Balzac, and Stendhal, not to mention such more recent figures as Anatole France, Proust, Romain Rolland, Gide, Martin du Gard. It is a quality esteemed by the French, who look upon the novel as not so much a form of entertainment as a source of instruction about life. The rôle of being a "conscience" attributed to Camus is one that has frequently been assigned to other French authors: Voltaire, Pascal, Zola, to name a few.

It is also relevant that Camus's major study at the university was philosophy. He was inclined toward serious thought early.

Speaking of German literature, Frank O'Connor asserts that Germany seems never to have turned out a novelist of the first rank. The reason suggested for this—and quoted and accepted by Mr. O'Connor—is that the teaching of philosophy in German universities is so thorough and prolonged, "that educated Germans are left unfit for the plastic, concrete form of thought required by the novel." Mr. O'Connor goes on to cite Turgenev as another one-time student of philosophy, who seems to have had trouble in ridding himself of its effects, if he ever did so.

I must say that Thomas Mann and Jakob Wassermann impress me as being very fine novelists, however, and Turgenev a superb one. But still the point might be valid: despite their sophisticated cultural background, the Germans have not produced many great novelists, other than Mann and Wassermann. Camus's early study of philosophy might have had the same artistically vitiating effect on him, for too much ethical analysis and an accompanying overfondness for psychologizing is apt to be at the expense of imaginative richness.

To sum up, Camus's deep moral concern and his interest in metaphysical questions and social problems follow in a French line. His preoccupation with large issues, and his fondness for scattering moral precepts and aphorisms throughout his work, are probably overvalued by non-Gallic readers, who believe him exceptional or preëminent in doing this. He is neither. At the same time, his fiction suffers from his being more interested in the general than the human particular.

If I may venture a guess, then, two factors have played a part in the accession of his sudden fame. One is his personal legend, and the other is his luck: his appearance on the novelistic scene was well-timed, and all by sheer chance.

Actually, his career was far from being always happy. He had to contend with many handicaps. Camus was born in North Africa, in the sun-bright Algeria he loved and celebrates in his work. He was of mixed blood, partly Spanish—on his mother's side. His father had been killed in World War I. The orphaned son was raised in poverty, and while he was still a young man—working to pay for his education, and deeply interested in athletics and amateur dramatics—he was cruelly struck by consumption, which was to dog him the rest of his life.

Even so, he went on to travel and write, and to produce and act in plays. He suffered the physical, mental, and spiritual horrors of World War II, all of which affected him strongly. He was a hero of the Resistance, leaving the safety of North Africa and returning to France to take his part in the struggle to free it. He continued in the forefront of political activities after the Liberation. From all accounts of those who knew him, he was handsome, charming, modest, sincere; a true liberal, humanitarian, idealist. He always lent his prestige and weight to good causes. To his friends he was very much the "lay saint" that he envisions man becoming in *The Plague*. Their high opinion of him was duly and generously set down in print and broadcast.

His tragic and ironic death, so soon after he won the Nobel accolade, was appalling news to his countrymen and the literate world; and it was a senseless death, since he was a passenger in a speeding automobile driven by his publisher's son. His name was immediately enhaloed with the piety that surrounds the newly dead; and besides, he was a man who had a clearly recorded passion for life and was death's eloquent enemy. He was lost at the height of his powers. Little but praise and regret has been spoken of him since his demise.

He did have the good fortune, however, of becoming almost unwittingly a spokesman for his generation. He had borne the hardships of World War II, and especially the Occupation, and questioned the meaning of those national disasters, and even of life itself. He was briefly a Communist, and also an atheistic Existentialist, the movements that other intelligent young men in France were bewilderedly joining. Consequently, what he wrote was of instant concern to them. He came to them well accredited, since he was one of them; and his work expressed their bitter mood exactly.

In defeated France a sense of frustration and hopelessness was everywhere. After that debacle, that betrayal, one could no longer believe in anything: patriotism, the wisdom of one's elders; and, apparently, God was indifferent or dead. The old standards of morality were but devices wielded by hypocrities to exploit the average man. The sanctions to which one submitted were not divinely inspired, but of clumsy human shaping. Was anything in society rational?

Then as now, the natural world, too, confronted man with a baffling silence: he could not hope to grasp it or his place in it, save by a mystical leap, which Camus looked upon as a form of self-deception by desperate minds unable to bear truth. "A world that can be explained even with bad reasons is a familiar world. But, on the other hand, in a universe suddenly divested of illusions and lights, man feels an alien, a stranger," he was to write in *The Myth of Sisyphus*.

Cast in his rôle as a stranger, then, man seeks a rational answer to things, but none is forthcoming; nothing that he sees about him—war and fratricidal strife, human selfishness and heedless egotism—suggests that rationality holds sway anywhere. Fearful, he looks to the heavens again for some revelation, but they still seem empty. He is assured of only one thing, that he has being, however briefly . . . his *existence* is the only thing he knows. He must make of it what he can, with no reference to supernatural guidance or reliance on an ultimate transcendence of this world and reward in the next. The certainty of death makes every human activity purposeless. Seen thus, life is absurd. Suicide might well be a logical solution to it.

It is shocking that a major writer finds it necessary to ask himself whether life is worth living. What is more, Camus felt this to be the fundamental question of philosophy: not "how to live?" but, "should one live at all?" This is the problem he debates in *The Myth of Sisyphus*.

Such pessimism hardly begins with Sartre, Camus, and the French Existentialists. Glance back at earlier chapters of this book, where Melville, Hardy, Conrad, and D. H. Lawrence say as much about man's inability to comprehend the world, and the burden of suffering he must bear, to him inexplicably. Indeed, identical plaints are voiced by Job, so sorely afflicted in the Old Testament, and by the author of Ecclesiastes; and by such saturnine Greek dramatists as Sophocles, who wrote that "Human life, even in its utmost splendor and struggle, hangs on the edge of an abyss. . . ." "Call no man fortunate who is not dead. The dead are free from pain." At random, one could gather like anguished outbursts from writers of such varied temperaments as Nietzsche, Tolstoi, Mark Twain, Galsworthy, Kafka, E. M. Forster, and Somerset Maugham, among the more recent.

Some of these authors later make a "leap," as Camus scornfully calls it, to religious mysticism, or accept a kind of "esthetic truce" with fate. But some do neither, and remain unreconciled to the harsh rôle assigned man by his mysterious Creator. Yet they do not glibly declare that "God is dead." Camus often repeats this, although nowhere does he define what he means by "God."

By comparison to these earlier novelists and philosophers, Camus and the French Existentialists with their fashionable pose of despair, from which they say they will not be seduced, may strike one as somewhat jejune in their intellectual analysis and formulation; although I shall not attempt a metaphysical discussion here. In any event, they have found no new truths.

Very possibly "absurd," the term so often employed by the Existentialists to sum up their feeling about experience, does not adequately convey to us their true meaning. In English the word connotes that there is an element of the amusing in man's plight; and this misapprehension has been further strengthened by the Dadaistic plays of Ionesco and others in the so-called "Theater of the Absurd," which are also Existentialist in spirit; and which frequently have moments of hilarious nonsense in them, to signify how incoherent and disordered life can be, facing us always with incongruities and inner contradictions. But for Camus and his fellow novelists, the "absurd" seems to contain no such nuance. He refers instead to the "absurd" or "blind" or "baffling" confrontation of man and the physical cosmos, in which pain rules and we are doomed to wither with age and die, or else, like Camus himself, be cut down beforehand; helpless, hopeless, and never understanding. Camus did not hold that either man or the physical world are in themselves irrational: it is in their predestined and purposeless encounter that all human reason is set at naught.

But then again, original ideas are difficult to come by. Perhaps it is impossible to have an opinion, intuition, or insight that has not been anticipated by someone else—indeed, by many wise men—throughout mankind's long history. It is also salutary that from time to time, from one generation to another, there should be this sort of reëxamination of values, to reassure ourselves of their current validity: we cannot take traditional concepts for granted simply because they have been approved in the past and handed down to us. This reëxamination the Existentialists do seek to provide us. Our question should be not whether Camus is an original thinker, or whether the Existentialists are, but only whether they are first-rate ones.

What is more, each new generation needs to have its values tested in up-to-date fiction, appropriate to its own day. Otherwise, the traditional conclusions seem to belong only to another age, not to the present. The demonstration has to be made anew, in contemporary terms. This ceaseless reëxploration and proof of what are essentially truisms and platitudes, goes on forever in the novel. Camus should not be blamed if we find platitudes in his work, for we come upon them in the work of most other novelists too, perhaps in the work of all. It is inescapable; it is also helpful and highly acceptable.

To look back again I have already suggested that Camus lacks a sharp personal accent in his prose. His style is much praised, and in many ways rightly. But always there are too many notes sounded by other writers in it. In his first work, *Noces,* much of his tone and pagan lyricism are frankly borrowed from Gide. The writing is vivid and sensuous, as in Gide's equally youthful *Fruits of Earth;* throughout Camus's work, exactness of image is a great virtue. He catches the scent and feel of things precisely, and he has a poet's eye for the hue and glint of environing objects. In *Noces* he is less thoughtful than Gide, and as yet less disciplined: his mystical awareness of physical sensation might be compared to D. H. Lawrence's: he could be called pantheistic, except that he avowedly disbelieves in God. But the style of *Noces* is in no degree *sui generis*. By the time he reaches *The Stranger,* he has abandoned this manner altogether. His model now, and he acknowledges it freely, is Hemingway. Indeed, he takes much from that whole school of American realists: Cain, Hammett, Steinbeck, O'Hara, who were then in vogue among the young *literati* in France. (What he thought of Hemingway's approach I shall discuss later.) Besides this, in *The Stranger,* one catches strong echoes of Kafka in the trial scene. The "oracular, over-elaborate" prose of *The Myth of Sisyphus* resembles Nietzsche's. *The Plague* shows an equally obvious debt to Defoe (conceded in the epigraph), to Melville (as I shall suggest more specifically on an ensuing page), and no less to Dostoevski. Camus had acted in a stage adaptation of *The Brothers Karamazov,* and afterwards he himself turned *The Possessed* into play form very successfully. He tells us that for twenty years he visualized and heard the characters in that book "talking" on the stage, and I do feel that his dialogues in *The Plague* markedly reflect those of Dostoevski's impassioned debaters in rhythm. *The Fall* bears the imprint of Pirandello, Strindberg, Kafka again; and lastly Maurice Barrès, whose combination of verbal sumptuosity with an effect of an overall plainness of style influenced Camus from the very beginning of his career. In *The Exile and the Kingdom,* each story employs a contrasting technique: a Faulknerian stream of consciousness and free use of flashbacks in *The Renegade,* for instance; a flatness of prose in *The Outsider* that again reminds us of Hemingway; while *The Adulterous Woman* reads like a sheaf of pages out of D. H. Lawrence, and *The Silent Men* sounds very Joycean. He has also openly acknowledged his admiration for Malraux and his discipleship there. None of this presents us with an author who has his own clear idiom.

All young artists tend to imitate those among their predecessors whom they esteem. As Malraux has put it, one of the principal sources of inspiration of young painters is "the studio," the challenging canvases of their predecessors. But in time the true young artist either rejects those influences, to assert his own vision and idiom, or absorbs them into his bloodstream by a process of osmosis; so that—while still present, perhaps—they are no longer clearly distinguishable. This Camus never succeeds in doing; in him, the borrowings are still disturbingly evident. Perhaps he did not write enough in a creative vein to work these influences out of his system. But it does come as a surprise to find them in a mature writer, and especially after the Nobel Prize had been awarded to him. I think it might be said of him that his books are full of echoes of others, and yet rather original at the same time. Camus does have his own voice, apart from the eclectic touches. How this could be, puzzled me a good deal. I have finally concluded that it is because his subject matter differs so much from those whom he resembles in style. His prose in *The Stranger* or *The Outsider* may be like that of Hemingway, but his story is nothing that Hemingway would ever have written: nor has *The Plague* a theme anything like one Melville would have chosen.

v

Camus must have been astonished by the immense and immediate success of *The Stranger*. It was published when he was twenty-nine, but he had actually written it four years earlier, when he was only twenty-five. At first its meaning and intent were not clearly grasped, but *The Myth of Sisyphus,* his philosophical essay on the "absurd," appeared a few months later; it seemed to cast light on Camus's purpose in writing his novel. Subsequently, *The Stranger* has gone through many editions, been translated into many languages. It is now widely studied in American colleges and generally thought to be, at very least, a minor masterpiece.

Sartre hailed Camus for having created in Mersault the true Existentialist hero, and having given expression in fiction to the philosophy of the "absurd" (a movement of which Sartre himself has been the acknowledged leader in France). He was also tremendously impressed by Camus's artistry. Since Sartre was then as now a dominant figure in literary Paris, such applause gave the book much impetus. Marcel Girard, another eminent French critic, declared that Camus had turned out "the best novel of his generation." Albert Maquet calls it, "one of the classics of our century." I could readily quote scores of other articles and reviews that praise it in terms quite as extravagant and excited.

Bernard De Voto has said, in another context, that "the interest of criticism in a novel is to find the novel that isn't there." I feel that this rather applies to *The Stranger*. After going through critical studies that purport to analyze Camus's story, I look back at *The Stranger* and try to verify the many high claims made for it, but I am unable to find support for them. It is a young man's book, and has virtues as a work of art, but it also seems to me very flawed: the characters are incredible, the plot implausible, and the moral—if any—illogical and unproved. It strikes me as very badly thought out —a very slight work, indeed.

Though *The Stranger* is often loosely described as a Symbolist novel, it is really allegorical, as we have defined the term here. It moves on only two levels. I have not come across any critics who find multiple meanings in it, or interpret it in more than one way. They are widely agreed that Mersault is a representative figure; he is innocent mankind, at the mercy of accident, destined to perish cruelly while still young. He is caught in a mesh of outmoded social and legal values. His crime is a senseless and unmotivated one, even more so than Lafcadio's in Gide's novel; but since his act was never intentional, his punishment is grossly disproportionate. All life, it appears, is without meaning or plan. It is impossible to attach the proper significance to anything, to know what weight to give it. Any moment may lead us to disaster. Henri Peyre recapitulates it thusly: "Man is a stranger in an alien world, and a stranger to himself." Running through the story are certain other themes which are close to Camus's heart: his hatred of social hypocrisy, civic bureaucracy, and capital punishment. He also conveys in excellently written passages his delight in sheer physical living: the beauty of sunlight and shadowed twilight in an Algerian town; and, above all, the joy of swimming, which the thoughtless Mersault prizes even more than love-making.

"Mother died today" are the first words of this laconic novel. Mersault goes reluctantly to the funeral, at an old peoples' home in the suburbs of Algiers; he is the only child, and presumptively the chief mourner, but he feels no grief. He has neither liked nor disliked his mother. He returns to the city, casually picks up a girl with whom he has had a few affairs in the past, spends the night with her; he agrees to marry her, at her rather offhanded suggestion, though he feels no emotion about it. He goes with a neighbor, a pimp, to a drunken beach party. There he is an onlooker at a quarrel between his neighbor and the Arab brother of a girl with whom the neighbor has been involved and is now at odds. The Arab attacks and wounds Mersault's companion. Later, Mersault himself borrows his companion's revolver, takes a solitary walk in the hot sun on the beach, again encounters the Arab, who threatens him with a knife. Without feeling or thought, Mersault shoots the Arab, and continues firing at the prostrate man. He is arrested and charged with murder. At the trial, he offers no defense or explanation. He is conscious of no remorse or guilt but is silent. The court procedure bores him. His lawyer is preposterously inadequate and offers only the barest case for him. Witnesses tell of his unfeeling conduct at his mother's funeral, and this irrelevant testimony sways the judges against him. He is condemned to die. In prison, he does experience fear and rebels at the thought of death. But he rudely refuses the consolation of a priest. Though he is unrepentant, unaware that he is to blame for anything, his last wish is that the crowds will jeer him at the moment of his execution. Supposedly, all this makes him the Existentialist hero, since nothing in life has value for him but physical life itself; he is a creature of impulse and blind chance; and yet he refuses to deceive himself with illusions, with religious beliefs, or to make a show of piety or respect or regret that he does not honestly feel.

Is this man heroic? Is he typical? Is he "innocent"? Is he even real? I would say that no man is quite such a stranger to himself as Mersault is portrayed as being, nor as indifferent to the opinions of others. No man is quite such a sensual, thoughtless automaton. Mersault is oversimplified to the point of caricature. As a result, he is too dull to serve as the focus of an important book. Camus is trying to shock us, of course, by having this anti-hero return from his mother's burial and then immediately pick up a girl and sleep with her, to take advantage of his day off from work. But his other heedless acts combine to give us a figure for whom we can hardly feel sympathy or with whom we can even identify. He helps Raymond, the pimp, play a cruel trick on the Arab girl whom Raymond has abandoned; he writes a misleading letter to her on Raymond's behalf. His choice of a brutal pimp as a companion hardly commends him, either. One soon perceives that Mersault, to the limited extent that he has any verisimilitude in our eyes, is a bundle of egotism. He is concerned with no one but himself. But is this true of all human beings, or even the majority of them? It would be shallow cynicism to believe so. Too many instances of altruism and idealism and self-sacrifice can be cited to deny it. Certainly, Camus himself was not that sort of man. Some commentators speak of Mersault as "Mr. Anybody," "the ordinary man living a humdrum existence." But I suggest that he is "Mr. Nobody," for no such person as amoral and self-centered as Mersault has ever existed. Camus has been greatly acclaimed for making his Existentialist hero not an articulate intellectual, but "a drab clerk in an office . . . a character out of a naturalistic novel." But I feel that he is not a living character at all. Finally, because we cannot sympathize with him, we cannot become too concerned about what happens to him; hence the book, though short, is tedious.

Nor is Mersault consistently or convincingly drawn, even within the acceptable limits of fictional oversimplification or caricature. Besides this, the plot really does not hold together. We might note a few such inconsistencies: Although Mersault is supposed to be an almost mindless automaton, we are also told that he has done well at the office and has just been offered a promotion and transfer to Paris. He has no feeling about this, either. Is this not hard to credit? If he is that intelligent on the job, he would be resourceful and competent in other ways, and no man would be completely emotionless about a job promotion or the prospect of moving from provincial Algiers to cosmopolitan Paris; or, again, about deciding to get married. Camus may tell us that his anti-hero is not stirred by such events or decisions, but he cannot persuade us that people are like that.

On the beach, his conduct is also inexplicable, save that he acts in certain ways to provide Camus with a plot. But we are entitled to ask questions about his strange behavior. Why, when Mersault sets out on an aimless walk, does he take Raymond's revolver with him? Indeed why does he leave the party and his stricken companion and set off on his own? Is he merely drunk? Why, when he encounters the Arab, does he not swerve away? The Arab has already shown himself dangerous by stabbing Raymond. Camus tries to explain this by having Mersault describe the effect of the noonday heat. "I could feel my temples swelling under the impact of the light. . . . It struck me that all I had to do was to turn, walk away, and think no more of it. But the whole beach, pulsing with heat, was pressing on my back." Much is made by commentators of the brilliant and effective writing of this scene. The idea is also put forth that Mersault's eyes are unduly sensitive to glare and this is partly responsible for his impulsive deeds. But is this enough to drive a man to murder? Anyhow, I do not find the argument persuasive. Mersault is a French *colon* who has lived in Algeria, in this bright sunlight, his entire lifetime. He is also fond of swimming and lying on the beach, and so he must be accustomed to its dazzle. How does it happen that it suddenly overcomes him, makes him take leave of his senses? This might have befallen a Northerner, but hardly a native of this sun-baked littoral.

At the trial, Mersault's lawyer is so inept that it is hard to believe that a criminal case would be entrusted to him. The judges are equally incompetent: they scarcely seem professional, and the reader might instruct them in basic legal procedure. Anyone might suppose that Mersault could successfully appeal to a higher tribunal, after a trial so poorly conducted. Oddly, Mersault and his lawyer never plead self-defense, although an excellent case might have been made for it, since the Arab had attacked and injured Raymond earlier and again drawn a knife. We are asked to accept that Mersault would be apathetic and even mute, during a trial at which his life is at stake. He has been presented as too self-centered, too physically aware, for that. He is also too intelligent not to speak up and protest on his own behalf. Although a weak attempt is made by the prosecutor to establish premeditation, the killing has obviously been one of impulse, and it hardly seems likely that Mersault would be decapitated on the evidence presented here, though he might have received a lesser sentence. The French critic Thody praises this trial as "a violent satire of a world of justice in which a man is condemned for murder because he did not weep at his mother's funeral." But this is begging the question, and the satire is not at all effective, because Mersault has committed a murder. Camus has Mersault recount his act in these words: "It crossed my mind that one might fire, or not fire—it would come to the same thing." Then Mersault does fire, and repeatedly pumps bullets into a fallen man. If Mersault feels that pressing a trigger and taking a man's life make no difference, he is either a psychopath or a monster. He is dangerous, and it is not safe for society to permit him at large. What sympathy can we be asked to accord him, other than that we grant to the tragically insane?

In prison, he does not want to die. Apparently only *his* life is important. We are expected to be sorry for him, but there is no feeling shown in the novel, even by the author, for the dead Arab, a young man who had been motivated by anger at the heartless trick played on his sister. And now, suddenly, in his last prison days, the inarticulate Mersault becomes surprisingly eloquent. He quarrels passionately with the priest and lucidly counters his arguments. He still feels himself "irreparably innocent." But is he? Should he go unpunished, after all? Earlier, he had falsely testified against the Arab girl at the police station: he was not chary of the truth about her. At the end, Mersault says that he wants to be greeted with "howls of execration" at his moment of death. I have looked in vain for any of Camus's admirers to explain this abrupt reversal of feeling by the condemned man. It is certainly a contradiction to his attitude heretofore. If he is indifferent, the true Existentialist anti-hero, he would not care whether his execution was observed by others or not. If he has changed, he would want sympathy from onlookers at the last moment. If he unexpectedly recognizes himself as guilty, then he might seek "execration" as he bows to the guillotine, but no critic suggests that moral enlightenment has visited Mersault. That would negate the whole theme of the novel. I suspect that in this final line Camus is engaging in a bit of mystification: he is apt to do that elsewhere, too.

Much has been made, as we know, of the prose style and fictional technique Camus has adopted here, partly following Hemingway's lead, partly Kafka's. Camus had certain doubts about the American school of realists identified with Hemingway. Later, at least, he deemed it too "external." I might paraphrase him as having said, "To be faithful to reality does not mean depicting simply its outer 'bark'; it means finding and completing a unity which runs through the interior of this reality." This he had already tried to do in the simplistic manner of *The Stranger*. Henri Peyre speaks of the result: "Seldom have the detached tone and the apparent lack of emotion reached such intensity in fiction. Seldom has the calm art of understatement succeeded in being so explosive." And, elsewhere, Professor Peyre writes:

> Mersault rises to tragic stature, without his creator's ever lifting his voice to a pitch of eloquence or poetry, without any naïve stress on symbolism (except the sweltering heat and glare of the sun), and without the intrusion of an analysis of his mind or of a commentary on his behavior. . . . The style is well-nigh infallible, and Camus displays the resources of a classical master who has already tamed the romantic exuberances of *Noces*. There are hardly any subordinate clauses or conjunctions linking one sentence to another. The compound tense to denote the past is used throughout, to render the senseless bursting of air bubbles on the surface of a stream and the lack of any real past surviving in the protagonist's consciousness. Nothing is said or hinted about Mersault's childhood, education, training, and parents. The narrative is carefully calculated not to endow the recorded events with any significance; this is contrary to most fiction, which, depicting the world, necessarily rebuilds it and hence explains it. Seldom has utter aimlessness in a character been suggested with such originality.

But Peyre, a very discerning critic, also has doubts that Mersault has been presented truly in the "round." He likens him to a "puppet" and deems him as "elementary" as the characters created by lesser, sentimental American "tough school" authors. He finds too much sleight of hand in Camus's emptying his anti-hero of "will power, of anger, of passion, even of psychological density." Why should not society be shocked by such a man, Peyre asks. Then by what means does Mersault rise, for the reader, to tragic stature? That is the question I must ask M. Peyre. By no definition of the "tragic hero" ever known to me, is Mersault—lacking will power, anger, passion, psychological density—qualified for that exalted rôle.

Albert Maquet tells us that *The Stranger* is memorable not for "the simple fable it relates, but for the sentiment . . . which emanates from it, and the art with which it proceeds, an art in which construction and technique perfectly adapted to its needs both play their part." It is not a novel with a thesis, he continues:

It explains nothing, proves nothing. . . . Mersault doesn't know the awakening of consciousness until the end of his adventure, on the last page; but it is remarkable that up to then his life has obeyed, according to all appearance, the absurd orthodoxy. He therefore presents this singular case of a conscious mind lulled to sleep but linked with a behavior that supposes a wide-awake state. With Mersault, the absurd is like a congenital infirmity, and this is what gives such weight of reality to his character. One might say that the absurd is in his blood. Entirely given over to sensation, he lives only in the successive moments; and with the sensation that disappears, the moment vanishes before a memory of it can be organized and registered. Thus we have this man's incapacity of experiencing a feeling, for to experience a feeling presupposes a continuity; he is without a past, but also without a future. The "It's all the same to me" that constantly returns to his lips is understandable. In order to express a judgment of value, it is necessary to base oneself on memory or have an imagination as to the future. In the flow of the present, all hierarchy is void of meaning.

This is impressive commentary, by a distinguished European critic, but I am afraid it does not withstand analysis. Such a person as M. Maquet says Mersault is, would soon be classified as "retarded" or "deficient." A man totally without memory or imagination could not function on a job, or even keep an appointment. If he had neither past nor future in his mind, he would quickly end in a mental institution. M. Maquet has let his delight in a logical concept run away with him. I believe that he goes much further than Camus himself intended. This confirms my fear that sometimes our best critics get carried away by enthusiasm for their own preconceptions. Actually, Mersault does have memories; a few of them, at least, visit him while he is in his prison cell; one sentence of twelve words, to be exact, evoking the world he loves: "warm smells of summer, my favorite streets, Marie's dresses and her laugh." He also does recall his father, who had once gone to see a man executed. We learn a little of Mersault's past relationship with his mother, his coldness and neglect, from him and the old people mourning at her funeral. So Mersault is not entirely without a background. Yet he does exist for us mostly in a vacuum of his own making (or of

Camus's making), and this too deprives him of a considerable degree of reality and dimensionality; because in fact people do not live only in the "now," they are at every instant compounds of many pressures from their remembered and even forgotten past and imagined future.

Philip Thody is another to write with enthusiasm of the prose in *The Stranger*. "The deliberate simplicity of Camus's style of narration does not only show the atomistic view of the universe as it appears to the absurd man. It also serves to underline the stupidity of many of society's assumptions in exactly the same way as does a similar technique in *Candide* or *Les Lettres Persanes*." Yes, but here we must remember, as M. Thody does not, that those works too deal with caricatures, not real people. And what are the stupid assumptions underlined here? Should society do away with the simple dignity of funerals? Or the necessity of arresting killers? "At the same time," Thody continues, "the style presents the hero of the story as a man whose attitude is justified and reasonable. . . ." I am curious, I must confess, as to how a narrative prose can do this. But the rest of M. Thody's commentary surprises me even more. Speaking of Mersault's disdain and indifference during the trial, this French critic explains: "He is accused, but he does not accept his guilt. If he shows little inclination to fight against his condemnation, it is because this would involve the loss of his honesty and integrity, and his acceptance, if only temporarily, of society's conventions. Mersault, condemned partly for his intransigent honesty, does not fail in his turn to judge society." But is it true that Mersault has this integrity? If he does not fake grief or remorse, is it not simply because he is too insensitive even to feel the need for them? We have no other evidence of his taking an intransigent stand against anything; faced with the concerns of others, he experiences only apathy. But M. Thody is of a different opinion: "Camus insists . . . not only upon Mersault's innocence but also upon his virtue." What virtue? M. Thody does not specify this, unless he refers to Mersault's "honesty." He goes on: "At the same time that Camus's use of Hemingway's technique helps him to satirize society, his own instinctively lyrical style expresses not only what Mersault has to live for, but also the reason for his shooting the Arab." This reason, it develops, is that the sun disturbed him.

He does not pull the trigger, the trigger gave way. . . . He is entirely possessed by the forces of nature and is passive under their influence. In an absurd world, where sensations and objects are all-important, they also have a double aspect. . . . One half of Camus's technique enables him to express the "weariness tinged with amazement" which is Mersault's attitude towards life, at the same time as his own highly poetical, personal style gives conviction that only physical existence matters or can influence action in an absurd world.

Sartre was one of the first to acclaim the "originality" of Camus's style, his deft use of Hemingway's rigid objectivity. Perhaps Sartre, too, overstressed its importance. After all, it is not the form but the content that counts. Admittedly, the first third of the book is brilliantly done. The details are etched with a sharp stylus. The mother's corpse lies in a white-washed chapel, watched over by a nurse with a tumor. The whole tone is one of coldness, emptiness, alienation. At the vigil beside his mother's body, Mersault is shown benumbed: he seems in the grip of an abnormal detachment almost schizoid: the old people who were his mother's friends, the drab place itself, are scarcely actual to him. His is a kind of catatonic stupor, a paralysis of feeling. He does not hear the old people talking, nor even himself, but he does see with remarkable clarity, noting everything. During the hot, perspiring funeral procession he catches the smell of horse's dung mixed with incense. The sun is shining. He even thinks it would be an agreeable day to take a walk in the country (if not to a cemetery). All this is rendered with great success. He returns to the city. The town episodes, and the beach scenes, up to the moment of the killing, are also vivid and effective. But thereafter the book runs down, becomes repetitive, the narrative pace slow despite its studied brevity, and the dialogue at times self-consciously literary. I have already commented on the baffling and inconsistent ending, which tells us nothing. Claude Mauriac has said that Camus does poorly with all his endings; he never quite seems to know how to round off or close a story.

Above all, from the moment Mersault says of himself, "I have never been able to regret anything in all my life," and also after he quotes—without disputing its obvious truth—the prosecutor's charge that "I had no soul, there was nothing human about me, not one of those moral qualities which normal men possess had any place in my mentality," the book loses for the average reader its representative character. If Mersault can be accepted as real at all, it must be as a very special type of being; there must be very few such freakish persons, if any. But most of the time we are forced to see him as merely an allegorical figure, in what is a seriously inadequate allegory. The premise is weak, and the reasoning throughout illogical.

Both Maquet and Sartre assert that this is not a novel with a thesis, seeking to prove or disprove anything. Indeed, Sartre feels that Mersault is an Existentialist hero for only a moment, for Mersault is not self-conscious enough and only belatedly and briefly analyzes his plight. But Sartre does see the story as presenting Camus's philosophy of the Absurd, which shortly afterward was more formally expounded in *The Myth of Sisyphus*. (Other critics have claimed that Sartre's attempt to equate *The Stranger* and *The Myth of Sisyphus* has misled many readers, for the two works are not as closely connected as Sartre first thought.) However, in *The Myth of Sisyphus* we do find Camus writing this about the Existentialist, or man confronting the "Absurd": "An attempt is made to get him to admit his guilt. He feels innocent. To tell the truth, that is all he feels—his irreparable innocence. This is what allows him everything. Hence, what he demands of himself is to live *solely* with what he knows, to accommodate himself to what he is, and to bring in nothing that is not certain." All this does seem to apply neatly to Mersault. And, again, Camus declares: "It was previously a question of finding out whether or not life had to have a meaning to be lived. It now becomes clear, on the contrary, that it will be lived all the better if it has no meaning. Living an experience, a particular fate, is accepting it fully." Some readers might think this hollow rhetoric, but at least it is a precise statement of Camus's position.

Peyre believes that Camus does uphold Mersault as an exemplary hero. Society, in condemning him, is more hypocritical and unjust than he is guilty. Again, Philip Thody sums up Mersault's attitude in these words: "His indifference is not towards life itself but only towards those emotions to which society, living on the dead belief that the world is reasonable and significant, attributes an arbitrary importance because he sees the emptiness of the rules." But are the rules empty? Should not the author remind us that they are based on five thousand years of human testing and experience? And what are the emotions to which society, living on "dead belief," assigns a merely "arbitrary importance"? Love for or at least filial obligation to one's mother, respect for the sacredness of the lives of others? Some very strange things are written by modern critics, and the reputations of novelists are sometimes lifted to eminence in odd ways, indeed.

Both *The Stranger* and *The Misunderstanding,* one of Camus's plays, are probed by Thomas Hanna, after personally discussing them with Camus. In Hanna's opinion, "Mersault has shown his revolt against the illusion of moral absolutism, he has affirmed his passion for the irreplaceable present moment of life, and he has become conscious of the boundless freedom that death grants to the living." For, "If we die, then what does it matter what we do in life?" This last statement, if implicit in a philosophy of the Absurd, strikes me as fatuous beyond belief. If we must die, then what we do in life is all-important. Even Camus recognizes this, by setting up as the criterion of the full life the *quantity* of one's experience (he was very slow in coming around to a more mature perception that the *quality* is also important).

Examining *The Misunderstanding,* in which a greedy sister kills her brother for money, Hanna continues: "But here the question arises, even as it has in *The Stranger,* as to the innocence of these people. In both instances a detestable act has been committed, but Camus does not condemn them. He has dramatically pushed the confrontation of man and the Absurd to a terrible extreme, and has left us to decide whether these people are not still innocent. If not, then what are the grounds for their guilt?" A remarkable question! Are not the grounds for the guilt of these two murderers obvious enough?

I would like to quote a bit further from Mr. Hanna, who in many ways seems to me a perceptive critic, but whose thinking here often puzzles me. "On this level of ordinary, humdrum life Mersault is really no different from any man. From this point it could have been *any* man, not just Mersault, who was to be judged and condemned by society. But what has happened is that this drifting life has carried Mersault to an action which was to force a judgment upon him. . . . An absolute moral criterion must be introduced into his life and an unequivocal judgment passed. . . . The world with which we are in sympathy (that of Mersault or Marie or *anyone*) is thrown into contrast with the world of the legalists, of the ethical absolutists." But I am of a very different opinion: Mersault is not an ordinary man, his world is not ordinary, nor is the judgment legalistic: many extraneous factors are weighed, such as Mersault's general attitude, his seeming callousness, the low people with whom he resorts, the circumstance of his having fired needless extra shots into his quite helpless foe. This is not confining the judgment to the facts alone. Three pages later, Hanna grants as much (though in Mersault's defense): "It is not—in the court's eyes—Mersault's murder which proves his guilt; it is his life which proves his guilt. This is to say that any life placed under the judgment of absolute moral standards is guilty and monstrous." I find Mr. Hanna's thought taking a big and illogical jump here. All men live imperfect lives, but not all pass aimless, unemotional ones, consort with panderers, have sex after coming from their mothers' funerals, or kill people calmly and heedlessly. Hanna concludes: "It remains for us to understand clearly that Mersault in committing murder still retains the innocence which has characterized him from the beginning, which is to say, the act of murder was consonant with all the other actions which indifferently issued from him." A strange kind of innocence? Is Mr. Hanna serious in arguing this way? Was Camus?

The absurdity here, Hanna avers, is "the attempt of society to justly apply absolute moral standards to the uncertain and chartless course of human life." What would be the alternative to judging Mersault by other than a court trial? Should he be allowed to say: "The sun bothered me, I was a bit affected by drink, so I killed the man. What difference does it make, after all?" Is not a legal code needed to assure such a man a fair trial? The code is doubtless not perfect, but it is the best that men have been able to formulate. The verdict is not mistaken. Mersault is not an innocent, except insofar as he is deficient in normal human feeling, and as such he is dangerous. Is it not perilous to elicit sympathy for him, or to describe him as guiltless? Is his incarceration unjust? Should he be allowed at large? (I have already suggested that I do not think an actual panel of judges would have condemned him to death.) Can we condone a casual murder by a man who is incapable of feeling remorse?

I have devoted much space to discussing *The Stranger* because this short novel is widely and slavishly admired, hailed by good critics; and yet I think its doctrine is pernicious. An ethical relativism such as Camus seems to ask for, leads only to moral anarchy. Can we let hedonists like Mersault determine solely for themselves what is right and wrong in this world? Other people would hardly be safe.

VI

Who can account fully why one book wins public acceptance, and another simply does not? But the faults of *The Stranger* are so obvious that it is difficult to explain why they were overlooked (and, I believe, willfully). But possibly it held an unconscious appeal, this "fantasy"—for it is hardly more than that—of an "ordinary" man committing a murder for almost no reason. We must recall the period and circumstances in which it was published: France had been conquered by the Nazis. Mersault's act and attitude may have expressed the feelings, repressed, of the average man in France during the Occupation. A hatred of authority, an emotion of stifled anger against all the imposed rules (many of which were logical), a sense of having to endure this experience by reverting to a kind of automatism in living, must have been widely shared. A personal deed of violence would have provided a deep release. I do not say that all the French people, always, had such feelings; but many of them must have, much of the time. Here, unwittingly, Camus may have created another multiple image whose full significance he himself did not appreciate. Furthermore, once a book is launched with acclaim, its chances for survival are naturally greater; it has earned, at least, a niche in literary history.

But why else has *The Stranger* continued to flourish? The Nazis no longer rule France. Why is this novel still so eagerly read? I am not a profound believer in the psychoanalytic interpretation of art, but neither do I turn my back on it. If no rational explanation of a book's popularity exists, we must look to an irrational one.

In fiction, which gives us so many vicarious experiences, there is bound to be enacted for us many of our daydreams and even more deeply hidden wishes. A man identifies himself with the "anti-hero" and sees himself as boldly promiscuous, or socially irresponsible, it may be. A woman follows the sexual adventures of the daring girl in the story and is herself wanton—while she reads. In such fiction, the author reflects our most anti-social fantasies and doubtless projects his own.

That is why quiet, gentle people are often avid readers of brutal books, and the prim and well-behaved may pore over scatological tales that detail the most shocking human depravity. Supposedly it is good for us to rid ourselves of our troublesome desires in this harmless way, which exacts no real or tangible toll of us. In our reading, a connection may be made with long-buried experiences and revolts that go back to our childhood, that are still active in our unconscious and needing an outlet, though our conscious mind might have forgotten them or deliberately shut them out. And similar needs are latent in the author, of which he is also not aware. Hence, an unacknowledged affinity may be established between some writers and some readers, particular ones in each instance. Of this deeper affinity, Bernard De Voto has said, "Novelists, whatever else they be besides, are also children talking to children in the dark." He also says very well that what takes place here "is not a complete identification or hallucination on the reader's part (or the writer's, probably), but only partial. It is in the spirit of *as if.* . . . In daydreams, everyone is his own novelist but an unsatisfactory one. An actual novelist . . . not only has a gift of phantasy more highly developed than other people, but also has an ability to organize his phantasies in coherent sequences and bring them closer to realities."

I would venture that this applies to the broad acceptance of *The Stranger.* It is an instance of what De Voto calls "a phantasy working itself out in a fantasy." I do not think that with this clue the novel can be reread and its attraction fully accounted for; I doubt that Camus ever had any conscious intention of creating a plot or character that would contain those oddly magnetic elements—the clue will be helpful to us only in certain passages. But it might explain why many readers condone Mersault's undutiful feeling toward his mother, his desire to have sex while in mourning, his aggressive *wish* to kill the Arab on the slightest provocation—and to shoot many times; his indifference toward the judges, toward the law, toward religion—all the things many of us are secretly bored with, resentful of, because all our emotions are ambivalent. I suspect that what Camus borrowed from Sartre's philosophy of the Absurd has had little to do with the success of *The Stranger,* actually. An author might explain what he sought to do in a book (and Camus was very articulate about his work), but very often he cannot know what it means to other people, which results in its being a success or a failure. And, just possibly, the youthful Camus might not himself have known fully what the book meant to him.

VII

Before long, Camus backs away from the implications of *The Stranger*, and even of *The Myth of Sisyphus*. He is always ready to correct himself; it is one of his admirable traits. If he is not a clear thinker, he is certainly an earnest and self-critical one. When he perceives his errors, he promptly confesses them. He may offer excuses for his mistakes, but he does not hide them.

Throughout his brief career, he first tries out his ideas in fiction and plays, and then—after that imaginative yet empirical test—sets them out in straightforward essay form. This is an interesting demonstration of the novelist's method, as I have described it earlier. His test of ideas in *The Stranger* did not quickly lead to his self-illumination, however, since that short novel is too confused. As might be expected, *The Myth of Sisyphus* is also mixed up and unconvincing, because it inherits the fundamental logical errors of *The Stranger*.

Camus has won fame as both novelist and philosopher. He sought to combine both talents in the same works. In the *Myth of Sisyphus*, he writes: "The great novelists are philosophical novelists—that is, the contrary of thesis-writers. Balzac, Sade, Melville, Stendhal, Dostoevski, Proust, Malraux, Kafka, to cite but a few. . . . They consider the work of art both as an end and a beginning." In other words, the novel "is the outcome of an often unexpressed philosophy, its illustration and its consummation." The moral problem implicit in a plot situation or the dilemma of a character has to be thought through. The story is "complete only through the implications of that philosophy. It justifies at last that variant of an old theme that a little thought estranges from life whereas much thought reconciles to life." This he was to learn after he had finished *The Stranger* and passed on to a better novel, *The Plague*. He also wrote later of the imaginary world of fiction as a "rectification" of reality, where all the things that are left incomplete or unsatisfactory in life are completed or corrected, it may be. In the novel is a kind of "wish-fulfillment." But unless he himself now saw the unconscious urges expressed in *The Stranger*, none of this fully enough applies to what he gained from that work.

I have often heard it put that Sartre is the philosopher who writes novels, and Camus the novelist who writes philosophy (a paraphrase, of course, of the well-known comment about Henry James and his psychologist brother, William). But possibly the quip is not so apt here, for Sartre strikes me as definitely superior to Camus on both counts. When I talk to friends about this, those of philosophical bent and training tell me that they prefer Camus's fiction to his essays; the storytellers invariably say that they respect his nonfiction more than his novels. The reason is simple. Camus writes very well for a philosopher; he philosophizes very well for a novelist. But he is not first-rank as either. In *The Myth of Sisyphus*, and later in *The Rebel*, a much more considerable work, his thinking is thin and eclectic. His arguments are often weak and cloudy. Though he disdains philosophers and artists who make "leaps," he endlessly makes illogical ones of his own, relying more on exhortation and rhetoric than demonstration and proof. His pseudo-Nietzschean style seems lucid at first, but on second glance its ambitious poetry often obscures his meaning and serves to cover up serious gaps in his argument. At times, he is remarkably perceptive; at other times, he sounds a bit naïve. I have not the space to substantiate this now, but any reader will find it amply illustrated in careful analyses of Camus's philosophy by Thomas Hanna and John Cruickshank, among others.

With all this, Camus's essays are highly stimulating: they are thoughtful (if not consistent and clear-thinking), elegantly phrased, often witty; and hold vivid and memorable insights. He is so gifted at aphoristic expression, indeed, and has scattered so many Pascalian epigrams on his pages, that he is likely to be much quoted out of context from here on, and thus earn a reputation for wisdom among the many who will not have actually read him.

In *The Myth of Sisyphus* we find some preposterous generalizations, both sweeping and shallow, which Camus himself soon realizes will not stand up. He corners himself by maintaining that man is innately innocent, since he lives in a meaningless cosmos; no matter what he does, no moral guilt can be charged to him. But this leads to ethical chaos. Since no truly divine or human sanction for morality exists, the most one can do is ask that men voluntarily accept social responsibility. How can one enforce it on those who refuse to conform? Camus has ruled out threats and judges. But can there be utter freedom for everyone? Clearly no. Camus is unable to provide any fresh logical base for new ethical standards, and finally falls back on old and conventional ones, after all. Still, he equivocates, and we get nowhere. Meanwhile, the reader keeps wondering why, if everything is "absurd" and meaningless, an author even bothers to write books or think about morality. This is a question that artists of the "Absurd" school are always being asked, to which they have not yet returned a convincing answer.

The best that Camus can reply is that art helps the artist to multiply his experience, and also to fix it—that is, immortalize it—"up to a point." (Later he is to give art a social purpose, a less egotistical one.) Along with this, his cult of pure physical existence, and his preachment that man should indiscriminately seek for a multiplicity of intense sensations and rôles in life—as the actor does, and the Don Juan—is embarrassingly sophomoric, or, at its best, Pateresque ("to burn ever with that hard gemlike flame"). In much of the early half of the essay he seems to be youthfully embracing a romantic pose of melancholy and despair. The young readers of France naturally welcomed it. His attack on so much that was orthodox, bourgeois, respectable, also delighted them. (Frank O'Connor remarks that whereas the English use the term "middle classes" in a neutral way, for the most part, and the Russians employ the somewhat equivalent "intelligentsia" in a tone of approval, "bourgeois" in French is a phrase of abuse. He quotes from Flaubert, "who laid it down as a principle that 'hatred of the middle classes is the beginning of wisdom' and compiled with loving detestation over many years a dictionary of the accepted ideas that he regarded as their particular code." This legacy from Flaubert shows in Camus's first two books.) I sense a parallel to his vogue among the young in France and elsewhere, in the similar popularity of J. D. Salinger, who also flatteringly presents the new generation as intellectually bolder and more candid than their elders. At all odds, with more emotional fervor than tight reasoning, he argues his way back from the philosophic necessity for suicide to a heroically flimsy but defiant *raison d'être*, which no doubt brings relief to his youthful readers.

Although *The Myth of Sisyphus* had a fine reception, his

various logical impasses and dilemmas were soon obvious to Camus. One reason given by commentators for his change of heart (and mind) is that he himself was now in France, under the Nazis' reign, and saw first-hand how necessary it is for men to have restraints, and for there to be enforceable laws to draw the line somewhere against crimes. Yet one supposes that Camus was intelligent enough to have come to this view eventually, even if he had never gone to Occupied France— the marvel is that it should have taken him so long.

He conducts his retreat from his former position with masterly skill; he turns a defeat into a victory. Once more he shows that he is honest, and his very candor disarms us. He now declares that *The Stranger* is not a novel that advocates an embrace of a philosophy of the Absurd—it merely reflects "the sentiment of the Absurd." Since this sentiment is part of the topical climate of ideas, it deserves to be recorded. But he himself does not subscribe to Mersault's hopeless point of view. "No, everything cannot be summed up in negation and absurdity. But we have first of all to pass through negation and absurdity because we have found them in our path, and because it is with them that our generation has to come to terms." Well, we might say, every generation has found them in its path, but no matter about that. Of *The Myth of Sisyphus*, Cruickshank reports: "The writing of the book lagged behind the development of his ideas. He himself has indicated that *The Myth of Sisyphus* does not quite accurately reflect the stage his own thought had reached at the period during which it was finally written." How is this possible? We might ask that. Can a serious essayist and novelist write books about his *former* ideas, when he is already in the process of forming new and contradictory ones? Cruickshank tells us further: "He also claims that the book (i.e., *The Myth*) was not a personal statement of faith but an attempt to understand ideas which he found current among his contemporaries." But Cruickshank is skeptical of this. "This last is incredible," he writes, "to anyone who reads *The Myth of Sisyphus*, with its personal bias so clearly and indelibly evident on every page." It does strike us as a naïve rationalization on Camus's part, or else a bit of facile self-deception. He later speaks of the "Absurd" as merely an "idea I found in the streets of our time."

The important thing, however, is that his ideas do advance. In *The Myth of Sisyphus* he had already taken note that when man enfolds a philosophy of the Absurd, "the initial anguish runs the risk of turning to comfort. The wound that is scratched with such solicitude ends by giving pleasure." This means to me that he was beginning to see through the romantic pose, to perceive that many intellectuals enjoy their self-designated solitude in the universe, to wallow in self-pity. He was no longer going to be one of them. In a preface to the *Myth*, he modifies his stand very substantially: "The Absurd, accepted until now as a conclusion, is considered in this essay as a point of departure. In this sense one can say that there is a tentativeness in my commentary: the position which it takes should not be prejudged. One simply finds here a description, in a pure state, of a sickness of spirit. No metaphysic, no belief is, for the moment, involved." This is no longer a retreat, but a rout. In *The Rebel*, he is to look back and admit: "Nothing remains in the absurdist attitude which can help us answer the questions of our time. The absurdist method, like that of systematic doubt, has wiped the slate clean. It leaves us in a blind alley." Furthermore, he now states: "To talk of despair is to conquer it. Despairing literature is a contradiction in terms." His work, for the future, will seek to be affirmative.

The great paradox is, of course, that Camus is most famous for *The Stranger* and *The Myth of Sisyphus*, and yet both books are built around ideas which he himself soon renounced.

VIII

In his *Caligula*, an early, prewar play, Camus had already reached the conclusion that "freedom has limits." The Roman emperor of this piece is again an Existentialist hero, who more than resembles Hitler and is quite as crazed, cunning, and cruel as the Nazi leader; but when Caligula carries too far his "freedom" to kill whom he pleases, he himself is killed. The others around him do this in self-defense. "Absolute domination by the law does not represent liberty," Camus acknowledges, still later, "but no more does absolute anarchy. . . . If the eternal law is not freedom, the absence of law is still less so. . . . Chaos is also a form of servitude. Freedom exists only in a world where what is possible is defined at the same time as what is not possible." He also concludes approvingly that "a profounder logic [in Nietzsche] replaces the 'if nothing is true, everything is permitted' of Karamazov by 'if nothing is true, nothing is permitted.'" In still another play, later, he has a character declare: "No, there is no justice, but there are limits. And those who claim to regulate nothing, like those who intend to regulate everything, equally go beyond the limits."

I have seen *Caligula* beautifully staged and acted, and read it twice; but though it has moments of theatrical excellence and flair, I felt its overall effect to be one of monotony and confusion. Perhaps only a student of philosophy could grasp at one showing what it is about. As a playwright, Camus's fault might be that he is—as a French reviewer, Leon Thoorens, has phrased it—*trop intelligent*. He is too metaphysical. The best advice ever given to such writers for the stage is that of W. B. Yeats, who told Sean O'Casey that when composing a play he should "burn" his opinions. But the main trouble is that Caligula is so clearly sadistic and insane, we pay no heed to the irrational pretexts he gives for his actions, and they are the chief intellectual burden of the work. If Camus wishes us to find them interesting or reasonable, at least, he should have given them to a more representative character, to whom we would be more willing to listen.

The new testing of his mature ideas occurs in *The Plague*, his only full-length novel and assuredly his major work of fiction. This is indeed a remarkable book, even though his eclecticism is again evident. It is easy to discern many of his sources for the novel—he openly acknowledges that one of them is Defoe's *Journal of the Plague Year*. The epigraph of the book, in fact, is taken from Defoe. Other novelists have written about characters who face and fight a dread epidemic. They tell how various people respond to it, and how some overcome their fear and selfishness, as Camus's Rambert is destined to do here. Maugham's *The Painted Veil*, about an outbreak of cholera in a Chinese province, and Cronin's *Keys of the Kingdom*, in a like setting, are instances. Both were popular successes. But no other writer has handled the theme with Camus's mastery or largeness of scope. The measure of this I shall try to indicate below. I have already mentioned that there are stylistic echoes of Melville in this book: the two sermons preached by Father Paneloux are very similar in tone and rhythm to Father Mapple's sermon on Jonah and the Whale in *Moby Dick* (and we know that Melville inspired Camus's handling of *The Plague* in even more significant ways). From *The Brothers Karamazov* Camus may have taken the crucial incident in which a loss of religious faith results from a horrified believer beholding the pointless death of an innocent child. Camus himself had played Ivan Karamazov in a dramatization of Dostoevski's novel, and it is Ivan who denounces the Christian God because He visits suffering and death upon pure and helpless little ones. A scene in which a child dies cruelly is to be found in Aldous Huxley's *Point Counter Point*, too, and doubtless Camus was familiar with that novel. I might have added to the list of literary influences that crop up in *The Plague*, that of Céline (*Journey to the End of the Night, Death on the Installment Plan*), who has also written in vivid language of the drab and repulsive side of life; but, of course, that choice of subject matter is in a French tradition, going back to Baudelaire. In a half-dozen other ways, however, Camus's book is very original; there is as yet no other novel quite like it.

It is one of the leading Symbolist works of our time. Camus had been reading Melville, and saw what could be done with a story that had a "multiple image" at its heart. What is particularly original is his choice of an outbreak of bubonic plague, spread by rats, as his focal symbol, from which he will reverberate his overtones. Initially, it hardly seems a poetic choice, but by a kind of necromancy Camus makes it one. . . . On the surface, then, *The Plague* is a naturalistic novel, which can be read as a strikingly imagined picture of the havoc an uncurbed and disruptive epidemic might bring to a modern city. This is wonderfully described, although the story—as befits a naturalistic work, perhaps—is almost plotless. Almost the only suspense arises from our asking ourselves which characters are fated to die during this siege, and which shall be spared, more or less at the Godlike whim of the author. Then, too, we are anxious to learn how long the pestilence will last, and how it will finally be brought under control. The narrative interest is not very strong, but suffices.

We soon realize, however, that Camus is writing about something other than the spread and ravages of the bubonic bacillus. In the early pages, he speaks as though the citizens of Oran are combating not a contagion of disease germs but the "plague" of war. For instance, the narrator remarks— equating the pestilence with political alarms, the threat of anything unpleasant—: "When a war breaks out, people say: 'It's too stupid; it can't last long.' But though a war may well be 'too stupid,' that doesn't prevent its lasting. Stupidity has a knack of getting its way. . . ." This could only remind French readers of their own reluctance to believe early enough in the seriousness of the Nazi menace. Just as the people of Oran shut their eyes to the first signs of the disease, the French had ignored Hitler.

In many other ways Camus allegorizes "war in the guise of a fearful epidemic." Once the city is overrun by the dying rats, and the inevitable quarantine begins, people are cut off from the outside world, as had been those in Occupied France. The infected are put in "concentration camps," and bodies are incinerated. Loved ones are torn asunder. Some citizens betray their cowardice, or their egotism and greed; others display the utmost sacrificial heroism. "Sanitary squads"—like the Resistance groups—are soon formed; and, on the whole, a feeling of solidarity grows up among those beset by this hideous ordeal behind the city's closed gates. That is why, when the book was published immediately after World War II, the French public first thought that it plainly alluded to the Nazi conquests in Europe, and found in it references to the bitter siege that France itself had endured.

Camus gave them his clue to this in the epigraph, taken from Defoe, which says: "It is as reasonable to represent one kind of imprisonment by another, as it is to represent anything that really exists by that which exists not." It was spelled out here that Camus intended to suggest two meanings in his work simultaneously, a particular and a general one.

But other readers quickly discerned that he hoped to imply not one specific and one general meaning, which would make this a clear allegory, but actually several general ones, all of them clear. One soon perceives that Camus is talking not only of the Nazis as the enemies of life and reason; through Tarrou, he denounces the Communists as well; indeed, he is plainly against any form of totalitarian despotism that perverts man's morality. Then, too, the presence and rôle of Father Paneloux in the story makes this book a religious debate: it is not merely the insidiously corrupting effect of political tyranny that the deadly bacillus germ symbolizes, but the existence of evil itself—pain, suffering—in a God-ruled cosmos. The guilt that is ascribed here is not mankind's alone, but even more, God's. The book thus begins to take on infinite perspectives and multiple dimensions, indeed. The separation and loneliness that the people of Oran experience is not only that enforced by an epidemic, but by the conditions of life itself, and by death with its harsh finality. One of his closest young friends in the Resistance had been caught and executed shortly before, and the shock of that had marked Camus.

Besides, did he not carry the tuberculosis bacillus in his lungs, and was he not himself doomed to early exile and death? Tuberculosis heightens morbidity, imagination, fear of dying. That Camus had an obsessive death-fear is very apparent. He touches on the subject of death wherever he writes, endlessly, disproportionately. It dominates his youthful *Noces*, overshadowing the pagan love of life that was also his. (Most authors who suffer from consumption—and this includes those we mentioned before, D. H. Lawrence, Kafka, O'Neill, Katherine Mansfield, as well as earlier figures such as Schiller and Keats—are deeply intent on realizing life to its full, too, and have an exacerbated sensibility. This is an equally important characteristic of Camus, and a corollary theme in much of his work.) Camus is death-haunted. He betrays it in his autobiographical essay, *Summer in Algiers*. In *The Stranger* he refers to the "dark wind" that comes to carry off all, and he told Hanna that it was the chief subject of the story. In *The Myth of Sisyphus* his discussion starts with thoughts of suicide. Whereas other people, in their early years especially, tend to take life and its joys for granted, unthinkingly, Camus's contemplation is seemingly drawn ceaselessly by his illness to problems of life and death. This darkens even his creative pleasure. Otto Rank suggests that the artist is more aware than others of the constant imminence of death: it compels him to create, in a frantic hope of achieving immortality. Camus's father had died young, and he always had the recollection of that, too, to cloud even his idle musings.

Melancholy, and a preoccupation with bodily functions, is also typical of consumptives. Why else would Camus have chosen so repulsive a subject as that of a plague for his major work? So odd and hideous a theme? Why else does he dwell so vividly on the loathsome details of the disease, and the ugly processes of death? Camus spares us nothing, and spares himself nothing. A reader might wonder how any author could spend months, even years, concentrating his efforts daily in describing the symptoms over and over, as successive characters become victims. For the same reason, because he was consumptive, Camus might identify himself with Dr. Rieux, the hero of *The Plague*, who unremittingly fights death. We note that Dr. Rieux says, "I have never managed to get used to seeing people die. That's all I know."

But there is also a strain of masochism in Camus. We shall see it manifested again in *The Fall*. It is perhaps a personal trait, but could also be derived from his reading of Dostoevski, Proust, Malraux, and Sartre. Both Frank O'Connor and Victor Brombert have observed in their studies of modern literature that sado-masochism runs through the works of those authors, and descends in part from the Marquis de Sade himself, by whom Camus was also much influenced. (He refers extensively to him in *The Rebel*.) Camus is clearly in this tradition. Writers of the Parisian school, Malraux and Sartre and Beauvoir in particular, are fascinated by the infliction of violence and the ordeal of suffering. Along with a neurotic and futile drive to lose themselves in Revolutionary activity, the success of which would for them be self-destructive, they seem to feel, as Brombert puts it, "a mystical desire to share the tortures of others, and hence to ease a sense of guilt at not having undergone it oneself." A novelist does this imaginatively by writing about it. One can assume that Camus died a thousand deaths while dwelling so intently with *The Plague*. In any event, the French intelligentsia are used to books as horrifying as his, and this might be another reason the novel found such a ready critical welcome in France, despite its sickening subject matter. (In his short story, *The Renegade*, Camus again gives vent to his compulsive interest in the sado-masochistic theme, at the same time that, with his usual ironic detachment, he satirizes it and his fellow intellectuals, especially those of the extreme Left, who fanatically seek "absolutes." He has a remarkable self-objectivity.)

In many ways *The Plague* is a badly constructed book. The story is told by an anonymous person, who at the end turns out to be the principal figure, Dr. Rieux. What is gained by this clumsy narrative device I do not pretend to know; but it does prevent us from beholding Rieux as the others see him, while at the same time he hides from us—being a reticent man—much that is required for us to share his emotions. The handling of this narrative device is even amateurish in tone: the opening chapter is especially awkward. The book is unbalanced, unequally proportioned. All the needed elements for a fine novel are here, but the characters are merely outlined; while the physical setting, the details of the disease and its progress, are set forth too fully and too often. This repetition makes for dullness and a slow narrative pace.

It is the same fault that we noted in *The Stranger*, but here it is worse. Less physical description of the town and the plague itself would have allowed time to create the people more roundly, and also have permitted Camus to give us even more characters: we follow the fortunes of too few (and most are too insignificant) for the story to convey a true sense of universality. Too much of the action is undramatized; it is only synopsized by the author—we do not experience it for ourselves.

The story might have had three powerful characterizations: Rieux, Tarrou, and Father Paneloux. But none is fully realized. Rieux, as has just been said, is kept too shadowy as the narrator who tells nothing about himself. A physical description of him is supplied only after twenty-five pages have gone by, perhaps an oversight, but anyhow, an artistic error (which is also repeated with Joseph Grand). It is important for us to appreciate how deeply Rieux loves his ill wife, but she leaves Oran in the opening pages of the book and is never again presented to us. The point is made that Dr. Rieux puts duty, to his profession, to humanity, before personal happiness and obligation. But we really do not feel the force of this, for the relationship of Rieux and his wife is hardly established. He scarcely ever thinks of her, or of their past life together, and therefore we cannot measure or sound the extent of his sacrifice. Later, Rieux keeps saying that Rambert, the journalist, is right to put love first, but this is not consistent with either Rieux's actions or other expressed attitudes. When the reason for his defense of Rambert is finally made explicit, and we learn how strongly Rieux felt about his dead wife, it is too late for it to have much impact in the story.

About Tarrou hangs a hint of mystery. This begins to annoy and frustrate us. Finally we learn who he is, and what his history has been. He might have been a principal figure, but is not allowed to be, because he does not play a large enough rôle. His death is magnificently described, but again he has been shadowy through so many chapters that he dies almost about the time he has begun to become real and deeply important to us. Once more, it is too late for this development in the story to have maximum value. His death coincides with that of Rieux's wife, though the two events are otherwise unconnected. Somehow, this appears too pat. We feel there must be some link, but none is discernible; it makes us think that either Camus is careless in planning his story, or else is seeking again to tease us with a false lead.

Father Paneloux is not a "priest" at all, but only a caricature of one. The same must be said of such Dickensian minor figures as Joseph Grand and Cottard, and the irascible, asthmatic patient whom Rieux still finds time to visit. They remind us of the old man with a dog who is Mersault's neighbor in *The Stranger*. Such eccentric characters always attract Camus. Philip Thody suggests that they fit in with Camus's overall theory of the "absurd," and points out that Tarrou, in his diary, identifies himself as a "connoisseur of the absurd," referring here to the term in the sense of odd people and odd events. They might also be persons out of Kafka, and in some ways *The Plague* offers us a Kafka-like world.

Another leading figure is Rambert, the journalist. His portrait is perhaps the least satisfactory of all. He lacks the intelligence and even common sense which would qualify him for his profession. It is hard to believe that any newspaper would hire him. He acts more like a spoiled child than an adult, and therefore hardly serves as a counterpoise to the dutiful, self-sacrificing Dr. Rieux. He cannot accept the rule that he may not leave the quarantined city. His thwarted efforts to escape from Oran, to rejoin the woman he loves in Paris, are also rather Kafka-esque. Suddenly he reverses his character. He decides to stay and play his part in fighting the pestilence. But Camus has not prepared us for this conversion in Rambert. His change of attitude does not seem to arise from any deep personal conviction; somehow we feel that it has come about chiefly because he is wearied by his repeated and futile attempts to get away.

Even Albert Maquet, whose admiration for Camus is almost worshipful, concedes that the people here lack solidity. "It must be admitted that the physical descriptions of the characters often smack of the passport or the identity card, rather than of authentic fictional creations. Are we otherwise instructed as to their personality, their type, the characteristics that make each individual a unique and irreplaceable human being? Not very much. Hence, when they confront each other in dialogue, we are always witnessing a confrontation, never a conflict of personalities." But Maquet argues that there is a good reason for this.

If their creator withheld from them the keen breath of a passionately imaginative life, it is because he did not propose to launch them into the free exercise of their lives, allowing them to accomplish their destinies in their own way by the simple operation of their feelings. The rôle he assigned to them is better defined and consequently more restricted, more linear. In effect, the life in which they are equally caught up has plunged them suddenly into a nightmare of misfortune, injustice, and suffering, and in this crisis the demand that is made is not upon the entire individual, but upon that part of him which concerns his dignity. Each one is expected to reply to the question that is put to all, at the same instant and in the same terms. And each one is a man confronting the condition of mankind, not an individual contending with his personal problems. That is why, though their faces and souls remain in shadow, they compensate by demonstrating so strong a moral personality.

But why should the demand not have been met by the "entire individual," and why should not each character confront "the condition of mankind" as a unique person as well as a social unit? The art of the novel calls for no less than that.

Throughout the book we are bothered by small implausibilities, which have an unfortunate cumulative effect. Why should there be serious shortages of food? The city could easily be supplied by having provisions left outside the gates, to be taken in. Also, from the air. One might expect a strenuous effort by other Algerian cities to be of help. But here Camus, perhaps unwittingly, is drawing too close a parallel to Vichy-ruled France, where food was scarce during the War and none could be sent in. (We might also ask whether a modern city has "gates." I do not know if Oran has, but this detail is not very important.) Again, we find it hard to believe that Cottard would welcome an epidemic, which might well cost him his life, simply because the quarantine may allow him to profit in the black market. Civilians, far from the fighting, often engage in smuggling and some do flourish, and so again the parallel is to a war rather than a pestilence. The same is true of the ironic assertion that business still goes on as usual in Oran. It could not have done so. Nor is it credible that cinemas and operas would remain open and be crowded during a time of bubonic plague, contagion easily transmitted. But theaters did draw audiences in Paris and elsewhere during the Occupation; obviously, Camus is thinking of that. He has an effective scene of an opera singer collapsing during a performance, but this is late in the course of the epidemic in Oran, and we cannot believe it could have happened then. At the very beginning, just after the outbreak, yes; but not at its peak.

Camus actually started to write this novel during the Occupation. He did not completely dissociate himself from it. Paneloux's first sermon, telling the congregation that they have brought this punishment on themselves for their sins, accords with similar preachments from French pulpits after the surrender of France. But it is one thing to tell a people that they have deserved their military defeat, and quite another to say that they have merited the indiscriminate ravages of a plague. The first is a man-made catastrophe, the latter is divinely ordained. This difference is partly responsible for the elements of caricature in Camus's portrait of Father Paneloux, and indeed of Christian teaching itself.

After all these strictures, with others to follow, one must still concede that this is an amazing novel. Once read, it haunts us. This is all the more unusual, because the style Camus chooses is incongruously flat. Thody calls it a "bureaucrat's prose," but of course the narrator is supposedly Dr. Rieux, hardly an office employee. But the description is apt. Camus, always a deliberate artist, does write as unemotionally here as is possible, though the subject could easily lend itself to over-colored rhetoric. Some of this aridity may have been inspired by his equally dry historical source, Defoe's *Journal*. Much of the writing is understated, and the language is full of banal phraseology and official jargon, as if we are perusing an administrative report of what occurred in beleagured Oran. Thody says that this impersonality allows the author to act on our sensitivity without ever revealing his own. He does not ask for our pity on behalf of this suffering humanity, but evokes it just the same. Peyre thinks that some of Camus's Spanish strain shows in his austere prose.

Camus himself declared it his intent to write a work in a classic vein. In such a classical piece, the primary emphasis is on the intelligence and control and restraint, which together impose on the material "a marvelous economy and a kind of passionate monotony. . . . To be classical," Camus continues, "means to repeat oneself and to know how to repeat oneself." I have already commented that even Camus's briefest products tend to be repetitive. Peyre too finds much of his work monotonous. Why a "passionate monotony" is a good effect

I do not quite grasp. This may well be another instance of Camus's rationalizing to himself—and others—a fault of which he has grown conscious. He is not alone in doing this. A host of other writers fall into the same habit. Artistic theories usually follow rather than precede the actual creation of a work, and may be clever apologies for its shortcomings.

Writing about Defoe's *Journal of the Plague Year*, Lathrop has pointed out how the author achieves an air of strangeness by putting a commonplace hero alone in the midst of extraordinary conditions—he is isolated in a plague-stricken city, just as Robinson Crusoe is also solitary on a tropical island. The marvel is external to the character, and this provides the author a chance to set down material details with a sharpness that gains an edge because an ordinary person is recording them. Camus does much the same in his novel, the chief difference being that Defoe's characters are not changed by what they experience, but Camus's heretofore commonplace people are, and some of them greatly. Camus's theory here is very sound. He later wrote: "There are works in which the event seems natural to the reader. But there are others (rarer, to be sure) in which the character considers natural whatever happens to him. By an odd but obvious paradox, the more extraordinary the character's adventures are, the more natural the story can seem: it is in proportion to the divergence we feel between the strangeness of a man's life and the simplicity with which that man accepts it."

To its credit, too—as Peyre notes—*The Plague* boldly ignores all the traditional baits of fiction: it offers no romantic escape, no "love interest" along with "seductive women characters," no melodramatic intrigues and surprises. Somewhat to his peril, Camus scorns all those age-old story appeals. His novel is lofty in conception, dedicated in purpose, and fulfills a zealous mission. Camus felt that the French novel, as distinct from all other literatures, has a special rôle: "restricting a story to a very limited number of situations, it should express and illustrate a certain view of man." This his story does accomplish.

Some critics complain that Camus is humorless, but to me a marked feature of *The Plague* is its touches of grim or ironic comedy. Some of this cynical humor arises from the narrator's tone. Thus he talks, in a passage near the opening of the book, of what it is like to die in a commercial-minded city like Oran.

The violent extremes of temperature, the exigencies of business, the uninspiring surroundings, the sudden nightfalls, and the very nature of its pleasures call for good health. An invalid feels out of place there. Think what it must be for a dying man, trapped behind hundreds of walls all sizzling with heat, while the whole population, sitting in cafés or hanging on the telephone, is discussing shipments, bills of lading, discounts! It will then be obvious what discomfort attends death, even modern death, when it waylays you under such conditions in such a dry place.

Some humor lies too in odd characters like Joseph Grand, who—as has already been said—is a Dickensian "grotesque." Joseph Grand is always planning to write a novel (clearly a bad one), the first sentence of which he can never get quite right. Over and over he attempts to phrase it. (All novelists will be able to identify themselves with him!) Similarly, M. Grand has been promised a promotion and never received it; he intends to send off a letter of protest to his superiors—but again he delays forever, not being able to word it quite to his satisfaction. In conversation, too, he is halting, always hesitating to find *le mot juste*. Especially good—for once—is Camus's physical portrait of him: his regional speech habits, his stammer, his toothlessness (he has an "ill-furnished mouth"), his dress. But he is also the book's most sympathetic figure: he has a simple, noble heart. He has forgiven the wife who has abandoned him; he loves his sister and nephews, and mourns his departed parents. He delights in listening to the chimes of a certain church bell at the vesper hour each day. He is affectionate, reliable. Camus himself had worked in government bureaus and doubtless knew such humble clerks doing their everyday jobs, unappreciated, yet having a "sensitive and virtuous" instinct. Grand falls victim to the plague, but recovers, as if Camus knew that the reader would demand it. Whether humor is appropriate in this novel is debatable, for at times it consorts badly with the action being depicted; but Camus's use of it is unexpected and highly original. It helps to mitigate the sustained horror of the book's subject.

But nothing can erase that horror. One of the brilliant touches in this fantasy is that Camus chooses to have it happen in a real city, Oran. A merely imagined place, with a fictitious name, would not have served him at all as well. This way, each page is endowed with a frightening authenticity. To deepen this aspect of realism, Camus adds a splendidly written passage listing and describing all the cities of antiquity that were ever besieged by plagues. Philip Thody points out another superb effect attained by Camus. "In earlier times, more primitive ones, the carts went around the streets to collect the dead, whose bodies were heaped in confusion one upon another. In Oran, the dead are scientifically collected, disinfected, loaded into trams and carried by night to the pits of quicklime." Are we not to take this as Camus's bitter satiric comment on German efficiency? Thody continues: "The excellence of Camus's description lies precisely in the contrast which he maintains between the physical, primitive horror of the plague, and the quiet, scientific administration of the modern city, between the awfulness of the events and the everyday places where they occur." We feel this, the moment Rieux steps on a rat on his staircase, and as the victims are stricken in restaurants, theaters, all the normal social settings. As the writing gathers strength, its metaphorical or allegorical significance is also given expression. Thus, referring to the outpouring and death of rats in Oran, the narrator tells us: "It was as if the earth on which our houses stood were being purged of its secreted humors; thrusting up to the surface the abcesses and puss-clots that had been forming in its entrails."

IX

Above all, *The Plague* is an atheistic tract. His antireligion is one of the issues that Camus is "testing," but again not very successfully, for some readers at least. The book is too didactic. It is not pure fiction, and hence not a pure experiential test.

From time to time the narrator inserts little essays. These hold interest briefly, then quickly grow dull; during them, we lose the drama of the personalized story. This is partly because, while the faceless and anonymous narrator pontificates, the stage is held by no clear, sympathetic character to whom these ideas are vital. The generalizations are also too sweeping: they lay down patterns of response and conduct that might apply to some or many people in the town, but not, as the impression is given here, to all the inhabitants. As we read, we grant the partial truth of the narrator's comments, but perpetually qualify them. Some of the insights are penetrating or witty, but again, some are less than first-rate; they sag under the weight of a heavy-handed cynicism and might better have been left out.

The story also pauses for philosophical exchanges between the characters—debates that have the tone and rhythm of talk in *The Possessed*. But these lack the sharpness and clarity of Dostoevskian analysis, and the dazzling illumination that Dostoevski often brings. Seldom, if ever, do the discussions carry through to a lucid conclusion, or clinch an idea. They are left hanging in air.

As Maquet observes, too, the talk does not spring fully and characteristically from the persons portrayed: an art at which Dostoevski excels, for his people say what we know they must say, being passionately who and what they are. The fault is that Camus's people are not enough flesh and blood for them to be interestingly and persuasively mental, too.

From his pulpit, at a wide interval of time during the epidemic, Father Paneloux delivers two sermons that are crucial to the argument of the novel. Both sermons are pitiless, and it is hard to believe that they typify what a priest would actually say in such circumstances. Indeed, the second sermon is "heretical," and therefore it is unfair for Camus to use it as representing the Christian point of view, and next to find fault with it.

Father Paneloux's first answer to the ravages of the plague is that God is pouring His wrath over the citizens of Oran for unspecified sins. He chides his congregation and offers no apology for the Divine will. The blame is theirs; they deserve to suffer. Rieux is led by this to say: " 'Paneloux is a man of learning, a scholar. He hasn't come into contact with death; that's why he can speak with such assurance of the truth—with a capital T. But every country priest who visits his parishioners and has heard a man gasping for breath on his deathbed thinks as I do. He'd try to relieve human suffering before trying to point out its excellence.' " Yet it is precisely because Paneloux is not a typical priest, but a scholar secluded from life, that he should not have been chosen by Camus to speak for the Catholic Church. On the other hand, there is a good deal of shrewdness in Tarrou's comment on this first sermon: " 'I can understand that type of fervor and find it not displeasing. At the beginning of a pestilence and when it ends, there's always a propensity for rhetoric. In the first case, habits have not yet been lost; in the second, they're returning. It is in the thick of a calamity that one gets hardened to the truth—in other words, to silence. So let's wait.' "

The pestilence rages on, and Paneloux is shaken by standing at the bedside of a dying child. He says to Rieux, " 'That sort of thing is revolting because it passes our understanding. But perhaps we should love what we cannot understand.' " Rieux replies angrily: " 'No, Father. I've a very different idea of love. And until my dying day I shall refuse to love a scheme of things in which children are put to torture.' " Unlike the priest, Rieux is not seeking man's salvation, only his health: " 'For me, his health comes first.' " (We must always remember that Camus's life was blighted by illness.)

Father Paneloux's second sermon, though slightly more charitable—he speaks to the congregation as "we" instead of "you"—is still uncompromising. In it are many echoes of Kierkegaard. Evil and pain exist for reasons beyond human comprehension. But man should not merely passively submit to them: his acceptance of his inexplicable punishment should be active. "Since it was God's will, we too should will it." He does not mean mere resignation, nor even humility. "It involved humiliation, but a humiliation to which the person humiliated gave full assent. . . . Thus, and thus only, the Christian could face the problem squarely and, scorning subterfuge, pierce to the heart of the supreme issue, the essential choice. . . ." It is wrong to say: " 'This I understand, but that I cannot accept'; we must go straight to the heart of what is unacceptable, precisely because it is thus that we are constrained to make our choice. The sufferings of children were our bread of affliction, but without this bread our souls would die of spiritual hunger." This Paneloux calls an "active fatalism." Again, he says: " 'Man must either love or hate God. And who would dare to choose to Hate Him? The love of God is a hard love. It demands total surrender. In a time of plague there is no island of escape from that choice.' "

Tarrou agrees with this. " 'Paneloux is right. When an innocent youth can have his eyes destroyed, a Christian should either lose his faith or consent to having his eyes destroyed. Paneloux declines to lose his faith, and he will go through with it to the end.' "

The harsh logic of this is, as Peyre remarks, "a distortion" of most Christian teaching. Furthermore Father Paneloux joins a volunteer "sanitary squad." Then he too falls ill. He has strongly urged the members of his congregation to take health precautions, as prescribed by the doctors and administration; they should avoid all self-destructive steps. " 'We should not sink on our knees and give up the struggle. No, we should go forward, groping our way through the darkness, stumbling perhaps at times, and try to do what good lay in our power.' " But now he himself refuses to have the help of a doctor or to take medication. The inconsistency of this is not clarified by Camus. Paneloux dies. His death is not definitely diagnosed as having been caused by the bubonic plague; Camus engages in another touch of the mystification of which he is so fond.

The fact is, Paneloux is a straw man set up as a ridiculous exemplar of Christian piety, and then knocked over. He is not a real person, nor a real priest. His refusal to have a doctor, because he will not try to circumvent what may be the will of God, is a *reductio ad absurdum*. The opposition between Paneloux and Rieux is false in many aspects, because men of God do not turn their backs on science and medicine. Although Paneloux's "active fatalism" may seem at first glance to be consistent, it is a simple truism that any consistency carried too far ends in a preposterous caricature, which is what Paneloux and his doctrine are. It is easy to make anything, atheism as well as belief, ridiculous by extending its logic beyond certain limits.

Camus's anti-religion is marked in all his writings. The essay which follows this novel, *The Rebel*, is studded with hostile epigrams by famed authors which he had apparently collected over a long period. Stendhal: "The only excuse for God is that He does not exist." Comte: "Set aside God in the name of religion." Lautréamont: "God is the criminal." Camus also quotes, in that book, Van Gogh's conviction that the world must be an imperfect sketch that God had discarded. But Camus himself told an interviewer that *The Plague* is his most anti-Christian writing.

The problem with which Camus seeks to cope in *The Plague* is that of the power of evil in the cosmos. This question has troubled philosophers and theologians for thousands of years; they have put questions and evoked answers that far surpass in subtlety and depth anything Camus offers us. Hence, we must feel that much of his religious thinking is exceedingly superficial. The choice of a plague as a symbol of this religious contradiction is a wonderful one: a pestilence seems to take its victims blindly—often the good perish, and the wicked survive. But Camus fails to exploit the full possibilities of this symbol. Perhaps both his generally prosy treatment and illogic are to blame. Peyre asks "whether Camus's classical restraint did not clip the wings of an allegory that, as *Moby Dick, Ulysses,* or *The Trial,* should have been expanded into a myth." I feel that it does reach the proportions of a "myth," but not one as large or bright as it might have been.

I have already indicated that nowhere does Camus define what he really means by "God." The concept of "God" is a highly varied one, differing from man to man, from culture to culture, from one epoch to the next. Elsewhere, Camus has written: "The fiercest type of revolt is that which is directed against a personal God." But even here a better definition is needed. When he apes the atheistic Existentialists and says, "God is dead," of which "God" is he speaking? Or does he refer to the end and disappearance of any kind of Spirit from the universe? Perhaps it is impossible to "prove" that there is a God, but it is equally impossible to "disprove" it. Agnosticism is an intellectually respectable stance, but atheism is a purely emotional attitude. The mystic says that God does exist, that he has "seen" Him, or "spoken" to Him, and great religious systems are founded on such mystical perceptions. Camus may have examined thoroughly all those systems, but has he? He gives no evidence of it anywhere in his writings. Can he positively "disprove" them? Or, in his personal historical context, is he accepting a bias against them which is merely an assumption on his part, a fashionable dogma he has borrowed, but little more? The basic contradiction of Camus's position is that he denies there can be positive knowledge of anything, yet assumes that he has it: that the cosmos is Godless and without meaning or purpose.

Other philosophers, like Bergson, who are not mystics, have nonetheless depended on "intuition" to inform them of the nature and reality of God. The difference between a mystical perception and intuition is, I hazard, that the latter is less ecstatic. But Camus scorns intuitive knowledge as well. He contends that the only source of knowledge is reason, and reason cannot treat with what is forever unknowable. But there are exacting "logical" demonstrations of God's existence, such as those put down by Aristotle and St. Thomas Aquinas, with which Camus must have been quite familiar, though he never mentions them. He should attempt to refute them, at very least, before he parades his atheism, if he wishes us to take his attitude seriously. Scientists also provide data to support (which is not the same as "proving") the "hypothesis" of a God, but Camus simply ignores them. This is why Gabriel Marcel has said that Camus's atheism is more a refusal of God than a proof of the impossibility of Him. "Certainly his atheism makes him refuse any effort to find a transcendent truth."

Similarly, Camus protests against prayer, which is an appeal to a power he considers nonexistent. He quotes Alain, who has declared: "Prayer is when night descends over thought." From this, Camus goes on exhortatively: "Yes, indeed, but . . . it should not be . . . that night that is born under closed eyelids and through the mere will of man—dark, impenetrable night that the mind calls up in order to plunge into it. If it must encounter a night, let it be rather that of despair, which remains lucid—polar night, vigil of the mind, whence will arise perhaps that white and virginal brightness which outlines every object in the light of the intelligence." It is a beautiful statement, but very theatrical—as all his thinking tends to be.

The reader should appreciate that I am not entering a brief for religious faith, any more than for an anti-religious attitude. I am merely suggesting that Camus does not handle his central argument with proper authority.

x

Still in a didactic vein, Camus moves on in *The Plague* to seek a humanistic set of ethics that shall be without supernatural sanction. "One will fight evil more deliberately if one does not believe in God," is one way he formulates this goal.

Tarrou, admiring Rieux's self-immolating zeal in trying to save the stricken, asks: " 'Why do you yourself show such devotion, considering you don't believe in God?' " Rieux replies that "if he believed in an all-powerful God he would cease curing the sick and leave that to Him. But no one in the world believed in a God of that sort; no, not even Paneloux, who believed that he believed in such a God. And this was proved by the fact that no one ever threw himself on Providence completely." (Actually, Paneloux has done that.) "Anyhow, in this respect Rieux believed himself to be on the right road—in fighting against creation as he found it." And, again, Rieux says almost sardonically: " 'Since the order of the world is shaped by death, mightn't it be better for God if we refuse to believe in Him and struggle with all our might against death, without raising our eyes toward the Heaven where He sits in silence?' " To this, Tarrou nods. " 'But your victories will never be lasting, that's all.' " Rieux's face darkens. " 'Yes, I know that. But it's no reason for giving up the struggle.' " " 'No reason, I agree. Only, I now can picture what this plague must mean for you.' " " 'Yes. A never-ending defeat.' " And later: " 'Who taught you all this, doctor?' " The reply comes promptly: " 'Suffering.' "

Both Rieux and Tarrou, then, are "rebels" as Camus now establishes the term; they do not passively submit to the onslaught of life, but struggle to discover and set up their personal and social values. In *The Rebel*, Camus adds: "The important thing is not, as yet, to go to the root of things, but, the world being what it is, to know how to live in it." Denying that he is a formal philosopher, he declares: "What interests me is how one should behave." Asking this question, he does indeed belong in the ranks of philosophical novelists.

His new ethical code is not to be based upon science, for he repudiates the logic, if not the data, of "science" too as a groundwork for moral certitude. "Modern unbelief is no longer based on science, as it was at the end of the last century. It denies the faith of science as much as that of religion. It is no longer the skepticism of reason in the face of miracles, but rather a passionate unbelief." Earlier he put it thusly: "Science that was to teach me everything ends up in a hypothesis. . . ." And, more pointedly, "We need to know if man, without the help of religion or of rationalist thought, can create his own values entirely by himself." But how? From what? If he rules out mysticism, intuition, science, and rational thought, what tools are left to him?

The solution is never very clear. In a fuzzy sort of way, he suggests that "art" is one path to the truth. He strews hopeful aphorisms concerning it throughout his nonfictional work. "What, in fact, is a novel but a universe in which action is endowed with form, where final words are pronounced, where people possess one another completely, and where life assumes the aspect of destiny? . . . Even if the novel describes only nostalgia, despair, frustration, it still creates a form of salvation." That is, I think, art provides us with an uplifting catharsis. As Thody closely paraphrases it,

> The ambition of the novelist is to take imperfect and unsatisfying reality and to transform it into a perfect, unified and satisfying whole. . . . Camus now looks in the novel for "the creation of a man-made universe which will rival the world of God and, in its order and coherence, compensate for the imperfections of God's creation." He finds the ideal novelist of revolt in Proust, who rescues his life from oblivion and gives it a lasting form in the perfect world of his own creation. Art, for Camus, corrects reality but does not deny it.

Whereas in his earlier view, in *The Myth of Sisyphus,* Camus had maintained that "an artist creates best when he is able at any moment to give up the whole enterprise . . . because he knows that creation is meaningless," he now asserts optimistically that "creation is the construction of meaning." He fondly quotes two *dicta* of Nietzsche: "No artist tolerates reality," and "Art and nothing but art. We have art in order not to die from truth." He is opposed to surrealism, because its practitioners search for and celebrate disorder. To the contrary, he feels that art should be a principal source of harmony and order. "The surest challenge which a work of this kind can present to the God-created world is to present itself as a whole, as a closed and unified world." He no longer maintains, as he did in *The Myth of Sisyphus,* that life should be described with *nothing* added to it. An artist must now show the world transformed, in terms of the values he holds or aspires to set up. Besides this, art cannot limit its concern to personal passions, but must embrace the "collective passion," "the human condition," which has been his attempt in *The Plague.*

Very fine words, but they really say little that is new. That art is the "imposition of order" we have heard many times from many others (even from Aristotle). The difficulty here is that Camus presupposes that an artist can create a closed world of order and harmony without his already having a clear or mature set of ethical values. Ideas are tested in a work of art, but seldom if ever originate there. They arise (or should arise) out of living, for which a more formidable moral guide than art is needed. In any event, the findings of art have little direct influence on the average man; in the realm of ethics, art plays no rôle equivalent to religion, except in the lives of a few. The nature of man is too anarchic and aggressive, and a far stronger sanction is required. The visionary and hopelessly impractical nature of much of Camus's thought is pitilessly revealed here.

When Camus speaks of *The Plague* as "anti-Christian," he is again using a broad, vague term. Many good Christians would join Rieux and reject Paneloux's theology. Several hundred million Christians are divided into scores of creeds and churches. Christians—so-called—have many different views of the world, depending on whether they are, let us say, Jesuits, Franciscans, Lutherans, Greek Orthodox, or Calvinists. By "Christianity" some refer to certain dogmas or doctrines of private salvation, or good works, or asceticism, about which other Christians have contrary beliefs. But paradoxically we find that the ethical ideas Camus arrives at in *The Plague* and *The Rebel* are of a kind held by Christians of almost all creeds, save that in his formulation they are not reinforced by a Divine fiat. Rachel Bespaloff says that Camus is proposing in these two books a "de-Christianized Christianity." That is a very exact description of his new "morality." One is reminded of Carl Becker's thesis, that when the eighteenth-century Rationalists exiled Christianity, its concepts crept in again to their ideology, but by the back door.

What was specific and startling in *The Plague,* and later in *The Rebel,* where it is central and much more fully developed, is Camus's attack on Stalinist ethics, largely considered the "humanist" position of his day. He had been identified with the Left, welcomed by Sartre and his influential group of Communist intellectuals, and himself had even briefly been a Party member when young; and now, in a manner that shocked his friends, he turned on Stalinism and its fundamental moral premise that "the end justifies the means." Tarrou finally dispels the mystery of his past: he had for a time been an active Communist and as such feels responsible for political murders, and bitterly repents it. Here, one symbolic aspect of the novel becomes very explicit.

Why had the young Tarrou joined the Party? Looking back, he can realize that it was a protest against his father's having been a public prosecutor who caused men to be guillotined. But the son eventually discovered that as a Communist he was sharing complicity in worse crimes, leading to more deaths.

"For many years I've been ashamed, mortally ashamed, of having been, even with the best intentions, even at many removes, a murderer in my turn.

"As time went on I merely learned that even those who were better than the rest could not keep themselves nowadays from killing or letting others kill, because such is the logic by which they live; and that we can't stir a finger in this world without the risk of bringing death to somebody. Yes, I've been ashamed ever since; I have realized that we all have plague, and I have lost my peace. And today I am still trying to find it; still trying to understand all those others and not to be the mortal enemy of anyone. I only know that one must do what one can to cease being plague-stricken, and that's the only way in which we can hope for some peace, or, failing that, a decent death. This and only this, can bring relief to men and, if not save them, at least do them the least harm possible and even, sometimes, a little good. So that is why I resolved to have no truck with anything which, directly or indirectly, for good reasons or bad, brings death to anyone or justifies others' putting him to death.

"That, too, is why this epidemic has taught me nothing new, except that I must fight it at your side. I know positively—yes, Rieux, I can say I know the world inside out, as you may see—that each of us has the plague within him; no one, no one on earth is free from it. And I know, too, that we must keep endless watch on ourselves lest in a careless moment we breathe in somebody's face and fasten the infection on him. . . . The good man, the man who infects hardly anyone, is the man who has the fewest lapses of attention. And it needs tremendous will-power, a never ending tension of the mind, to avoid such lapses. Yes, Rieux, it's a wearying business, being plague-stricken. But it's still more wearying to refuse to be it. That's why everybody in the world today looks so tired; everyone is more or less sick of the plague. But that is also why some of us, those who want to get the plague out of their systems, feel such desperate weariness, a weariness of which nothing remains to set us free except death. . . .

"Pending that release, I know I have no place in the world today; once I'd definitely refused to kill, I doomed myself to an exile that can never end. I leave it to others to make history. I know, too, that I'm not qualified to pass judgment on those others. There's something lacking in my mental make-up, and its lack prevents me from being a rational murderer. So it's a deficiency, not a superiority. But as things are, I'm willing to be as I am; I've learned modesty. All I maintain is that on this earth there are pestilences, and there are victims, and it's up to us, so far as possible, not to join forces with the pestilences. That may sound simple to the point of childishness; I can't judge if it's simple, but I know it's true. You see, I'd heard such quantities of arguments, which very nearly turned my head, and turned other people's heads enough to make them approve of murder; and I'd come to realize that all our troubles spring from our failure to use plain, clean-cut language. . . ."*

In this remarkable speech, Tarrou comes very much alive. Its Schweitzer-like sentiments also won Camus a wide audience. His commentary on being an ex-Communist and on living in the age of the Cold War and the H-bomb had much pertinency to European intellectuals, who with Camus had turned to pacifism and put equal blame on both camps for their hostility.

After *The Plague*, however, in *The Rebel*, the effort is to destroy the heretofore plausible claims of Marxism. It is shown as a "horizontal religion" and a false one, that "relegates to the end of history the Garden of Eden and the Revelation, which tradition had always placed at the beginning." Again: "Marxism replaces the promise of the 'Beyond' with the 'Later on.'" Yet, for its false promise, men are enslaved and slaughtered. He calls for a better form of revolt, which will "refuse the temptation of absolute Utopias

---

*Excerpts from *The Plague* (translated by Stuart Gilbert) and *The Fall* (translated by Justin O'Brien) reprinted by permission of Alfred A. Knopf Inc.

which leads Marxism to progress to the perfect city through a succession of crimes." He begs for an end of lies, oppression, and killings perpetrated in the name of "political realism," which anyhow is not realism but only a new kind of baseless illusion. Of the Marxists, who deem themselves "privileged executioners," because their acts will be sanctified by history and their ultimate purpose is humane, he says: "All executioners are of the same family," and couples them with the Fascistic oppressors of the Right. "Official history has always been the story of great murderers. It is not today that Cain is killing Abel. But it is only today that Cain is killing Abel in the name of logic and then claiming the ribbon of the Legion of Honor. . . ." He buttresses his case with a long historical review of "revolt" and Marxist deceptions.

On its appearance *The Rebel* was greeted with anger and retaliatory insult by the Leftists of Paris. One result was the famous break between Sartre and Camus, followed by bitter polemics in the Parisian newspapers. In our Anglo-Saxon world it is a bit hard to see why Camus was so long coming around to his anti-Communist views (which are less forcibly expressed than those of other ex-Communists such as Arthur Koestler, George Orwell, Ignazio Silone); but it must be understood that Marxism had never been as fully accepted in England and America, as in France and Italy, among the leading intellectuals there, headed at first by Gide, Malraux, Aragon, and Sartre. Even today, Communism is far more respectable in an important clique in Paris than in most other Western capitals. His former Leftist friends did not hesitate publicly to accuse Camus of "selling out" to Yankee money. He did not ignore the attacks, as he perhaps should have done, but replied in earnest. The debates that followed between Sartre, Breton, and Camus were not on a very high level, nor always to the point. Indeed, the quality of thinking in Paris at this time, as I have intimated before, does not strike one as first-rate. In that supposed Olympus of Reason and Lucidity, the intelligentsia often seem to be engaged in quarrels that are astonishingly childish. Much of the argument offered us is Talmudic, filled with squabbles over trifles, semantics, personalities. It might even be said that many of the ideas of André Breton and his followers sound rather demented.

We shall not analyze *The Rebel* here, as that leads us away from literature to history and political science. Camus's most objective critics find the book not very original, and needing fuller documentation. It is very repetitive, with a good deal of fustian. The style lacks the restraint of the novels; it is grandiose. Cruickshank states that Camus waxes lyrical to cover weak ideas or transitions of thought. He will begin to build a logical structure, then abruptly abandon it to issue moral fiats, or to coin an epigram. All the time, Camus's "sense of conventional morality" keeps cropping up, often without relevance or concrete demonstration. But Thody points out that Camus *is* original "in the way in which he comes to the same conclusions as the liberal humanist while setting out from absolutely different premises." That is, his conclusions are not fresh, but his strategy is. He never identifies himself as bourgeois or even as a humanist, but always refers to himself as a "rebel," and thus takes the other "rebels"—the well-entrenched Marxists—"from the rear." Says Thody, also: "In France, during his last years, Camus was almost alone the voice of liberal humanism." But I am not sure this is true: there were others. In any event, in an age of violence and intellectual attraction to totalitarian and often dangerously abstract solutions, he did range himself on the side of individualism, freedom, and "limits." He now saw that to place a "limit" on man's impulses, even on his impulse to do "good" to others, is the all-important task. What one man considers "good," his fellow man might not.

Contrasting *The Myth of Sisyphus* to *The Rebel*, Camus writes: "In the age of negation, it was of some avail to examine one's position relative to suicide. In the age of ideologies, we must examine our position relative to murder." In his quest for a new ethical code, the problem of "political assassination" always haunts him. Perhaps it had been borne in upon him during his years in the Resistance. He recognizes clearly that at times only a violent act will remove a tyrant —a Caligula, a Mussolini.

But how can he reconcile this with his compulsive respect for the sacredness of human life, his objection to capital punishment? "If this world has no higher meaning, if man is only responsible to man, it suffices for a man to remove one single human being from the society of the living to automatically exclude himself from it. When Cain kills Abel, he flees to the desert." (But, of course, Cain slays his brother for no good reason—it is typical of Camus that he chooses a colorful image, but does not probe it very carefully.)

Camus now determines that an assassin should expect to pay with his own life for the life he takes. This will let him atone for his act. In essence, this is only the old Mosaic code, self-administered—the *lex talionis,* of an eye for an eye, a tooth for a tooth. But Camus's troubled mind is soothed by the poetic justice of it. (There is also a masochistic strain here.) He writes a play, *The Just,* to illustrate his moral concept, depicting the idealistic Russian Terrorists who in 1905 nobly gave their lives to murder a Grand Duke. Theirs is the "aristocracy of sacrifice."

As a general rule, it might be hard for a revolutionary party to recruit assassins who know in advance that inescapably they must die for their bold patriotic deed. Such killers may accept a risk, but will they face up to a certainty of early death? It calls for a Japanese psychology, rather than a Western one. Most of the tyrants of history would probably have lived out their years and died in bed, if Camus's rule-of-thumb had prevailed then. His high-mindedness, incarnated in this argument, brought hoots from the Parisian Leftists, who perhaps rightly deemed him wholly impractical.

XI

Other positive values are suggested in *The Plague.* One that is mentioned—but really, only touched on—is Tarrou's yearning for "sanctity."

> "It comes to this," Tarrou said almost casually, "what interests me is learning how to become a saint."
>
> "But you don't believe in God."
>
> "Exactly! Can one be a saint without God?—that is the problem, in fact the only problem, I'm up against today."

What "secular sainthood" would consist of is not developed in the story; in fact, this brief but arresting exchange between Tarrou and Rieux is as far as the subject is carried. Later, Tarrou writes in his diary: "Perhaps we can only reach approximations of sainthood. In which case we must make

shift with a mild, benevolent diabolism." (I must confess that
the sense of this entry quite eludes me, unless Camus is saying
that anything less than sainthood is a form of diabolism.)
There is an essay by Henri Bergson, in which that philosopher
defines "secular sainthood"—and names Socrates as one
who attained that state. Possibly Camus borrows the idea
from him.

Tarrou is not an "active fatalist." When he falls ill, he
struggles with all his strength against death, but dies. Afterwards, Rieux considers Tarrou's history and final lonely fate.
Rieux "realized the bleak sterility of a life without illusions.
There can be no peace without hope. Tarrou had lived a life
riddled with contradictions and had never known hope's sol-
ace." Whether this implies a retreat from Camus's celebration
of a life without illusions, is hard to know.

Another value strongly affirmed in the closing pages of the
novel is "human love." Rambert, Tarrou, and Rieux are engaged in a three-sided discussion. Rambert is talking:

"I know that man is capable of great deeds. But if he
isn't capable of a great emotion, well, he leaves me cold."

"One has the idea that he is capable of everything,"
Tarrou remarked.

"I can't agree; he's incapable of suffering for a long time,
or being happy for a long time. Which means that he's
incapable of anything really worth while." He looked at the
two men in turn, then asked: "Tell me, Tarrou, are you
capable of dying for love?"

"I couldn't say, but I hardly think so—as I am now."

"You see. But you're capable of dying for an idea; one
can see that right away. Well, personally, I've seen enough
of people who die for an idea. I don't believe in heroism;
I know it's easy and I've learned it can be murderous. What
interests me is living and dying for what one loves."

Rieux had been watching the journalist attentively. With
his eyes still on him he said quietly:

"Man isn't an idea, Rambert."

Rambert sprang off the bed, his face ablaze with passion.

"Man *is* an idea, and a precious small idea, once he turns
his back on love. And that's my point; we—mankind—have
lost the capacity for love. We must face that fact, doctor.
Let's wait to acquire that capacity or, if really it's beyond
us, wait for the deliverance that will come to each of us

anyway, without his playing the hero. Personally, I look no farther."

When Rambert confides to Rieux his fixed decision to flee the city, by whatever means, to join his beloved in Paris, the scene goes like this: "Rieux rose. He suddenly appeared very tired. 'You're right, Rambert, quite right, and for nothing in the world would I try to dissuade you from what you're going to do; it seems to me absolutely right and proper." And, again, Rambert expresses his doubts about his course of action. " 'Maybe I'm all wrong in putting love first.' Rieux looked him in the eyes. 'No,' he said vehemently, 'you are *not* wrong.'" Near the end of the novel, too, the narrator tells us that this ordeal has taught the populace a great lesson: "They knew now that if there is one thing one can always yearn for and sometimes attain, it is human love." We can hardly credit Camus, however, for having been the first to enunciate this idea.

But we already know that Rambert does not leave the city, after all. He gives up his plans and joins the fight against the pestilence.

Although Rieux has praised personal love, and acknowledged its claims, he puts it aside for a higher duty. In his conversation with Rambert, he has voiced his own feeling:

" 'However, there's one thing I must tell you: there's no question of heroism in all this. It's a matter of common decency. That's an ideal which may make some people smile, but the only means of fighting a plague is—common decency.'

" 'What do you mean by "common decency"?' Rambert's tone was grave.

" 'I don't know what it means for other people. But in my case I know that it consists in doing my job.'"

What Rieux is really speaking of is a sense of "solidarity" or "brotherhood" with others. He has replied to Tarrou, " 'I know I feel more fellowship with the defeated than with saints. Heroism and sanctity don't really appeal to me, I imagine. What interests me is being a man.'" This is the new tone of Camus's thought. In *Noces, The Stranger,* and *The Myth of Sisyphus,* his preoccupations are remarkably self-centered; but he has finally outgrown this and become more conscious of other people. He himself says: "If there is any evolution from *The Stranger* to *The Plague*, it is in the direction of solidarity and participation." Elsewhere, he also states: "The world in which I live is repugnant to me, but I feel a solidarity with the men who suffer in it." From this feeling arises the principal affirmation of the book. The characters in *The Stranger* live in a complete and unreal detachment. Very great is the difference between Mersault, with his egoism, emotional dullness, and social indifference, and Dr. Rieux, who concedes the need for human love and altruistically seeks to serve mankind. Camus, in *Noces,* had declared: "There is no shame in being happy." But now Rambert says for the author: " 'There can be cause for shame in being happy all alone.' "

In *Le Monde,* in an interview, Camus disclosed that of all the characters in *The Plague,* "the closest to myself is not Tarrou the saint, but Rieux the doctor." He felt sympathy for Paneloux, yes; and for Tarrou, too. But "above holiness without God as Tarrou conceives it" is opened up "another human possibility, the one that Rieux is seeking." Consequently, Pierre-Henri Simon says of *The Plague*: "It affirms in the clearest manner a pure humanism, a religion of human nobility without God and even against God."

The same plea for "solidarity" and "brotherhood" begins to appear in some of Camus's short stories as well, notably in *The Silent Men,* which describes a labor strike and the fellow feeling of the workers, not only between themselves but with their employer, who is worried about a sick child; and in *Jonah,* which is about an artist who tries unsuccessfully to withdraw from the world; and even in *The Growing Stone.* As Malraux puts it, mankind belongs to "a deep and tragic fraternity." All men share guilt for social ills, all must accept the same weight of responsibility for them, all must join forces to combat them. "These ethics of guilt and responsibility have in fact helped to create a new type of hero and a new type of tragedy," which Camus now seeks to write. Of the people in *The Plague,* he tells us: "There no longer existed any individual destinies, but only a collective history. . . ." He enlarges this concept philosophically: "It often happens that we cannot bear to see offenses done to others which we ourselves have accepted without rebelling. This is not merely a question of identification or a feeling of community of interests. Injustices done to men whom we consider enemies can, actually, be profoundly repugnant to us. . . . When he rebels, a man identifies himself with other men and so surpasses himself, and from this point of view human solidarity is metaphysical."

Along with this, Rieux is modest. Sympathy, honesty, dedication to duty are the chief feelings he permits himself. Rieux is a rationalist, not seeking to set up any substitute religion. A modest man, a modest aim, a modest reward—this sums up his character and his style of life. The same is true of Joseph Grand, who with quiet courage persists in keeping the statistics of the plague; the little man doing his job, making his personal contribution.

On the final page of the book, the narrator names himself at last—as Rieux—and tells us that he

> resolved to compile this chronicle, so that he should not be one of those who hold their peace but should bear witness in favor of those plague-stricken people; so that some memorial of the injustice and outrage done them might endure; and to state quite simply what we learn in a time of pestilence: that there are more things to admire in men than to despise.
>
> None the less, he knew that the tale he had to tell could not be one of a final victory. It could only be the record of what had to be done, and what assuredly would have to be done again in the never ending fight against terror and its relentless onslaughts, despite their personal afflictions, by all who, while unable to be saints but refusing to bow down to pestilences, strive their utmost to be healers.

To some critics, this is taken as a momentous advance on Camus's part. Victor Brombert observes:

> Above all, Camus has reaffirmed in lyric fashion the need to return to the modest "mortal" condition. His intellectual pilgrimage evokes the journey of Ulysses; it is a return from the world of monsters to the world of men. . . . This struggle against abstractions, this concern for the stark realities of the "human condition," have made of Camus— at least so it seemed—the heir of the best in Malraux. . . . In *The Plague*, he proposes *modest* heroes. The doctor wishes to be neither a hero nor a saint, but merely to do an honest and useful job. He proves that there are humble virtues more precious than heroism. . . . The simple humanity of Camus's characters thus stands in direct contrast

to the haughty, strident, somewhat aristocratic tone of Malraux's "heroic" heroes.

And Philip Thody says:

> For ordinary people it [*The Plague*] satisfied the yearning for the normal, the humanly acceptable, the sensible and the practical after an epoch of excess and murderous fanaticism. Camus struck a note of optimism in man and in human nature, of faith in a purely practical and empirical code of values that came like a breath of fresh air after the pessimism of Sartre, Kafka, Faulkner, Gary and other writers of the post-war in France.

Now, in fact, all this praise is elicited by only a few paragraphs in the novel. Camus's output has been very narrow, as we have remarked, and in his fiction not much space is given to the discussion of ideas. We must wonder if a tremendous amount of meaning is not read into Camus by critics, and whether—artistically, at least—his small body of work can carry it all, and whether his fiction makes its points tellingly enough. Like Eliot's *The Waste Land*, the novels and short stories of Camus depend a great deal on exegesis. This is true of any Symbolist work, of course; and perhaps is less true of Camus's novels than of many others. But, at the same time, few other writers have such extravagant claims of merit and depth made on their behalf.

In any event, is this a great insight at which Camus has arrived? Is it anything new? In Conrad we find expressed a similar need for men to display solidarity, in a hostile universe —symbolized by the stormy ocean—and the importance of each man doing his job well. The theme runs throughout his work, but the critics have commented little on it. Conrad once summed it up for himself in a letter:

> The fact is, that one becomes useful only on realizing the insignificance of the individual in the scheme of the universe. When one well understands that in oneself one is nothing and that a man is worth neither more nor less than the work he accomplishes with honesty and purpose, and within the strict limits of his duty towards society, only then is one the master of his conscience, with the right to call himself a man.

But listen to John Galsworthy (to whom few of these critics would accord much honor): "Life for those who still have vital instinct in them is good enough in itself even if it lead to nothing, and we humans have only ourselves to blame if we, alone among animals, so live that we lose the love of life for itself. As for the parts we play, courage and kindness seem to me the only virtues. . . ." In *The Patrician,* too, a Galsworthy character says: " 'Society is held together by the natural decency in man. The democratic principle, which you despise, at root means nothing at all but that.' "

If sentimentality is Galsworthy's besetting sin, is it any the less that of Camus in *The Plague* (as earlier in *The Stranger*)? It is very well for him to say, at the end of his novel, that "there are more things in men to admire than to despise," but hardly anyone in the book qualifies for that accolade: the behavior of the townspeople is mostly described harshly, cynically. Indeed, one of Camus's shrewdest observations is of how the populace responds to the siege and its danger. "In the early days, when they thought this epidemic was much like other epidemics, religion held its ground. But once these people realized their instant peril, they gave their thoughts to pleasure." That is, they go to films, make love with reckless hedonism; or plunge into the black market, almost frantically. Only a handful of the characters—Paneloux, Rambert (belatedly), Rieux and a fellow doctor, and Tarrou, and finally M. Othon, act well or with awareness and dignity.

Of Camus's doctrine of "modest heroes," one may ask if it is not inadequate? Does it offer man a challenge, a chance of greatness? Is it fitted to the truth of human nature, which has other needs, impulses, aspirations? Rieux fears unreason, fanaticism, stupidity. But these destructive forces are in man, and perhaps more than "modest heroism" is required to cope with them.

The French critics were divided about *The Plague.* Some admired its artistic achievement but found it intellectually insubstantial. They saw in it little more than a "Quaker morality," a "medical humanism," a "plea for the International Red Cross." Among those critics is one who argues that "Camus refuses to hold men responsible for the evil they cause, nor to show they might have to be resisted by violence —he opposes to his characters not the personal Nazis but impersonal microbes. He doesn't honestly confront the problem of how long you remain in solidarity with your fellow men, when your fellow men threaten your life." (This is, of course, the evasion practiced by all pacifists.) Camus's whole belief that man only errs because he is misled or ignorant is highly superficial, again. He does not seem to grasp the willful mischief man can create, and even *loves* to create, as Dostoevski saw.

But the claims made for Camus are really far greater than those he made for himself. His own modesty and candor always win us over. After he saw where he had gone astray in his philosophy of the absurd, he made a frank admission: "The perception of the absurd is one perception among many. . . . That it has colored so many thoughts and actions between the two wars only proves its power and validity. But the intensity of a perception does not necessarily mean that it is universal. The error of a whole period of history has been to enunciate . . . general rules of action founded on emotions of despair whose inevitable course, in that they are emotions, is continually to exceed themselves." Then he proceeded to reject most of what he had stood for up to that time. Now, of *The Rebel,* he is to say again:

All those for whom the problems aired in this book are not merely theoretical have comprehended that I was analyzing a contradiction which had first been mine. The thoughts of which I speak have nurtured me and I wanted to carry them further by ridding them of what I believe prevented them from advancing. I am not, in effect, a philosopher, and I can speak only of what I have experienced. I have experienced nihilism, contradiction, violence, and the vertigo of destruction. But at the same time I have hailed creative powers and the privilege of living. Nothing authorizes me to judge in a detached way an epoch of which I am completely a part. I judge it from within, merging myself with it. But henceforth I reserve the right to tell what I know about myself and others, on the sole condition that what I say shall add nothing to the intolerable wretchedness of the world, but merely with the object of pointing out, within the dim imprisoning walls where we are groping, the still visible points where doors may open. . . . I am interested only in a new renaissance.

In other words, he excuses himself by saying that he is the child of his epoch, and its popular errors are his, too. To judge by the public acceptance of his books, he is right.

It is not as a philosopher, then, nor even as a prose novelist of ideas that he excels, but fundamentally as a poet with prophetic gifts. That is why he is at his best in a Symbolist work; it is his true *métier*. In that more shadowy world, his sight is sharpened, and his earnest portents carry more weight. They echo, as they should in a Symbolist novel. We listen and shudder as he warns us in the last lines of his best piece of fiction, that the plague bacillus, by which we know he means evil, never dies or disappears for ever, but lies dormant and can "rouse up its rats again and send them forth to die in a happy city."

XII

After the Nobel Prize was awarded to him, bringing him world-wide attention, Camus offered his final novel, *The Fall*. The critics, who were now prepared to hail him, actually received this little work rather quietly. Its appearance was something of an anticlimax. The reason was, *The Fall* baffled all its readers. Whatever new direction the author was taking was not sharply indicated in this new story. Even its tone is ambiguous: it is light, playful, mocking, although the theme is dark. How seriously is *The Fall* to be judged? All sorts of meanings and intentions are found in it. It invites repeated scannings, to get at its heart; but to read it over is easy, because it is very short.

Despite all his personal success, including the unexpected Nobel award, Camus appears in this book to have fallen back into deepest gloom. Thody says that we can only identify Camus with the hero, Clamence, if we forget all that Camus had written up to this time. Claude Mauriac discovers in it "a renunciation of the paradoxical optimism of his preceding books, the hope born of despair to which *The Myth of Sisyphus, The Plague*, and *The Rebel* testify." But Maquet disagrees with them: "*The Fall* seems less aimed at instructing than at disturbing us. Camus's rejection of all complacency, all subterfuge, all compromise overwhelms us with revelations that are at times intolerable . . . but such intransigency, through the absolute purity to which it refers, heals and stimulates us in the long run, and far from casting us down into despair, whips up our energy to live a life finally disintoxicated and freed from the imposure of false satisfactions."

So it goes—a Symbolist work is bound to be hard to circumscribe! Thus it conveys one idea to this reader or critic, and another to that reader or critic. Maquet reports that Camus himself, in a personal comment to R. Quillot, described *The Fall* as "an undertaking of 'moderate demoralization.' It repeats to consciences that they are not without blemishes." Some of us, however, might quarrel with the adjective "moderate." This little book is profoundly disturbing.

J-B. Clamence, the narrator and principal figure, is a highly successful and widely admired lawyer. He has followed a career of exemplary public virtue. In court, he is famed for volunteering to handle the defense of the poor and oppressed. Like Tarrou in *The Plague*, he always takes the side of "the victims." In other aspects of social life, he is equally kind to the old and the ill. One night, walking home late after some hours of delightful love-making, he crosses a bridge and upon reaching the further side, hears a cry of distress. A girl is attempting suicide by throwing herself into the Seine. At least, that is what Clamence thinks is happening. On impulse, however, he does not look back. He continues walking. But this night and this impulsive act change his life. He has discovered the truth about himself, that he is not the noble person and humanitarian he has pictured himself, and which others regard him to be. He begins to neglect his law practice, avoid his friends. He enters into debauchery. He is soon down and out, morally, financially, socially. He finally leaves Paris, goes to Amsterdam, where he sets himself up as a sort of "saloon lawyer" in a waterfront bar called, most fancifully, the "Mexico City." Here he becomes the companion of the most degraded human beings: pimps, prostitutes, uncouth merchant sailors, wealthy sensation-seekers.

In the "Mexico City" his custom is to corner visitors, talk to them, and reveal the story of his "fall." But he does this in such a strange and involved way, that it is impossible for the listener—or the reader—to know whether or not anything he says about himself is factual. He calls himself a "judge-penitent," by which he implies that he is both the judge and the repentant malefactor. In particular, he asks forgiveness for having judged others, and for having defended them in court under the hypocritical pretense that he was being kind and generous—he was merely creating a flattering image of himself, for his own enjoyment, and for others.

He was—and still is—vain and deceitful, as well as deeply selfish and lecherous. But he is now openly dishonest and immoral, thereby proving himself essentially more honest and moral, more nearly true to his basic human nature. He invites his listener, each evening a different person, to play the same rôle of "judge-penitent" with himself. By influence, the reader too is asked to enter into this moral charade or game, in which a man strips all pretense from himself, accuses himself, judges himself; and then, perhaps, goes on to live a life as degenerate as that of J-B. Clamence. The story is merely an account of one such conversation—actually, a monologue—between Clamence and an unidentified listener, who is also a lawyer from Paris. But the listener is given no name, never speaks, and has no characteristics. The effect is almost as though he were not there at all, and Clamence is speaking directly to us.

In *The Fall* we have displayed again all of Camus's short-comings as a conventional storyteller. There is no present plot or action, only an account of an event that has occurred in the past. Very short, the narrative is also slow-moving. Our attention is held only by a promise that something interesting will be told to us, but that never does occur. Clamence's self-characterizing monologue is repetitive: he makes the same point over and over in variations, some of them clever, but none advancing the action. Too devious to be credible, Clamence is really a caricature. The book betrays Camus's tendency to seek for types, rather than to offer rounded individuals.

At times Clamence is cynical, scathingly so; but often this barely conceals the author's sentimentality *au fond*. Many of Clamence's epigrams are highly effective, and quotable out of context; but, as with those spoken by Tarrou in *The Plague*, too many just fail to come off, or are crude, or lack illumination and point. The formula for them finally becomes slightly apparent, until they begin to sound a bit mechanical (as also happens with Oscar Wilde). They raise a question, too: does Camus totally reject Clamence's sardonic opinions (most unlikely), or does he approve of some? If so, which ones? The narrator expresses many views, and we are given no clue as to how the author feels about them. Again, many of Clamence's comments lose force by being overstatements; and, finally, some are rather overfamiliar, mere truisms.

Certainly *The Fall* is not ordered and well-made fiction. But then, it is clear by now that Camus had no ambition to become a conventional novelist. Perhaps he did not have the gifts to be one, but in that event he wisely channeled his talents to personal art forms that suited him best. *The Fall* has the virtue of being a constant provocation of thought, agreement or disagreement. The device of the transparent listener— we are always looking through him or past him, at Clamence —is highly original and skillfully handled. The more we reread this little book, too, the more depth of meaning it holds for us. It begins to fascinate us, tantalize us, dog us. What exactly is Camus saying? A *tour de force,* and perhaps also a *jeu d'esprit,* is *The Fall.* Its elusive intentions, its multiplanes of ironic suggestion, its sharp humor contrasting with its dark poetry, are attributes that make it a unique Symbolist work of art. Lastly, it is on a subject which is of the utmost personal importance to us all. As someone has said, "*The Fall* does not annul the truths of *The Plague.* . . . What human dignity can accomplish against historical and collective evil is one thing, what remains for human dignity to accomplish against the evil of the individual conscience is another thing." That is the challenge this *récit* poses. Certainly here Camus has come a long way from the naïvete and oversimplification of moral issues that we met in *The Stranger.*

Is *The Fall* autobiographical? Is it a "confessional narrative"? That was the first question asked by Camus's fellow-Parisians. In his epigraph, which is from Lermontov, he indicates that his "judge-penitent," like the principal figure of *A Hero of Our Time,* is "in fact a portrait, but not of an individual; it is the aggregate of the vices of our whole generation in their fullest expression." That would seem to exclude the author, except insofar as he too is typical of his times. But French readers, at least the more knowing ones, found many signs that the narrator of *The Fall* bears sharp resemblances to Camus himself. For instance, the very name "Clamence" sounds like "Camus." An even plainer clue is given by the "judge-penitent," who tells us that he loved sports, and during his army days often acted in plays. Camus has written elsewhere of his own youthful delight in these two activities. The only two places in the world where he ever felt truly innocent, Clamence says, were in "the stadium and the theater."

Clamence also keeps in his room a stolen panel, from Van Eyck's tripartite "Adoration of the Lamb." It has been suggested that Camus's three novels too constitute a triptych, with *The Plague* the center work, *The Stranger* and *The Fall* on either side: Mersault representing one extreme aspect of the author's personality, Clamence the other extreme, and Dr. Rieux exemplifying a better balanced, middle-way of life. That both the Mersault and Clamence sides of his nature are allowed to go unchecked, to such extremes, might constitute for Camus a self-warning or at least measure of self-criticism, fictionally expressed.

Claude Mauriac believes that one of the inspirations of *The Fall* was Sartre's quarrel with Camus. When *The Plague* and *The Rebel* appeared, attacking Marxist morality, Sartre began one of his replies by demanding publicly, "But I ask you, Camus, *who* are you to be so lofty?" What, indeed, was Camus's claim to moral superiority? This question, and the hostile reception of his work by erstwhile friends, who had been his great admirers, deeply shook his self-assurance. He felt betrayed. This led him to a serious self-examination. Still another challenge to his self-image was the manner in which news of his Nobel Prize was received in Paris. Camus himself had not expected to win it: he was of the opinion, and perhaps rightly, that his idol André Malraux was much more deserving. His doubts about his own worthiness could only have been confirmed by the coolness, spitefulness, and even open fury with which many of the Parisian critics greeted his sudden success. Many of his close companions had become venomous adversaries, and he was shocked by this.

Significantly, *The Fall* is filled with bitter, cynical comments on "friendship." Clamence is not shown as having experienced any large degree of betrayal by his friends, but Camus himself had. This might account for the train of complaints about them that follows in the monologue: "Men are never convinced of your reasons, of your sincerity, of the seriousness of your sufferings, except by your death. So long as you are alive, your case is doubtful; you have a right only to their skepticism." And: "Just listen to the table conversation during August in those summer hotels where our charitable fellow citizens take the boredom cure. . . . Let's not give them any pretext, no matter how small, for judging us! Otherwise,

we'll be left in shreds. We are forced to take the same precautions as the animal trainer. If, before going into the cage,
he has the misfortune to cut himself while shaving, what a
feast for the wild animals! I realized this all at once the
moment I had the suspicion that maybe I wasn't so admirable.
From then on, I became distrustful. Since I was bleeding
slightly, there was no escape for me; they would devour me."
And, again, "One can wage war, ape love, torture one's
fellow man, or merely say evil of one's neighbor while
knitting." Or, of the avidity of friends: "Your success and
happiness are forgiven you only if you generously consent to
share them." And still more harshly: "God is not needed
to create guilt or to punish. Our fellow men suffice. . . . I
have known what is worse than the Last Judgment, the
judgment of men. For them, no extenuating circumstances.
. . ." Clamence further asks, "How could sincerity be a
condition of friendship? A liking for truth at any cost is a
passion that spares nothing and that nothing resists. It's
a vice, at times a comfort, or a selfishness. Therefore, if
you are in that situation, don't hesitate: promise to tell the
truth and then lie as best you can. You will satisfy their
hidden desire and doubly prove your affection. . . . This is
so true, that we rarely confide in those who are better than
we. Rather, we are more inclined to flee their society. Most
often, on the other hand, we confess to those who are like us
and share our weaknesses. Hence we don't want to improve
ourselves or be better, for we should first have to be judged
in default. We merely wish to be pitied and encouraged in the
course we have chosen." His misanthropy grows darker on
every page.

But if his friends have treated him harshly, he is as
scathing in his evaluation of them. Is not Clamence speaking
of Sartre and the Communists now? He says: "Take our moral
philosophers, for instance, so serious, loving their neighbor
and all the rest—nothing distinguishes them from Christians,
except that they don't preach in churches. What, in your
opinion, keeps them from being converted? . . . They don't
want to start a scandal, so they keep their feelings to
themselves. For example, I knew an atheistic novelist who used
to pray every night. That didn't stop anything: how he gave
it to God in his books!" Of such weak-kneed Existentialists,
who wish only to follow the intellectual fashion, he relates a
cynical anecdote (probably aprocryphal): "Their satanism is

virtuous. It's not at all surprising that their minds are confused and that one of my friends, an atheist when he was a model husband, got converted when he became an adulterer!"

All the Party-liners come in for his scorn: "The truth is that every intelligent man, as you know, dreams of being a gangster and of ruling over society by force alone. As it is not so easy as the detective novels might lead one to believe, one generally relies on politics and joins the cruellest party. What does it matter, after all, if by humiliating one's mind one succeeds in dominating everyone?" He sees them, above all, as power-seekers. "Power settles everything. It took time, but we finally realized that. For instance, you must have noticed that our old Europe at last philosophizes in the right way. We no longer say as in simple times: 'This is the way I think. What are your objections?' We have become lucid. For the dialogue, we have substituted the communiqué: 'This is the truth,' we say. 'You can discuss it as much as you want; we aren't interested. But in a few years there'll be the police who will show you we are right.' "

Clamence again refers to Communism (and perhaps Gaullism or any leadership, too, by implication?) as a "vertical religion": "They are free and hence have to shift for themselves; and since they don't want freedom and its judgments, they ask to be rapped on the knuckles, they invent dreadful rules, they rush out to build piles of faggots to replace churches. Savonarolas, I tell you. But they believe solely in sin, never in grace." It is a fierce indictment of his intellectual foes: "So hurray for the master, whoever he may be, to take the place of heaven's law. 'Our Father who art provisionally here. . . .' In short, you see, the essential is to cease being free and to obey, in repentance, a greater rogue than oneself. When we are all guilty, that will be democracy. Without counting, *cher ami,* that we must take revenge for having to die alone. Death is solitary, whereas slavery is collective. The others get theirs, too, and at the same time as we—that's what counts. All together at last, but on our knees and with heads bowed." His disgust is too strong to be contained. "Anyone who has considerably meditated on man, by profession or vocation, is led to feel nostalgia for the primates. They at least don't have any ulterior motives."

Yet, what is more important, Camus seems to turn on himself for an even more thorough search of his own motives, a scorching second look. As Clamence depicts his past, we quickly recognize its allegorical likeness to the author's own. In his career, as a lawyer: "I had a specialty: noble causes. . . . Yes, it was enough for me to sniff the slightest scent of the victim on a defendant for me to swing into action. You'd have thought that justice slept with me every night." Is this not Camus, the humanitarian crusader? "Nature favored me as to physique, and the noble attitude comes effortlessly. . . . I was buoyed up by two sincere feelings: the satisfaction of being on the right side and an instinctive scorn for judges in general." And, again, he tells how he built up his reputation by "two or three manifestoes, perhaps even more, launched and signed at the least excuse."

His fondness for moral loftiness had been, indeed, a compulsive personal trait. He always had to be high, dine on a terrace. He was, as he puts it, a "top deck pacer." He hated to be or to read or hear of things far down. He felt singled out, or marked by fate, to be fortunate, superior to others. "My profession satisfied most happily that vocation for summits. . . . It set me above the judge, whom I judged in turn, above the defendant whom I forced to feel gratitude." But he now realizes how impure were his reasons. "I learned at last that I was on the side of the guilty, the accused, only in exactly so far as their crime caused me no harm. Their guilt made me eloquent because I was not its victim." But he goes even further. If, as a lawyer, he defended the "noble murderers" —as Camus had done in *The Stranger* and his play, *The Just*—was he not perhaps gratifying his own inherent criminality and love for attention? Criminal acts, such as murders, cost the perpetrator too dear. But defending criminals in the name of humanity allowed one to participate in their acts vicariously, while at the same time winning a name for being on "the right side of the bar," and all this was done by far more economical means. Of course, this indictment of having deviously satisfied an innate impulse of aggression while gaining esteem as a humanitarian would apply not only to Camus but to all the holier-than-thou Leftist intelligentsia of Paris.

Being nice to others, Clamence tells us, was to him like an *apéritif*. (He does not deem himself unique in this instance.) It fed his self-love. He then gives us an Homeric catalogue of his petty deeds and gestures, as he played the rôle of a "benefactor of humanity": he helped the blind across the street, visited the sick, attended funerals of unimportant people; courteously directed strangers, lent a hand to vendors with heavy pushcarts, paid generously for flowers bought from an old peddler. He always gave up his seat to elderly passengers in a bus or tram. But all this was a selfish disguise of his true nature, his persistent egoism, his continuous living from "I" to "I" to "I." In sum, "I realized by delving in my memory, that modesty helped me to shine, humility to conquer, and virtue to oppress."

Clamence remarks on how well he wrote. In describing his prose, he makes it sound very much like Camus's again. That is, he had the same fondness for the subjunctive mood, for fine phrases. But then he bursts out, in self-excoriation: "Style, like sheer silk, too often hides eczema." He consoles himself by thinking that "after all, those who murder the language are not pure, either." Or, as he also puts it: "I am well aware that an addiction to silk underwear does not necessarily imply that one's feet are dirty." That is, he is not going to indulge himself in the false, inverted pride of putting on sackcloth and ashes.

And does all this self-accusation make him feel inferior to others? But hardly, for he is still too bitter. Besides, the human mind is too wily to acknowledge its full guilt. "After all I have told you, what do you think I developed? An aversion for myself? Come, come, it was especially with others I was fed up. To be sure, I knew my failings and regretted them. Yet I continued to forget them with a rather meritorious obstinacy. The prosecution of others, on the contrary, went on constantly in my heart."

What should we make of this? Is Camus saying to his hostile critics, "You're right. I'm a hypocrite. But I'm not the only one, since we all are"? Is this a sincere confession, a true *mea culpa*, by someone still striving to become a secular saint, a Pascal without Christ? Is this the goal of Clamence's monologue in *The Fall*? Perhaps there is also a strain of masochism in it.

Says Hanna, of the character of Clamence:

> Some of it is very clearly Camus himself, but not the major part. In no other work has Camus so enjoyed playing with his readers, alternately speaking rather obviously about himself and abruptly shoving the mask of Clamence between himself and the reader without so much as a comma or period of warning . . . in playful irony. It is

always uncertain whose history and whose sins he is confessing. And the net result is that this, the most personal of Camus's works, is the least revealing. It seems that he's not as concerned about adding to the Camus "legend" as he is to confound any attempt of others to build a legend around him. . . . The portrait of the Camus we do know is as astonishing as it is admirable in its self-deprecating irony.

Thody takes a different tack. He notes that Camus wrote *The Fall* in his forty-third year, which is apt to be a time of self-doubt and examination. Thody thinks that the novel began as a satire, but involuntarily turned into Camus's "scathing self-portrait." Further:

It might have been an attempt, such as Gide's in *The Immoralist* and *Strait Is the Gate*, to work out personal problems through art, to get rid of certain personal obsessions. . . . A disquieting book, more disquieting than anything else which Camus has written. A book that was purely ironic would not disturb the reader quite so much, and while it is not possible to accept Clamence as a wholly serious creation, he does incarnate an aspect of Camus's character which had remained hidden in his earlier works.

But Claude Mauriac is inclined to read a quite different intention into *The Fall*. "Camus does not pretend to be indifferent to incomprehension and jealousy. He confesses his anxiety that some of these hostile reactions might at times be justified." Then what? "If he goes to the extreme of making Clamence odious, isn't it done with the ulterior motive of compromising himself along with his hero? Albert Camus no longer wants to be taken for someone else. He prefers to espouse the opinions of his judges, since, in fact, if he feels innocent on the points for which he is reproved, he knows he is guilty of others. Since there are no innocents, this is perhaps a subtle way of pleading not guilty in spite of everything. Each one of us must accommodate himself as best he can to the anxiety of life." And: "By making such confessions, Camus of course would increase his nobility instead of threatening it. The man who sets himself up as a judge suffers in turn being judged, and draws a lesson from that." In other words, Mauriac suspects that Camus is playing a wily game. He wards off criticism by rushing to acknowledge his every shortcoming. He strips himself naked. He purposely identifies himself with Clamence, so as to establish his basic honesty, by publicly admitting all the faults with which his enemies charge him, and even other sins that were not suspected. He willingly offers himself to "bear the brunt of their reproaches. Thanks to this subterfuge, not only identified by him but there by choice, Albert Camus can poke fun at himself nicely and efficaciously. His humor becomes, for the duration of a book, his particular way of *consolidating his position with his reverses.*"

We are watching another brilliant retreat, a trick at which we have seen Camus excel before. The author's motives are very mixed: some are characteristically straightforward, some are sly. But that is probably true of our every act. Camus is very complex, jealous of fame and immortality, yet as sincere as anyone can be. What he has done here, if Mauriac's insight is true, is not in my eyes in the least discreditable. Camus is merely being human.

XIII

Other dimensions of the character of "Clamence" are seen by critics. He is not Camus himself, but Everyman. Maquet considers *The Fall* to be "a calculated confession, in which the anecdote goes beyond its particular reference to reach the human species through the individual and unmasks man's deepest nature. In short, it is humanity entire that confesses through the mouth of this curious penitent; 'the mirror into which he gazes, he finally holds up to others.' "

I must agree with Maquet and others, that Clamence is meant to have this universality. In consequence, *The Fall* is a theological allegory, as its very title implies: does it not dramatize a "fall" from divine or else from some form of human grace? The hero's first name is also obviously significant: Jean-Baptiste. He is John the Baptist, and "Clamence" bears an onomatopoetic likeness to the French word for "clamoring." Thody suggests shrewdly that this leads us directly to *"vox clamans in deserto,"* which makes the hero of this tale "a voice crying in the wilderness." We note too that the setting is Amsterdam (with a beautifully rendered atmosphere of rain and mist), and an emphasis is placed on a description of that North European city's inner circle of nine canals, which clearly resemble those of "Dante's concentric Hell." Thody further points out that "the obsession of man's unworthiness links *The Fall* closely to the Catholic novels of Graham Greene or François Mauriac, and it seems to be a deeply felt cry *de profundis* for salvation." But "Clamence" is also an echo of "clémence," which is the French for "mercy" or "forgiveness." How much is Camus seeking to have us infer from his hero's name?

Then we have the puzzling symbolism of the stolen panel which Clamence keeps in his room. The reference is to "The Righteous Judges," a panel actually made off with a decade before, from Van Eyck's Triptych "Adoration of the Lamb," an ornament of the Cathedral of Saint-Bavon in Ghent. It is witty (is that the right word?) of Camus to claim that his fictional Clamence has helped to steal this *real* masterpiece and is hiding it from sight. Now, separated from the central panel, the Righteous Judges can no longer adore the Lamb of God. Is Camus saying by this that human judges cannot perceive true innocence? Why does Clamence keep the precious and sought-for painting in his room? He offers five different reasons. Most of them are minor, but the chief one is intensely masochistic: the picture serves as a sort of *memento mori*; he *likes* to feel that he may be arrested and even risks decapitation at any time for his part in the theft. It is an odd form of self-torture, destined to attain a frenzied climax.

Another question is the identity of the listener. Clamence speaks of him as a lawyer, and then refers to himself as a lawyer, too. But we get the impression that had the listener been a doctor, Clamence might have introduced himself as a doctor, instead—to heighten the psychological bond between listener and speaker. The "judge-penitent" varies his profession each time, to match that of the visitor whose attention he snares. But this, again, broadens his audience, and the application of what he narrates. Some critics think, on the other hand, that nothing Clamence says is to be taken literally: he is talking to no one but himself. In the same way, the mocking laughter that he asserts he heard on the street, after the girl's cry for help, was actually his own sardonic laughter, self-derisive.

Is anything in Clamence's account to be deemed factual by the reader? Supposedly, the crucial event in Clamence's life is the suicide of the girl on the bridge at midnight. But he never looks back to confirm that she had indeed perished. Perhaps she actually did not. It is not essential, because what really counts is his failure to respond to her call—that exposed his true nature, how he would act when no one was there to judge him. He discovered what a sham he was. The notion that some readers and critics get is that Clamence changes his story—as well as his profession—each time he tells it, to each new victim waylaid in the bar. He concocts a different picture of his past. Also, he does confess that "Clamence" is not his real name, but a false one. He says, too, that he fabricates a mask for himself: "a portrait which is the image of all and no one."

Says Clamence:

A person I knew used to divide human beings into three categories: those who prefer having nothing to hide rather than being obliged to lie, those who prefer lying to having nothing to hide, and finally those who like both lying and the hidden. I'll let you choose the pigeon-hole that suits me.

But what do I care? Don't lies eventually lead to the truth? And don't all my stories, true or false, tend toward the same conclusion? Don't they all have the same meaning? So what does it matter whether they are true or false if, in both cases, they are significant of what I have been and of what I am? Sometimes it is easier to see clearly into the liar than into the man who tells the truth. Truth, like light, blinds. Falsehood, on the contrary, is a beautiful twilight that enhances every object.

The physical setting contributes to this hallucinatory aspect of the narrative: the smoky "Mexico City" bar, such a strange place in which to meet a "judge-penitent" who passes a moral sentence on himself and others; and, outside, foggy Amsterdam, its outlines hazy, all as ambiguous as the facts themselves.

Is Clamence really contrite, or only pretending to be? If he reveals the shameful details of his life, it is not to make amends by humility, but only so that the listener—together with the reader—will admit to having the same faults. By his frankness, at least, Clamence feels superior to his reticent listeners. He looks down at those who lack the courage of self-knowledge and public confession. By degrading others in this way, he recovers a measure of his own self-confidence. Everyone else is as guilty as Clamence himself—that is what he asserts. "Isn't it good likewise to live like the rest of the world, and for that doesn't the rest of the world have to be like me?

Threat, dishonor, police are the sacraments of that resemblance?" He repeats this accusation many times. "I say 'my friends,' moreover, as a convention. I have no more friends; I have nothing but accomplices. To make up for this, their number has increased; they are the whole human race. And within the human race, you first of all. Whoever is at hand is always the first."

He describes his exact method: "I set up my office in a bar in the sailors' quarter. The clientele of a port-town is varied. The poor don't go into the luxury districts, whereas eventually the gentlefolk always wind up at least once, as you have seen, in the disreputable places. I lie in wait. . . ." When he has engaged his victim in talk, he tells them: " 'I was the lowest of the low.' Then imperceptibly I pass from the 'I' to the 'we.' " Still later: "The more I accuse myself, the more I have a right to judge you. Even better, I provoke you into judging yourself, and this relieves me of that much of the burden." All this excites him. "I mingle what concerns me with what concerns others. I take our common features and the experiences we have endured together, the weaknesses that we share, the good behavior, the man of the time, in short, as he exists in me and in others." For this he is amply rewarded. "How intoxicating to feel like God the Father and to hand out definitive testimonials of bad character and habits." His trick is that he pretends to abase himself, in order to get others to do so and then passes judgment on them: hence, his hyphenated phrase, the "judge-penitent." He explains it in this fashion: "Inasmuch as every judge some day ends up as a penitent, one had to travel in the opposite direction and practice the profession of penitent to be able to end up as a judge." He will, "like Copernicus, reverse the reasoning to win out."

This is Clamence exercising his perverse guile on his victim. Is this not also Camus doing the same with the reader? Creating "a portrait which is the image of all and of no one"? If Clamence feels the intoxication of playing God and passing moral judgments, does not Camus feel it, too? Or is he also making a reference here to Sartre and the Communists, and to the Christian moralists whose orthodoxy he challenges? All those who are quick to condemn others? Thody hints that Clamence might be a caricature of the kind used by both the Marxists and the Churchmen to win converts, and Camus might be ironically making fun of the caricature itself. Like Clamence, both Marxism and Christianity—says Thody—try to crush men with a sense of their sinfulness. "What he is principally attacking is the feeling of guilt which brings many middle-class intellectuals not only to Catholicism but also to Communism." Rather than believing in the wickedness of mankind, Camus might be satirizing that attitude on the part of others. Several times, Clamence describes himself as "a false prophet, seeking to enslave men," and Thody cites this in support of his reading of the character. The following, too: "I invite the good people to submit to authority and humbly to solicit the comforts of slavery, even if I have to present it as true freedom." This certainly sounds as though Clamence's creator is opposing the imposition of an absolute ethic, from whatever source. "Camus is attacking the idea of universal guilt by showing the despicable uses to which it may be put." This implies that no human attitude is so free from error as to require our complete allegiance. We must remain "modest" and acknowledge the relativity of all the ideals we embrace. Still, even Thody is not sure that Camus's purpose should be interpreted in just this way and no other.

XIV

In literature, a long-time favorite has been the Satanic hero. In an essay on Romantic fiction, Dorothy Van Ghent has referred to him as the Lucifer figure. He descends from the Devil of the Middle Ages. The later-day Lucifer, however, "has an ambivalence that the medieval Devil doesn't. The medieval Devil is a really ugly customer, so ugly that he can even become a comedy figure. . . . The demonic archetype of which we are speaking here is deeply serious in quality because of his ambivalence: he is a fertilizing energy and profoundly attractive, and at the same time horribly destructive to civilized institutionalism. It is because of his ambivalence that, though he is the 'enemy,' ethically speaking, he so easily takes on the stature and beauty of a hero, as he does in the Satan of *Paradise Lost*." Such Lucifer figures include Richardson's Lovelace, Byron's Manfred, Brontë's Heathcliff, Mann's Dr. Faustus. The novels of Dostoevski and André Gide are populated with him. "The Fallen Angel in whom a bit of the divine still shines." It is clear, I believe, that Camus intended to have the "fascinating" Clamence included in that company. But Clamence, though perversely interesting, fails to achieve this bright stature, and this may be to Camus's credit, rather than not. The demonic "judge-penitent" who preaches in the "Mexico City" bar is too sick, too neurotic, and lacks the radiance of a Lucifer. He admits: "Alas, after a certain age every man is responsible for his face." Camus has not glamorized him: his setting is sordid, his mordant humor is often cheap. "I had principles to be sure, such as that the wife of a friend is sacred. But I simply ceased quite sincerely, a few days before, to feel any friendship for the husband." His sins are too petty. He is no "arch-fiend." Of criminals, he says:

> I find them more moral than the others, those who kill in the bosom of the family by attrition. Haven't you noticed that our society is organized for this kind of liquidation? You have heard, of course, of those tiny fish in the rivers of Brazil that attack the unwary swimmer by thousands and with swift little nibbles clean him up in a few minutes, leaving only an immaculate skeleton? Well, that's what their organization is. "Do you want a good clean life? Like everybody else?" You say yes, of course. How can one say no? "Ok. You'll be cleaned up. Here's a job, a family, and organized leisure activities." And the little teeth attack the flesh, right down to the bone.

The image is brilliant, but on second glance one finds it inaccurate—it does not illustrate murder by slow attrition—and the gibe is small and callow. Clamence is not a Nietzschean character; nor is he in the bold mold of the Marquis de Sade, whom—as we know—Camus had studied closely.

All this leads us quite far from the notion that Camus and Clamence are the same person; for Clamence possibly embodies, as Thody suggests above, a social problem; and also very definitely is a slight variation of a familiar literary type. He is also partly Pirandellian, in his frequent self-contradictions, his paradoxes. I stated before that to me he is so complex, so involuted, that we soon cease to believe in him: we cannot bind him up into a plausible human being. He just does not add up to one. I think we also feel that a man sensitive enough to be agonized by guilt about his failing to respond to an anonymous cry of distress, would not thereafter act as Clamence does, would not fall as far into depravity, would not become as sly, unscrupulous, and even cruel. The seeds of that are not portrayed in the earlier Clamence. He would not have waited until middle age before discovering such qualities in himself. If he had them before, and gave previous expression to them, then no significant "fall" has occurred. Granted that he was less hypocritical in his private life than in public, his "fall" is only social and public—and self-willed. Indeed, the point has already been made that in becoming more frank, more *open* in his depravity, Clamence has not "fallen" at all: he has, instead, become a more honest, more worthy person. But here we are back with the pseudo-Pirandellian paradox. Meanwhile, the story—or "argument"—has become so involved, along with the character, that it dismays the reader. Camus's intellectual cleverness is to a degree self-defeating. He has made his message too difficult to grasp.

But even if the character is not wholly credible, the manner in which Camus handles his monologue is often masterly. It is repetitive, yes—and its wit is uneven. Yet most of the time it has an air of improvisation; it sounds as though Clamence is listening to himself, and rapidly thinking aloud. Although he claims to have planned every syllable of his approach, his words and thoughts run away with him. The effect is remarkably lifelike. His emotions show through. He is aware that he is giving himself away and seeks to cover it up. He begs the listener to pay no attention to an involuntary digression. "It's an overflow; the minute I open my mouth words flow out." And then: "But I'm letting myself go, I'm pleading a cause!" Excusing himself: "Well, now, I'm getting excited, I'm overdoing it." Or, disarmingly: "Don't pay too much attention to my ravings; they're controlled." But he is not really in control, and all this lack of restraint means that he is talking to himself: his monologue has as its goal self-discovery; despite his boasted self-knowledge, he is still exploring himself.

In *The Myth of Sisyphus* Camus had written:

> A work of art calls for a daily effort, self-mastery, a precise estimate of the limits of truth, measure, and strength. It constitutes an *ascesis.* . . . But perhaps the great work of art has less importance in itself than in the ordeal it demands of a man and the opportunity it provides him of overcoming his phantoms and approaching a little closer to his naked reality.

Clamence, then, is an artist—like Camus himself. He attempts each day, with each new listener, a new version of himself. He is "overcoming his phantoms" and approaching a little closer, with each memory and question, to what is at least a symbolic self-portrait. The mirror image he holds up to himself, and presumably Camus holds up to himself, too, and which is held up for us to see ourselves as well, is distorted, as Mauriac phrases it, by "certain picturesque exaggerations and intentional caricatures." (Since it is *symbolic*, we have no warrant to take any of its details as factual.) But though distorted, though cracked and magnified, it is meant to be the "naked reality." It is "a painful 'voyage to the limits of oneself,' " which so taxes Clamence that he grows physically feverish from it, as a consumptive person might.

xv

The Fall is the complete antithesis of *The Stranger*, for here Clamence accepts responsibility for the death of someone he does not even know—and, in fact, punishes himself for it even though he is not certain how the suicide attempt has ended. So strong is his sense of guilt, at his heedless conduct, that his feeling toward himself turns rapidly from self-love to self-doubt and almost as quickly to bitter self-loathing. This *récit* is also more Existentialist in tone than *The Plague,* for all the problems it poses are personal ones, and the solutions to which it leads (though it never does find any) must be personal, too. Hanna says: "The author is no longer dealing with the romanticized individual facing a fragmented universe nor with the rebellious individual facing an oppressive metaphyscal or political system. For the first time Camus is concerned with the individual (i.e., the reflective individual) as he faces himself, attempting to bring his personal history or destiny into accord with his understanding of himself and his world."

In all of Camus's work, there is an intense drive toward self-knowledge. He gives voice to it over and over. "Man is concerned with hope. But that is not his business. His business is to turn away from subterfuge." But the quest can be frustrating: "If I try to seize this self of which I feel so sure, if I try to define and summarize it, it is nothing but water slipping through my fingers." The subject is too intangible. "In psychology as in logic, there are truths but no truth. Socrates' 'Know thyself' has as much value as the 'Be virtuous' of our confessionals."

How then shall one arrive at the facts of personality? "It is probably true that a man remains forever unknown to us and that there is in him something irreducible that escapes us. But *practically* I know men and recognize them by their behavior, by the totality of their deeds, by the consequences caused in life by their presence." But this will strike some readers as a prescription of only limited worth. Who can ever know the "totality" of any man's deeds, or all the consequences of them? More original and perceptive is Camus's suggestion: "A man defines himself by his make-believe as well as by his sincere impulses." That is, in the analogy Camus offers, one can judge an actor by the parts he chooses to play repeatedly. And surely we form an idea of Clamence by his pretenses, his lies, as well as by the truths he utters. To this Camus adds once more: "All true knowledge is impossible. Solely appearances can be enumerated and the climate make itself felt."

Self-knowledge requires psychological insight. In *The Fall* Camus displays such insight far more than in his other fiction. Clamence as a whole does not convince us, but many of his remarks have been described as "psychological vignettes" of great keenness. An example: "True debauchery is liberating because it creates no obligations. In it you possess only yourself; hence it remains the favorite pastime of the great lovers of their own person. It is a jungle without past or future, without any promise above all, nor any immediate penalty. The places where it is practiced are separated from the world. On entering, one leaves behind fear and hope. Conversation is not obligatory there; what one comes for can be had without words." I can hardly imagine that being better worded.

The dominant note of *The Fall*, however, is Clamence's all-pervasive sense of guilt. The author seems to have rediscovered "original sin": man is largely hypocritical and depraved. Clamence's almost suicidal ignominy is stressed ceaselessly. His catalogue of his share of human failings is frightening. But is not the harsh mood of the monologue abnormal? Emile Henriot, saying that Clamence takes "masochistic pleasure in degrading himself," finds his such self-hatred and self-cynicism "disgusting." It is certainly true that Clamence seems to enjoy torturing himself: and the preoccupation with self-inflicted pain—here, psychological—is again consonant with the sado-masochistic trait manifested in so much of Camus's writing. Note how mercilessly Clamence attacks himself and others:

> No excuses, ever, for anyone, that's my principle at the onset. I deny the good intention, the respectable mistake, the indiscretion, the extenuating circumstance. With me there is no giving of absolution or blessing. Everything is totted up, and then: "It comes to so much. You are an evil-doer, a satyr, a congenital liar, a homosexual, an artist, etc."

Look, too, how Camus apparently turns on himself—a humanitarian—in the following anecdote told by Clamence:

> I knew a pure heart who rejected distrust. He was a pacifist and libertarian and loved all humanity and the animals with an equal love. Well, during the last wars of religion in Europe he had retired to the country. He had written on his threshold: "Wherever you come from, come in and be welcome." Who do you think answered that noble invitation? The militia, who made themselves at home and disemboweled him.

Clamence also relates how he now lives, figuratively, in a "little-ease," the mental and spiritual equivalent of a medieval prison cell:

> It was not high enough to stand up in nor yet wide enough to lie down in.

This is a metaphor for his haunted conscience, his conviction of guilt. And it applies not only to himself:

> We cannot assert the innocence of anyone, whereas we can state with certainty the guilt of all. Every man testifies to the crime of all the others—

In *The Plague* we are told that, "the language he [Rieux] used was that of a man who was sick and tired of the world he lived in—though he had much liking for his fellow men—and had resolved, for his part, to have no truck with injustice and compromises with the truth." This could be Camus speaking of himself, for he has openly identified himself with Rieux. In *The Fall* a sardonic yet bitterly accusatory Clamence refers to the irrationality of everything and everybody: "Do you know what has become of one of the houses in this city that sheltered Descartes? A lunatic asylum."

Coupled with this self-poisonous sense of personal guilt and contempt for his fellow man, Clamence betrays a yearning for a lost innocence. Can it ever be recaptured? The same note is sounded by Tarrou, in *The Plague*. It is another of Camus's most persistent themes, especially in his plays. His characters long for purity of heart. Clamence cries: "Yes, we have lost track of the light, the mornings, the holy innocence of those who forgive themselves." But we note the hopeless cynicism of the last part of the phrase—"who forgive themselves." Is true innocence ever attainable by human beings? It is the desire for sainthood; but it must be secular, for Camus dwells in a Godless universe.

The guilt which dogs Clamence might be described as "neurotic"—it is Kafka-like, in being so omnipresent. Claude Mauriac says, of the crucial incident of the drowning girl,

> . . . the critic must remain discreet here and not try to imagine what personal matter Albert Camus wished to express by this allusion to a fault which, from the evidence at hand, he did not commit and which one ought to attribute to his protagonist alone. No doubt this invented trait is there in place of a real one.

(A good example of what Mauriac implies here, I suppose, might be Philip Carey's clubfoot, which is generally taken as an allusion to Somerset Maugham's own stammer in his autobiographical novel, *Of Human Bondage*. Novelists frequently resort to such "transfers" for discretion's sake.) "Perhaps Camus simply wanted to suggest the feeling of guilt that he had always had and which we all share," Mauriac continues. An approach like this to a novel tempts critics, especially when the full biographical facts are known: but it is often misleading—and, besides, at the present time no facts *are* as yet known to justify it. Mauriac himself, writing while Camus was still alive, did not pursue the point further.

Hanna sees Clamence's "guilt" as a purely social or metaphysical one. For him, Clamence is a scapegoat.

In *The Fall* we discover more sharply than in any other of his works the Camusian scene of a single indi-

vidual given over to a lucid acceptance of "his times"—
allowing the social anguish of his times to become the
personal anguish of an individual moment. . . . In a very
real sense he *is* the times. Accepting within himself the
rich and conflicting currents of a whole age and not
simply living this but suffering it, because of a conscience,
a sense of rightness and proportion. . . . What we see here
is an illustration of Nietzsche's dictum: If the old tablets
of the law have been broken, then we must make new ones.
No man can live in absolute freedom. . . . Clamence is left
in an interim period, attempting, as a judge-penitent, at
least to make it clear to all men exactly what it is in which
they are caught. And perhaps by clarifying the problem he
has taken the first step toward the creation of the "new
law." He longs for the innocence he once knew, while
rejecting the "virtue" he once practiced. . . . He seeks an
old innocence and a new law (both he and his age do that).
He is the suffering of history. Certainly there is no suffering
of history except as it is embodied in an individual. He
suffers not just history, but *our* history. . . . He is essentially
a Christ-like figure who accepts the common sins and ills of
every man. Like Christ, he suffers for us. And perhaps this
is the only kind of Christ that Camus could ever conceive,
suffering without hope of final assurance; perhaps this is the
only Christ possible for an age which has suffered the
fall. . . .

A remarkable statement by a critic! Whether Clamence
can be recognized as a Christ-figure, or that he was intended
by Camus to be a substitute for one, I do not know: but
several rereadings of this strange little novel do not persuade
me to accept Hanna's view. But that the guilt conveyed by
this story is meant to typify a social emotion rather than a
personal one of Camus himself, I am more ready to believe.
In his earlier works, he does not write as though he had a
neurotic obsession of that kind. Indeed, he has heretofore insisted on a pagan concept of the utter innocence of man, in a
malign but impersonal universe, to an extent that has seemed
oversimplified and sentimental. Mersault has no guilt feelings
whatsoever: that is what makes him quite incredible. Tarrou,
in *The Plague*, does characterize the evil incarnate in men as
"the pestilence" they carry with them. But a careful distinction
is made by the author. Tarrou is innocent of any responsibility

for the physical plague raging around him, and guilty only for having helped to spread the pestilence he bears within himself. And he is still hopeful of purging himself of it by arriving at sainthood. Yet, on the whole, Camus sweepingly absolves most of the population of Oran of inherent sinfulness. Rieux pointedly declares that men are more good than wicked; the evil in them mostly results from ignorance, and hence can probably be eradicated. In none of this are there signs that our novelist has a sustained neurotic fixation on guilt.

In *Art and Artist* Otto Rank separates the true neurotic from the partially neurotic artist, who overcomes any inhibiting compulsions he might have. The true neurotic is psychologically paralyzed: he wants to create, but cannot. He becomes the *artiste-manqué*. The practicing artist, on the other hand, successfully liberates himself of his obsessions by pouring them into his often prodigious output. His imagination may be colored by his somewhat neurotic emotions, but it far outstrips them. If Camus had guilt feelings, they were certainly not crippling. A Nobel Prize for Literature testifies to that. Perhaps not to harbor some sense of guilt, to be wholly adjusted and happy, would result in an artist remaining superficial. Again, if Camus was neurotic, it was just enough so to deepen his art. Nor should one overlook the lyric joy that so often flows through his work!

In discussing *The Plague*, I have already referred to the tradition of sado-masochism in nineteenth- and twentieth-century French literature, which comprises a major part of Camus's background. A better instance, even than *The Fall*, of how this is reflected in his fiction, is his cruel story, *The Renegade*. The chief figure in this harsh parable is an apostate, a former seminarian, who attempts to join a desert tribe that celebrates hideous sexual rites. They betray him; he becomes their captive and slave. He is tortured horribly: he is degraded, given humiliating tasks, which he performs with a perverse ecstasy; his tongue is ripped out, and his mouth salted. He is finally set loose to die of thirst in the hot desert, beneath the intense, beating sun; but first he seeks to kill a would-be rescuer. The story is taken as a clear allegory, aimed at those Marxists and other Leftists in Parisian circles who hungered for "absolutes": whose self-destructive impulses also made of them "hunters of pain." (See the novels of Malraux, Sartre, and others.) As the admiring Brombert puts it, the renegade of the story is "a brain-washed absolutist, his mind castrated and raped as much as his body."

Such Left-oriented intellectuals had what Paul Nizam terms a sense of "social original sin." Brombert, who quotes him, adds: "It is near-pathological. A foreboding or prescience of the death of bourgeois society and values. . . . The very sons of the bourgeoisie suffer from the stench, deny their family ties, and set out to forge for themselves a fresh virginity." In *The Plague* Camus offers Tarrou as the perfect exemplar of such a rebellious son, a young idealist protesting against his father (a public prosecutor) and all "paternal morality." Among young Frenchmen a further furious protest was evoked by the "political opportunism of the elder generation's handling of foreign affairs in Spain, Czechoslovakia, and Austria," in Hitler's time.

The power-seeking tendencies of the modern intellectuals, as well as their twisted suicidal propensities, are satirized by Camus in *The Renegade*. In the same way, it might be, Clamence is—again—a caricature of the guilt-ridden intellectual. Here his love of degrading himself, berating himself, and offering to sacrifice himself, is depicted with detachment and mocking humor. It is quite possible to read *The Fall* in this very different light. Camus had belonged to the same intellectual circles for a time, and played his prominent part in them. He had shared their exaggerated sense of "original social sin." Then it is not Camus only who grotesquely suffers from too much guilt, but also his former friends, whom he portrays with enviable self-objectivity.

XVI

Are any positive values propounded in *The Fall*? We saw that those brought forth in *The Plague* are thin and unoriginal. In this new book, at least, a definition of human "purity" is given to us. It is to investigate and appraise ourselves fully, ruthlessly, to learn what we are; and then to accept ourselves for that, and to bare ourselves to others as we are, so that sincerity is our dominant trait. As with Captain Brierly in *Lord Jim*, one can only escape the judgment of others and their derisive laughter, by first judging oneself unsparingly, which finally permits one to judge them in turn. But is this enough? Has *The Fall* nothing more to offer than this, on the positive side?

Clamence's relentless self-probing has not brought him relief from his dilemma. He is still miserable, and his life is if
anything even more depraved. He himself hopelessly confesses this. But he feels helpless about his prospects. "When
you don't like your life, when you know that you must change
it, you don't have a choice, do you?" Caught, impotent,
Clamence tries at moments to pretend that he is satisfied with
his new self-image and degenerate mode of living. "I'm happy,
I'm happy, I tell you. I forbid you not to believe that I'm
happy. I'm dying of happiness!" But his is a gnawing despair.
Has he betrayed too much of himself? He seeks to hide it
from his listener. "I'm afraid to let myself go; but I'm not
crying. We let ourselves go at times, we doubt the evidence,
even when we've discovered the secrets of a good life. My
solution, of course, is not the ideal." It is, indeed, no answer
at all, to his desperate situation. Has his self-knowledge led to
his improvement, or merely to his disintegration? "How to
become another person? Impossible. What one must be is nobody, one must forget oneself for someone, at least once. But
how?" That sounds as though "love" might be the key to some
form of personal redemption, but Camus does not follow or
develop this idea, possibly because it would be much too
platitudinous.

The final lines of the novel bring us to a barrier, a dead
end. Clamence declares that everyone pleads for a "second
chance" but does not really want one. Would he turn back
and plunge to save the girl in the Seine, if he had another
choice? "The water's so cold! But let's not worry! It's too late
now. It will always be too late. Fortunately!"

Clamence has too much freedom, more than he can bear.
That is his problem, and by implication it is everybody's problem in the twentieth century. He recognizes no rule by divinity, no supernatural ethical sanction. He is an Existentialist,
a groping stranger in a threatening world. His plight is that of
a fathomless loneliness, with no God to command and guide
him. "On the bridges of Paris I, too, learned that I was afraid
of freedom." Freedom brings moral responsibility. His decision on the bridge revealed to him how empty of moral virtue
his heart was. That imposes on him a personal guilt which is
beyond acceptance. He can turn nowhere for absolution, except to himself: and self-forgiveness is only a dishonest evasion. He confronts himself as he really is, but backs away with
revulsion from the truth about himself. "Ah, *mon cher,* for

anyone who is alone, without God and without a master, the weight of days is dreadful. Hence one must choose a master, God being out of style." (The echo of Dostoevski is very strong at moments.) Clamence never suggests who *his* new master might be, though the inference is that the Marxists have found one. And again: "At the end of all freedom is a court sentence." (This is the point so eloquently made by Dostoevski and Erich Fromm, that freedom is a burden too heavy for the average man to carry.) Beyond this, *The Fall* does not go.

Should we not wonder that Camus has so little faith in man's ability to order his life and his world? Ever to better himself, to aspire to high ethical goals, and sometimes attain them? He clearly had that hope in *The Plague*, but now he has lost it. "An optimist on the value of man and a pessimist on his destiny," is how he once described himself.

A particular symbol of his despair about mankind's capacity to conceive and mete out perceptive justice is the figure of the "judge," against which his anger is steadily aimed. Judges are cruelly satirized as stupid and incompetent in *The Stranger* and *The Plague*, even before *The Fall*. When he dramatized *The Plague* for the stage (rather unsuccessfully) as *State of Siege*, he proposed that "The Plague" be represented by an actor dressed as a bureaucrat in a high hat, although the director of the play put him into a Nazi uniform, instead. Why does Camus feel so strongly that legal justice is quite different from true justice, and why does he have such a bitter opinion of judges? It might be owing to his experiences, things heard and seen, when he was young and worked as a clerk in police headquarters in Algiers. Was he disillusioned there? Is the French system of justice actually so perverted?

Sometimes by "judges" he also seems to refer to Sartre and the Marxists, those who had passed "sentence" on *him*. Thus, he writes in *The Artist and His Time*: "Today judges, accused, and witnesses exchange positions with exemplary rapidity. My choice, if you think I am making one, would at least be never to sit on a judge's bench, or beneath it, like so many of our philosophers." He resents the way in which others assume airs of moral superiority and presume to judge their fellows. Clamence also says:

He who clings to a law does not fear the judgment that reinstates him in an order he believes in. But the keenest of

human torments is to be judged without a law. Yet we are
in that torment. Deprived of their natural curb, the judges,
loosed at random, are racing through their job. Hence we
have to try to go faster than they, don't we? And it's a real
madhouse. Prophets and quacks multiply; they hasten to get
there with a good law or a flawless organization before the
world is deserted.

Then Clamence includes himself among them, speaking of
himself as "an empty prophet for shabby times." Here the
application seems to be both specific—to the Marxists—and
much broader. A whole study could be made of Camus's use
of the "judge" as a symbol with multiple meanings, to say
nothing of his more complex concept of the "judge-penitent."

XVII

Despite his anticlericalism, French Catholic critics were
usually kind to Camus. They approved of him personally, his
public earnestness and sincerity, his espousal of good causes;
and they particularly applauded his attack on Marxism. That
he had once been in Sartre's camp made his political shift all
the more welcome to Catholic intellectuals. They now hailed
the appearance of *The Fall*, with its religious symbolism and
heartrending baring of intimate faults, as a possible preface to
Camus's conversion to Catholicism.

That a religious vein runs through Camus, the poet and
moralist, is obvious. To the extent that he joyed in the physical
world, and in the sensations of living almost mystically, he is
a pantheist. But I can find no signs in *The Fall* that it is a
preface to the author's acceptance of a conventional faith of
any sort. Very possibly it is true, as Hawthorne once said of
Melville, that Camus is extremely uneasy in his unbelief. Yet
all the references to Christ in the novel are to a figure who is
not divine. Whereas Mersault rails against Christian beliefs in
The Stranger, Clamence treats them with more sympathy
here. But he is far from ready to subscribe to any creed; he
speaks of religion as "a huge laundering venture," and he
indulges in trivial gibes at its expense. The attribution of
"guilt" at second remove to Christ Himself for the Slaughter
of the Innocents (which occurred at the very time of His
birth) could only be taken as blasphemous by most orthodox
Christians. as would Clamence's claim that the Gospels were
partly censored by the Disciples. The best Clamence can say

is, "He was not superhuman, you can take my word for it. He cried aloud in his agony, and that's why I love him, my friend who died without knowing." From this he goes on to attack the overzealous and overpious, among whom must be clerics. "Too many people now climb onto the cross merely to be seen from a greater distance, even if they have to trample somewhat on the one who has been there so long," meaning on Christ Himself. "Too many people have decided to do without generosity in order to practice charity." And: "They have hoisted him onto a judge's bench, in the secret of their hearts, and they smite, they judge above all, they judge in his name." Where Christ was compassionate, these Christian moralists "condemn without absolving anyone." He also interprets some of Christ's most important utterances as meant to be no more than ironic jokes.

At the very beginning of his career, Camus had decried those Existentialists (Dostoevski, Kierkegaard) who ended their bold metaphysical search with a "leap" to faith. To him, such a "leap" was but a form of "philosophical suicide." He recognized that, "Man is the only creature who refuses to be what he is," but there is no evidence in *The Fall* that mystical transcendence is even being considered as a way out of the twentieth-century spiritual crisis. Camus is too committed to rationalism. He is too indignant at the submission to suffering of the human lot that he deems is preached by Christianity. To him, the Christian solution is too easy, lacks courage; he calls for a more rebellious attitude, a ceaseless protest.

In place of religious consolation and guidance, Clamence offers nothing. Says Hanna of *The Fall*: "It ends with no ready answer which makes all things right. Camus has brought us a whole vision of trouble and given us little more with which to deal with it than a certain irony and cynicism, and a searing honesty." I think this is a fair summary. *The Fall* ends in an unresolved cynicism. But perhaps it was, again, a testing ground for Camus's newest ideas. Possibly his sudden tragic death came before he could formulate his latest and more mature perceptions in another essay.

XVIII

But he was turning away from philosophy. In 1956 he told an interviewer that he looked upon himself as "first and foremost an artist." He added: "Problems of style and composition never cease to preoccupy me, especially when I refuse to cut myself off from the questions of our day."

The extraordinary brevity of *The Fall* (which partly contributes to its ambiguity) is to a degree the result of his further brooding on artistic form. He was more and more attracted to the principles of classical economy. He illustrates his feeling by an anecdote, the reply of a guard to Louis XVI, when that monarch was on his way to the guillotine. The king, asking the guard to bear a message to the queen, was told: "I am not here to do your errands, but to take you straight to the scaffold."

Besides the classical virtue of economy, Camus felt that a novel should not make its point explicitly, although *The Plague* does so. "He is not the artist who speaks, but who causes to speak." The moral of a story must be conveyed by the plot, the action, and fate of the characters, the tone and atmosphere; it should never be boldly declaimed.

The true work of art is always on the human scale. It is essentially the one that says "less." There is a certain relationship between the global experience of the artist and the work that reflects that experience, between *Wilhelm Meister* and Goethe's maturity. That relationship is bad when the work aims to give the whole experience in the lace-paper of an explanatory literature. That relationship is good when the work is but a piece cut out of experience, a facet of the diamond in which the inner luster is epitomized without being limited. In the first case there is overloading and pretension to the eternal. In the second, a fecund work because of a whole implied experience, the wealth of which is suspected.

I have ventured that a writer's theory usually follows rather than precedes a particular work. When he finishes his story, he looks at it and sees what he has intuitively done. What he learns from that he may consciously apply to his next work, though there will be a further intuitive innovation there, and so on. Along with this, his theory is all too often a rationalization and defense of what he has done. Most likely, all this is true of Camus. The chief reason he wrote so briefly is because that was his temperamental bent.

Brevity is not always an artistic virtue. It may result in oversimplified characters, in ideas that are not sufficiently explored, in skimpy settings. These are faults in all of Camus's fiction. He does compensate for his overcompression by the vividness of his phrasing, the exactness of his description. ("To write is already to choose," he said, meaning that the artist must be highly selective about each detail.) His true virtuosity is shown by the skill with which he creates the story's *milieu*, in damp, benighted Amsterdam, which is so unlike the hot, dry beauty of the North African scenes in which are enacted his other plots. But if *The Fall* were twice as long, it might be twice as good.

Nor is it always best to have one's message implicit only. The reader may fail to get it. If what a writer has to say is important to him, he should not be afraid to express it openly. Quite apart from its symbolic aspect, *The Fall* is too enigmatic. Clamence's self-arguments are too devious to follow. He is forever doubling on his tracks. Much of *The Fall* is confusing, not because the plot and principal figure are symbolic, but simply because the author offers too many paradoxes and is too oblique in presenting his theme.

Some of Camus's other comments on "writing" are interesting. For example, in *The Rebel* he says: "Genuine classicism is only romanticism subdued." And: "Genius is a rebellion that has created its own limits." These strike me as valuable epigrams, and they show his classical bias. That a writer is always striving to say more than he can is well put in this challenging statement, with its overtone of frustration: "Art is an impossible demand given expression and form."

Here is another significant passage:

A creative period in art is determined by the order of a particular style applied to the disorder of a particular time. It gives form and formulas to contemporary passions. Thus it no longer suffices, for a creative artist, to imitate Mme. de La Fayette in a period when our morose rulers have no more time for love. Today, when collective passions have stolen a march on individual passions, the ecstasy of love can always be controlled by art. But the ineluctable problem is also to control collective passions and the historical struggle. The scope of art . . . has been extended from psychology to the human condition. [And he adds:] In order to dominate collective passions they must, in fact, be lived through and experienced, at least relatively. At the same time that he experiences them, the artist is devoured by them.

This seems an excellent self-description.

I would quote one more comment by Camus, which appears to apply to *The Fall*, though it was crystallized by him before he wrote that novel. "Great style is invisible stylization, or rather stylization incarnate. 'There is never any need,' says Flaubert, 'to be afraid of exaggeration in art.' But he adds that the exaggeration should be 'continuous and proportionate to itself.' " That is, the exaggeration here refers to the shaping, clarifying, rectifying that is involved when the artist takes his material from real life. I suspect that this kind of exaggeration —or stylization—occurred in Camus's planning of the heightened character and melodramatic career of Clamence.

XIX

Camus noted and rejected two extremes in fictional art, the formal and the realistic. "The former attempts a total negation of reality and the latter attempts its total acceptance, both of which are impossibilities."

Nonetheless, he was moving steadily away from realism, which is the style in which *The Stranger* is couched, toward a more formal kind of art. A footnote in *The Rebel* reports the painter Delacroix's dictim, "For realism not to be devoid of sense, all men must have the same minds and the same way of conceiving things." The mature Camus did not picture men as being cast in such a uniform mold. Besides that, he saw that, "to be truly realistic a description would have to be endless. To reproduce the elements of reality without making any kind of selection would be, if such an undertaking could be imagined, nothing but a sterile repetition of creation." He mentions how Stendhal can describe his hero's entrance into a room in one phrase, without need of a long catalogue of details.

He had composed *The Stranger* while strongly under the influence of Hemingway, Cain, Caldwell, and Steinbeck. He had won acclaim as the foremost practitioner in France of that type of virile or "tough" and terse writing. But now he begins to find fault with it. "The American novel claims to find its unity in reducing man either to elementals or to his external reactions and to his behavior. It does not choose feelings or passions to give a detailed description of, such as we find in classic French novels." He refers here only to twen-

tieth-century American fiction of the Hemingway school, and
also cites the much-admired Faulkner as belonging to it. "It
rejects analysis and the search for a fundamental psychological motive that could explain and recapitulate the behavior
of a character." All that he says here could very well be applied to Mersault, and it seems almost as though he is aiming
this criticism at himself. From such a rigidly objective story,
he continues, we get "only the flash of recognition. Its techniques consist of describing men by their outside appearances,
in their most casual actions; of reproducing, without comment, everything they say, down to their repetitions; and
finally by acting as if men were entirely defined by their daily
automatisms." This is called "realism," he protests, but is
actually

> the most arbitrary form of stylization. It is born of a mutila-
> tion, and of a voluntary mutilation, performed on reality.
> The unity thus obtained is a degraded unity, a levelling off
> of human beings and of the world. . . . To deny the interior
> reality of a character is to refer oneself to an imaginary
> man. . . . The life of the body, reduced to its essentials,
> paradoxically produces an abstract and gratuitous universe,
> continuously denied, in its turn, by reality. This type of
> novel, purged of interior life, in which men seem to be
> observed behind a pane of glass, logically ends, with its
> emphasis on the pathological, by giving itself as its unique
> subject the supposedly average man. In this way it is pos-
> sible to explain the extraordinary number of "innocents"
> who appear in this universe. The simpleton is the ideal sub-
> ject for such an enterprise since he can only be defined—
> and completely defined—by his behavior.

The perfect example of such "innocents" might be Lenny,
in Steinbeck's *Of Mice and Men,* and some of the loose-
jointed idiots who populate the novels of Caldwell and Faulkner, and the monosyllabic prizefighters and countermen in
Hemingway's stories. "He is the symbol of the despairing
world in which wretched automatons live in a machine-ridden
universe, which American novelists have presented as a heart-
rending but sterile protest." This disapproving summary does
lead him far from the inspiration of *The Stranger.*

"Literary art," he concludes elsewhere, "can neither totally consent to reality nor turn aside from it completely. It simply adds something that transfigures reality." In Proust there is a world of "interior reality" and "memory . . . that is, the memory of the past plus the immediate sensation" which gives a far less distorted picture of people. But Camus's creative faculty is not stopping here, with Proustian analysis, but is now excited by a new vision. "The West, in its great creative works, does not limit itself to retracing the steps of its daily life. It consistently presents magnificent images which inflame its imagination and sets off, hotfoot, in pursuit of them." I have stressed the point, repeatedly, that Camus never did forsake a close connection with the real scene, with urgent contemporary problems; that is one of his great strengths as he enters the symbolist realm. Germaine Brée says of him: "The lucidity which sustains his fiction is far closer to the lucidity of hallucination or dream than to the mechanically rational lucidity for which it is often mistaken." Essentially, this had always been true—even of *The Stranger*; and certainly of the nightmarish *The Plague*, of which Michel Mohrt has written that it is "bathed in allegory" and that "the city of Oran in it . . . becomes a fabulous city halfway between the real and the imaginary." In *The Fall* he finally finds his true medium. Though this little novel is far from perfect, it is amazingly successful, for it embraces so much, suggests so much, and lingers so long in the reader's mind.

Rachel Bespaloff proposes that Camus uses multiple images because he has no other way "to remain faithful in authentically describing the human condition and, at the same time, to suggest the philosophical values which he relates to that condition. Thus, Camus's symbolism is the result of his obstinate realism." But I believe this is only a partial explanation. Symbolism beckoned to him, and he excelled at it, for yet other reasons. Precise thinking was not his forte, and he must have come to realize it, after having found himself in so many serious logical contradictions. He then learned that he appeared at his best in works in which a degree of ambiguity added to the artistic effect and was also legitimate. Besides, I suspect that it also appealed to his perverse or impish fondness for mystification. He himself, speaking of Kafka, confesses with his usual modesty and candor: "A symbol always transcends the one who makes use of it and makes him say in reality more than he is aware of expressing."

Index